Vortex of Conflict

Vortex of Conflict

U.S. Policy Toward Afghanistan, Pakistan, and Iraq

Dan Caldwell

STANFORD SECURITY STUDIES

An Imprint of Stanford University Press

Stanford, California

FOUNDATION®
BOOKS

Delhi • Bengaluru • Mumbai • Kolkata • Chennai • Hyderabad
Pune • Thiruvananthapuram

Published by
Cambridge University Press India Pvt. Ltd.
under the imprint of Foundation Books
Cambridge House, 4381/4 Ansari Road, Daryaganj, **New Delhi** 110 002

Cambridge University Press India Pvt. Ltd.
C-22, C-Block, Brigade M.M., K.R. Road, Jayanagar, **Bengaluru** 560 070
Plot No. 80, Service Industries, Shirvane, Sector-1, Nerul, **Navi Mumbai** 400 706
10 Raja Subodh Mullick Square, 2nd Floor, **Kolkata** 700 013
21/1 (New No. 49), 1st Floor, Model School Road, Thousand Lights, **Chennai** 600 006
House No. 3-5-874/6/4, (Near Apollo Hospital), Hyderguda, **Hyderabad** 500 029
Agarwal Pride, 'A' Wing, 1308 Kasba Peth, Near Surya Hospital, **Pune** 411 011
T.C. 25/ 2731 Lukes Lane, Ambujavilasam Road, **Thiruvananthapuram** 695 001

This edition has been published by Cambridge University Press India Pvt. Ltd. by arrangement with Stanford University Press.

First South Asia Edition 2012

ISBN 978-81-7596-927-8

Published by Manas Saikia for Cambridge University Press India Pvt. Ltd. and Printed at Sanat Printers, Kundli, Haryana

To those who have served in
Afghanistan and Iraq and their families,
With appreciation and gratitude

Contents

Preface and Acknowledgments xi

Part I HISTORY

1 From Cold War to War on Terror 3
2 The United States and Islamic Countries 9
3 Afghanistan, Pakistan, and the United States 30
4 Iraq: From Cradle of Civilization to Republic of Fear 53
5 The Development of Terrorism, 1991–2001 71
6 The Bush Doctrine 91

Part II ISSUES

7 Assumptions 111
8 Intelligence 127
9 War Plans 153
10 Postwar Reconstruction 171
11 Policymaking 189
12 Allies 207
13 Strategy 225

Part III CONCLUSION

14 Lessons and Legacies: Twenty-Six Articles 247

APPENDIXES

A Maps of Afghanistan, Pakistan, Iraq, and the Middle East Region 269
B Chronology 274

C	Bibliography	288
	Terrorism, Counterterrorism, and Counterinsurgency	288
	Afghanistan and Pakistan	294
	The Iraq War	304
	Notes	335
	Index	379

Tables

2.1	Shia Population by Country	12
2.2	U.S. Petroleum Imports by Country of Origin, 1970–2008	27
3.1	Statistical Profiles of Afghanistan and Pakistan, 2010	34
3.2	Afghan *Mujahideen* Groups, Leaders, and Supporters	43
3.3	Aid Requested and Received for Afghanistan, 1996–99	46
4.1	Statistical Profile of Iraq in 1990	57
5.1	Chronology of Al Qaeda Attempted and Actual Terrorist Acts, 1992–2010	80
10.1	Provisional Reconstruction Teams (PRT) in Afghanistan and Iraq	186
12.1	U.S. and Coalition Troop Deployments in Iraq, 2003–9	215
12.2	Percentage of Respondents Who View the U.S. Positively, September 2003	221
12.3	International Security Assistance Force (ISAF) Deployments to Afghanistan, January 2007, February 2010, and November 2010	223

Preface and Acknowledgments

In 2007, at the suggestion of my friend and colleague Bruce Jentleson, the editors of Columbia International Affairs Online commissioned me to write an article on the Iraq War. They gave me significant leeway concerning the substance of my piece, and I wrote an article entitled "The Wrong War at the Wrong Time with the Wrong Strategy."[1] The title was the characterization of the Iraq War by former Central Command commander General Anthony Zinni, and the article was a long, sad work detailing the mistaken assumptions and intelligence failures that led to the U.S. invasion of Iraq in March 2003.

I wrote most of the article in San Clemente, California, at my family's beach house, which is located on the northern boundary of Camp Pendleton, a large Marine Corps base. One day after writing for five or six hours I needed a break, so I went for a walk on the beach. I saw two young men in their early twenties with very short hair ("white sidewalls") who were obviously Marines, and they were building a sand castle at the edge of the shore. Immediately I thought, how nice; these two young men have probably seen and experienced a lot in their young lives, and it's good that they can recapture part of their childhood. Then I looked up on the beach and saw two prostheses; I looked back at the two sand castle builders and saw that one of them was missing both legs from the knees down.

In retrospect, I am ashamed that I did not go over to the young Marine, introduce myself, and thank him for his service to and sacrifice for his country. I have been motivated to write this book by that young man. A second motivation came from a friend and Iraq veteran. Several years ago this friend, who was in the U.S. Army Reserves, was called up for active duty service in Iraq. At the time, he was in his mid-forties with three grown children and a wife to leave at home. He spent fifteen months in Iraq, and when he returned, I took him to lunch to welcome him home. After we had talked a little while, he looked at me square in the eyes and said that he had a personal question: "Why was I there?" A third motivation came from two friends—Juliette George and Rodney Honeycutt—both of whom after reading my article on Iraq encouraged me to expand it into a book.

The young Marine on the beach, my friend who served in Iraq, and my friends motivated me to write this book in order to describe and explain U.S. policy toward the war on terror, Afghanistan, Pakistan, and Iraq. As the bibliography at the end of this book clearly demonstrates, there are many, many articles and books about each of these subjects; these are the invaluable "first cuts" of history. Despite all of these, however, there is no one volume treatment that will provide the interested reader with an understanding of the reasons why and how the United States got to where it is in Afghanistan and Iraq. Pakistan is a key piece in this puzzle, and it has not yet been fully incorporated into our understanding of the U.S. involvement in both wars. I believe that, in the future, the wars in Iraq and Afghanistan, including its border with Pakistan, will be viewed as integrally related to the war on terrorism.

Several of those with whom I have spoken, including Ambassador Ryan Crocker and former Army brigade commander Colonel Peter Mansoor, have said that they would not write about Iraq because it is too soon to do so. They may be right; however, I believe that it is important to tell the story on the basis of available data. Undoubtedly, more data will become available, and history will have to be rewritten, but that is the perennial task of historians. So I offer this "second cut" of history with the expectation that it will have to be expanded, revised, and corrected as additional information becomes available.

Writing a book is like running a marathon; it requires many hours of training and also requires the help and forbearance of others, particularly one's family. Pepperdine University granted me a sabbatical leave during the fall semester of 2009 that enabled me to do much of my writing. Timothy Crawford and Paul Viotti read and commented in detail on the entire manuscript and offered a number of helpful suggestions. Joseph J. Collins, professor at the National Defense University, good friend, and former Army officer and member of the Rumsfeld Pentagon, also commented on the entire manuscript and shared his own writings on subjects of mutual interest. I was particularly heartened by his study of the decision to invade Iraq because, starting from opposite ends of the political spectrum, he and I reached similar conclusions.[2] That gives me hope that truth will prevail. Others who read and commented on the complete manuscript were Pierce Brown, Lora Caldwell, Howard Eldredge, Frank Hawke, Jim

Osterholt, and Emerson Siegle, and I thank each of them. I would also like to express my appreciation to the following colleagues who read and commented on one or more chapters of the book: Khalil Jahshan, Robert Jervis, Jami Miscik, Pat Morgan, and Greg Treverton. I have tried my best to respond to the suggestions and criticisms that I have received; however, any errors that remain are my responsibility.

When I had completed the draft of the book, I asked my daughter, Ellen Caldwell, who is an art historian, to find a photograph that would be appropriate for the book, and she found the compelling photo on the cover. I thank her for her artistic insight, formatting the draft manuscript, and preparing the index.

I would also like to thank Geoffrey R. H. Burn, the director of Stanford University Press, who has provided encouragement and guidance for this project from the outset. In addition, I would also like to thank editors Jessica Walsh, John Feneron, and Martin Hanft for their insight and suggestions.

During a ceremony posthumously granting the highest U.S. military decoration to Sergeant First Class Jared C. Monti for his heroic actions to try to rescue one of his wounded comrades in a battle in Afghanistan in 2006, President Obama noted that Sergeant Monti and his fellow soldiers "remind us that the price of freedom is great. And by their deeds they challenge every American to ask this question: What can we do to be better citizens? What can we do to be worthy of such service and such sacrifice?"[3] Knowing a number of those who have served in Afghanistan and Iraq, I have some idea of the sacrifices that they and their families have made for these wars, and they have paid disproportionately more than their fellow citizens. Many members of the military have served multiple tours; one Marine I met had served six consecutive tours.

It has taken me the equivalent of a year of full-time work to write this book, about the same amount of time of a tour of duty in Iraq or Afghanistan. Of course, the surroundings in which I have worked do not compare with Iraq or Afghanistan. Nevertheless, in reading, thinking, and writing about these wars I have vicariously experienced, however distantly and in a minor way, some of what the more than 2 million American citizens who have served in Iraq or Afghanistan experienced.

As a citizen, I am not sure that I could ever "be worthy" of the sacrifice of Sergeant Monti or the more than 5,800 other members of the U.S. military who have died in these wars, but I want to try, and I have done two things. First, I dedicate this book to those who have served in Afghanistan or Iraq and their families with my heartfelt thanks. Second, I will donate all of the royalties from the sale of this book to the Wounded Warriors Project, which provides support and encouragement to wounded veterans, and I hope that the readers of this book and other citizens will think about how they can support our troops in tangible, meaningful ways.

Dan Caldwell

San Clemente, California
November 2010

Part I: History

U.S. Marine Corps officer shaking hands with tribal elder. Source: U.S. Marine Corps photo by Lance Corporal Matthew P. Troyer, USMC

Iraqi car dragging a statue of Saddam Hussein in Baghdad. Source: U.S. Marine photo by Sergeant Paul L. Anstine II, USMC

1 From Cold War to War on Terror

It is always difficult to evaluate the legacies, lessons, and implications of the wars in which the United States has been involved, and for a number of reasons this is even more difficult with the wars on terrorism and in Afghanistan and Iraq. In many ways, World War I set the stage for the ensuing drama of the twentieth century; the empires of the Romanovs in Russia, the Hohenzollerns in Prussia, the Ottomans in Turkey, and the Habsburgs of Austria-Hungary were destroyed by the war, and new technologies—the "revolution of military affairs" of that day—both prolonged the war and made it more devastating than previous wars. The conclusion of the war halted the fighting and killing, but it did not bring peace to the world. Woodrow Wilson's attempt to establish a new system and organization for managing power in international relations, the League of Nations, faltered and ultimately failed due in part to the refusal of the United States to join the new international organization.

The vindictive peace treaty following World War I contributed to the onset of the worldwide depression and the crippling of the international economy and the rise of hyperinflation, which, in turn, increased the desperation that led the people of one of the most advanced countries in the world, Germany, to turn to a marginally sane, racist megalomaniac, Adolf Hitler. The "second Thirty Years War" (1914–45) ended with the detonation of the most destructive weapons ever invented over Hiroshima and Nagasaki. In the shadow of the nuclear mushroom clouds, the doctrine of nuclear deterrence was developed which, contrary to the predictions of many, resulted in the "long peace" of the cold war. Nuclear deterrence was supplemented by the farsighted programs of the Marshall Plan, which enabled the victorious and vanquished countries of Europe to rebuild and develop, contributing to the cohesion and stability of the Western alliance of democratic, capitalist states.

For more than four decades, the cold war between the United States and the

Soviet Union dominated the attention of policymakers, academics, analysts, and members of the public. As observers of the U.S. at least since the time of Alexis de Tocqueville have noted, most Americans are neither knowledgeable about nor interested in international relations. U.S. cold war policy, however, provided a simple equation for understanding foreign policy: communists were bad, and anticommunists were good. One did not need to know where a particular communist country was or even who its leader was; the important thing was whether it was communist or part of, as it was known during the cold war, the Free World.

The central objective of American cold war policy was to contain the spread of communist influence throughout the world. In pursuit of this goal, the United States concluded both bi- and multilateral alliances with many noncommunist countries, the most important of which was the North Atlantic Treaty Organization (NATO). When North Korea attacked South Korea, a U.S. ally, in June 1950, the United States and the United Nations responded by sending troops. This was the first modern, limited war in which the U.S. was involved, and it resulted in a stalemate. In fact, even today the war has not formally been ended; only an armistice exists. Ultimately, more than 36,000 Americans were killed in the Korean War.

Despite warnings from many quarters, the U.S. became involved in a second major war in Asia during the cold war, Vietnam, and although the stalemated outcome of the Korean War was frustrating to Americans, the loss of the Vietnam War was even more traumatic. Up until that time, the Vietnam War had been "America's longest war," and it was the first war that the United States had lost. The outcome of the war had a number of implications. More than 58,000 Americans were killed in this war, which was costly in both human and economic terms: it literally and figuratively broke the American military. It took more than a decade to repair the damage that was done. In addition, it affected, as all wars do, the way that Americans thought about war. To many, the Vietnam War showed that the U.S. should not intervene in foreign conflicts in almost any circumstances. The war, in the words of General David Petraeus, who wrote his doctoral dissertation on the lessons of the war, was "indelibly etched in the minds" of those who had fought in it.[1]

After more than four decades, the internal stresses and strains of communism, ironically the very things that Marx would have called the "internal contradictions" of capitalist countries, resulted in genuine proletariat revolutions, with the fall of the Berlin Wall in November 1989 followed by the disintegration of the world's first communist state, the Soviet Union, in December 1991.

With these two events, the four and a half decades–long cold war came to an end, and academics and policy analysts scrambled and competed with one another to develop a new paradigm for explaining and prescribing the next U.S. strategy for dealing with the rest of the world. These new ways of thinking included Francis Fukuyama's "end of history," Samuel Huntington's "clash of civilizations," Kenneth Waltz's "neo-realism," Robert Keohane's and Joseph Nye's "neo-liberalism," and other approaches as well. Although each of these approaches had its supporters, none gained majority support. As a result, the period following the disintegration of the cold war was known for what it was not, namely, the cold war. The new era was labeled the post–cold war, but there was no agreement on what that meant.

The New Age of Terrorism

Former Secretary of Defense Caspar Weinberger and later Colin Powell, who served two tours of duty in Vietnam, developed criteria to be met if the United States were to involve itself in a war: vital national interests of the U.S. were involved, there should be clear, achievable objectives, there was significant public and congressional support for doing so, military force was to be used with the intent of winning, the use of military force should be a last resort, and there was an exit strategy for the war. In January of 1991, these principles of the Weinberger-Powell doctrine were applied spectacularly successfully when the United States and more than thirty other countries forced Saddam Hussein's Iraq to withdraw from Kuwait following its invasion and occupation of that country. Public opinion supported the coalition of forces; massive force was used; and Iraq was forced out of Kuwait. But the coalition stopped short of Baghdad and left Saddam in power. There were several reasons for this, most notably that the United Nations coalition did not have a mandate to change the regime in Iraq. Most American officials, including President George Herbert Walker Bush, believed that removing Saddam and overthrowing his Baath Party would create a power vacuum in the region that Iran would fill. Americans nervously recalled the takeover of the American embassy and taking of U.S. hostages in Tehran in November 1979, and they did not want to see Iran achieve regional hegemonic status. In addition, the United Nations and the U.S. coalition partners had not approved of a policy for changing the regime in Iran. There were, however, some U.S. officials, most notably Paul Wolfowitz, who called for the overthrow of Saddam from the time of the first Gulf War.

The September 11, 2001, attacks on the United States definitively ended the post–cold war epoch of U.S. foreign policy and changed everything. The U.S. was no longer invulnerable to attack on its continental homeland, as it had been since 1812. In addition, the attacks were waged by what international relations specialists call a "nonstate actor," and this meant that the attackers had no territory of their own, no permanent "return address." In al Qaeda's case, however, the Afghan government under the Taliban had provided sanctuary and refused to turn over its leaders according to the American demand. On October 7, 2001, U.S. military forces attacked Afghanistan, destroying al Qaeda's terrorist training camps and overthrowing the Taliban government.

In March 2003, the United States invaded Iraq and quickly defeated Iraqi military forces. What the military calls the "kinetic phase" of the war was akin to Thomas Hobbes' state of nature: "nasty, brutish, and short." The postwar phase of the war proved to be far more difficult than anyone had expected or predicted. When the U.S. reacted to the September 11 attacks by attacking both Afghanistan and Iraq, a new era of American foreign policy had clearly begun, and policymakers, analysts, and journalists have already written many articles and books about these challenges to the United States (see the bibliographies in Appendix C).

This book examines the ways in which, and to what extent, these conflicts were related. In many respects, the wars on terrorism, and in Afghanistan and Iraq are separate and discrete, but on another level, they are integrally linked; it is likely that in the future they will be viewed in that way. The underlying premise of this book is that the wars in Afghanistan and Iraq can only be understood in relation to 9/11 and the ensuing war on terrorism, just as the wars in Korea and Vietnam can only be understood in relation to the cold war.

The Organization of the Book

This book is divided into three major parts. Part I focuses on the history and background of the principal countries involved in the wars against terrorism, Afghanistan, Pakistan, and Iraq. Part II focuses on the major issues concerning these conflicts including assumptions, intelligence, war plans, postwar reconstruction, policymaking, allies, and strategy. Part III of the book draws conclusions concerning the lessons to be learned from these conflicts for the future.

The central focus of this book is on U.S. policy toward terrorism, Afghanistan, and Iraq. The book does not focus in great detail on each of the countries involved in South Asia; rather, it focuses on U.S. policy toward that vital region. In order to explain contemporary American policy, it is important to provide the historical context.

Therefore, Chapter 2 describes U.S. dealings with Islamic countries with particular emphasis on American policy toward the Middle East and the epochal changes that took place in 1979, including the overthrow of the Shah of Iran, the conclusion of the Egyptian-Israeli peace treaty, the rise of radical Islamism, and the Soviet invasion of Afghanistan.

Chapter 3 focuses on Afghanistan and Pakistan, and particularly the Soviet-Afghan conflict from 1979 to 1989, the rise of the Taliban in Afghanistan, the development of nuclear weapons in Pakistan, and the relationship of Pakistan's Inter-Services Intelligence organization to Islamic radical groups.

Chapter 4 describes the geography, demographics, economics, and politics of Iraq during the reign of Saddam Hussein. It also focuses on the first war with Iraq in 1990–91 and the aftermath of that war.

Chapter 5 focuses on the development of terrorism in the 1991–2001 period, with particular emphasis on the rise of Osama bin Laden and al Qaeda. In addition, several opponents to al Qaeda are examined, including Afghanistan's Northern Alliance headed by Ahmed Massoud. The chapter concludes with a description of another day that will "live in infamy," September 11, 2001.

Chapter 6 describes the foreign policy of the George W. Bush administration, both before and following the attacks of September 11. The chapter describes the principal elements of the Bush Doctrine and the policies for attempting to deal with the threats posed by terrorism and weapons of mass destruction.

In Part II, the focus changes from a consideration of history to the central issues of the wars in Afghanistan and Iraq, including assumptions, intelligence, war plans, postwar reconstruction operations and planning, policymaking and the interagency process, relations with allies, and the strategies of the two wars.

Chapter 7 outlines the assumptions of the Bush administration, including the linkage of 9/11 and Iraq, the duration of military operations, Iraqis' reception of American soldiers, the role of expatriate leaders, the establishment of democracy, the costs of the wars, and best case assumptions.

Chapter 8 focuses on intelligence issues concerning the conflicts, including intelligence failures, intelligence regarding Afghanistan, Pakistan, and Iraq, and U.S. governmental investigations of the use and abuse of intelligence. Information and analysis concerning supposed weapons of mass destruction (WMD) in Iraq is examined.

Chapter 9 focuses on the ways that the U.S. government considered dealing with al Qaeda, Afghanistan, and Iraq, including containment and deterrence, assassination and coups, the use of Special Forces, conventional military attack, or the utilization of mobile, lightly armored forces. This chapter focuses on the acute phase of military conflict, what the military refers to as the "kinetic" phase of conflict.

Chapter 10 focuses on Phase IV of the military operations—postwar reconstruction issues, programs, and problems—in both Afghanistan and Iraq. The shortcomings of U.S. postwar planning in both Afghanistan and Iraq are examined. In addition, Provincial Reconstruction Teams (PRT) are described and assessed.

Chapter 11 describes policymaking coordination and problems in the conflicts under investigation. The chapter focuses on the interagency process within the executive branch, the National Security Council, and the role and involvement of Congress. The coordination between and among these agencies, departments, and governmental branches is evaluated.

Chapter 12 describes the support for the wars in Afghanistan and Iraq by various allies of the United States. In addition, the ways in which the United States dealt with its allies in these conflicts and the withdrawal of non-American forces from Afghanistan and Iraq are desccribed.

Chapter 13 describes the significant change in strategy from a conventional counterterrorist strategy to a counterinsurgency approach in both Afghanistan and Iraq. Some observers have noted that this change marked a strategic counterrevolution. The "surges" of U.S. military forces in both Afghanistan and Iraq are described.

In Part III of the book, the conclusion presents a number of the strategic lessons to be drawn from the wars in Afghanistan and Iraq. These lessons are presented as twenty-six articles, an approach borrowing from T. E. Lawrence. In addition, the likely legacies of these two wars are described.

The three appendices to the book are integral parts of it. Appendix A contains maps of Afghanistan, Pakistan, Iraq, and the Middle East region. Appendix B is a chronology of the major events related to the subject of the book with an emphasis on the period since September 11, 2001. Appendix C contains selected bibliographies on: (1) terrorism, counterterrorism, and counterinsurgency, (2) Afghanistan and Pakistan, and (3) the Iraq War.

2 The United States and Islamic Countries

United States policies toward Afghanistan, Pakistan, and Iraq cannot be understood without considering broader American involvement with other Islamic countries including the greater Middle East. Of course, this is a vast subject about which many articles and books have been written. In this chapter, I describe some of the major contours of the relationship between the United States and the Muslim world. I do so not as a Middle East specialist but rather from the perspective of someone with a primary interest in American foreign policy. I specifically focus on the following questions: (1) What are the emerging characteristics of the Islamic world? (2) What are the major historical events and divisions within the Islamic world? (3) What impact do the politics and divisions within the Islamic world have upon U.S. policy toward Afghanistan, Pakistan, and Iraq? and (4) What are the major U.S. interests in the Muslim world?

The United States has dealt with Islamic countries since its founding; indeed, Morocco was the first country to recognize the United States as an independent country, in 1777. This overview of the interaction of the United States with Islamic countries is simplified; yet, it provides the essential contours of the backdrop of U.S. policies toward Afghanistan, Pakistan, and Iraq. Just as one cannot understand U.S. policies toward the Soviet Union, the People's Republic of China, and Eastern Europe from 1947 through 1991 without an understanding of U.S. cold war policy, one cannot comprehend American policies toward Afghanistan, Pakistan, and Iraq without an understanding of U.S. interactions with individual Muslim countries and the Islamic world in general, including Muslims within non-Islamic countries.[1]

For most of its history, the United States did not have a coherent strategy toward the Muslim world because its interests were neither threatened nor at stake. With the growth of radical Islamism, American interests are clearly at stake, and the U.S. has had to respond to this challenge.

At the crux of U.S. Middle Eastern policy, and increasingly U.S. relations with the Muslim world at large, is the Arab-Israeli relationship. Some have contended that if the Arab-Israeli problem were resolved (whatever that would mean), conflict in the Middle East and South Asia would subside. Others believe that the Palestinian issue is the core of the Arab-Israeli conflict and once resolved, conflict in the region would decrease significantly. A central value of Muslims is a belief in justice, and Muslims have a corresponding belief in fighting injustice. Reflecting their extreme interpretation of the meaning of justice and how to obtain it, Islamists call for an end to Arab-Israeli conflict or even the elimination of Israel; however, it is not likely that either improbable possibility, even if effected, would put an end to terrorism or demands for the complete withdrawal of the U.S. from the region.

Radical, political Islamists dramatically emerged on the world scene in 1979 and influenced world politics from that time on. Although there were differences among Islamists, they generally were opposed to Westernization, and particularly Western notions of democratization, globalization, and secularization of society. Some Islamists had their own irreconcilable vision of the West and its perceived evils and called for the establishment of a new caliphate.

Emerging Characteristics of the Islamic World

In the seventh century C.E., the Prophet Muhammad founded the religion of Islam. According to Muhammad, the five pillars of Islam consisted of the monotheistic proclamation of faith (the *Shahada)*, prayer, pilgrimage to Mecca (the *Hajj*), charity, and the fast during the month of Ramadan. The principles of Islam, one of the world's principal religions, were laid down in the Quran. Islamic law, the *Sharia*, was contained in six thousand Quranic verses and the sayings and example of the Prophet Muhammad (the *Sunnah*), and these were supposed to constitute the basic foundation of all Islamic communities. Quranic verses provide guidance for the behavior of believers in topics as diverse as punishments for crimes such as adultery and drinking alcohol to the permissibility of wearing jewelry. Those Muslims who espouse a political agenda and whose goal is to establish an Islamic state are called Islamists, and they believe that the *Sharia* cannot be improved upon and are in favor of its becoming the foundation of laws in Muslim societies. This conception of the basis of law as deriving from God contrasts markedly with the Euro-American, Enlightenment view of popular sovereignty: that law derives from people rather than God. Thus, in many Islamic societies, politics, law, and religion are closely inter-related, and separation of church and state, a hallmark of Christian doctrine and Western Enlightenment, is foreign to almost all Islamic countries.

The influence of *Sharia* is clear in a number of Islamic countries. For example, Saudi Arabia has no formal constitution other than the Quran, and its flag bears the Islamic proclamation of faith, "There is no god but God, and Muhammad is his Messenger." In addition, the former rulers of Saudi Arabia, King Khalid and later King Fahd, ordered that they not be referred to as "King" but rather as "the Custodian of the Two Holy Places": Mecca (the birthplace of Muhammad and the holiest site in Islam) and Medina (the location of the Prophet's Mosque and the second holiest city). Saudis consider themselves to be the protectors of the most sacred cities in Islam and have assumed responsibility for fulfilling that role. For example, until 2004, the Saudi government did not issue tourist visas to visit Saudi Arabia; the only exceptions to this were visas issued only to Muslims to visit Mecca on pilgrimage, the *Hajj.* International airliners flying from Asia to Europe often refueled at Saudi airports in Dhahran or Jeddah, and when they did so, passengers were not allowed to deplane for both security reasons and because their presence would defile the sacred land of the Prophet. When King Fahd allowed the military forces of the United States and its allies to enter Saudi Arabia to oppose Iraq in 1990 and to use Saudi military bases, radical Islamists were outraged. Reflecting this view, Osama bin Laden wrote, "The most recent calamity to have struck Muslims is the occupation of the land of the two sanctuaries, the hearth of the abode of Islam and the cradle of prophecy, since the death of the prophet and the source of the divine message—the site of the holy Kaaba to which all Muslims pray. And who is occupying it? The armies of the American Christians and their allies."[2]

Following the death of the Prophet Muhammad in 632 C.E., Muslims could not decide whether to choose Muhammad's direct descendants or his close companions as his successor. Sunni Muslims believe that Abu Bakr succeeded the Prophet as ruler of all Muslims, or caliph. Shia Muslims believe that authority over the caliphate should have passed through Muhammad's descendants beginning with the Prophet's cousin and son-in-law, Ali. In contrast, Sunnis supported the election of caliphs. Four years after the Prophet's death, Ali's Shia followers killed the third caliph, and soon after, Sunnis killed Husain, Ali's son. This began the often-violent history of Shia-Sunni interaction. Since their initial split, the Shia and Sunnis have developed a number of cultural, theological, and political differences.

TABLE 2.1
Shia Population by Country

Country	Percent Shia	Total population (millions)	Shia population (millions)
Afghanistan	20	28.4	5.9
Azerbaijan	75	8.0	6.0
Bahrain	75	0.7	0.52
India	1	1,095.4	11.0
Iran	90	68.7	61.8
Iraq	65	26.8	17.4
Kuwait	30	2.4	0.73
Lebanon	45	3.9	1.7
Pakistan	19	165.8	33.2
Qatar	16	0.89	0.14
Saudi Arabia	10	27.0	2.7
Syria	1	18.9	0.19
UAE	6	2.6	0.16

Source: Compiled by author from data in Central Intelligence Agency, *World Factbook*, www.cia.gov; Council on Foreign Relations, *The Chronicle* (September 2006), p. 7.

Today, there are 1.3 billion Muslims in the world, and 85 to 90 percent of these are Sunnis. Table 2.1 provides a listing of the Shia population by country and shows that Iran has the greatest number of Shia and the largest Shia population as a percent of population of any other country. Ninety percent of Iranians are Shia, two-thirds of Iraq's population consists of Shia, and approximately 20 percent of both Pakistan and Afghanistan is Shia. Thus, in both Iraq and Iran, Shia constitute a majority.

The split between Shia and Sunnis has been a significant factor in the relationships of Islamic countries and within particular countries. Saddam Hussein was a Sunni, and from the time he came to power in Iraq in 1968 until the U.S. invasion and overthrow of Saddam in March 2003, Sunnis controlled the major state organizations including the military and security agencies. Throughout this period, Saddam's government repressed the Shia segment of the population. Both al Qaeda and the Taliban are Sunni and hold anti-Shia views.[3]

Dr. Vali Nasr, an authority on Shia and an adviser to the U.S. government, has shown that the Shia demand for fair representation is not a localized phenomenon but is, rather, a broader endeavor.[4] He has also noted that the "Shia revival" is likely to incite a Sunni extremist response. Indeed, one can readily see the way that this has occurred in Iraq. Following the overthrow of Saddam, Shia who had been repressed for decades reasserted their power and in some cases persecuted Sunnis.

The split between Shia and Sunnis is not the only division within the Muslim world. Journalist Thomas Friedman has noted that politics in the Islamic world is "tribe-like"; that is, groups either in power or seeking power consist of an actual tribe, clan, religious sect, or a village group.[5] Some anthropologists and sociologists contend that "tribe-like" organization resulted from the behavior and practices of actual tribes living in the harsh environment of the desert. In such a setting, it was essential that people in the same social group cooperate in order to survive. There was no centralized authority in this setting, and consequently, the tribe became the primary social group and determined how and in what ways society should operate. Given this view, behavior that could be (and often is) ascribed to some Islamic countries resulted from bedouin culture and the harsh challenges of living and surviving in the desert. From this setting, the Arab proverb evolved: "My brother and I against our cousin; my cousin and I against the stranger." Reflecting this view, Osama bin Laden wrote, "The Iraqi who is waging *jihad* against the infidel Americans or Allawi's [former Iraqi Prime Minister Ayad Allawi] renegade government is our brother and companion, even if he was of Persian, Kurdish, or Turkoman origin."[6] Bin Laden, a Sunni, therefore believed that opposing the U.S. was more important than opposing the Shia.

Tribes or families still rule many Islamic governments today. For example, Abdul Aziz bin Saud was the founder of the Kingdom of Saudi Arabia, and since his death in 1953, his sons have continued to fill the top positions of the Saudi government. The current king, Abdullah bin Abdul Aziz, is one of the fifty-three sons of the kingdom's founder. The al-Sabah family has ruled Kuwait since 1752 and remains in control today. In Iraq, Saddam Hussein chose his subordinates and long-time close associates primarily from his native village of Tikrit and assumed that he could trust them more than outsiders. Similarly, Osama bin Laden selected subordinates only from among known associates whom he trusted. This form of personnel selection made it extremely difficult to gain intelligence about Osama bin Laden and al Qaeda or Saddam and his government.

The Ideational Foundation of al Qaeda

Bin Laden, Ayman al Zawahiri, and other members of al Qaeda were strongly influenced by three Islamist writers: Taqi al-Din ibn Taymiyya, Muhammad ibn Abd al-Wahhab, and Sayyid Qutb. Although separated by centuries, these writers focused on similar themes that influenced radical contemporary Islamists.

Taqi al-Din ibn Taymiyya was born in 1263 about 350 miles northeast of Damascus in what today is Turkey. Both his father and grandfather were respected theologians, and ibn Taymiyya followed in their footsteps. He was educated in Damascus, and his family had to flee the city in order to escape the invasion of the Mongols, who had ostensibly converted to Islam by professing belief in God and the Prophet Muhammad. The Quran prohibits warfare between Muslims, but this did not prevent Muslim Mongol converts from attacking and taking over Muslim dynasties throughout the Middle East. In his writings, ibn Taymiyya developed three major themes. First, he believed in a narrow, strict interpretation of the sources of Islam; namely, that only the teachings and deeds of the Prophet (the *Sunnah*) should be used to provide guidance for individuals and Islamic societies. Those such as ibn Taymiyya and later his followers, such as Osama bin Laden and Ayman Zawahiri, who believed in only the teachings of these "pious" ancestors, the *salaf*, are called *salafis*. Second, ibn Taymiyya believed in the intermingling of religion and politics. As terrorism experts Daniel Benjamin and Steven Simon have noted, "The modern notion of separate realms of the religious and secular world would have been inconceivable to ibn Taymiyya, and to all Muslims of his time. Indeed, an integral part of Islam's glory was the figure of the caliph—the divinely mandated leader whose forces led a lightning conquest of much of the known world for the faith."[7]

Ibn Taymiyya's refusal to subordinate religion to politics had several important implications. He believed that leaders should reflect true and literal beliefs of Islam, and if they did not, then they were guilty of apostasy and not worthy to lead. In a curious way, ibn Taymiyya's view was similar to that of European Enlightenment philosophers John Locke and Jean Jacques Rousseau, who believed that rulers had a "social contract" with their subjects that, if broken, justified revolution.[8] The third belief that ibn Taymiyya developed concerned *jihad*, holy war. Perhaps reflecting the threat posed by attacking Mongols and contrary to traditional Islamic teachings, ibn Taymiyya sought to place *jihad* as a "pillar of Islam," second only to the declaration of faith. In going against traditional Islamic teachings, ibn Taymiyya challenged the authority of religious scholars, just as his later disciple, Osama bin Laden, would also do. In an essay published in 1994, bin Laden wrote, "The Imam ibn Taymiyya says, 'When it comes to *jihad*, we must take into consideration the correct opinion of religious scholars who have experienced what is confronting the worldly men, except for those who focus solely on the ritual aspects of religion; their opinion should not be taken, nor should the opinion of religious scholars who have no experience in the world.'"[9] In other words, bin Laden argued that Muslims should follow him rather than those who were formally trained in religion. Bin Laden repeatedly refers to ibn Taymiyya throughout his writings and statements, referring to him as the "Sheikh of Islam." In his 1998 proclamation of a *jihad* against "Jews and Crusaders," bin Laden approvingly quotes ibn Taymiyya, "As for fighting to repel an enemy, which is the strongest way to defend freedom and religion, it is agreed that this [*jihad*] is a duty. After faith, there is no greater duty than fighting an enemy who is corrupting religion and the world."[10] Ibn Taymiyya emphasized the literal, strict interpretation of Islamic beliefs, the unification of religion and politics, and support for *jihad*, and these three central beliefs strongly influenced contemporary *salafis* such as Osama bin Laden.

A second major influence on contemporary Islamists came from Muhammad ibn Abd al-Wahhab, who was born in 1703 in al-Uyayna, Arabia, then a part of the Ottoman Empire. His father and grandfather were both judges, and rather than following in their footsteps, al-Wahhab studied religion in Medina, Baghdad, Isfahan, Qom, and Basra, where he was forced to leave for accusing its population of apostasy. Al-Wahhab was strongly influenced by the works of ibn Taymiyya, who had lived four centuries before him and who called for a return to the basics of early Islam—the Quran and the *hadith*, the sayings and teachings of the early followers of Muhammad. Any legal ruling or pronouncement issued on the basis of anything except the classics constituted apostasy. As author Lawrence Wright has noted, al-Wahhab "believed that God clothed Himself in a human form; he rejected the intercessory prayer of saints and expressions of reverence for the dead; and he demanded that Muslim men refuse to trim their beards. He banned holidays, even the Prophet's birthday, and his followers destroyed many of the holy sites, which he considered idols. He gave a warrant to his followers that they could kill or rape or plunder those who refused to follow his injunctions."[11] In simply listing these prohibitions, one can see the influence that al-Wahhab had on a later radical Islamist group, the Taliban, which instituted many of these rules when they took over Afghanistan. When al-Wahhab vandalized popular shrines in his hometown of al-Uyayna as being idolatrous, he was thrown out of town, much as he had earlier been ostracized by Basra; he went to Dariyya, a small town close to modern Riyadh, where he met the ruling sheik, Muhammad ibn Saud, who wanted to extend his control over central Arabia. Al-Wahhab viewed ibn Saud as a leader with whom he could work to promote his view of Islam, and, thus, as Benjamin and

Simon point out, "[an]"An alliance of power and faith was born."[12] Al-Wahhab's influence was so great that those who believe in his strict version of Islam are referred to as "Wahhabis." This was a sometimes tense alliance that would nevertheless endure into present-day Saudi Arabia. The theocratic character of Saudi Arabia is evident in a number of ways; for example, the Quran is the constitution and law within the kingdom, and there is a religious police force, the *Mutawain*, that even today patrols Saudi streets ensuring that women are covered up properly with an *abaya*, that shopkeepers observe the call to prayer five times per day, and that other Islamic laws in the Quran are observed. The *Mutawain* illustrates the melding of state and religion; it is governed by the Committee for the Protection of Virtue and the Prevention of Vice, which, in turn, is controlled by the governmental Ministry of the Interior. In essence, the *Mutawain* represents the cooptation of a religious cadre by the government.

Following the 1938 discovery of oil and the resulting wealth from the oil industry, Saudi Arabia was transformed from an undeveloped country of roving bedouins into a modern nation-state. However, despite this remarkable transformation in a matter of a few decades, the alliance between political and religious leaders endured, and the Saudi government and population, buoyed by petro-dollars, supported the alliance in several different ways. Saudi Arabia's population, constituting 1 percent of the 1.3 billion world's total Muslim population, nevertheless provides more than 90 percent of the aid to construct and maintain thousands of mosques, schools, and colleges throughout the world.[13] Wahhabi clerics and teachers are the ones who staff these institutions and propagate *salafi* beliefs.

Sayyid Qutb, an Egyptian writer, theoretician, and member of the Muslim Brotherhood, exerted the third major influence on contemporary Islamist thinking. Referring to Qutb, Professor John Calvert has noted, "No other Islamist ideologue . . . exerted a comparable influence on the phenomenon, both in his day and in the generations that followed"[14] How did Qutb achieve such prominence within the Islamic world?

Born in 1906 in a small town in upper Egypt, Qutb as a young person was not particularly religious, although he had memorized the Quran by the time he was ten years old. As a young man, he worked as an inspector for the Egyptian ministry of education, which sent him to the United States for higher education and to improve his English language skills in November 1948, just six months after the establishment of the state of Israel. Qutb studied English in Washington, DC, during the first half of 1949, and then moved to Greeley,

Colorado, to attend Colorado State College of Education (now the University of North Colorado). Qutb was appalled by what he observed in the U.S., which he viewed as sexual licentiousness, rampant materialism, pervasive racism, excessive individual freedom, and secularization. He wrote to a friend, "The soul has no value to Americans. There has been a Ph.D. dissertation about the best way to clean dishes, which seems more important to them than the Bible or religion."[15] For many foreign students, including many from Muslim countries, study in the U.S. gave them an appreciation for American ideals and institutions; for Qutb, his time in the U.S. alienated and radicalized him.

Soon after he returned to Egypt in August 1950, he joined the Muslim Brotherhood, a popular movement that had begun in Egypt in 1928 to promote its credo: "God is our objective; the Quran is our constitution; the Prophet is our leader; struggle is our way; and death for the sake of God is the highest of our aspirations."[16] The Brotherhood had political as well as religious objectives, and beginning in 1948, its members attacked British and Jewish businesses in order to pressure Britain to withdraw from Egypt and to protest the establishment of the state of Israel. The Egyptian ruler, King Farouk, ordered the dismantling of the Brotherhood, which responded by assassinating the Egyptian prime minister. The government then killed the founder of the Brotherhood, Hassan al-Banna. It was in this environment that Qutb developed his ideas, many of which were based on those of ibn Taymiyya and ibn Abd al-Wahhab. Like the two earlier writers, Qutb believed in the restoration of an earlier, purer form of Islam. Central to Qutb's thought is his idea of *jahiliyya*, an Islamic concept describing the period before the development of Islam and a general state of ignorance of Islam. Applying this term to modern Muslim societies, Qutb believed that "the influence of European imperialism had left the Muslim world in a condition of debased ignorance similar to that of the pre-Islamic era."[17] According to this view, many Muslims in the modern world had "fallen into a pre-Islamic state of barbarity, especially those where Muslims have forsaken God's law in favor of man-made laws."[18] Believing that the Egyptian government had forsaken the Islamic way and becoming involved in the Muslim Brotherhood's attempt to overthrow Gamal Abdel Nasser, Qutb was arrested, tried, found guilty of subversion, and executed in 1966. But his ideas did not die with him. Qutb's biographer John Calvert characterizes Qutb as the "most famous thinker" of the Muslim Brotherhood, and Benjamin and Simon write that Qutb "is the Islamic world's answer to Solzhenitsyn, Sartre, and Havel, and he easily ranks with all of them in influence."[19]

Taqi al-Din ibn Taymiyya, Muhammad ibn Abd al-Wahhab, and Sayyid Qutb were the most influential thinkers in the *salafi* school of Islam, and a number of contemporary Islamists, including Osama bin Laden, Ayman Zawahiri, and Mullah Omar, attempted to implement their ideas in contemporary society. However, there were other schools of thought in Islam that differed with *salafiyya* in religious doctrine and practice. Sufism is a mystical, tolerant form of Islam brought to South Asia from Arabia, and it is more inward looking than *salafism*. Some Pakistani and many Afghan Muslims are Sufis, and they often have serious and deep-seated doctrinal or religious differences with their *salafist* coreligionists.[20] Sometimes these differences develop into problems and even conflicts. For example, *salafist* members of al Qaeda in Afghanistan, in keeping with their beliefs, would sometimes destroy memorials to the dead, and this caused problems with Afghan Sufis, who believe in revering dead relatives.

Basing their views on radical interpretations of Islam, militant Muslims opposed modern trends toward Westernization, globalization, secularization, and democratization. For example, Islamic societies have been characterized by authoritarian rule in which power is concentrated in a single ruler or elite and not bound by any constitutional framework or strictures, save the guidelines of the *Sharia*. Various types of authoritarianism can be viewed on a scale ranging from relatively benign to malevolent. In benign authoritarian governments, the leaders hold open meetings with their subjects called *majlis*, which simultaneously perform the functions of legislature, executive, and judiciary, and this provides some connection and interface between the government and its citizens. At the other extreme are malevolent authoritarian governments that are centralized and dominated by a single leader or restricted elite. Clearly, Saddam Hussein and Taliban leader Mullah Omar were all characteristic of the second type of ruler, and even though he has never been the ruler of a country, Osama bin Laden is a malevolent authoritarian leader.

History and Politics

No country can escape its past, and those in the Middle East and South Asia are no exception to this generalization. Following the death of Muhammad, the first caliph, Abu Bakr, successfully unified the Arabian Peninsula and then attacked and took over Palestine by 636. Jerusalem, and particularly Haram al-Sharif (also known as the Temple Mount to Jews), is the third most sacred place in Islam after Mecca and Medina and is the site of two major Muslim shrines, the Dome of the Rock, where Muslims believe Muhammad ascended to heaven, and the al-Aqsa mosque, the largest in Jerusalem.

Jerusalem is the cradle of three of the world's religions—Islam, Judaism, and Christianity. In 1100, European crusaders captured Jerusalem, and a century later a Turkish-speaking warrior named Osman, who had converted to Islam, took over the fringes of the Eastern Roman or Byzantine Empire. Thus the Ottoman (or Osmanli) empire was established. By the fifteenth century, Osman's successors had conquered and replaced the Byzantium Empire. In the north, they had expanded into Crimea; in the south, to the Arabian Peninsula and the Persian Gulf; in the east, to Baghdad and Basra; and in the west, to Egypt and North Africa. By the sixteenth century, the Ottoman Empire included what we know of today as the Middle East, North Africa, the Balkans, and the countries of Greece, Serbia, Croatia, Albania, Romania, Bulgaria, and much of Hungary. Within this empire there were more than twenty different nationalities, and it stretched from the Persian Gulf to the Danube River. The estimated population of the Ottoman Empire was around 40 million at the time when England's population was 4 million.

During the last part of the nineteenth century, Ottoman control of its far-flung empire began to wane, and during and after World War I, control of the Middle East shifted from the Turks to the British and French.[21] As a result of a number of agreements, by 1922 the Ottoman Empire was no more, and the residual political entity was Turkey. Since the fall of the Ottoman Empire, centralized Muslim authority, which Muslims call the caliphate, ceased to exist. According to Sayyid Qutb, a new caliphate governed by *Sharia* would emerge only after there was a revival of Islam in one country. Once the Taliban took over in Afghanistan, bin Laden and other Islamists believed that it could become a new caliphate.

During World War I the British had opposed the Turks, and the most famous of the anti-Turkish British officers was the brilliant, but idiosyncratic, T. E. Lawrence, one of the first of the twentieth-century insurgency strategists and practitioners. It was Lawrence of Arabia who famously noted, "To make war upon rebellion is messy and slow, like eating soup with a knife."[22] Lawrence wrote "27 Articles," a distillation of the lessons he had learned leading Arabs in combat against the Turks. Several articles were particularly pointed. In Article 15 Lawrence presciently advised, "Do not try to do too much with your own hands. Better the Arabs do it tolerably than you do it perfectly. It is their war, and you are to help them, not to win it for them. Actually, also, under the very odd conditions of Arabia, your practical work will not be as good, perhaps, as you think it is."[23]

In May 1916, Britain, France, and Russia reached an agreement by which Palestine would be internationalized. In November 1917, British Lord Balfour sent a letter to Lord Rothschild, the head of the Zionist Federation in Great Britain, promising British support for the establishment in Palestine of a national home for the Jewish people on the understanding that "nothing shall be done which may prejudice the civil and religious rights of existing non-Jewish communities in Palestine." Under the Palestine Mandate, Britain controlled Palestine on both sides of the Jordan River; however, in 1922, the two-thirds of Palestine lying to the east of the Jordan River became the autonomous state of Transjordan. At this time, there were 84,000 Jews in Palestine. As repression of Jews increased in Europe, Jewish refugees immigrated in large numbers to Palestine, and by 1939, there were 445,000 Jews in Palestine.

World War II and the genocidal murder of 6 million Jews in the concentration camps of Nazi Germany gave further impetus to the Zionist movement to establish a Jewish state in Palestine. With the outbreak of war, the Nazi slaughter of European Jews began, and in May 1942, the Zionist conference in New York City formally called for the establishment of a Jewish state.[24] At the end of the war, President Truman supported the creation of a Jewish country, and in May 1947, the newly founded United Nations established a special committee to investigate the calls for the founding of a new state. In November, the UN General Assembly voted to partition Palestine into separate Arab and Jewish states. On May 14, 1948, the state of Israel declared its independence, and within a matter of hours, both the Soviet Union and the United States, the two most powerful states in the world at that time, formally recognized Israel's statehood.

Arab-Israeli Relations

The founding of the state of Israel created a homeland for the estimated 650,000 Jews who had immigrated by 1948, but at the same time it displaced Arabs who had lived in Palestine for generations; this underlying tension contributed to ongoing conflict between Arab countries and Israel. Soon after the founding of Israel, armed forces from Egypt and Jordan with some troops from Syria, Lebanon, and Iraq jointly invaded Israel in a failed attempt to destroy the newly established state. The Arab countries signed separate armistices with Israel, and as a result of these, Jordan occupied the Jordan River's West Bank and Jerusalem, and Egypt occupied the Gaza Strip. During the 1950s, there was a massive ethnic migration throughout the Middle East; hundreds of thousands of Jews left Arab countries for Israel, and an estimated 750,000 Arab Palestinians left Israel, going primarily to Jordan.

Sir Lawrence Freedman has identified two radical waves of change in the Middle East since the end of World War II: the first of these was led by Arab nationalists, and in particular Gamal Abdel Nasser, who became Egypt's leader following the overthrow of King Farouk in 1952.[25] The second radical wave was led by radical Islamists and began with the 1979 Iranian revolution. Both the first and the second waves were anticolonial and anti-Zionist, and both formed the backdrop to American relations with Islamic countries for decades to come.

On the surface, American political ideals and Nasser's anticolonial orientation should have been complementary or at least not inconsistent; however, Nasser strongly supported both the emerging nonaligned movement and Algeria's rebellion against France. Reflecting his emphasis on Arab nationalism and power, in 1956 Nasser nationalized control of the Suez Canal, which had been run by a Franco-British company. In response, Israel, Britain, and France invaded Egypt to reassert control over the canal in November 1956. President Eisenhower publicly condemned the action by the three U.S. allies, and they were forced to withdraw. The United Nations established a peacekeeping force that implemented a ceasefire and occupied the Sinai Peninsula.

Nasser attempted to reassert his claims for Arab nationalism in June 1967 by forcing the UN force to withdraw from Sinai and by imposing a blockade of the Straits of Tiran. Responding to these actions, Israel attacked and forced Egypt to withdraw from the Sinai, taking over the Gaza Strip, Syria's Golan Heights, and the West Bank of the Jordan River, including the old city of Jerusalem, in only six days of fighting. As Freedman notes, "More than anything else, it was the June 1967 war with Israel that undermined Nasserism. . . . Suddenly Israel was more than three times its previous size. Nasser's bombastic rhetoric of glorious victory was revealed to be without foundation."[26] After six days, a United Nations ceasefire ended the fighting.

Nasser remained in power until his death in 1970, when he was succeeded by Anwar Sadat; however, the Arab defeat in the Six Day War of 1967 marked the beginning of the end of the first wave of radicalism in the Middle East.

There were signs that a new wave was emerging. For example, on July 22, 1968, terrorists who were part of George Habash's Popular Front for the Liberation of Palestine (PFLP) hijacked an Israeli El Al flight bound from Rome to Tel Aviv. Most of the passengers were released in Algiers, and the remaining twelve hostages were eventually released unharmed after Israel agreed to the release of Palestinian militants who had been held in Israeli prisons. Many consider this to be the first act in the annals of modern terrorism.[27] This was followed in September 1970 by the hijacking of several planes, which were held at an old Royal Air Force base in Jordan. King Hussein ordered an attack on the planes and a crackdown on radical Palestinians, who came to refer to Jordan's attack as "Black September." Pakistani General Zia ul Haq commanded a Pakistani counterterrorism training mission in Jordan, and its members helped to defeat the militant Palestinians.[28] This event dramatically marked the distinction between moderate Arabs such as King Hussein, who were willing to accept the existence of the state of Israel, and radical Muslims who called for the elimination of Israel. The debate between these two factions would continue unabated for decades.

Frustrated by their defeat in the Six Day War, Egypt and Syria sought to regain the territory that they had lost. On October 6, 1973, on Yom Kippur, the holiest day of the Jewish year, Egypt and Syria launched a combined, simultaneous surprise attack on Israel from the south and the north. Initially, Egyptian and Syrian forces made great gains against Israeli forces; this was definitely not a repeat of the Six Day War. Within two weeks, however, Israel was successful in driving the Syrians back and retaking the Golan Heights and forcing the Egyptians back across the Suez Canal. Once again, a United Nations peacekeeping force enforced a ceasefire, and in January 1974 Israel withdrew from the Suez Canal's west bank. With Henry Kissinger serving as intermediary, Israel signed two disengagement agreements with Egypt and one agreement with Syria concerning the Golan Heights. Even though Israel defeated Egypt and Syria on the battlefield, the Yom Kippur War demonstrated that Arab countries could challenge Israel. But this war did not resolve any of the long-standing issues between Israel and its Arab neighbors, which continued to reject the very existence of the Jewish state.

In 1977, President Anwar Sadat announced that he would visit Jerusalem, the first significant indication of reconciliation between Israel and an Arab state. The reaction by other Arab states was vociferously negative. For example, Iraq condemned Sadat's move and cut its ties with Egypt. The League of Arab States suspended Egypt's membership from 1979 to 1989 and moved the League's office from Cairo to Tunis.

Relations between Israel and the Arab world worsened in 1978, when Israel assisted Lebanese Christian forces in their civil war against Lebanese Muslims. After a terrorist attack by the Palestinian Liberation Organization based in Lebanon, Israel invaded southern Lebanon. Subsequently, Israel voluntarily withdrew from Lebanon and allowed United Nations forces to take over; however, Israel continued to support Lebanese Christian militia forces, the Phalangists. Following more terrorist attacks against Israel, it occupied southern Lebanon in 1980.

1979: The Year of Transition and the Second Wave of Islamic Radicalism

Many times in history, the significance of events is clear only in retrospect; that is certainly the case with 1979. In the course of that year, the Shah of Iran was deposed; Iranian radicals took over the U.S. embassy in Tehran; Saddam Hussein became president of Iraq; Israel and Egypt signed a peace treaty; radical Muslims seized the Grand Mosque in Mecca; Pakistani radicals attacked and burned the U.S. embassy in Islamabad; and the Soviet Union invaded Afghanistan.[29] In short, the events of 1979 dramatically marked the beginning of the second wave of Islamic radicalism, and this wave was characterized by anticolonialism, a resurgence of radical, political Islam, and the beginning of acceptance of Israel by the largest Arab state, Egypt. It was as if the driver of history had one foot on the brake and one foot on the accelerator; the centrifugal and centripetal forces of history were battling each other.

Since the overthrow of Iranian Prime Minister Muhammad Mossadegh in 1953 with the help of the CIA, the Shah of Iran had exercised firm control over his country, and the United States supported and relied on the Shah. For years, the U.S. considered Iran to be one of the three pillars, along with Saudi Arabia and Israel, of U.S. policy in the Middle East. Although most Iranians were Muslims, they differed from many of their Arab neighbors in two ways. First, they were ethnic Persians and not Arabs, and the two groups resent being confused with each other. Second, 90 percent of Iranians are Shia Muslims, the most concentrated Shia population of any country in the world (see Table 2.1). The divide within Islam between Shia and Sunnis has been and remains an important fissure among Muslims. Iran shared a characteristic with a number of its Arab

Muslim neighbors—vast oil and gas reserves. Iran possessed 10 percent of the world's proven oil reserves and, because of its substantial revenue from oil sales, became one of the biggest purchasers of American weapons. The Nixon administration approved the sale of more than $20 billion worth of U.S.-produced weapons. President Carter considered Iran to be "an island of stability in one of the more troubled areas of the world," and of the Shah, Carter said, "[T]here is no leader with whom I have a deeper sense of personal gratitude and personal friendship."[30] Thus, when the Shah was deposed in January 1979, it came as a surprising shock to U.S. policymakers.[31] Eleven months later, radical Iranians took over the American embassy in Tehran and took sixty-six Americans hostage in apparent retaliation for the United States admitting the Shah to the U.S. for medical treatment. Freeing the hostages dominated the foreign policy agenda of the Carter administration from the time that the hostages were seized on November 4, 1979, until Carter left office in January 1981. The Iranian hostage crisis significantly weakened Carter among the U.S. electorate and contributed to his defeat by Ronald Reagan in the 1980 presidential election, and in this sense the crisis helped to usher Reaganism into American politics.

Radical Islamists were also active in Afghanistan. On February 14, 1979, the U.S. ambassador to Afghanistan, Adolph Dubs, was kidnapped by a Tajik separatist group, Setami-i-Milli (Oppressed National Movement). Tajiks were a different ethnic group than the dominant Pashtuns of Afghanistan and were opposed by the Pashtuns. Dubs was later killed during a rescue attempt by Afghan security forces. One week following the killing, the Carter administration announced that it was going to make deep cuts in the U.S. aid program for Afghanistan because of Dubs' killing and because of the "abysmal human rights record" of the Afghan government.

Not all of the news concerning the Middle East was bad in early 1979, though, for in March, Israeli Prime Minister Menachem Begin and Egyptian President Anwar Sadat signed a peace treaty that ended more than thirty years of unmitigated hostility between the two states. Significantly, Egypt became the first Arab state to recognize Israel and its right to exist. Egyptian President Sadat recognized the significance and danger of what he was doing, and in October 1982, a radical member of the Muslim Brotherhood assassinated the Egyptian visionary who had dared to pursue peace with Israel. A mirror image of this tragedy occurred in Israel thirteen years later when a radical Jewish nationalist assassinated Yitzhak Rabin, the Israeli visionary who had pursued peace with Egypt with the Oslo Accords.

The rise of Shia fundamentalism concerned the Sunni leadership of Iraq, and in July Saddam Hussein became president and solidified his control through a combination of patronage, terror, and the cynical use of religion for his own purposes.

The events of early 1979 illustrated the conflicting tendencies of Islam in this period. Although the Egyptian-Israeli peace treaty was an indicator of moderation, the overthrow of the Shah and takeover of the U.S. embassy in Tehran were indicators that radical Islamists were on the rise. A further indicator of this occurred in Saudi Arabia, one of the most conservative Islamic countries, where in November a group of almost 500 Saudi terrorists, inspired by the writings of ibn Taymiyya and Abd al-Wahhab, took over the Grand Mosque in the holiest city of Islam, Mecca, and held hundreds of pilgrims hostage.[32] The attack had taken the Saudi government by surprise, and it did not respond for more than a week. The government requested the architectural plans of the Grand Mosque from the Bin Laden Brothers for Contracting and Industry (the company founded by Osama bin Laden's father), which was in charge of many construction projects in Mecca, and government forces planned their counterattack on the basis of these plans. When the government's attack was launched, it was brutally effective. Official estimates indicated that the number of people killed was in the hundreds; unofficial estimates are in excess of 4,000 killed.[33] More than sixty leaders of the uprising were captured, tried, convicted, and decapitated, the largest mass execution in Saudi history.[34]

The day after radicals attacked the Grand Mosque, other radicals in Pakistan attacked the American embassy in Islamabad and two American cultural centers in Rawalpindi and Lahore. According to reports, the attackers were responding to radio broadcasts from Iran indicating that the U.S. and Israel were involved in the takeover of the Grand Mosque. The anti-American/anti-Israeli rioters consisted mostly of students from Quaid-I-Azam University and were connected with the Islamic Party, Jamaat-e-Islami, which, in turn, was influenced by the radical Muslim Brotherhood. Fifteen thousand people surrounded the embassy while 139 embassy personnel hid in the basement, and it looked as if events in Islamabad were going to mimic those in Tehran. Eventually, the anti-American riot played itself out, and the crisis ended with four deaths. But events in both Iran, which was hostile to the U.S., and Pakistan, whose government was friendly toward the U.S., indicated that radical Islam was playing an increasingly important role in Middle Eastern politics.

The year 1979 also marked the emergence of "political Islam," whose adherents are called "Islamists." In its development, Christian doctrine addressed the relationship between religion and government, and there have been several notable Christian theocracies in which church and state were one, including John Calvin's Geneva and the Puritan Massachusetts Bay Colony. However, the predominant Christian doctrine called for the separation of church and state. In contrast, many Islamic countries have followed long-held practices of mixing religion and politics.[35] Islamism is a political movement, and complicating the problem is the fact that central religious authority in Islam is nonexistent or ambiguous. Sunnis, which constitute 90 percent of the world's Muslims, have no universally recognized religious leaders, although Shia do. This ambiguity opens the door for those inclined to use religion for their purposes. Saddam Hussein, for example, was essentially a secular leader, but when it suited his purposes, just as Stalin had done in the Soviet Union, he used religion. Similarly, Osama bin Laden issued religious edicts *(fatwa)* with no formal religious authority to do so.

U.S. Interests in the Middle East and South Asia

Given the ferment of issues and events in the Middle East and South Asia highlighted by the events of 1979, it would have been timely and relevant to consider American interests and priorities in the Middle East and South Asia, and there was some consideration of these issues in the U.S. government. But the significance of the events of 1979 was not immediately recognized. There are four major U.S. interests in the greater Middle East region.[36]

First, the United States over time became increasingly interested in the oil in the region. Prior to World War II, the U.S. was actually an exporter of oil; in fact, one of the factors that contributed to Japan's decision to attack American forces at Pearl Harbor in December 1941 was the U.S. decision to stop exporting oil to Japan.[37] Given the increasing consumption of oil by the United States, over time it became a voracious importer of oil, and much of this came from Middle East oil producers, which possessed the lion's share of the world's proven oil reserves: Saudi Arabia possessed approximately 25 percent, Iraq possessed 10 percent, Iran possessed 10 percent, and Kuwait possessed 10 percent.[38] As Table 2.2 demonstrates, the United States became increasingly dependent on the Middle East as a source of petroleum. In addition, many of the shipping routes for transporting oil from the Middle East to the U.S., Europe, and Japan

TABLE 2.2

U.S. Petroleum Imports by Country of Origin, 1970–2008

Year	Persian Gulf*	Iraq	Saudi Arabia	Total OPEC	Total non-OPEC	Imports from Persian Gulf as % of total imports	Imports from OPEC as % of total imports
1970	121	0	30	1,294	2,126	3.5	37.8
1972	471	4	190	2,046	2,695	9.9	43.2
1974	1,030	0	461	3,256	2,856	17.0	53.3
1976	1,840	26	1,230	5,066	2,247	25.2	69.3
1978	2,219	62	1,144	5,751	2,612	26.5	68.8
1980	1,519	28	1,261	4,300	2,609	22.0	62.2
1982	696	3	552	2,146	2,968	13.6	42.0
1984	506	12	325	2,049	3,388	9.3	37.7
1986	912	81	685	2,837	3,387	14.7	45.6
1988	1,514	345	1,073	3,520	3,882	20.8	47.6
1990	1,996	518	1,339	4,296	3,721	24.5	53.6
1992	1,778	0	1,720	4,092	3,796	22.5	51.9
1994	1,728	0	1,402	4,247	4,749	19.2	47.2
1996	1,604	1	1,363	4,211	5,267	16.9	44.4
1998	2,136	336	1,491	4,905	5,803	19.9	45.8
2000	2,488	620	1,572	5,203	6,257	21.7	45.4
2002	2,269	459	1,552	4,605	6,925	19.7	39.9
2004	2,493	656	1,558	5,701	7,444	19.0	43.4
2006	2,211	553	1,463	5,517	8,190	16.6	40.2
2008	2,373	627	1,532	5,958	6,914	18.4	46.3

Source: U.S. Department of Energy; http://www.eia.doe.gov/emeu/aer/txt/ptb0504.html.

*Persian Gulf category includes Bahrain, Iran, Iraq, Kuwait, Qatar, Saudi Arabia, United Arab Emirates, and the Neutral Zone between Kuwait and Saudi Arabia.

bordered Middle Eastern countries, increasing the vulnerability of oil importers to a possible oil cutoff.

The second interest of the United States in the Middle East and South Asia was related to the first: namely, promoting stability in the region. The U.S. would not have assured access to Middle Eastern oil without stability; consequently, the United States sought to support stable governments in the region, and this goal was purchased at the cost of ideological consistency for the U.S. For example, most governments in the region were authoritarian, hardly consistent with the American policy, since the days of Woodrow Wilson if not before, of supporting the self-determination of people; yet, in Saudi Arabia, Iran, and the Gulf states, the U.S. supported authoritarian governments. Why? Because they were stable and assured the United States access to oil, the lifeblood of any modern, advanced, industrial state.

But the U.S. government and society are not monolithic, and there was a strong tradition in American political culture of supporting democratic processes and ideals, and this tradition led many Americans both in and out of government to support a third objective in the Middle East and South Asia: democratic values. As a part of this approach, the U.S. supported democratic movements and parties, and the most prominent of these was Israel. Given the horrific losses of the Holocaust and the significant Jewish constituency within the U.S., it is not surprising that a prominent American objective in the Middle East was the survival and security of Israel. Many Muslims have no direct experience with democracy, do not believe democracy is the best form of government, and the American support of Israel as a democratic state simply heightened Islamic hostility to the idea of democracy. In the minds of many Islamists the United States, Israel, and democracy are integrally related leading them to reject democracy as an acceptable political system.

In addition, as part of its emphasis on ideals in the Middle East and South Asia, the United States supported what it viewed as a fourth interest: fundamental human rights. Indeed, one of the most distinctive aspects of the U.S. approach to international relations, if not the most distinctive, is its moralistic approach to foreign policy. Of course, the actual level of support for human rights has waxed and waned with each presidential administration, but to a greater or lesser degree, human rights has been a constant attribute of American foreign policy since the founding of the republic. Jimmy Carter was the president who most emphasized human rights in recent decades, and some have argued that the pressure that he placed on the Shah of Iran actually contributed to the Shah's downfall. For example, Carter condemned the use of torture by the Shah's secret police, SAVAK. For most of its history, the United States strongly opposed the use of "cruel and unusual punishment." In many Islamic countries corporal punishment, such as cutting off a hand for thievery or decapitation for capital crimes, is still practiced. Even close U.S. allies, such as Saudi Arabia, have engaged in such practices, causing tensions between the two countries.

There was, of course, no problem with any one of these four American objectives; however, the problem was trying to balance and even reconcile these goals. For example, the U.S. wanted access to Middle Eastern oil, which required stability in the region. But the U.S. also supported Israel, and at times these goals were mutually exclusive and both could not be accomplished simultaneously. During the Yom Kippur War of 1973, the United States resupplied Israel with military equipment, and in response, the Arab members of the

Organization of Petroleum Exporting Countries (OPEC) imposed an embargo of shipments of oil to the U.S., resulting in a fourfold increase in the price of oil from three dollars per barrel in September 1973 to twelve dollars a barrel two months later. The United States also supported the promotion of democracy and human rights, but this goal conflicted with the orientations of many of the authoritarian oil suppliers in the Middle East.

3 Afghanistan, Pakistan, and the United States

Afghanistan and Pakistan have been linked in various ways for many years, and as Stephen Philip Cohen has noted, "Any comprehensive policy toward Pakistan must also address Pakistan's relationship with Afghanistan. The two states have a long-standing and complex relationship, which took an astounding turn when American forces removed the Taliban government with Pakistan's reluctant assistance."[1] General David Petraeus has pointed out, "One cannot adequately address the challenges in Afghanistan without adding Pakistan into the equation."[2] Respected Oxford University Professor Adam Roberts has pointed out, "Granted the indissoluble connection between Afghanistan and Pakistan, any policy in respect of the one has to be framed in light of its effects on the other."[3] Counterinsurgency expert David Kilcullen has noted, "Afghanistan is one theater in a larger confrontation with transnational *takfiri* terrorism . . ."[4] According to journalist Bob Woodward, President Obama noted in late 2009, "We need to make clear to people that the cancer is in Pakistan."[5]

Afghanistan under the Taliban was the country that provided sanctuary to al Qaeda and enabled its members to train an estimated 60,000 terrorists.[6] According to the 9/11 Commission, "Afghanistan was the incubator for al Qaeda and for the 9/11 attacks."[7] In May 1998, Pakistan detonated six nuclear explosions definitively demonstrating that it possessed nuclear weapons and contributed to the development of the U.S. objective, to use President George W. Bush's words, "to keeping the world's most dangerous weapons out of the hands of the world's most dangerous terrorists."[8]

Pakistan: The Fulcrum of Asia?

Geopoliticians such as Sir Halford MacKinder contend that geography is destiny, and throughout its history, Pakistan has been strongly influenced by its geographic location at the juncture of South Asia, West Asia, and Central Asia. Because of its geostrategic position, the former head of Saudi intelligence, Prince Turki al-Faisal, has called Pakistan "a kind of Central Asian fulcrum . . . a pivot point for trade and energy supplies."[9] General Anthony Zinni, the former commander of the Central Command, testified that Pakistan "may hold the key to stability in Afghanistan and Central Asia."[10] U.S. ambassador to Pakistan Anne Patterson has claimed, "Pakistan is ground zero for threats against the United States."[11] Therefore, the importance of Pakistan cannot be over-rated.

Any country's past affects its present, and Pakistan is no exception to this generalization. Over time, a number of different groups invaded what is currently Pakistan; these groups included the Persians, Greeks, Scythians, Arabs, Afghans, and Turks. Alexander the Great was one of those who invaded. In 330 B.C. Alexander defeated the Persians and marched through Sindh and Balochistan (what is now southern Pakistan) and then on to Babylon in what is today Iraq, where he died in 323 B.C. Muslim traders in the eighth century brought Islam to Sindh. The Mughal Empire (southern Indian subcontinent) dominated the sixteenth and seventeenth centuries, and the British came to rule in the eighteenth century. In 1842 the first Anglo-Afghan War was fought, with the result that the British annexed Sindh, Hyderabad, and Khairpur. Several years later, as a result of the Sikh Wars, the British annexed Punjab, and in 1858, the British East India Company, which had controlled the lucrative opium trade with China, dissolved and was replaced by the British Raj (the rule of India by the British Crown). In 1878–80, the second Anglo-Afghan War was fought, and in 1893 Sir Mortimer Durand and Amir Abdur Rahman Khan of Afghanistan negotiated a partially surveyed boundary, which came to be known as the Durand Line, between British India (including what is now Pakistan) and Afghanistan. As Owen Bennett Jones has noted, "Ever since partition, Kabul has argued that the Durand Line was never meant to be an international boundary and has complained that it deprived Afghanistan of territory that historically had been under its control."[12] The boundary area between Afghanistan and Pakistan has remained controversial and problematic down to the present day.

Great Britain controlled present-day Pakistan as part of its imperial holdings in India. In the first half of the twentieth century, Muslims pressed for autonomy from India, which was predominantly populated by Hindus. On March 23, 1940, Muslims in India asked for a separate homeland, a request that was summarily denied. The situation reached crisis proportions in June 1947, when legislation was introduced into the British Parliament calling for the partition of India, legislation that resulted in mass rioting and unrest in India. Within months, there were 250,000 deaths from rioting and demonstrations, and an estimated 24 million refugees roamed the countryside. In August 1947, British India was partitioned into two major parts: (1) India, which included West Bengal and Assam, and (2) Pakistan, which included East Bengal (East Pakistan) and territory in the northwest (West Pakistan). Within two months, India and Pakistan went to war over the sovereignty of Kashmir, a Muslim majority state not included in newly partitioned Pakistan and ruled by an Indian maharaja. In January 1948, India submitted the dispute over Kashmir to the United Nations, which implemented a ceasefire and called for a plebiscite to determine Kashmir's future. As a prerequisite for the plebiscite, both India and Pakistan were supposed to withdraw their military forces from the region, but neither did so. As a result the plebiscite never occurred; India and Pakistan fought another war over Kashmir in 1965, and it remains a volatile issue today. Why? Stephen Cohen has noted several reasons. First, Pakistani nationalists "feel that their identity is wrapped up in the fate of Kashmir, a region that reflects their own personal and political histories."[13] Second, Pakistanis believe that if India gave up Kashmir, Indian Muslims would immigrate to Pakistan, perhaps even resulting in the breakup of India. Third, Kashmir has become a symbolic issue of identity between Pakistan and India and has assumed great significance in both countries.

In December 1971, India invaded East Pakistan and almost immediately recognized the new country to emerge following the invasion, Bangladesh. According to Pakistani Field Marshal Mohammad Ayub Khan, "The separation of Bengal, though painful, was inevitable and unavoidable. The majority of those people [in East Pakistan] had been duped into believing that West Pakistan was their enemy.... I suppose the Hindu morale is now very high. It is the first victory they have had over the Muslims for centuries. It would take us a long time to live this down."[14]

In 1974, India tested what it called a "peaceful nuclear device," which differed from a rudimentary nuclear weapon in name only. Given the rivalry, competition, and lack of trust that has characterized Indian-Pakistani relations, it is not surprising that the Indian test stimulated Pakistan to follow in India's proliferation footsteps, and in May 1998, Pakistan detonated six nuclear explosions, demonstrating its nuclear capability.[15] In doing so, Pakistan became the first Islamic country to obtain its own nuclear weapons.

Pakistan's army has been central to the development and maintenance of stability. Since its founding in 1947, four different military regimes have ruled Pakistan. For the army, Pakistan's security rests on three pillars: "resisting Indian hegemony in the region and promoting the Kashmir cause; protecting and developing the nuclear [weapons program]; and promoting a pro-Pakistani government in Afghanistan."[16]

Pakistan today is a country of about 800,000 square kilometers, almost twice the geographic size of California. It borders four countries: Afghanistan, India, Iran, and China. Pakistan has a total population of 175 million, making it the fifth largest country in the world. Pakistan's military is the sixth largest in the world, and by 2020, Pakistan is projected to be the fifth largest nuclear weapons power in the world.[17] It has six major ethnic groups that constitute 94 percent of the population: Punjabi (45% of the population), Pashtun (15%), Sindhi (14%), Sariaki (8%), Muhagirs (8%), and Baloch (4%). In 2008 its gross domestic product was $167.7 billion and per capita GDP was $2,500. Further characteristics and statistics for both Pakistan and Afghanistan are shown in Table 3.1.

Several of the statistics in this table deserve elaboration. First, Afghanistan has a significantly higher population growth rate than Pakistan, 2.58 percent versus 1.56 percent. Second, Pakistan is more urbanized than Afghanistan, 36 percent versus 24 percent. Third, Afghanistan's per capita gross domestic product is only 40 percent ($1,000 versus $2,500) that of Pakistan. Perhaps reflecting harsher economic conditions, Afghanistan's literacy rate is almost half that of Pakistan, and average life expectancy is 70 percent of Pakistan's (45 versus 65 years). Cumulatively, these statistics indicate that economic and political development is more likely to be significantly more difficult to achieve in Afghanistan than Pakistan.

Afghanistan: The Cockpit of Asia?

Similar to Pakistan, Afghanistan's geographic position has strongly influenced its history. Arnold Toynbee, one of the most respected historians of the twentieth century, wrote, "Afghanistan has been deluged with history and been devastated by it."[18] In ancient times, many believed that the region of Afghanistan was the center of the world. Lord Curzon referred to Afghanistan as "the cockpit of Asia," and Indian poet Muhammad Iqbal called it "the heart of Asia."[19] Archaeologists have found evidence of human habitation in the region dating back to 3,000 B.C. Situated on the trade routes between the Middle East and South Asia, Afghanistan became the focal point for invasion, and invaders

TABLE 3.1
Statistical Profiles of Afghanistan and Pakistan, 2010

Attribute	Afghanistan	Pakistan
Geographic size	652,230 sq. km. Slightly smaller than Texas	796,095 sq. km. Less than twice the size of California
Bordering countries and length of borders	Pakistan (2,430 km) Tajikistan (1,206 km) Iran (936 km) Turkmenistan (744 km) Uzbekistan (137 km) China (76 km)	Afghanistan (2,430 km) India (2,912 km) Iran (909 km) China (523 km)
Population	28, 395,716	174,578,558
Median age	18 years	21.2 years
Population growth rate	2.58%	1.555%
Urban population	24%	36%
Life expectancy	44.4 years	65.26 years
Literacy rate	28.1%	49.9%
Ethnic groups	Pashtun (42%) Tajik (27%) Hazara (9%) Uzbek (9%) Aimak (4%) Baloch (2%) Turkmen (3%) Other (4%)	Punjabi (44.68%) Pashtun (Pathan) (15.42%) Sindhi (14.1%) Sariaki (8.38%) Muhagirs (7.57%) Baloch (3.57%) Other (6.28%)
Religious groups	Sunni Muslims (80%) Shia Muslims (19%) Other (1%)	Sunni Muslims (75%) Shia Muslims (20%) Other (5%)
Economics: GDP	$14.04 billion (2009)	$166.5 billion (2009)
GDP per capita	$1,000	$2,500
Export partners(2008)	U.S. (26.47%) India (23.1%) Pakistan (17.36%) Tajikistan (12.5%)	U.S. (15.87%) UAE (12.35%) Afghanistan (8.48%) UK (4.7%) China (4.44%)
Import partners	Pakistan (26.78%) U.S. (24.81%) Germany (5.06%) India (5.15%) Russia (4.04%)	China (15.35%) Saudi Arabia (10.54%) UAE (9.8%) India (4.02%) Kuwait (4.73%) Malaysia (4.43%)
Disputes	Border with Pakistan	Kashmir Control over Tribal Areas
Other information	World's largest opium producer	Major transit route for Afghan drugs producer

Source: Data from Central Intelligence Agency, *World Factbook*; available at www.cia.gov/library/pulications/the-world-factbook/index.html.

of Afghanistan have included the British, Sikhs, Mughals, Persians, Mongols, Macedonians, Soviets, and Americans.[20]

In 329 B.C. Alexander the Great conquered Afghanistan, Central Asia, and India. In A.D. 645 Arabs came and introduced Islam into the region. From 874 to 999, Persia controlled the area, and in 1219 Genghis Khan attacked. In 1222, he conquered Herat, considered to be the "cradle of Afghanistan's history and civilization." In this attack, Khan spared only 40 of the 160,000 residents of Herat.[21] In 1383 Timur (called Tamerlane in the West) conquered and occupied the region. In the sixteenth century, the Mughal king Babur (who was a descendant of Genghis Khan) invaded from what is today Iran and captured first Kabul and then Kandahar and introduced elements of Persian culture into Afghanistan.

In the nineteenth century, Britain made three attempts to take over Afghanistan in order to halt the expansion of Russian influence in the region. The first Anglo-Afghan War lasted from 1839 to 1842 and resulted in a disastrous defeat for Britain. In their retreat, British forces were reduced from 16,000 to 1, and William Brydon, the sole survivor, remembered, "This was a terrible march, the fire of the enemy incessant, and the numbers of officers and men, not knowing where they were going for snow-blindness, were cut up."[22] Following the war, at the recommendation of the Viceroy of India, John Lawrence, the British chose to follow a policy of "masterful inactivity" with regard to Afghanistan, and in 1867 Lawrence warned that "to try to control such a people is to court misfortune and calamity. The Afghan will bear poverty, insecurity of life; but he will not tolerate foreign rule. The moment he has a chance, he will rebel."[23] In 1873, Britain and Russia signed a treaty making Afghanistan a buffer state between the Russian- and British-controlled empires; however, in 1878 Russia violated the treaty by sending a mission to Kabul. In response, Britain sent an expeditionary force of more than 33,000 soldiers to secure important mountain passes including the Khyber Pass, which connects Pakistan and Afghanistan. After several years of fighting with mixed results, the British withdrew in 1880. A British officer who had served in Afghanistan noted "the extreme difficulty in administering a satisfactory thrashing to a mountain-bred people who have an ever open door behind them."[24] At the end of World War I, following the collapse of the Romanov dynasty in Russia, Britain attacked Afghanistan, beginning the third Anglo-Afghan War. Later that year, in August 1919, Britain and Afghanistan signed the Treaty of Rawalpindi, granting independence to Afghanistan. As journalist Ahmed Rashid has noted, "[T]he British made three attempts to conquer and hold Afghanistan until they realized that the intractable Afghans could be bought much more easily than fought."[25] This was a lesson that the United States would later learn in its occupation of Iraq when it paid Sunni insurgents—dubbed the "Sons of Iraq"—not to fight against American forces.

Politics in Afghanistan reflect the ethnic divisions and conflicts within the country. The majority group, constituting 42 percent of the population, consists of Pashtuns. Twenty-seven percent of the population consists of Tajiks, 9 percent Hazaras, and 9 percent Uzbeks, in addition to a smaller number of Aimaks, Balochs, and Turkmen.[26] These groups are distributed geographically. A majority of Pashtuns lives live south of the Hindu Kush (the 500-mile mountain range that covers northwestern Pakistan to central and eastern Pakistan) and with some Persian speaking ethnic groups. Hazaras and Tajiks live in the Hindu Kush area, and north of the Hindu Kush are Persians and Turkic ethnic groups.

For the first decade following independence, Afghanistan was ruled by a Pashtun, Amanullah Khan, who, according to Louis Dupree, "struck at the roots of conservative Islam by removing the veil from the women, by opening co-educational schools, and by attempting to force all Afghans in Kabul to wear Western clothing."[27] One of the king's advisers, Mahmud Tarzi, commented, "Amanullah has built a beautiful monument without a foundation. Take out one brick and it will tumble down."[28] And this is what happened in 1929 when Habibullah Kalakani, a Tajik, took over the government. But he only lasted nine months and was overthrown by King Mohammed Nadir Shah, who ruled from 1929 to 1933, when he was assassinated and replaced by King Mohammed Zahir Shah, who became the last king of Afghanistan and was on the throne for forty years. But, as the respected expert on Afghanistan, Louis Dupree, noted, "King Mohammad Zahir Shah reigned but did not rule for twenty years. His uncles, as befitted Islamic cultural patterns, ruled."[29] After this, Zahir Shah's cousin, Mohammad Daoud Khan, ruled, and Zahir Shah accepted his tutelage. Under Daoud's rule, relations between Afghanistan and Pakistan worsened, and diplomatic and economic relations were severed. In March 1963, King Zahir Shah asked for Daoud's resignation, and at long last after three decades the king came to rule as well as reign Afghanistan.

Two weeks after Daoud's resignation, the king appointed a committee to write a new constitution, and by the spring of 1964 a new constitution had been written.[30] The king convened a *Loya Jirga*, a meeting of the members of the National Assembly, the Senate, the Supreme Court, and the constitutional commissions. On September 20, 1964, the new constitution was signed by the 452 members of the *Loya Jirga*, and on October 1 by the king. Dr. Joseph Collins has noted that the signing of the 1964 constitution marked "the golden age for Afghan governance. It was the best part of the twentieth century. Afghanistan had a chance."[31]

Following the adoption of the constitution, "the Afghan political system remained suspended between democracy and monarchy, though much closer to the latter."[32] The Parliament became "lethargic and deadlocked" in the 1969–73 period, and in 1973 Daoud, supported by the military, staged a coup d'état and took power while the king was out of the country for medical treatment.

In April 1978, radical leftists in the Afghan army overthrew the Daoud's civilian government in a violent coup, which Dupree characterized as "more Groucho than Karl." Within days, the leader of a procommunist party and a leader whom the Soviets supported, Nur Mohammed Taraki, emerged as the most powerful leader in Kabul. On a visit to Moscow, the Soviets told Taraki that he should get rid of his subordinate, former Foreign Minister Hafizullah Amin; however, Amin found out about the plot against him, turned the tables, and killed Taraki in a coup in September 1979. Religious fundamentalists had called for the overthrow of the Taraki government, and they were pleased with the overthrow and death of Taraki.

With 20 percent of the Soviet Union's population consisting of Muslims and with the apparent spread of Islamic fundamentalism, Soviet leaders grew increasingly concerned about the implications of these developments for their country, and they wanted an Afghan leader who would cater to their wishes and restrain the growth and spread of Islamic radicalism. There were dangerous developments on the horizon. In November 1979, the Ayatollah Khomeini took over the government of Iran and criticized Soviet meddling in the domestic politics of Iran. Important figures such as the Iranian Grand Ayatollah Shariatmadare publicly supported Afghan resistance fighters who opposed the Soviet-supported Taraki regime.[33] In November 1979, a group of radical Islamists took over the Grand Mosque in Mecca, a mob attacked and burned the U.S. embassy in Islamabad, and the American embassy in Libya was attacked and burned. Although none of these events directly involved the Soviet Union, they indicated the depth of hostility and commitment of some radical Muslims, and this greatly concerned Soviet leaders.

On December 24, 1979, Soviet military units entered Afghanistan. In a report to the Central Committee of the Communist Party of the Soviet Union, the top leaders noted, "[E]fforts were made to mend relations with America as a part of the 'more balanced foreign policy strategy' adopted by Kh. [Comrade] Amin. Kh. Amin has held a series of confidential meetings with the American *charge d'affaires* in Kabul . . . . Kh. Amin attempted to buttress his position by reaching a compromise with leaders of internal counter-revolution. Through trusted persons he engaged in contact with leaders of the Moslem fundamentalist opposition."[34] To the top leadership, Amin demonstrated two major weaknesses: he was wavering in his support of the USSR, and he met with Muslim fundamentalists. Because of their ongoing concern about the spread of Islamic radicalism, Soviet leaders made plans to replace Amin with an Afghan leader who would be more dependable.

The Soviet Invasion and Occupation of Afghanistan

In the days following the initial invasion, the Soviet Union sent approximately 75,000 soldiers to replace Hafizullah Amin with Babrak Karmal, and eventually, 120,000 troops were sent to Afghanistan. Because the Soviet republics of Turkmenistan, Uzbekistan, and Tajikistan bordered Afghanistan, it was relatively easy for Soviet troops to enter the country and to be resupplied from bases in the USSR. The reaction to the Soviet invasion from the United States was quick and definitive. Two days after the invasion, U.S. National Security Affairs adviser Zbigniew Brzezinski wrote a classified memo to President Carter:

> We are now facing *a regional crisis.* Both Iran and Afghanistan are in turmoil, and Pakistan is both unstable internally and extremely apprehensive externally. If the Soviets succeed in Afghanistan, and [security deletion] the age-long dream of Moscow to have direct access to the Indian Ocean will have been fulfilled. Historically, the British provided the barrier to that drive and Afghanistan was their buffer state. We assumed that role in 1945, but the Iranian crisis has led to the collapse of the balance of power in Southwest Asia, and it could produce Soviet presence right down on the edge of the Arabian and Oman Gulfs. Accordingly, the Soviet intervention in Afghanistan poses for us an extremely grave challenge, both internationally and domestically. While it could become a Soviet Vietnam, the initial effects of the intervention are likely to be adverse for us . . .[35]

American officials thus viewed the Soviet invasion of Afghanistan through the lenses of the cold war. President Carter sent Soviet leader Leonid Brezhnev what he called "the sharpest message" of his presidency on the hot line telling him that the invasion was "a clear threat to peace" and "could mark a fundamental and long-lasting turning point in our relations."[36] Within days of the invasion, President Carter signed a covert action order authorizing the CIA to send weapons to the Afghan resistance clandestinely. According to former CIA agent Milt Bearden, "[O]ur effort in Afghanistan had now become a central component of the endgame of the Cold War. Driving the Soviets out of Afghanistan was the goal; the welfare of the people of Afghanistan would be improved along the way, it was hoped, but that was not essential."[37] Journalist Steve Coll noted, "For many in the CIA the Afghan jihad was about killing Soviets, first and last."[38] In addition, memories of Vietnam and the role that the USSR had played in the American defeat there animated U.S. policy.

Both the Soviets and the *mujahideen* fought the war in a brutal, vicious manner. The USSR had clear technological superiority in conventional military terms and particularly in airpower and sought to capitalize on this; for example, "[W]hen the Soviets bombed Herat in 1979, they inflicted even more damage on the city than the Mongols had done."[39] Particularly effective was the heavily armed MI-24D "Hind" helicopter gunship, which could carry 128 rockets and four napalm or high-explosive bombs. Its machine guns could fire 1,000 rounds per minute, and with this impressive firepower, the Hind wrought havoc against the *mujahideen* until 1985. In addition to Hind helicopters, Soviet forces also employed landmines extensively and devastatingly. During the more than nine-year Soviet-Afghan War, the Soviets laid between 5 million and 10 million landmines throughout Afghanistan, and these had a long-lasting effect.[40] It is estimated that from 1979 to 1999, more than 400,000 Afghans were killed and another 400,000 injured from mine explosions.

According to one analyst of Afghanistan, "The frustration of waging what appeared to be an 'unwinnable war' against unconventional guerilla forces, denied the Soviets the prospect of ever hoping to permanently pacify the countryside or to expand the areas under their control. Civilians were driven out of their homes as Soviet forces indiscriminately bombed villages, destroyed crops, orchards, and irrigation systems, and scattered anti-personnel mines over large tracts of the country-side where a guerilla presence was suspected."[41] Mao Zedong, the brutal leader of the Chinese communist revolution and a theorist of insurgency warfare, famously wrote, "The people are like water, and the army is like fish . . . . The guerilla must move among the people as a fish swims in the sea."[42] The *mujahideen* were like Mao Zedong's insurgent fish in the Afghan sea, and the Soviets in the mid-1980s began to adopt a policy aimed at draining the sea itself.

For their part, the *mujahideen* fought the type of insurgency that they had previously fought against the British, consisting of hit-and-run attacks by guerillas who could not be differentiated from the civilian population. The *mujahideen* showed little mercy with captured Soviet forces. There were numerous accounts of captured Soviet soldiers being skinned alive. Captured pilots were subject to particularly harsh treatment. According to Milt Bearden, a former CIA agent who dealt with the *mujahideen*, "Soon after I arrived in Pakistan, I was shown a photograph of a Soviet pilot in a silver flight suit, up to his waist in snow, skin burned by the relentless sun, with a bullet hole in the side of his head. His Tokarev semiautomatic [pistol] was still clutched in his hand. He had killed himself rather than be captured. The greatest fear was not so much being hit as falling into *mujahideen* hands."[43]

In the fight against the USSR, ethnic and religious differences were subordinated to the most important immediate task: to defeat the infidel Soviet invaders. As a result, Uzbeks under General Aburrashid Dostum, Hazaras under Karim Khalili and Pahlawan Malik, Tajiks under Burhanuddin Rabbani, General Ahmed Shah Massoud, and Pashtuns under Gulbuddin Hekmatyar, Abdul Haq, Hamid Karzai, Jallaladin Haqqani, and Mullah Omar joined forces in order to oppose the Soviets. The United States, Saudi Arabia, and Pakistan provided military aid to the *mujahideen*. In fact, one arm of the Pakistani government, the Inter-Services Intelligence directorate (ISI)—which the late former Pakistani Prime Minister Benazir Bhutto referred to as a "state within a state"—had long-standing contacts with a number of the rebel groups and served as the conduit for aid primarily to fellow Pashtuns. As journalist Ahmed Rashid has noted, "[W]hen the Soviets invaded Afghanistan in 1979, Pakistan already had effective Islamic radicals under its control which would lead the jihad [against Soviet forces]."[44] At the time of the Soviet invasion, diplomatic relations between the United States and Pakistan were at a low point, but the U.S. depended upon the connections of the Pakistani and Saudi intelligence agencies, which maintained most of their contacts with the fundamentalists including Hekmatyar's Islamic Party, Mullah Omar's Taliban, Tajiks Younis Sayyaf and Jalaluddin Haqqani. Although the ISI provided support for a number of fundamentalist groups, they did not favor Tajik leaders Burhanuddin Rabbani—the head of Jamaat-e-Islami—and his deputy Ahmed Massoud.

Ronald Reagan brought a very different national security team to Washington once he was inaugurated in January 1981. One of the most important members of this new team was CIA Director William Casey, who had served as an officer of the Office of Strategic Services (OSS) in World War II. Casey, a devout Catholic, was intensely anti-Soviet when he became director. Milt Bearden, who worked for the CIA as a clandestine officer, noted, "Casey and the hard-liners were convinced that the Soviets had been behind the assassination attempt against Pope John Paul

II."[45] As his then special assistant, Robert Gates, noted, "Bill Casey came to the CIA primarily to wage war against the Soviet Union."[46] And he actually did so. During the spring of 1985, with CIA backing *mujahideen* groups staged cross-border raids into the USSR.[47] As journalist Steve Coll noted, "More than any other American, it was Casey who welded the alliance among the CIA, Saudi intelligence, and [Pakistani leader] Zia's army. As his Muslim allies did, Casey saw the Afghan jihad not merely as statecraft, but as an important front in a worldwide struggle between communist atheism and God's community of believers."[48]

Between 1981 and 1983, the CIA provided $60 million to the *mujahideen*, an amount that the Saudi government matched.[49] In providing this aid, the U.S. hoped to further its cold war position *vis-à-vis* the USSR, and in support of this objective, Casey encouraged the *mujahideen* to recruit radical Muslims from all over the world to come to Pakistan to join the *jihad* against the Soviet Union. It is estimated that between 1982 and 1992, 35,000 Muslim radicals from forty-three countries came to Pakistan and Afghanistan to fight with the *mujahideen*.[50] In addition, Casey approved attacks by *mujahideen* forces against Tajikistan and Uzbekistan, and at one point secretly went to Pakistan to meet with *mujahideen* groups.[51]

Despite the joining together of insurgent forces and the support from the U.S., Saudi Arabia, and Pakistan, things were looking bleak for the *mujahideen* six years into the war. The Soviets' use of airpower was particularly effective against the insurgents. At the urging of a flamboyant American congressman, Charlie Wilson, the CIA sent via Pakistan's ISI agency a portable, shoulder-fired, surface-to-air missile, called the Stinger, to the Afghan insurgents in February 1986.[52] On September 25, Afghan Engineer Ghaffar ordered his team to take aim and fire on Soviet helicopters based at Jalalabad airfield. Within minutes, Ghaffar sent his report to his ISI handlers: "Three confirmed kills at southeast end of the target airfield. Four missiles fired. One missile failure."[53] With this attack, the advantage shifted to the Afghans, and during the rest of the war, it is estimated that the U.S. provided between 2,000 and 2,500 missiles to the *mujahideen*,[54] and that a total of 270 Soviet aircraft were shot down with Stingers.[55] It is important to note that U.S. aid to the *mujahideen* for numerous reasons was funneled through the ISI, which was staffed, like the *mujahideen*, by many who held radical, Islamist beliefs. But the American desire to defeat the USSR and to turn the corner on the "Vietnam syndrome" trumped other concerns and would ultimately come back to haunt the United States.

In March 1985, following the deaths in office of three general secretaries of the

Communist Party—Leonid Brezhnev, Yuri Andropov, and Konstantin Chernenko—the Soviet Politburo turned to its youngest member, Mikhail Gorbachev, and selected him as the next leader of the Communist Party of the USSR. One can compare Gorbachev to a medical doctor who was confronted with a seriously ill patient, the Soviet body politic. Gorbachev had a crucial choice: he could treat the symptoms and not the underlying causes of the country's problems, which was the strategy that his three predecessors had chosen, or he could attempt to deal with the underlying causes of the problems. To return to the medical metaphor, "Dr." Gorbachev confronting a patient with a serious infection, say gangrene in one limb, could tell the patient, "Go home, drink plenty of water, get lots of rest." Or, he could opt for a more radical approach and amputate the infected limb. Gorbachev opted for the second approach and, once in office, announced a radical program of reform marked by four initiatives: *glasnost* (openness), *perestroika* (economic restructuring), democratization, and a new approach to foreign policy. Calling Afghanistan a "hopeless military adventure" and a "bleeding wound,"[56] Gorbachev believed "that problems there could not be solved with the use of force. Such attempts inside someone else's country end badly. But even more, it is not acceptable to impose one's own idea of order on another country without taking into account the opinion of the population of that country. My predecessors tried to build socialism in Afghanistan, where the central government was very weak. What kind of socialism could that have been?"[57] On February 9, 1988, Gorbachev announced that the Soviet Union would withdraw its forces from Afghanistan over a ten-month period. In his memoirs, Gorbachev noted, "If one recalls how many lives this war cost us, how many young people were crippled for life, and the loss and sufferings of the Afghan people, one can understand the explosion of hope that came from the promise to end this conflict that had brought shame on our nation."[58]

The Soviet Union had been in Afghanistan for nine years and fifty days, and on February 15, 1989, the last Red Army units crossed the Termez Bridge from Afghanistan to Uzbekistan, one of the Soviet republics. Lieutenant General Boris Gromov, the commander of the 40th Army, was the last to cross the bridge and was greeted by his young son.[59] This ended the Soviet-Afghan War, which had resulted in enormous costs for both Afghanistan and the USSR. By this time, 620,000 Soviet soldiers had served in Afghanistan and 14,453 had died; 53,753 were wounded; and 415,932 suffered serious illnesses.[60] In July 1990, Eduard Shevardnadze, then foreign minister of the USSR, noted that the war had cost the Soviet Union 60 billion rubles, equal to approximately $96 billion.[61]

The losses were even more staggering for the Afghans: between 1 and 1.5 million had been killed, 5 million went abroad, and as many as 3 million had been forced to leave their homes, all in a country with a total population of 22 million at the time of the Soviet invasion.[62] These losses had a profound impact on the political, social, and economic sectors of Afghan society.

The countries involved in the Soviet-Afghan War had also invested enormous amounts of money. Between 1980 and 1992, the United States spent between \$4 and \$5 billion, an amount that was matched by European and Islamic countries.[63] In the nine years of the war, the *mujahideen* received approximately \$10 billion. At the end of the war, however, U.S. aid to Afghanistan was quickly reduced; between October 1989 and October 1990, the U.S. decreased its aid by 60 percent. By 1992, the United States had stopped sending military aid to Afghanistan, and the previously united *mujahideen* had splintered into ethnic factions that fought one another. Table 3.2 lists the major *mujahideen* groups, their leaders, and principal supporters.

TABLE 3.2
Afghan *Mujahideen* Groups, Leaders, and Supporters

Group	Leaders	Ethnicity	Supporters
Islamic Party	Gulbuddin Hekmatyar	Pashtun	Muslim Brotherhood
Office of Support Services	-		Jamaat-e-Islami ISI (Pakistan) GID (Saudi Arabia) CIA Osama bin Laden
Northern	Burhanuddin Rabbani	Tajik	Muslim Brotherhood
Alliance	Ahmed Shah Massoud		MI-6 (UK) CIA (1984 and after) Rafsanjani (Iran)
Northern Alliance	Aburrashid Dostum	Uzbek	
Hizb-e-Wahadat	Karim Khalili Abdul Haq Hamid Karzai	Hazara Pashtun Pashtun	 CIA (until late 1980s)
Haqqani Network	Jalaluddin Haqqani	Pashtun	ISI (Pakistan) GID (Saudi Arabia) CIA Muslim Brotherhood
Hezb-e-Islami (Yunis)	Yunis Khalis Pahlawan Malik Abdurrab Rasul Sayyaf	 Hazara	ISI (Pakistan) ISI (Pakistan) GID (Saudi Arabia) Muslin Brotherhood

Source: Compiled by author.

The most important of these various groups were the Islamic Party headed by Gulbuddin Hekmatyar, Uzbeks led by General Dostum, Tajiks led by Burhanuddin Rabbani, al Qaeda headed by Osama bin Laden, and Hazaras led by Pahlawan Malik. In addition, there were a number of prominent tribal leaders who allied with different *mujahideen* groups, including Abdul Haq, Hamid Karzai, Jalaluddin Haqqanni, and Yunis Khalis. Even though *salafi*, fundamentalist, Muslim groups were opposed to much of what Western countries represented, they were willing to accept the West's aid in order to defeat Soviet forces in Afghanistan.

As the last Soviet soldier left Afghanistan, the beginning of a new era was evident. The U.S. had pursued its cold war objectives in its support of the *mujahideen* in Afghanistan, but as General Gromov crossed the bridge into Uzbekistan, the United States faced new challenges and new opponents. Ironically, the *mujahideen*, the Islamic fundamentalists of Afghanistan, had been the allies of the United States in the war against the Soviets in Afghanistan. But American support of the *mujahideen* in Afghanistan contrasted markedly with U.S. policy in Iran. As Lawrence Freedman has noted, "Whereas in Iran, the United States found itself working against the Islamists, in Afghanistan they supported them, in concert with Pakistan and Saudi Arabia."[64] Indeed, for many years, the Pakistanis and Saudis had supported Islamic fundamentalists in Afghanistan. As former National Security Council (NSC) terrorism expert Richard Clarke noted, "Pakistani military intelligence funded by the U.S. and Saudi governments and 'charitable' organizations, had turned groups of nineteenth-century Afghan tribesmen and several thousand Arab volunteers into a force that had crippled the mighty Red Army."[65] The Pakistanis did so as a way of bolstering its position *vis-à-vis* India, particularly regarding Kashmir, which both India and Pakistan claim. By supporting Islamic fundamentalists, the Pakistani government increased its leverage relative to India. The Saudis supported Muslim fundamentalists out of religious motivation; namely, to support fellow conservative Muslims. And the U.S. did so to put pressure on the USSR, its erstwhile cold war opponent. Toward the end of the Afghan War, Soviet Foreign Minister Shevardnadze prophetically warned his American counterpart, Secretary of State George Shultz, "A neutral, nonaligned Afghanistan is one thing, a reactionary fundamentalist Islamic regime is something else," but American policymakers did not take Shevardnadze's warning seriously because they thought that he was primarily worried about the threat of Islamic radicalism to republics in the USSR.[66]

The Rise of the Taliban in Afghanistan

The type of Islam that the Saudis observe, as noted in Chapter 2, was a conservative branch founded by Abd al-Wahhab, and the movement he founded, Wahhabism, is a strict form of Islam that bans alcohol, segregates the sexes, and emphasizes *Sharia* law. The Saudi government and wealthy Saudi citizens sent money to radical Islamic groups in Pakistan to set up and maintain Islamic schools called *madrassas*, and many of these were established along the border of Pakistan and Afghanistan. In 1971, there were an estimated 900 *madrassas* in Pakistan, but by 1988, these had grown to 8,000 registered and 25,000 unofficial *madrassas*.[67] Because Pakistan's public educational system was not very good, *madrassas* were the only educational alternative for many males from poor Pakistani families. The curriculum consisted exclusively of studying the Quran, and no part of the curriculum went beyond this.

Many students from *madrassas* were attracted to the Taliban movement in Afghanistan. *Talib* (plural, *Taliban*) translates as an Islamic student, one who seeks knowledge. A *mullah* is one who gives knowledge. Some *mujahideen* who later became Taliban leaders were actively involved in the war against the Soviets from 1979 until the withdrawal of Soviet forces in 1989, and they physically reflected the costs of war, for many of them were seriously wounded. The leader of the Taliban, Mullah Muhammad Omar, lost his right eye when a rocket exploded close to him, and he was wounded by shrapnel. The former justice and foreign ministers of the Taliban were also one-eyed, and the former Taliban mayor of Kabul, Abdul Majid, had a leg and two fingers missing.[68]

The Taliban were Sunni Pashtuns, and therefore shared an ethnic and religious background with many Pakistanis. Fifteen percent of the Pakistani population was Pashtun, and an even higher percentage of the Pakistani army—20 percent—was Pashtun. In addition, the Pakistani government had long supported the Taliban, many of whom had attended *madrassas* in Pakistan. The Pakistani military considered its support of the Taliban as a key means of supporting its strategic interests, which were primarily focused on India. When Soviet forces left Afghanistan, aid from Western countries and the United Nations dropped precipitously, as Table 3.3 indicates.

In this environment, the Taliban were able to expand their control of Afghanistan. In October 1994, the Taliban took over Spin Boldak in southern Afghanistan and a month later took over Kandahar. In September 1995, the Taliban took over the ancient city of Afghanistan, Herat, and within a year had

TABLE 3.3
Aid Requested and Received for Afghanistan, 1996–99
(in millions of U.S. dollars)

Year	UN request	Actual amount	Percent
1996	124	65	52%
1997	133	56	42%
1998	157	53	34%
1999	113		

Source: Data derived from Ahmed Rashid, *Taliban: Militant Islam, Oil and Fundamentalism in Central Asia* (New Haven: Yale University Press, 2000), p. 108.

taken over Kabul. With their victories, the Taliban instituted a harsh version of *Sharia* law. For example, following the takeover of Kabul in September 1996, the head of the religious police issued a decree that included: "Women you should not step outside of your residence. If women are going outside with fashionable, ornamental, tight and charming clothes to show themselves, they will be cursed by the Islamic *Sharia* and should never expect to go to heaven." The Taliban's harsh views were applied to other ethnic groups as well; to the Sunni Taliban, the Shia Hazara Muslims were considered to be apostates and were persecuted. Laws were enacted requiring men to grow their beards a prescribed length, banning kite flying, and other extreme examples. As Ahmed Rashid has noted, "Ironically, the Taliban were a direct throwback to the military religious orders that arose in Christendom during the Crusades to fight Islam—disciplined, motivated and ruthless in attaining their aims."[69]

By the late 1980s, the region consisting of Afghanistan, Iran, and Pakistan had replaced the "Golden Triangle" of Laos, Myanmar, and Thailand as the major producer of opium in the world. Opium production was begun in Pakistan in the mid-1980s, and by 1986, Pakistan produced more than 800 tons of opium per year, approximately 70 percent of the world's heroin supply. The importance of drug sales is illustrated by a 1986 case in which two Pakistani military officers were caught with a combined total of 440 kilograms of high-grade heroin worth an estimated $600 million, an amount equivalent to all U.S. aid to Pakistan for that year.[70] There were, of course, significant results of Pakistan's involvement with drug production: the addiction of its population. In 1979, there were few, if any, heroin addicts in Pakistan; by 1986, there were 650,000; by 1992, 3 million; and by 1999, 5 million.[71] American officials were concerned about the increase in drug production in Pakistan and allocated more than

$100 million for poppy eradication programs following the Soviet withdrawal from Afghanistan. These programs were effective; opium production dropped to 24 tons in 1997 and to 2 tons in 1999.[72] Despite this program, British Prime Minister Blair estimated in 2001 that "ninety percent of the heroin on British streets originates in Afghanistan."[73] Several experts have estimated that Afghanistan provided more than 93 percent of the world's supply of opium from 2006 to 2008.[74]

With the U.S. drug eradication programs in Pakistan and greatly reduced aid available from the U.S., Saudi Arabia, and Pakistan, the Taliban and al Qaeda sought to finance their operations by taxing opium exports from Afghanistan, the world's largest opium producer. Of course, the use of narcotics is prohibited by *Sharia* law; however, the head of the Taliban's counter-narcotic force, Abdul Rashid, noted, "Opium is permissible because it is consumed by *kafirs* [unbelievers] in the West and not by Afghans."[75] In 1990, Afghanistan produced 1,570 tons of opium, an amount that increased to 2,800 tons by 1997. By 1997, almost all of Afghan poppy production was under the control of the Taliban, and the Taliban received an estimated $75 million from drug smuggling between Afghanistan and Pakistan.[76] Afghan intelligence officials estimated that 30 percent of the Taliban's income came from drug trafficking.[77]

U.S. Policy toward Afghanistan and Pakistan

From 1947 until the disintegration of the USSR in December 1991, concerns over the cold war dominated the relations of the United States with other countries including Pakistan and Afghanistan. American strategists appreciated Pakistan's geostrategic position and sought to ally with Pakistan through several agreements. In 1954 Pakistan and the U.S. signed a mutual defense agreement, and later Pakistan joined a U.S.-sponsored multilateral defense organization, the Southeast Asia Treaty Organization (SEATO), a kind of Asian analogue to the European North Atlantic Treaty Organization (NATO). The United States used Pakistani airbases to stage reconnaissance flights with U-2 aircraft over the USSR, and it was from one of these bases in Peshawar that CIA pilot Gary Powers took off before he was shot down and captured over the Soviet Union in 1960.[78]

Because the U.S. considered Pakistan to be an important ally against the USSR, it provided significant aid to Pakistan; however, when India and Pakistan went to war in 1965, the U.S. placed an embargo on weapons shipments to both warring countries, a policy that continued until 1975. In July 1971, the Pakistani leader, Yahya Khan, assisted President Nixon and Dr. Henry Kissinger in their efforts to contact the government of the People's Republic of China and to open discussions about normalizing relations between the two countries. In February 1971, Dr. Kissinger flew to Islamabad where U.S. press officials said he was going to discuss Pakistani-American relations. In fact he flew secretly to Beijing, where he met with top Chinese officials and arranged for the February 1972 Sino-American summit meeting.

During the 1971 Indian-Pakistani war, the United States "tilted" toward Pakistan, although the Pakistani leader at the time, Zulfiqar Ali Bhutto, believed that the U.S. could have pressured India not to intervene into Pakistan's civil war. As a result, relations between Pakistan and the U.S. cooled under Bhutto, and he withdrew his country from SEATO.

In May 1974, India detonated a nuclear device, an event that stimulated Pakistan to pursue development of its own nuclear weapons. In April 1979, President Carter cut off economic assistance (except food aid) to Pakistan, as required by the Symington Amendment to the Foreign Assistance Act of 1961. In November 1979, thinking that the U.S. had been involved in the takeover of the Grand Mosque in Mecca, rioters attacked and burned the American embassy in Islamabad, killing four people.

In December 1979, when the Soviet Union invaded and occupied Afghanistan, which shares a 2,430-kilometer border with Pakistan, the United States offered Pakistan $400 million in economic and military aid, which Pakistani President Zia-ul-Haq dismissed (but accepted) as "peanuts." American aid to Pakistan grew in the 1980s, increasing to $3.2 billion in 1981 and to $4 billion in 1986. In March 1985, President Reagan authorized covert aid to the *mujahideen* in National Security Decision Directive-166.

Throughout the 1980s, the U.S. president had to grant Pakistan waivers from the requirement that aid not be given to any country pursuing a nuclear weapons program. In 1985 the Pressler Amendment was passed, which required the president to certify that a country receiving U.S. aid was not developing nuclear weapons. Until the USSR withdrew from Afghanistan, the president issued this certification; however, when the Soviets withdrew from Afghanistan, the U.S. adopted a stronger position on the issue of nuclear weapons. In 1990 President George H. W. Bush refused to issue the certification, and U.S. aid to Pakistan was stopped.

The time period from 1989 to 1991 was critical for Pakistan. The Soviet Union had withdrawn from Afghanistan and then disintegrated in December 1991. With these events, the cold war no longer provided the impetus for the U.S. to support Pakistan economically and militarily. In addition, without the Soviet threat looming in the background, the U.S. increased pressure on Pakistan to halt its development of nuclear weapons. Without the backing of its principal cold war ally but still optimistic as a result of the defeat of Soviet forces in Afghanistan, Pakistan turned increasingly to other sources for ensuring its security—Islamic fundamentalists in Afghanistan. The Pakistani army saw the *mujahideen* as an excellent force to oppose its long-time enemy, India, in the most contested region in Indo-Pakistani relations, Kashmir. In 1989, officers of the Pakistani intelligence organization, ISI, told Prime Minister Benazir Bhutto that they wanted to employ the same methods that they had used against the Soviets—namely, to support Islamic fundamentalist groups' campaign of *jihad*—to drive India out of Kashmir.[79] Within several years, ISI was training *mujahideen* in training camps in Afghanistan run by Gulbuddin Hekmatyar for covert operations in Kashmir. Thus, the ties between Pakistan and the *mujahideen* deepened following the Soviet-Afghan War.

At the end of the Soviet-Afghan War, in Afghanistan the *mujahideen* groups formed a new government consisting of Islamic Party leader Burhanuddin Rabbani as president, Ahmed Massoud as minister of defense, and Gulbuddin Hekmatyar as foreign minister. But this coalition government was short-lived, and civil war broke out in 1992. Hekmatyar and Aburrashid Dostum led the two factions on one side and Rabbani and Massoud on the other. CIA operative Milt Bearden recalled, "Hekmatyar was the darkest of the Afghan leaders, the most Stalinist of the Peshawar Seven, insofar as he thought nothing of ordering an execution for a slight breach of party discipline."[80] The Pakistanis favored and continued to support their fellow Pashtun, Hekmatyar, and opposed Tajiks Rabbani and Massoud. Hekmatyar went from fighting the Taliban to being one of their main military commanders. Relations among the various *mujahideen* groups, however, grew increasingly conflictual and violent. In May 1992, there was open fighting on the streets of Kabul. Without the direct threat of Soviet forces, issues of tribal or clan loyalty, religious dogma and observance, and ethnic identity came to the fore. Following the end of the Soviet-Afghan War and for many years after, Afghanistan was one of the poorest countries in the world.

It was in this environment that the Taliban emerged as a force that united Islamic piety and Pashtun power, and many Pashtuns were attracted to this movement. Steve Coll has noted that Taliban "were as familiar to southern Pashtun villagers as frocked Catholic priests were in the Irish countryside, and they played a similar role. They taught schoolchildren, led prayers, comforted the dying, and mediated local disputes."[81] Even though he was not from a particularly wealthy family, Hamid Karzai donated $50,000 to the Taliban, gave them weapons, and introduced them to important Pashtun leaders around Kandahar.[82] Others were also positively impressed with the Taliban; Zalmay Khalilzad, a key American adviser on Afghanistan, wrote, "The Taliban does not practice the anti-U.S. style of fundamentalism practiced by Iran. It is closer to the Saudi model."[83]

With the support of Pakistan, Saudi Arabia, Muslim fundamentalists, and some Americans, the Taliban emerged as the most powerful of the Afghan Pashtun groups, and Pakistan's ISI gave it substantial aid. This meant that the "lion of Panjshir," Ahmed Massoud, was left out in the cold. He was a Tajik and not a Pashtun supported by Pakistani intelligence. According to most sources, Massoud was the most capable military commander of all of the *mujahideen* leaders, and his followers revered him. According to long-time CIA operative Gary Schroen, Massoud was "the finest tactical commander on either side of the fighting" and the "premier military figure in Afghanistan, and his prestige and influence stretched into all areas of the country."[84] Part of the reason that Massoud was so influential is that he would not leave Afghanistan except for short periods of time; he was not like the "Gucci *mujahideen,*" who lived abroad and only came to Afghanistan for brief public relations forays.

Despite his mostly stellar reputation in the West, Massoud engaged in nefarious activities, including smuggling drugs and gems and the murder of thousands of Hazaras in Kabul during the mid-1990s.[85] In addition, Iran's Ministry of Intelligence and Security (MOIS) provided support to Massoud and his Northern Alliance. According to CIA operative Gary Berntsen, "I'd spent years working against MOIS and considered them the equivalent of Middle Eastern Nazis. Either directly or indirectly, they had been responsible for deaths of many U.S. citizens since the Islamic Iranian Revolution."[86] Despite the nefarious reputation of MOIS, Massoud accepted aid from it.

By 1994, Northern Alliance forces had defeated the Afghan Islamic fundamentalist groups led by Hekmatyar, and the Pakistanis increased their support for the Taliban and al Qaeda. In September 1995, the Taliban captured Herat and in September 1996 took over Jalalabad and then the capital city, Kabul, becoming the de facto government of Afghanistan although only three countries formally recognized it. By the end of 1996, several significant events had occurred. First, the Taliban controlled two-thirds of Afghanistan. Second, Osama bin Laden arrived in Afghanistan and established his al Qaeda training camps. And third, Massoud broke with his former mentor, Rabbani, and retreated into his homeland, the Panjshir Valley, just as he had done when pressed by the Soviets. By that time, Massoud's Northern Alliance controlled about 10 percent of Afghanistan.

"Is That Thing Still Going On?"

In 1991, a senior CIA agent briefed President George H. W. Bush about covert U.S. aid to Afghanistan that was being funneled through Pakistani intelligence. The president seemed surprised by the operative's comments and asked, "Is that thing still going on?"[87] In one sense the president's reaction was not surprising because few Americans paid attention to Afghanistan following the end of the Soviet-Afghan War. In fact, American policy largely consisted of bolstering Pakistan's ISI support of former *mujahideen* leaders. During the 1992 presidential campaign, neither the Republican nor the Democratic campaign platforms even mentioned Afghanistan. Once in office, few of President Clinton's national security advisers showed any interest in Afghanistan; it was old business and largely forgotten. According to CIA operative Schroen, "The events in Afghanistan in the mid-1990s were back-page news at best, just another civil war among squabbling warlords in a country so devastated and backward that there was little or nothing to fight over."[88] For most Americans, Afghanistan in the 1990s was, like Czechoslovakia for most Britons in the 1930s, "a far away country about which we know little."

There were, however, some disturbing trends beneath the calm surface. In 1989, the CIA's office in Islamabad estimated that there were approximately 4,000 Arab *mujahideen* volunteers in Afghanistan, and these were largely under the control of Younis Sayyaf, who was a product of the Muslim Brotherhood and who was intensely anti-American.[89] In addition, the 1991 Gulf War had created strong anti-American feelings in much of the Islamic world, including among Muslim fundamentalists in countries allied with the U.S., Pakistan, the Gulf emirates, and Saudi Arabia. By 1995, CIA analysts described Osama bin Laden's headquarters in Sudan as "the Ford Foundation of Sunni Islamic terrorism, a grant-giving source of cash for violent operations."[90]

American officials became concerned that this "foundation" or another group could obtain some of the leftover Stinger shoulder-fired, surface-to-air missiles that the U.S. had given to the *mujahideen* during the Soviet-Afghan War. The United States had shipped between 2,000 and 2,500 missiles, and at the end of the war, somewhere between 350 and 600 were missing; no one really knew the exact number.[91] U.S. intelligence reports indicated that the Taliban possessed 100 Stingers as of 2002.[92] NSC counterterrorism coordinator Richard Clarke minimized the importance of the missing Stingers because he believed that they had been expended in the war, destroyed in an enormous explosion at a Rawalpindi weapons depot, or that their batteries had expired.[93] Other U.S. government officials were not as sanguine as Clarke; terrorists or agents of a government hostile toward the U.S. could use Stingers against military or civilian passenger aircraft. The CIA had reports that Stingers had been sent to Somalia, that Mullah Omar possessed 53 Stingers and that Iran had acquired around 100 of the missiles.[94] Presidents George H. W. Bush and Bill Clinton authorized a covert CIA program to buy back Stingers at a going rate of $70,000 to $150,000 per missile.

In September 1996, CIA operative Gary Schroen flew to Kabul to meet with Northern Alliance leader Ahmed Shah Massoud to enlist his help in buying back Stinger missiles and to cooperate with the CIA in keeping track of Osama bin Laden and Arab terrorists in Afghanistan. Massoud was wary of Schroen's approach because he felt that the U.S. had abandoned Afghanistan following the defeat of the USSR, and he had justification for this feeling. But Massoud was also in a difficult position; by 1996 his forces were forced to retreat into the Panjshir Valley, and they controlled only 10 percent of Afghanistan. The U.S. could offer Massoud the financial help that he desperately needed. According to Schroen, Massoud "agreed to cooperate to the full extent of his ability, but he noted that he was engaged in a bitter struggle with the Taliban and was hemmed in by drawn battle lines. Going directly after bin Laden would be difficult for his forces, positioned as they were . . ."[95] Schroen's meeting with Massoud opened the door to U.S. relations with the Northern Alliance, a relationship that would continue for the next five years and beyond.

4 Iraq: From Cradle of Civilization to Republic of Fear

In 1920, the British officer and insurgency expert T. E. Lawrence wrote of the Arabs:

> They lack system, endurance, organisation. They are incurably slaves of the idea, men of spasms, instable like water, but with something of its penetrating and flood-like character. They have been a government twenty times since the dawn of history, and as often after achievement they have grown tired, and let it fall: there is no record of any force except success capable of breaking them. The history of their waves of feeling is significant in that the reservoir of all ideas, the birth of all prophecies are shown in the deserts. These empty spaces irresistibly drive their inhabitants to a belief in the oneness and omnipotence of God, but the very contrast of the barrenness of nature, the lack of every distraction and superfluity in life.[1]

In writing these observations, Lawrence undoubtedly had in mind the desert bedouins with whom he collaborated to oppose the forces of the Ottoman Empire, yet much of what he has written applied to the Arab world more generally and to Iraq particularly.

Geography, Demographics, Economics, and History

Geography plays an important role in the history and development of states and international relations, and Iraq is no exception. Iraq occupies an area that historians and anthropologists consider to be the "cradle of civilization." The Tigris and Euphrates rivers, which bounded the "fertile crescent," provided the physical environment for the earliest known civilization, Sumer, to develop 5,000 years ago. This ancient civilization ended 2,500 years ago, and much of the area's history since that time has been influenced by geographic factors. Iraq has no natural geographic barriers, as does mountainous Switzerland, and as a result has been invaded and occupied many times throughout its long history.

The Prophet Muhammad's new religion came to this area soon after his death, and Islam reached its cultural apogee under the Abbasid Caliphate, which lasted from 750 to 1258. The Mongol leader Hulagu, who was the grandson of Genghis Khan, ended the Abbasid era by attacking and taking over Baghdad in 1258. In 1658 the Ottomans took over and ruled until 1917. As historian Charles Tripp has observed, "During the sixteenth and seventeenth centuries the lands that were to become the territories of the modern state of Iraq were gradually incorporated into the Ottoman Empire as three provinces, based on the towns of Mosul, Baghdad and Basra."[2]

Britain and the Ottoman Empire declared war on each other in October 1914, several months after the formal beginning of World War I. In order to protect its interests in the Persian Gulf region, Britain sent an expeditionary force initially to Basra and then on to Mosul and Baghdad. In 1916 Britain and France signed an agreement, named after its negotiators, Francois Georges Sykes and Sir Mark Picot, which called for the division of the Ottoman Empire at the end of World War I. At the Versailles conference at the end of the war, U.S. President Woodrow Wilson strongly advocated the idea of self-determination. The British government, however, had its own plans for Iraq and its other colonies and prevented an Iraqi delegation from attending the conference. At the San Remo conference in April 1920, the Mandate for Iraq was awarded to Great Britain, "clearing the way for the British to set up a ruling Council of State, composed largely of British officials, with Iraqis in strictly subordinate positions."[3] At the beginning of the Mandate, the population of Iraq was approximately 3 million, and of these more than half were Shia, 20 percent were Kurds, 20 percent Sunnis, and the remainder were Jews, Yazidi, Christians, and Turkmen. The Ottomans excluded Shia from participating in government, and the British appointed Sunnis to the most important administrative positions.

Oil was discovered close to Kirkuk in 1927, a factor that was to become far more significant than anyone at the time suspected. In the first twenty years of oil production in the Kirkuk area, more than 100 million tons of oil were produced.[4] In 1932, Britain formally agreed to end its Mandate and nominally granted Iraq independence, but it continued to run the country behind the scenes, similar to the way that it ran Iran as well.[5] Iraqis were supposed to provide for domestic stability and the defense of Iraq, and Great Britain retained the right to use military bases in Iraq in the event of war. It was an arrangement that in some respects resembled the later infamous Soviet policy of "Finlandization," according to which the USSR would control Finland's foreign relations while Finland would manage its domestic policy.

When Britain granted independence to Iraq, King Faisal became the ruler, but was in power only a year, and his son, Ghazi, succeeded him. In 1936 the army staged a coup d'état and became the arbiter of Iraqi politics, even though King Ghazi remained in power. This coup was the first of many to follow. In 1939 the king was killed in an automobile accident, and Ghazi's infant son was named king. Many Iraqis believed that the British had murdered the king, a feeling that led to anti-British attitudes. The prime minister at the time, Rashid Ali, led the opposition to Britain.

British Lord Curzon noted that, in World War I, "the Allies floated to victory on a wave of oil."[6] When World War II began, Britain and the other combatants were well aware that access to oil would be crucial, and Britain sought to increase its influence and control over Iraq and established a Royal Air Force base fifty miles from Baghdad. Considering the base a violation of its sovereignty, Iraq sought to close it down, and in response the British attacked the Iraqi army on May 2, 1941. Rashid Ali sought allies to oppose the British, but only Germany and Vichy France were willing to assist Iraq. Following the British defeat of Iraqi forces at the end of May, Rashid Ali escaped to Germany and was replaced by pro-British Iraqi leaders.

Throughout this period, the United States called for Iraq to cooperate with Great Britain and pledged to do all that it could "short of a declaration of war" to help Britain. As a result, Iraqis came to view the United States and Great Britain in a similar way; namely, as countries that favored colonial status for Iraq.

The relations of the United States with Iraq following World War II were dominated by the cold war. Given the country's geographic position, American policymakers viewed Iraq as a valuable ally against the Soviet Union and in 1954 began sending military aid to Iraq. This was followed a year later by the founding of the Baghdad Pact, a mutual defense treaty among Iraq, Turkey, Iran, Pakistan, and the United Kingdom that was a kind of Middle Eastern analogue of NATO or SEATO. Even though the U.S. was not formally a member, it had supported the creation of the agreement.

Contemporary Iraq is a country that is geographically a little larger than California, or about half the size of Pakistan. It is bordered by six countries: Iran, Jordan, Kuwait, Saudi Arabia, Syria, and Turkey. Although all of these neighboring countries are Islamic, there are some significant differences among them. While Jordan, Kuwait, Saudi Arabia, and Syria are overwhelmingly populated by Arabs, Iran is populated by Persians and Turkey by Turks, who are ethnically different from Arabs. Social scientists define a nation as a group of people who identify themselves as members of the same group unified by a common language, history, and culture. Islam is a transnational religion common to a number of different nations and ethnic groups. In the Ottoman Empire, Greeks, Bulgarians, Armenians, Romanians, and Turks were unified by a common history, culture, and geography. In contrast, Arabs did not share many of these attributes. Ethnic differences have played an important role in Iraq's past and are likely to continue to be an important factor for the foreseeable future. Important differences also exist within the Arab countries. For example, even though Iraq and Syria were ruled by the Baath Party dating back to the 1960s, the long-time leader of Syria, Hafez al-Asad, and Saddam Hussein were bitter rivals.

As noted in Chapter 2, there are a number of branches and sects within Islam, the two most important being the Sunni and Shia Muslims. Although the population of Iraq is overwhelmingly Muslim—97 percent—there are major divisions among three principal religious groups: Sunnis, who constitute about 35 percent of the Iraqi population; Shia, who constitute 60 percent; and Christians and others, who constitute 3 percent. Kurds, who are Muslim Sunnis but not Arab, constitute 15 to 20 percent of the population. These religious and ethnic differences have played important roles at various times in Iraqi history. Until recently, the division between Sunnis and Shia was less noticeable, and intermarriage between the two groups was relatively common. Four Iraqi cities—Najaf, Karbala, al-Kazimiyya, and Samarra—are four of the most venerated towns in Shia Islam. Shia were mostly excluded from administrative positions during the Ottoman period because the Ottomans were Sunni, and throughout Iraq's modern history, the officer corps of Iraq was disproportionately filled with Arab Sunnis. Sunni Kurds were largely excluded from the officer corps because they were not Arab.

The discovery of oil in Kirkuk and later in Saudi Arabia and the Persian Gulf was a development that would transform the history, politics, and economics of the entire region. Countries that the industrial revolution had previously bypassed experienced spectacular economic growth following the discovery of oil. By the early 1970s, it was estimated that Iraq possessed approximately 10 percent of the world's proven oil reserves. In 1972, Saddam Hussein nationalized the Iraq Petroleum Company, and a year later Iraq, Saudi Arabia, and other

TABLE 4.1
Statistical Profile of Iraq in 1990

Geographic size	438,317 sq. km
Bordering Countries	Iran (1,458 km) Jordan (134 km) Kuwait (240 km) Saudi Arabia (495 km) Neutral Zone with Saudi Arabia (191 km) Syria (605 km) Turkey (331 km)
Population	18,781,770 (July 1990)
Population growth rate	3.9% (1990)
Life expectancy	67
Literacy rate	55–60% (1989 estimate)
Ethnic groups	Arab (75–80%) Kurdish (15–20%) Turkoman, Assyrian, other (5%)
Religious groups	Sunni Muslims (32–37%) Shia Muslims (60–65%) Christian or other (3%)
GNP	$35 billion
GDP per capita	$1,940
Export partners	U.S., Brazil, USSR, Italy, France, Japan, Yugoslavia
Import partners	Turkey, U.S., Germany, UK, France, Japan, Romania, Yugoslavia
Disputes	Sovereignty over the Shatt al Arab waterway with Iran; control over the Kurds in northern Iraq; Neutral Zone with Saudi Arabia; ownership of Warbah and Bubiyan Islands with Kuwait. Upstream water rights with Syria

Source: Data from Central Intelligence Agency, *World Factbook*; available at www.cia.gov/library/pulications/the-world-factbook/index.html.

Arab members of the Organization of Petroleum Exporting Countries (OPEC) embargoed exports of oil to any states that supported Israel in its war with Egypt and Syria. The resulting drop in supply drove the price of oil up substantially and resulted in an eightfold increase in oil revenues for Iraq, which by 1975 had annual oil revenues that equaled $8 billion. Table 4.1 provides a statistical profile of Iraq in 1990, the year that Iraq attacked and occupied its Arab neighbor, Kuwait.

Iraq under Saddam Hussein and the Baath Party

Born on April 28, 1937, in the Sunni town of Tikrit, Saddam Hussein was aptly named "Saddam," which in Arabic means "one who confronts." When he was just nineteen years old, Saddam participated in an abortive coup. He finished high school at age twenty-four in 1961, and in the summer of 1964, Hasan al-Bakr appointed his young relative, Saddam, as a Baath (meaning "renaissance" in Arabic) party official; however, several months later the leaders of a Baathist coup ordered that al-Bakr, Saddam, and others be arrested. Saddam remained in prison until 1966, when al-Bakr once again appointed him to be the deputy secretary-general of the regional command of the Baath Party in Iraq. In July 1968, al-Bakr and several other Baathist officials and Arab nationalist officers overthrew the government and established a new one with Hasan al-Bakr as president and Abd al-Razzaq al-Nayif as prime minister. For al-Bakr and Saddam, "the Baath Party was an extension of their personal power through a patronage system which they alone would control."[7] At the time of the Baathist coup, the party had only 5,000 members. The Baathists, like the Bolsheviks of the Soviet Union, demonstrated that a small minority fanatically committed to revolution could be successful. In November 1969, Saddam was appointed the deputy chairman of the Revolutionary Command Council, and in the ensuing years, he continued to expand his power, becoming a general in 1976, assuming control of Iraq's oil policy in 1977, and ruthlessly purging the leadership of the Baath Party in 1978. In July 1979, Hasan al-Bakr suddenly announced that he was resigning from office, and within hours Saddam became president, ushering in a reign of terror. In September 1980, Iraqi forces invaded Iran, beginning the eight-year-long, enormously costly Iran-Iraq War.

By 1984 the membership of the Baath Party had grown to 25,000, and there were another 1.5 million supporters of the party. Although Iraq, like other states, had a complicated array of government ministries, agencies, and organizations, the real power stemmed from Saddam Hussein, and he depended heavily on relatives, those who had supported him, and individuals from the clan of rural Iraq around Tikrit, his hometown. According to George Polk, Saddam gave the tribal "chiefs he appointed money and arms and put them to work to watch even the Baath party; thus he created a new form of tribalism on top of the old. At the center of this new organization of prestige and power was the clan of Saddam himself, al-Majid, which was a part of a larger, more diffuse, less closely related tribe known as the Al Bu Nasir."[8]

Throughout his political career, Saddam demonstrated a "personality constellation" that former CIA psychiatrist Jerrold Post contends was characterized by "messianic ambition for unlimited power, absence of conscience, unconstrained aggression, and a paranoid outlook."[9] Despite his modest beginnings in Tikrit, Saddam traced his lineage to the Prophet Muhammad. According to historian Charles Tripp, "A continuous line of political succession was established between the rulers of the ancient kingdoms of Mesopotamia, the Abbasid caliphs and Saddam Husain himself."[10] Once in power, Saddam ordered the rebuilding of the ancient city of Babylon and commanded that all of the bricks used in the reconstruction be stamped: "The Babylon of Nebuchadnezzar was re-constructed in the era of Saddam Hussein." Saddam also had ambitions to be the successor of Gamel Abdel Nasser in promoting pan-Arab nationalism; in short, he wanted to be the preeminent leader of the entire Arab world.[11]

Saddam maintained his power through several means. Saddam was essentially a secular leader, but he would use religion for his purposes at times. In order to consolidate his power, Saddam utilized the widespread and systematic use of terror. On July 16, 1979, Saddam became president of Iraq; six days later he held a meeting of senior members of the party. A former opponent of Saddam, Abd al-Hussein Mashadi, appeared before the group and confessed that he had led a Syrian-backed plot against Saddam, who then named fifty-four additional alleged coconspirators and asked for volunteers to participate in the firing squads of those who were named, thus making coconspirators of those who participated in the trumped up charges. According to Kanan Makiya, "Neither Stalin nor Hitler would have thought up a detail like that. What Eichmann-like refuge in 'orders from above' could these men dig up in the future if they were ever to marshal the courage to try and depose their Leader? . . . With the act, the party leadership was being forced to invest its future in Saddam."[12] In essence, by acquiescing in Saddam's evil actions, members of the Baath Party became complicit. An estimated 500 senior members of the Baath Party were executed as part of these purges. Saddam's actions were reminiscent of the infamous "show trials" of the Soviet Union under Stalin, a playing out of what Dr. Jerrold Post called Saddam's "malignant narcissism."

Just four months after Saddam became president, the conservative clerics of Iran were able to topple the Shah from power, an event that marked the rise of Shia fundamentalism. Given the Shia majority of the Iraqi population, the Iranian Revolution posed a very real threat to the stability and Sunni-dominated Baathist control of Iraq. In reaction to the rising influence of Shia, Saddam resolved to keep his fellow Sunni Arabs in the most important positions in his government and was concerned about any indications, real or imagined, that the other two most prominent ethnic-religious groups in Iraq, Shia and Kurds, were engaged in actions opposed to the dominant Sunni regime. Saddam used poison gas on the Kurds for the first time in April 1987 and then at Halabja on March 15, 1988, an attack that killed an estimated 5,000 people.[13] Evidence collected after the attacks indicated that several different types of chemical agents had been used, including mustard gas and the nerve agents sarin, soman, tabun, and VX, all of which are considered to be weapons of mass destruction.[14] According to *Washington Post* reporter Patrick Tyler, "Entire families were wiped out and the streets were littered with the corpses of men, women and children. Other forms of life in and around the city—horses, house cats, cattle—perished as well."[15] Long-time Middle Eastern expert William Polk noted, "Not only Iraqi troops but Kurdish militiamen, recruited from those with grievances against other Kurds, acted out tribal vendettas and engaged in theft, rape, and murder on a scale not witnessed since the Mongol invasions."[16]

Plato once wrote, "A tyrant is always setting some war in motion so that the people will be in need of a leader." As noted above, Saddam wanted to be considered the most important Arab leader and for Iraq to be the pivotal Arab state. The major geopolitical rival of Iraq was Iran, which was Persian and predominantly Shia, both anathema to Saddam. Validating Plato's observation, Saddam embarked on an effort to pressure the Iranian government to recognize that the regional balance of power had changed in Iraq's favor. Saddam sought to do this by abrogating the 1975 treaty and asserting Iraqi control over the complete Shatt al-Arab, the tidal river formed by the confluence of the Tigris and the Euphrates rivers that forms part of the Iraq-Kuwait border. In keeping with his plans, on September 22, 1980, Saddam ordered pre-emptive attacks on Iranian military airfields and a ground invasion of Iran, actions that began the eight-year, enormously costly Iran-Iraq War. As Judith Miller and Laurie Mylroie noted, "Many commentators compared the war, in its devastating and senseless fury, to the Great War of 1914–18 which so traumatized an entire European generation. . . . The casualties that resulted were greater than all of the Arab-Israeli wars that have taken place over the past forty years."[17]

The war cost Iraq approximately $15 billion per year, and the human costs of the war included an estimated 250,000 Iraqis killed, more than 300,000 seriously wounded, and almost 50,000 prisoners of war. With its population of 18 million, these losses would be equivalent to 10 million Americans killed or wounded in war.[18] By comparison with the United States, approximately 620,000 were killed in the Civil War, and 405,000 Americans died in World War II. In terms of casualties as a percentage of total population, only Soviet losses of 20 to 25 million in World War II rivaled the losses of Iraq and Iran in their eight-year war. The economic losses of the war were also substantial. Iraq's oil exports fell from 28 million barrels in 1980 to 3 million barrels in 1982, with corresponding revenues of $26 billion and $9 billion.[19] At the end of the war, Saddam blamed Kuwait, Saudi Arabia, and the United Arab Emirates for driving down the price of oil, thus preventing Iraq's economic recovery after the war.[20] Iraq demanded that Kuwait pay it $10 billion,[21] and Saddam repeatedly asked Saudi Arabia and Kuwait "to declare that the $40 billion financial aid that they had given to Iraq during the war with Iran should be considered a grant and not a loan."[22]

The First Gulf War

With Saddam blaming his Arab brethren for Iraq's economic problems, he turned to the means of solving his problems that Plato had suggested centuries before: taking over a neighboring, militarily weak country. In this case, Saddam's target was Kuwait. In 1990, Iraq's share of the world's proven oil reserves was an estimated 10 percent; Kuwait had another 10 percent; and Saudi Arabia had 25 percent. By invading and occupying Kuwait, which many Iraqis considered a province of Iraq, Saddam would control one-fifth of the world's oil supplies. In addition, Iraq has a coastline of only 26 miles, and Kuwait has a coastline of 120 miles. By taking over Kuwait, Iraq would increase its coast more than fourfold. The Iraqi takeover of Kuwait would also eliminate the substantial debt that Iraq owed Kuwait as a result of the Iran-Iraq War. Of course, Saddam could not go to war without considering Iraq's relations with other countries.

The two non-Arab countries with the closest ties to Iraq were the Soviet Union and France. The Soviet Union and Iraq signed a Treaty of Friendship in 1972, and at the time of the Iraqi invasion of Kuwait in August 1990, there were approximately 8,000 Soviet citizens in Iraq. The Soviet Union had sold Iraq a great deal of military equipment throughout the 1980s, and by 1990, Iraq owed the USSR more than $10 billion and France more than $7 billion.[23] France had sold the nuclear reactor to Iraq in 1976 that the Israelis attacked and destroyed in 1981. By 1982, 40 percent of French arms exports were going to Iraq.[24]

U.S. President George Herbert Walker Bush had served in a number of foreign policy positions; in fact, he had more extensive and varied foreign policy experience than almost any other American president; he had served as a member of Congress, de facto ambassador to China, U.S. representative to the

United Nations, director of the CIA, and eight years as vice president. As a result of these experiences, Bush believed strongly in the importance of cooperating with other countries in addressing vital issues. In addition, and in contrast to President Ronald Reagan whom he served as vice president for eight years, George H. W. Bush believed in a pragmatic approach to foreign policy. He and his closest circle of advisors were "realists," who emphasized a pragmatic rather than ideological approach to dealing with international issues.

At a meeting of the Arab Cooperation Council in February 1990, Saddam demanded that the Gulf states declare a moratorium on the loans that Iraq had accepted to finance the Iran-Iraq War. He also wanted OPEC to establish stricter quotas that would result in increased revenues from the sale of oil and asked for an additional loan of $30 billion from the Gulf states, saying, "Let the Gulf regimes know . . . that if they do not give this money to me, I will know how to get it."[25] During the spring of 1990, American intelligence agencies discovered evidence of a substantial military buildup in Iraq, and by July 19, 35,000 soldiers from three divisions had been deployed ten to thirty miles from the Iraq-Kuwait border.[26] This deployment concerned both Arab and American officials; however, following his July 24 visit to Baghdad as a mediator appointed by the Arab League, Egyptian President Hosni Mubarak concluded that Saddam did not intend on invading Kuwait, and Saddam agreed to negotiations in Jeddah, Saudi Arabia. As an attempt to deter Iraqi aggression, the United States announced joint military maneuvers with the United Arab Emirates, and in response, Saddam summoned the U.S. ambassador to Iraq, April Glaspie, to discuss U.S. actions.[27] The ambassador did not have time to request and receive detailed instructions from Washington and had to respond to Saddam's questions and criticisms on the basis of existing U.S. policy.[28] At this time, the United States government had not decided to threaten military action in order to deter Iraq. Without authorization to make a credible threat, the best Ambassador Glaspie could do was to restate existing U.S. policy calling for the countries in the region to resolve their own problems. Saddam believed that Vietnam had traumatized the American people and their leaders and that the U.S. would be unlikely to respond to an Iraqi invasion of Kuwait. By July 27, Iraq had massed 100,000 soldiers from eight divisions on the Iraq-Kuwait border, and despite this substantial show of force, U.S. officials still believed that Saddam was simply trying to intimidate Kuwait.

On August 2, 1990, Iraq attacked Kuwait. This invasion saw one Arab state attacking another, an event that President Mubarak of Egypt called "shocking."

A force of 300,000 Iraqi troops attacked and occupied Kuwait within twenty-four hours. The members of the al-Sabah ruling family of Kuwait and an estimated 300,000 other Kuwaitis escaped and sought sanctuary in Saudi Arabia and other Arab states. The invasion concerned Western, advanced industrialized countries because many of them depended upon oil exports from the Middle East. Thus, with its invasion and occupation of Kuwait, Iraq controlled approximately 20 percent of the world oil reserves, and its military forces were posed on the border of Saudi Arabia, the country with the largest oil reserves in the world.

Most observers and international lawyers did not accept Iraq's territorial claim to Kuwait; indeed, the al-Sabah family had ruled Kuwait since 1752, and most viewed Iraq's invasion and occupation as a clear case of blatant aggression. This certainly was true of President George Herbert Walker Bush, a member of "the greatest generation" who had served as the youngest pilot in the U.S. Navy in World War II. To Bush and others, Iraq's action was reminiscent of the aggression perpetrated by Nazi Germany, and Saddam was, according to President Bush, "Hitler revisited." On August 5, 1990, the president declared, "This will not stand, this will not stand, this aggression against Kuwait."[29] Prime Minister Margaret Thatcher held a similar view: "[A]ggressors must be stopped, not only stopped, but they must be thrown out. An aggressor cannot gain from his aggression. He must be thrown out and, . . . I thought we ought to throw him out so decisively that he could never think of doing it again."[30] For Bush, Thatcher, and members of their generation, the lesson of World War II was clear: dictators like Hitler and Saddam cannot be appeased, and aggression must be met with strong resolve and, if necessary, military force.

Following Iraq's invasion and occupation of Kuwait, Bush contacted numerous foreign leaders in order to solicit their support in opposing Iraq's takeover of Kuwait. Ultimately, thirty-eight countries allied with the United States, including long-time, influential allies of the United States: the United Kingdom, Germany, and France. Even though the Soviet Union had strong ties with Iraq, it did not oppose the United States or its coalition members' actions. In fact, there is strong evidence that Iraq's invasion of Kuwait came as a surprise to the USSR. At the time of the invasion, Secretary of State James Baker was visiting his Soviet counterpart, Eduard Shevardnadze, in Siberia, and Shevardnadze told him: Saddam "is perhaps a sort of a thug, but he is not irrational, and [an attack on Kuwait] would be an irrational act and I don't think that could happen."[31] Later in the crisis, the Iraqi foreign minister, Tariq Aziz, sent Mikhail

Gorbachev a message that Iraq would welcome a more active Soviet role, and Gorbachev responded, "What you [Iraq] did was an act of aggression and we cannot and will not back you in any way. We are ready to help . . . on the basis of complete withdrawal [from Kuwait]."[32]

The leaders of Saudi Arabia were justifiably concerned about the invasion and occupation of a neighboring Arab state, and yet, they were hesitant to invite those whom they considered unbelievers into territory that is considered the most sacred in Islam. Despite this hesitance, however, Saudi leaders were genuinely concerned about the threat to the kingdom posed by Iraqi military forces in Kuwait. The most pressing immediate question to Saudi leaders was how they could deter an Iraqi attack on their country. Broadly speaking, there were two options: either depend on their own forces supplemented with other Muslim forces including, possibly, former members of the *mujahideen* or to accept American and European forces as allies against Iraq.

For its part, the United States worked with the members of the United Nations in order to isolate and pressure Iraq and formed an extensive coalition. The UN passed a number of resolutions calling for international sanctions against Iraq. The CIA estimated that such sanctions would take years to be effective, and for his part, General Colin Powell, who served as chairman of the Joint Chiefs of Staff in the George H. W. Bush administration, was willing to try sanctions for two years. A veteran of Vietnam, Powell was concerned about the casualties that would result from such an invasion; fatalities were estimated to be in excess of 10,000 American troops. Another Vietnam veteran involved in Gulf War planning, General Charles Horner, noted, "I don't think there was a day during this [Gulf] war that we didn't touch back and sort of touch those sore points from Vietnam. One of the first casualties in Vietnam was integrity, the people, our generals, it wasn't so much of not telling the truth but when they were faced with impossible situations they tried to make do . . . . Vietnam was a ghost we carried with us."[33] Powell's concern led him to support the use of American military force only if four criteria were met: clear objectives, the deployment of overwhelming force, strong public and congressional support, and a clear postwar strategy.

In November 1990, the United Nations passed Security Council Resolution 678, which demanded Iraq's unconditional withdrawal from Kuwait by January 15, 1991, six weeks from the passage of the resolution. At the end of November 1990, James Baker met with Tariq Aziz to discuss a possible withdrawal from Kuwait, and Aziz gave no indication that Iraq was interested in a withdrawal. In response to Aziz's refusal to compromise, it appeared that war was imminent, and Baker took the opportunity to warn Aziz that the U.S. would respond forcefully, including possibly using nuclear weapons, were Iraq to use chemical or biological weapons.[34] Despite both American and international pressure, however, Saddam Hussein did not withdraw, and President Bush issued an ultimatum to Iraq that contained the three classic elements of any ultimatum: (1) the action required of the opponent (withdraw from Kuwait and restore the al-Sabah monarchy), (2) a time limit (January 15, 1991), and (3) the threat of action that will be taken if the action demanded of the opponent is not met (the U.S. and its coalition partners will force withdrawal from Kuwait). Apparently, Saddam did not believe that President Bush and his advisers were serious; they were. In fact, prior to the start of the war, Secretary of Defense Dick Cheney ordered General Powell to draw up plans for the possible use of nuclear weapons against Iraq.[35]

On January 17, 1991, at 1 A.M., American Apache helicopters attacked and destroyed Iraqi radar sites, which paved the way for an extensive air and cruise missile attack; the "mother of all battles," as Saddam called it, had begun. The air attack lasted thirty-nine days and was then followed, beginning on February 24, with a ground attack, which drove to within 150 miles of Baghdad. The acute, kinetic phase of the war was essentially completed within 100 hours of its beginning, with a total of 139 American fatalities. A ceasefire was signed at Safwan on February 28, 1991. The cost for Iraq was substantial: an estimated 10,000 Iraqi civilians and 30,000 Iraqi soldiers were killed, a number that proportional to population was five times the casualties that the United States suffered in the Vietnam War.[36]

The economic cost of the war was also substantial; within six weeks, the U.S. destroyed more of Iraq's infrastructure than was destroyed during the eight years of the Iran-Iraq War. The economic cost of the war to the coalition was $55 billion; however, U.S. allies, most significantly Kuwait, Saudi Arabia, and Japan, reimbursed the U.S. $50 billion.

The UN resolutions under which the U.S. and its coalition partners were operating called for Iraq to withdraw from Kuwait, and these resolutions did not call for the overthrow of Saddam, the complete defeat and disarmament of the Iraqi military, or the takeover of Baghdad. As a result, American forces stopped at the thirty-third parallel, about thirty miles south of Baghdad. Much of Iraq's military equipment was destroyed, although some Iraqi military forces retreated to Baghdad for sanctuary. According to Secretary Baker, "We have done the job. We can stop. We have achieved our aims. We have gotten them out of Kuwait."[37] Defense Secretary Dick Cheney commented, "We could have gone on . . . [but] I don't know how we would have let go of that tar baby once we had grabbed hold of it. . . . How many additional American casualties would we have had to suffer? How many additional American lives is Saddam Hussein worth? And the answer I would give is not very damn many."[38]

In contrast to the end of most other wars in American history, not everyone was satisfied with the results, including the commander-in-chief, President George H. W. Bush, who commented, "Why do I not feel elated? But we need to have an end. People want that. They are going to want to know we won and the kids can come home. We do not want to screw this up with a sloppy, muddled ending."[39]

Leaving Saddam in power was in keeping with the UN's resolutions, and there were also geopolitical reasons for allowing Saddam to remain in power with significant military forces still under his control. Other than Iraq, the major power in the region was Iran. Following the takeover of the Shah's government by radical, fundamental clerics headed by the Ayatollah Khomeini in November 1979, a group of young Iranian radicals took sixty-six Americans hostage and held fifty-two of them captive for 444 days. This action strongly influenced American attitudes toward Iran, and the pragmatic members of the George H. W. Bush administration recognized that a counterbalance to the radical, Iranian theocracy was needed both for regional stability and to maintain assured access to oil in the Gulf region. Therefore, American forces limited their actions against Saddam's Iraq. Indeed, many of the members of George H. W. Bush's foreign policy advisory group would later criticize the decision to stop short of Baghdad and to leave a residual Iraqi military force intact, but in January 1991, this was viewed as a sensible decision in keeping with the wishes of the broader international community.

Most viewed the coalition's victory over Iraq as definitive and decisive; however, Saddam Hussein claimed victory in the conflict. In one sense, he was correct: he and his Baath Party had survived. Indeed, within several years, he was the only leader of a major combatant from the war who was still in office. Bill Clinton defeated George H. W. Bush in 1992, Margaret Thatcher left office in 1990, and King Fahd of Saudi Arabia suffered a debilitating stroke in 1995 and relinquished his power to his brother, Abdullah.

The outcome of the war also enabled Saddam to continue his reign of terror in Iraq. At the end of the war, the coalition imposed a no-fly zone in the northern part of Iraq above the thirty-sixth parallel to protect the Kurds and in the southern parts of Iraq below the thirty-second parallel to protect the Shia; however, this ban did not apply to helicopters. The U.S. had encouraged the Kurds and the Shia to oppose Saddam's dictatorial rule, and when protests broke out, Saddam responded brutally and decisively. In the crackdown, an estimated 30,000 to 60,000 Shia were killed.[40] In the north, approximately 20,000 Kurds were killed and another 2 million fled their homes fearing another genocidal campaign, similar to the one waged against Halabja in 1988.

The Intermission between the First and the Second Gulf Wars

The 1991–2003 period between the first and second American wars against Iraq may be viewed as a long intermission between two "acts" or episodes of the same war. Some members of the cast remained the same and some changed, and some, though they were in both wars, played different roles.

In April 1991, at the end of the combat phase of the first Iraq War, the United Nations passed Resolution 687 that called for the creation of the UN Special Commission on Iraq (UNSCOM) to monitor and verify the demilitarization of Iraq, including the destruction of weapons of mass destruction, which the commission found Iraq unquestionably possessed at that time. The resolution tied the lifting of economic sanctions on Iraq to providing reparations to Kuwait and to Iraq's degree of cooperation with UNSCOM's efforts. Within a month of the resolution's passage, the commission had inspectors on the ground in Iraq conducting no-notice inspections of suspicious sites, installing cameras, sensors, and seals at these sites and reviewing all imports of technical materials into Iraq. Most observers believe that UNSCOM did an effective job in eliminating items prohibited by Resolution 687, including more than 800 SCUD missiles of the type that had been used against both Israel and Saudi Arabia during the war, stockpiles and plans for chemical and biological weapons, plans for nuclear research, and plans for the "Condor Project" (a joint Egyptian-Argentine-Iraqi project to develop ballistic missiles), as well as the destruction of great quantities of conventional munitions.[41] In fact, following the end of the first Gulf War, UNSCOM destroyed more Iraqi weapons than the coalition forces destroyed during the war, including "28,000 munitions, 480,000 liters of agent, 1.8 million liters of liquid chemical precursors, and a million kilograms of solid precursor chemicals."[42]

In January 1993, Iraq refused to remove missiles that the U.S. contended it had moved to southern Iraq, and American and allied aircraft attacked a suspected nuclear facility and missile sites south of Baghdad. Six months later, the U.S. government announced that it had discovered an Iraqi plot to assassinate President George H. W. Bush during a visit to Kuwait, and in response, President Clinton ordered an attack of twenty-three Tomahawk cruise missiles on the Iraqi intelligence headquarters in Baghdad; according to Iraqi sources, eight were killed in the attack. To critics of the Clinton administration, such as Paul Wolfowitz, this response consisted of ineffectual "pin-pricks."[43]

In October 1994, Iraq moved troops toward Kuwait, and the U.S. dispatched an aircraft carrier battle group, 54,000 troops, and combat aircraft to the region to prepare for possible conflict with Iraq. Following the American deployment, Iraq pulled its troops away from the Iraq-Kuwait border. In August 1996, Iraq sent military forces into northern Iraq and captured Irbil, a city within the Kurdish "safe haven" in northern Iraq protected by American-led forces. In response to the Iraqi incursion, U.S. forces fired twenty-seven cruise missiles at Iraqi military targets and extended the southern no-fly zone from the thirty-second to the thirty-third parallel just south of Baghdad.

In October 1997, Iraq accused the American members of UNSCOM of spying and expelled them from Iraq. President Clinton ordered a carrier battle group to the Persian Gulf, and the United Nations threatened new economic sanctions if Iraq did not cooperate with UN inspectors. When Iraq ejected the remaining American inspectors, the UN withdrew its other inspectors in protest. The United Kingdom and the U.S. built up their military forces in the Gulf, and Iraq readmitted UNSCOM inspectors, including the Americans. Iraq then announced that it would exclude from inspection "palaces and official residences," areas that UN officials had suspected concealed forbidden items.

In January 1998, an influential group of former policymakers wrote to President Clinton to urge him to overthrow Saddam. This letter was sponsored by the Project for a New American Century and was signed by eighteen individuals, many of whom would become important members of the George W. Bush administration, including Donald Rumsfeld, Richard Armitage, John Bolton, and Paul Wolfowitz. In their letter, the signers warned that the Clinton administration's policy of deterrence was failing and that

> [t]he only acceptable strategy is one that eliminates the possibility that Iraq will be able to use or threaten to use weapons of mass destruction. In the near term, this means a willingness to undertake military action as diplomacy is clearly failing. In the long term, it means removing Saddam Hussein and his regime from power.[44]

In several ways, this letter was a harbinger of themes that would emerge in George W. Bush's administration three years later: in particular, its emphasis on the threat of weapons of mass destruction and the need to remove Saddam from power.

This letter indicated the level of frustration of former members of the George H. W. Bush administration, neoconservative foreign policy analysts, and a growing number of members of Congress who increasingly called for a change of regime in Iraq. In February 1998, a group consisting of both Republicans and Democrats and co-chaired by former Congressman Steve Solarz and Richard Perle sent an open letter to President Clinton calling for "a determined program to change the regime in Baghdad." In September 1998, a bill to provide $97 million for military and educational training for opponents of Saddam was introduced. The bill passed by a vote of 360 to 38 in the House of Representatives and unanimously in the Senate. Many had assumed that the Iraqi people would rise up and topple Saddam following the disastrous first Gulf War. The CIA had tried to sponsor opposition leaders to overthrow Saddam, but all of these efforts failed. By exercising brutal control over Iraqi society, Saddam was able to remain in power, a fact that deeply frustrated many Americans.

The inspection situation worsened throughout 1998. In January, Iraq blocked an UNSCOM inspection team led by an American, and later the same month, President Clinton called on Iraq to open all sites to inspection. In February, UN Secretary General Kofi Annan announced that he had worked out a deal with Iraq promising to remove UN economic sanctions in exchange for greater transparency for the inspectors.[45] Six months later, Iraq announced that it did not see any move to lift sanctions and that it was halting the work of the UN weapons inspectors. In response, the U.S. and UK announced that they were considering possible military strikes in order to force Iraq to cooperate with the inspectors. On November 5, 1998, the UN Security Council passed a resolution condemning Iraq's actions as "flagrant violations" of UN resolutions. In mid-November, Iraq allowed the inspectors to return, but three weeks later, the chief UN inspector, Richard Butler, announced that Iraq was impeding inspections and that the UN inspection team would leave Iraq. Upon his return from Iraq, Butler issued a report in which he stated that Iraq did not fully cooperate with the UN inspectors, and in response, American and British forces embarked on Operation Desert Fox, attacking key targets for a four-day period.[46]

To some, the timing of the attacks was suspect; impeachment proceedings against President Clinton, stemming from the sordid Monica Lewinsky affair, had begun one day before the attacks on Iraq. Senate Majority Leader Trent Lott commented, "While I have been assured by administration officials that there is no connection with the impeachment process in the House of Representatives, I cannot support this military action in the Persian Gulf at this time. Both the timing and the policy are subject to question."[47] Other critics drew a parallel between Clinton's action and the popular movie *Wag the Dog*, in which a fictional president hires a Hollywood producer to start a war in order to divert the public's attention from a sex scandal. Many thought that reality was imitating fiction and yearned for a change in political leadership.

T. E. Lawrence wrote, "Mesopotamia [Iraq] will be the master of the Middle East, and the power controlling its destinies will dominate all its neighbors."[48] One of the earliest known civilizations was founded in the area that today constitutes Iraq, and throughout much of recorded history Iraq has played a significant role. Its importance increased with the discovery of oil and the increasing importance of this commodity to industrialized states in the twentieth century. Rising to power, Saddam Hussein sought to make Lawrence's prediction true and fought a long, costly war with Iran, invaded and occupied a neighboring Arab country, Kuwait, and fought and lost two wars with the United States and its allies. In perpetrating these actions, it may well be that Saddam in fact affected the destinies of all its neighbors as well as many other countries for years to come.

5 The Development of Terrorism, 1991–2001

Terrorism is as old as recorded human history, and is, therefore, not a new phenomenon to much of the world. The terrorist attacks on the United States on September 11, 2001, however, were devastatingly unique for Americans. Professor Walter Laqueur has defined terrorism as "the illegitimate use of force to achieve a political objective when innocent people are targeted."[1] RAND Corporation analyst Brian Jenkins has defined it as "the use or threatened use of force designed to bring about a political change."[2] The U.S. government has defined terrorism as "premeditated, politically motivated violence perpetrated against noncombatant targets by sub-national groups or clandestine agents, usually intended to influence an audience."[3] Terrorism may be sponsored or perpetrated by states or nonstate actors, and it is the growth in number and lethality of the latter type of terrorism that distinguishes the contemporary age from previous eras. In this chapter, I trace the development of terrorism, emphasizing the changing nature of terrorism and the emergence of al Qaeda and its leader, Osama bin Laden.

Terrorism in History

Both the Old and New Testaments of the Bible recount a number of cases of what would today be defined as terrorism; for example, in the book of Numbers, God commands, "Now therefore, kill every male among the little ones, and kill every woman who has known man intimately. But all the girls who have not known man intimately, spare for ourselves."[4] One method of terrorism is assassination, and the word "assassin" derives from an Arabic word meaning "the followers of Hassan i-Sabbah," who was known to kill his political opponents. When modern nation-states began to emerge following the Thirty Years War (1618–1648), political leaders ultimately rejected state-sponsored terrorism and assassination, if for no other reason than that they wanted to protect themselves.[5] However, over time, states began to employ terroristic methods against both their own populations and other countries.

State-sponsored terrorism was traditionally the most common and lethal variant of terrorism, but throughout history, there have also been individuals and nonstate groups that have utilized terror as a means to achieve their goals. Nonstate terrorists have included anarchists, Marxist revolutionaries, ethnic nationalists, religiously motivated groups, pathological individuals and groups, and radical political movements such as neofascists. As noted in Chapter 2, various Muslim thinkers had written about *jihad* (holy war) and the use of violence, including terrorism.

Many historians date the emergence of modern terrorism to the 1968 hijacking of an Israeli El Al airliner by George Habash's Popular Front for the Liberation of Palestine. This event was followed by a number of other terroristic acts perpetrated by both state and nonstate actors. The takeover of the American embassy in Tehran in November 1979 was another significant event in the development of terrorism, and in 1979, the U.S. government publicly identified seven state sponsors of terrorism: Cuba, Iran, Iraq, Libya, North Korea, Sudan, and Syria. Following its takeover of Afghanistan in 1996, the Taliban government was added to the list. As of November 2010, Cuba, Iran, Sudan, and Syria were still on the list.[6]

During the 1980s and 1990s, a total of 666 American citizens died from international terrorism, and during the same twenty years, a total of 190 Americans died from domestic terrorism for a total of 856 fatalities.[7] Deaths of all nationalities during the same period were substantially higher: 7,132 were killed and 31,000 were wounded. On the one hand, these are significant casualties, particularly for the families affected by these losses; on the other hand, these losses paled in comparison to fatalities from other causes. For example, during this period an average of 40,000 Americans per year were killed in traffic accidents, and it was more likely for Americans to be struck by lightning, die from bee stings, or drown in bathtubs than to be killed by terrorists in this period of history.[8] In the 1990s, the number of terrorist events actually declined as the following statistics indicate: 484 (1991), 343 (1992), 360 (1993), 353 (1994), 278 (1995), and 250 (1996).[9] According to Paul Pillar, a former CIA official and deputy chief of the Counterterrorism Center, the terrorists of this period were primarily "young adult males, unemployed or underemployed with poor prospects for economic improvement or advancement through legitimate work."[10]

In addition, most of the terrorists of this period had little formal education and were not married.

The U.S. government responded to the terrorist incidents of the 1980s and 1990s by adopting a law enforcement approach to dealing with the problem. In particular, U.S. government policy was based on the following principles: (1) make no concessions and do not conclude any agreements with terrorists, (2) apprehend and bring to justice perpetrators of terrorist acts, (3) isolate and pressure state sponsors of terrorism to change their behavior, and (4) assist countries which work with the U.S. to improve their counterterrorist capabilities.[11]

The Emergence of Osama bin Laden and Al Qaeda

As noted in Chapter 3, during the more than nine years of fighting the Soviets in Afghanistan, the *mujahideen* developed a well-trained military force that, with the material assistance of Pakistan, Saudi Arabia, the United States, and other Islamic countries, was able to defeat one of the most powerful states in the world at that time. With the defeat of the USSR, the U.S. turned its attention elsewhere. Of course, there were good reasons to do so, given the fall of the Berlin Wall in November 1989, Iraq's invasion and occupation of Kuwait in August 1990, and the disintegration of the Soviet Union in December 1991.

The *mujahideen* and their supporters were buoyed by their success and looked for ways to apply their guerilla tactics, strategy, and experience to support and advance the objectives of Islam, but there were few opportunities to do so or to integrate into normal society. As Omar Saghi, a scholar at the Institute for Political Studies in Paris, has pointed out, "The 1990s, in many Arab countries and especially in Saudi Arabia, may be seen as the decade of failed veterans who would remain unable to reintegrate into civilian life."[12] Like other religiously motivated individuals and movements, they believed that their success in defeating the Soviets indicated that God really was on their side. It was easy to conclude that if the Soviets could be defeated, then perhaps the last remaining superpower in the world, the United States, could also. In 2000, bin Laden reflected this view: "Using very meager resources and military means, the Afghan mujahedeen demolished one of the most important human myths in history and the biggest military apparatus. We no longer fear the so-called Great Powers. We believe that America is much weaker than Russia."[13]

Iraq's invasion and occupation of Kuwait in August 1990 represented not the "clash of civilizations," as coined by Bernard Lewis and popularized by Samuel Huntington, as much as a clash within a civilization, for it was an invasion of one Arab state by another Arab state. Many concluded that Saddam Hussein would not stop at Kuwait's borders but could continue into Saudi Arabia, the country with the largest oil reserves in the world. The modern Kingdom of Saudi Arabia was founded in 1902, and in 1938 vast oil deposits were discovered that provided the financial base to build the infrastructure of a modern state. The founding ruler of Saudi Arabia, King Abdul Azziz al Saud, depended on a hard-working immigrant from Yemen, Muhammad bin Laden, and his construction company to build many of the major projects in the new country, and these projects resulted in enormous revenues for the Bin Laden Construction Company.

Osama bin Laden was born in 1957, the seventeenth son of twenty-four sons and fifty-four children total of Muhammad bin Laden. According to Professor John Calvert, the Soviet-Afghan War was the "defining experience" of bin Laden's life,[14] and during the war he raised substantial amounts of money for the *mujahideen* and reportedly fought, but only in a single battle. Why did bin Laden follow this path rather than the more common path for young Saudis from wealthy families, of attending university overseas and frequenting the clubs and casinos of Beirut, London, Paris, and Monaco? In 1976, when bin Laden was eighteen years old, he entered King Abdul Aziz University in Jeddah and studied business administration.[15] In addition, bin Laden read and was strongly influenced by several radical Islamists, including those whose views are described in Chapter 2—Taqi al-Din Ibn Taymiyya, Muhammad ibn Abd al-Wahhab, and Sayyid Qutb. Bin Laden was at university at the same time that Abdullah Azzam, a West Bank Palestinian member of the Muslim Brotherhood, taught at the university, and the two may have met there, although this is not known for certain. Like bin Laden, Azzam was strongly attracted to and influenced by radical Islamists; in fact, he wrote a book about ibn Taymiyya.

After Osama left the university, he and Azzam and their wives became close friends; according to Osama's bodyguard, theirs was "a meeting of money, will and youth, represented by Osama Bin Laden, and knowledge, direction and experience represented by Abdullah Azzam."[16] Azzam believed that holy war, *jihad*, was a sacred obligation for Muslims, and when the Soviets invaded Afghanistan, Azzam, a charismatic speaker, became one of the most influential recruiters and fundraisers for the *mujahideen*. According to Professor Fawaz Gerges, Azzam became the "spiritual father of the so-called Afghan Arabs."[17] In addition, with donations worth millions of dollars from wealthy Saudi and

Gulf Arabs, Azzam established an organization called the Maktab al-Khadamat (Services Office) in Peshawar that housed and trained an estimated 10,000 Muslims who came to Peshawar to fight against the Soviets in Afghanistan. It is also estimated that the Maktab al-Khadamat disbursed approximately $2 billion to its offices throughout the world.[18] Although most of the *jihadi* volunteers were from Egypt and Saudi Arabia, there were also volunteers from almost twenty other Islamic countries, including Iraq, Kuwait, Turkey, Jordan, Syria, Libya, Tunisia, Morocco, Lebanon, Yemen, Algeria, Sudan, Pakistan, Malaysia, and Indonesia. Azzam's standard message was "Jihad and the rifle alone: no negotiations, no conferences and no dialogues."[19] As part of his fundraising efforts, Azzam visited the United States more than twenty times in the 1980s in order to raise support for the *mujahideen*.[20] By the late 1980s, there were thirty-three American cities with branches of Azzam's and bin Laden's Services Office, including Brooklyn, St. Louis, Kansas City, Seattle, Sacramento, Los Angeles, and San Diego.[21] In November 1989, Azzam and two of his sons were killed in a bombing outside a mosque in Peshawar, Pakistan. Those responsible for the killing were never identified, although some suspected that Ayman al-Zawahiri or even bin Laden had played a role.[22] Bin Laden blamed Azzam's assassination on the "Judeo-Crusader alliance."[23]

Osama and Azzam had worked closely together throughout the 1980s; some knowledgeable observers believed that Azzam was bin Laden's "spiritual guru," and Azzam had said of bin Laden that "a whole nation [was] embodied in one man."[24] Osama had raised money for Azzam's Maktab al-Khadamat, and the year before Azzam was killed, Osama founded a new organization, which he called al Qaeda. In Arabic, this has two meanings: "the base" or "the rule." Following Azzam's assassination, radical Egyptian Islamist Ayman al-Zawahiri became bin Laden's most important associate. As Gerges has noted, "With the exception of Azzam, Zawahiri contributed the most to the radicalization of bin Laden and the deepening of his politicization and versatility in *jihadist* tactics."[25]

Following the Iraqi invasion of Kuwait, bin Laden met with Prince Sultan, the defense minister of Saudi Arabia, and told him, "I am ready to prepare one hundred thousand fighters with good combat capability within three months. You don't need Americans. You don't need any non-Muslim troops. We will be enough."[26] The minister pointed out that there were no caves in Saudi Arabia, which the *mujahideen* had effectively used in Afghanistan, and declined bin Laden's offer. After an impressive briefing by Secretary of Defense Dick Cheney, complete with classified satellite photos showing Iraqi military units in Kuwait, King Fahd invited the United States and its coalition of thirty-eight other countries to enter his country. Bin Laden and other Muslim radicals were incensed, for the country that they considered to be the most sacred in Islam would be, in their view, occupied by infidels, including Jews and women, who were uncovered and would even drive vehicles. At this time, Saudi women were not allowed to drive even if they were members of the royal family. In a scathing public attack on Sheik Abd al-Aziz bin Baz, the chief mufti of Saudi Arabia, who had issued an edict approving the deployment of foreign troops to Saudi Arabia, bin Laden wrote: "When the forces of the aggressive Crusader-Jewish alliance decided during the Gulf War—in connivance with the [Saudi] regime—to occupy the country in the name of liberating Kuwait, you justified this with an arbitrary juridical decree excusing this terrible act, which insulted the pride of our *umma* and sullied its honor, as well as polluting its holy places."[27] Saudi governmental authorities were concerned about bin Laden's increasingly militant statements and kept him under house arrest for a while. Then in late 1991 they allowed him to go to Sudan, where he lived under the protection of radical Islamist leader Hassan al-Turabi. Saudi authorities hoped to solve a Saudi domestic problem by exiling him to Sudan but in doing so created the beginnings of a significant international problem. Bin Laden was joined by his friend, al-Zawahiri. Because of bin Laden's continuing condemnation of the Saudi regime, the Saudi government on several occasions attempted to assassinate bin Laden, but without success.[28] For his part, bin Laden used Sudan as his training base and staging area to send *mujahideen* secretly to various hotspots including Somalia, Kenya, Yemen, Bosnia, Egypt, Libya, and Tajikistan.[29] Although not known at the time, it was al Qaeda members who taught Somali fighters how to shoot down American helicopters in October 1993 in Mogadishu using rocket-propelled grenades.[30] In the ensuing fighting and the attempted rescue of downed helicopter pilots, eighteen American soldiers were killed, and President Clinton ordered the withdrawal of U.S. forces from Somalia in early 1994.

On February 26, 1993, a car bomb detonated in the parking garage of the World Trade Center in New York killing six people and injuring more than one thousand. Significantly, this was the first Islamic terrorist attack on American territory. Ramzi Yousef, a Pakistani citizen who had trained in an al Qaeda camp in Afghanistan, was identified as the leader of the operation, and three others assisted him. All four were associated with the Al Kifah Center in Brooklyn, which was funded by and affiliated with the Mahktab al-Khadamet, the organization founded by Abdullah Azzam and supported by Osama bin Laden. Richard Clarke, the former National Security Council counterterrorism coordinator, contends that the bombing was an al Qaeda operation and that Yousef had communicated with bin Laden from New York.[31] Although some question the degree of involvement of bin Laden and al Qaeda in the 1993 World Trade Center bombing, attention was nevertheless focused on bin Laden.[32] The Saudi government took away bin Laden's Saudi citizenship in March 1994 and pressured the bin Laden family construction company to reduce its payments to Osama. For its part, the U.S. government responded with a law enforcement approach; according to the 9/11 Commission, "Legal processes were the primary method for responding to these early manifestations of a new type of terrorism."[33]

In June 1995, there was an unsuccessful assassination attempt on Egyptian President Hosni Mubarak during an official visit to Addis Ababa, Ethiopia. Investigators concluded that the plotters came from and were supported by Sudan, and this conclusion galvanized Egypt and the United States to pressure Saudi Arabia to have Sudanese leader al-Turabi expel bin Laden from his country. In May or June of 1996, bin Laden, Zawahiri, his family, and supporters went to Afghanistan and settled south of Jalalabad in the Tora Bora mountains where the *mujahideen*, with bin Laden's financial help, had built an extensive series of tunnels during the Soviet-Afghan War. Several months after bin Laden returned to Afghanistan, the Taliban took over Kabul, establishing their control of most of the country. Although relations between bin Laden and the Taliban were not always friendly or close, each had reason to support the other. Both were radical, *salafi* Sunnis, and for bin Laden, the Taliban provided a sanctuary where he could train young Muslims for *jihad;* for the Taliban, bin Laden provided financial support, estimated to be $10 to $20 million per year, and the prestige of hosting and supporting someone who was becoming one of the most influential radical Muslim leaders in the world.[34] As an undated National Security Council (NSC) memo put it, "Under the Taliban, Afghanistan is not so much a state sponsor of terrorism as it is a state sponsored by terrorists."[35]

It is curious that the otherwise retrogressive leaders of radical Islamic movements recognized and capitalized on the capabilities of modern mass communications technologies. For example, during his fifteen years of exile from Iran, the Ayatollah Khomeini, who seemed to want to drag Iran back into the fourteenth century, recorded and secretly distributed into Iran cassette tapes of his fiery, anti-Shah sermons, building support for his perspective and, ultimately, his return to Iran. Technology marched on, and radical Islamists were quick to recognize its potential for spreading their ideology. For several years prior to his forced exile from Sudan, Osama bin Laden wrote a series of articles on a wide range of topics. An organization founded and supported by Osama in London in July 1994, the Committee for Advice and Reform, faxed Osama's statements throughout the world, but focused primarily on Saudi Arabia, the Gulf, and international media groups.[36] Ironically, this use of fax machines resembled the way in which young Chinese reformers communicated prior to and during the Tiananmen crisis of 1989, but, of course, they were striving for greater freedom, while the terrorists called for *jihad.* In the 1990s, terrorists were quick to recognize the advantages that the internet offered to them. As the 9/11 Commission noted in its report, "The emergence of the World Wide Web has given terrorists a much easier means of acquiring information and exercising command and control over their operations."[37] Bin Laden effectively and strategically utilized the internet as a recruiting tool, to disseminate propaganda, and to promulgate his pronouncements and diatribes against the U.S. and its allies.

Bin Laden has stated that *jihad* is "an individual duty" for every Muslim who is able to go to war, and al Qaeda ranks *jihad* as second only to *iman* (belief) among the five pillars of Islam.[38] On August 23, 1996, bin Laden issued a declaration of war against the United States, a call for violent *jihad* against Americans, and the overthrow of the Saudi regime. In bin Laden's view, "[T]he greatest disaster to befall Muslims since the death of the Prophet [is] the occupation of Saudi Arabia, the cornerstone of the Islamic world."[39] Bin Laden focused particular attention on the U.S. and its citizens: "Killing the Americans and their allies—civilian and military—is an individual duty for every Muslim who can carry it out in any country where it proves possible, in order to liberate the Al-Aqsa Mosque and the holy sanctuary [Mecca] from their grip, and to the point where their armies leave all Muslim territory, defeated and unable to threaten any Muslim."[40] In calling for the killing of civilians, bin Laden negated centuries-old Islamic and Christian conceptions of just war prohibiting the murder of innocent civilians.[41] At the conclusion of his statement, bin Laden issued a clarion call: "I say to our Muslim brothers across the world: your brothers in Saudi Arabia and Palestine are calling for your help and asking you to share with them in the *jihad* against the enemies of God, your enemies the Israelis and Americans. They are asking you to defy them in whatever way you possibly can, so as to expel them in defeat and humiliation from the holy places of Islam .... Cavalry of Islam, be mounted!"[42]

Bin Laden's "cavalry" dramatically responded to his order on August 7, 1998, when members of al Qaeda simultaneously attacked the American embassies in

Tanzania and Kenya, killing eleven in Dar es Salaam and 213 in Nairobi; of the killed, twelve were Americans. An additional estimated 5,000 were wounded in the two attacks, which served as a wake-up call for the U.S. government. These attacks were devastatingly impressive and sophisticated, carried out nearly simultaneously though separated by hundreds of miles. After the African embassy attacks, it was clear that al Qaeda had both the capability and intention to implement bin Laden's call for action against the United States. According to Professor Fawaz Gerges, "The embassy bombings marked a turning point for bin Laden and his associates and greatly advanced their cause."[43] In response to the embassy attacks, the United States launched thirteen cruise missiles against a pharmaceutical plant in Sudan that was suspected of producing biological weapons and sixty-six missiles against al Qaeda training camps in Afghanistan. In addition, the U.S. placed a $3 million bounty on bin Laden, who responded by placing a $3 million bounty on any CIA officer brought to him alive or dead.[44]

Even after the bombings of the embassies, al Qaeda had been responsible for fewer than fifty American deaths; however, it was becoming clear that a new type of terrorism was emerging. Long-time RAND Corporation terrorism expert Brian Jenkins pointed out in 1975, "Terrorists want a lot of people watching and listening and not a lot of people dead . . . . Terrorism is theater."[45] After the African embassy bombings, NSC counterterrorism staff members Daniel Benjamin and Steven Simon amended Jenkins' canonical statement contending that contemporary terrorists "want a lot of people watching *and* a lot of people dead."[46] In fact, a "new terrorism" was emerging that was: (1) increasingly networked, (2) more diversely motivated, (3) more global in reach, (4) more lethal, and (5) increasingly targeted at Americans, including civilians.[47] Table 5.1 shows a chronology of attempted and actual al Qaeda terrorist acts between 1992 and 2010.

As the 1990s went on, there were other changes in the nature and character of terrorism, and over time several different types of terrorists could be identified. The first group of terrorists in the contemporary era emerged from the Afghan War and consisted of *mujahideen* veterans. They were professional, disciplined, experienced, and ideological, and Osama bin Laden was their principal leader and spokesman. A second group of terrorists was less organized and trained and engaged in criminality as their preferred modus operandi. The would-be "millennium bomber" of Los Angeles International Airport, Ahmed Ressam, was characteristic of this group. The third type of terrorists consisted of amateurs, what counterinsurgency expert David Kilcullen has called "acci-

TABLE 5.1
Chronology of Al Qaeda Attempted and Actual Terrorist Acts, 1992–2010

Date	Event	U.S. as target?	Killed	Wounded
12/29/92	Bombing of two hotels in Aden, Yemen	Yes	2	
2/93	World Trade Center bomb	Yes	6	1,000
10/93	Mogadishu, Somalia	Yes	18	73
12/11/94	Attempted bombing of Philippine airliner	No	1	
11/13/95	Car bomb exploded outside Saudi National Guard office	Yes	7	60
6/96	Al-Khobar towers (Hezbollah and Al-Qaeda?)	Yes	19	372
11/97	Tourists in Luxor, Egypt	?	62	
8/7/98	U.S. embassies in Kenya and Tanzania	Yes	224	5,500
10/00	USS *Cole*	Yes	17	30
9/11/01	Pentagon and airliner	Yes	189	106
9/11/01	World Trade Center	Yes	3,065	
9/11/01	United Airlines	Yes	92	
11/22/01	Attempted bombing of airliner with "shoe bomb"	Yes	0	
4/11/02	Synagogue in Djerba, Tunisia bombed	No	17	
7/14/02	Car bomb, U.S. consulate, Karachi, Pakistan	Yes	11	45
10/6/02	French-registered tanker sailing off the coast of Yemen is damaged	No	0	
10/12/02	Three bombs exploded in Bali, Indonesia (Jemaah Islamiyah responsible)	No	202	1,500
11/28/02	Bombing of Hotel Mombassa, Kenya	No	13	
5/12/03	Car bombs in Riyadh, Saudi Arabia	No	34	
8/13/03	Car bomb, Jakarta, Indonesia	No	13	149
3/11/04	Madrid trains (Moroccan Islamic Combatant Group)	No	191	1,400
10/1/05	Bombing in Bali, Indonesia	No	20	100
11/26/08	Attacks in Mumbai, India (Lashkar e-Tayba)	No	163	
8/28/09	Suicide bomber attempted to kill Saudi counterterrorism director	No	0	
7/16/09	Two hotels bombed in Jakarta (Jemaah Islamiyah responsible)	?	9	50
12/25/09	Attempted blowing up of U.S. airliner	Yes	0	0

Source: Compiled by the author from various sources.

dental guerillas."[48] These consisted of locals who were not trained and who for reasons of tribal or clan loyalty or money became involved in terrorism.

Since the days of Theodore Roosevelt's "Great White Fleet," American naval ships have been used to "show the flag," to establish presence, and to protect the sea lanes of communication and commerce. In keeping with these classical missions, American leaders have ordered ships to visit ports around the world. In January 2000, a U.S. destroyer, the USS *The Sullivans*, made a port visit to Aden, Yemen. A member of al Qaeda attempted to blow up the ship but was unsuccessful. Nine months later, another U.S. ship, the USS *Cole* (a 550-foot Arleigh Burke class destroyer) made a port visit and was approached by a launch carrying two people who benignly waved to the American sailors on the deck. Then the launch turned suddenly toward the middle of the *Cole* and detonated a large explosion that ripped a hole twenty feet high and forty feet wide in the ship. Seventeen sailors were killed and forty were wounded, and it was only because of the heroic actions of the ship's crew that it did not sink. The attack on the *Cole* was a significant indicator of al Qaeda's modus operandi; namely, that it returned to try and succeed at previous, unsuccessful operations. But this was not recognized as a pattern following the attacks on *The Sullivans* and the *Cole*. If American intelligence officials had recognized such a pattern, they would have been more attuned to al Qaeda's interest in returning to the World Trade Center following the failed 1993 operation.

Dating back to 1998, several actual and attempted terrorist attacks galvanized American officials' attention on the need to address directly the threat from al Qaeda and Islamic terrorists: the attacks on the U.S. embassies in Tanzania and Kenya, the attempted attack on the USS *The Sullivans*, the abortive millennium attacks and particularly Ahmed Ressam's failed attack on Los Angeles International Airport, and the bombing of the USS *Cole*. The question, of course, was how the United States should go about dealing with al Qaeda. The cruise missile attacks on Iraq following the unsuccessful assassination attempt on George H. W. Bush and on Sudan and Afghanistan following the embassy bombings had not stopped or even slowed down the terrorists. In addition, President Clinton and his key national security advisers wanted actionable intelligence before ordering another cruise missile attack or other actions against bin Laden. As Clinton's national security advisor, Samuel Berger, testified to a congressional inquiry in 2002:

> Unfortunately, after August 1998, we never again had actionable intelligence information reliable enough to warrant another attack against Bin Laden or his key lieutenants. If we had, President Clinton would have given the order. The President ordered two submarines loaded with cruise missiles on perpetual deployment off the coast of Pakistan for that very purpose. We also were engaged in a number of covert efforts I cannot discuss in this unclassified format.[49]

In the fall of 2000, chairman of the Joint Chiefs of Staff (JCS) Henry Shelton ordered the preparation of a paper outlining twelve or thirteen options for employing military force against bin Laden, including several "boots on the ground" options.[50] General Shelton indicated that these options could be implemented "very quickly," but that they depended on intelligence agencies providing reliable actionable intelligence. NSC counterterrorism advisor Richard C. Clarke recalled, "[T]he overwhelming message to the White House from the uniformed military leadership was 'we don't want to do this' . . . . The military repeatedly came back with recommendations that their capability not be utilized for commando operations in Afghanistan."[51] General Shelton believed that a large military force would be necessary to conduct effective operations against al Qaeda in Afghanistan, and he was skeptical about Rumsfeld's ideas about "transformation." In addition, he had disagreed with Rumsfeld, who had wanted to abolish the JCS' legislative liaison and public affairs offices. When Shelton retired at the end of September, the option to send U.S. military forces into Afghanistan was dead in the water.

The military's hesitance to send troops to Afghanistan opened the door to the CIA to develop a plan for dealing with bin Laden in Afghanistan, and there were no great options; each had a number of negatives, confronting the CIA with a classic dilemma. After discussion of a number of options, CIA planners focused on the possibility of working with Ahmed Shah Massoud, the charismatic, Tajik leader of the Northern Alliance.

Ahmed Shah Massoud: The Lion of Panjshir

According to Gary Schroen, the CIA operative who had dealt with Afghan leaders since the end of the Soviet-Afghan War, "[T]he only serious military opposition to the Taliban rested in Ahmed Shah Massoud and his Northern Alliance forces."[52] The Taliban were composed of Pashtuns, and they were opposed by the non-Pashtun forces of the Northern Alliance that consisted of Massoud's Tajik troops, General Rashid Dostum's Uzbek forces, Herat's Ismael Khan, and Hazara commanders of central Afghanistan. Richard Clarke supported Massoud and indicated his reason for doing so: "If Massoud posed a serious threat to the Taliban, bin Laden would have to devote his arms and men to fight against the Northern Alliance rather than fighting us."[53]

How did Ahmad Shah Massoud become the Afghan leader that the CIA and Clarke looked to? Born in 1952 or 1953 in Jangalak, a town in the Panjshir Valley about sixty miles north of Kabul, Massoud was the son of a colonel in the military of King Zahir Shah. He attended a French-sponsored school, the Lycee Istiqlal, where Massoud learned French and did well enough academically to win a scholarship to study in France. Massoud turned down the scholarship offer and applied for Afghanistan's military academy but was turned down.[54] Instead, he attended the Soviet-sponsored Kabul Polytechnic Institute, where he came into contact with radical Islamists who were connected to the Muslim Brotherhood in Egypt. These included Burhanuddin Rabbani, Abdurrab Rasul Sayyaf, and others who had studied in Egypt, picked up the radical, Islamist ideas of the Brotherhood, and returned to Afghanistan. In 1973 this group founded the Muslim Youth Organization, which was dedicated to the revolutionary ideas of Sayyid Qutb. In July 1973, the group attempted to seize power, and when the coup failed, fled to Pakistan to seek sanctuary. The Pakistan government welcomed them and provided military training for the Afghan exiles and their followers.[55] According to later Soviet intelligence reports on Massoud, in 1974–75 he was further trained in guerilla warfare tactics in Egypt and Lebanon, where "he took part in combat operations and committed terrorist acts in armed Palestinian groups."[56] There were also reports that Massoud participated in an uprising in the Panjshir district in June 1975. Massoud was both a man of action and of theory; he read and studied the works on guerilla warfare written by Mao Zedong, Che Guevara, and French revolutionary theorist Regis Debray. He was also devoutly religious; as journalist Ahmed Rashid noted, "Ahmad Shah Masud leads breaks from directing a battle to pray and then goes into a deep spiritual silence as booming guns and wireless chatter fill the air."[57]

Between 1975 and 1978, Massoud went back and forth between Pakistan and Afghanistan, but in 1978, he returned to his home in the Panjshir Valley with twenty to thirty supporters, seventeen rifles, the equivalent of $130 in cash, and a letter requesting that the local population declare holy war against the Soviet-backed government.[58] But Massoud came with more: a charismatic personality and commitment to his country. According to Soviet intelligence analysts, "[He] has proved this to everyone: he is a strong-willed and energetic person who displays persistence and purposefulness in achieving set tasks."[59]

Once the Soviet Union invaded and occupied Afghanistan in December 1979, Massoud's "set task" became the defeat of what he viewed as infidel, foreign occupiers. By almost all accounts, Massoud was the most talented *mujahideen* military leader. In October 1986, Robert Gates, then deputy of the CIA, characterized Massoud as "the very effective Mujahedin commander."[60] NSC staff members Daniel Benjamin and Steven Simon called Massoud "a superb general" and a "legendary battlefield commander."[61] Some contended that Massoud's ultimate ambition was to become king of Afghanistan.[62] Pulitzer Prize–winning journalist Lawrence Wright called Massoud "one of the most talented guerilla leaders of the twentieth century."[63] Even Osama bin Laden's mentor and adviser, Abdullah Azzam, called Massoud "the most brilliant leader in Afghanistan,"[64] a compliment that may have been one reason that Azzam was assassinated.[65]

Despite these laudatory views of Massoud, there were other critical reports. Although he was later lionized following his assassination, there were, in fact, a number of problems in working with and supporting Massoud. As Richard Clarke noted, "[He] had sold opium, abused human rights, and had killed civilians."[66] Massoud had raised money by smuggling both gems and drugs.[67] Massoud had also accepted support from Pakistan, India, and Iran. In fact, there were reports that Iran's notorious Ministry of Intelligence and Security helped Massoud because Shia Iran was strongly opposed to the Sunni Taliban.[68]

Once the Soviets departed Afghanistan in 1989, the surface unity of the *mujahideen* exploded into civil war, and from 1992 until the Taliban took over Afghanistan in 1996, Massoud fought the forces of the Taliban, Hekmatyar, and Dostum. There was, however, little doubt in Massoud's mind who posed the principal threat. In October 1998, in testimony to the Senate Foreign Relations Committee, Massoud warned:

> This is a crucial and unique moment in the history of Afghanistan and the world, a time when Afghanistan has crossed yet another threshold and is entering a new state of struggle and resistance for its survival as a free nation and independent state . . . . Today, the world clearly sees and feels the results of such misguided and evil deeds. South Asia is in turmoil, some countries on the brink of war. Illegal drug production, terrorist activities, and planning are on the rise. Ethnic and religiously motivated mass murders and forced displacements are taking place, and the most basic human and women's rights are shamelessly violated. Fanatics, extremists, terrorists, mercenaries, and drug Mafias have gradually occupied the country. One faction, the Taliban, which by no means rightly represents Islam, Afghanistan or our centuries-old cultural heritage, has, with direct foreign assistance, exacerbated this explosive situation.[69]

By 1998, despite the reports of drug dealing, gem smuggling, human rights abuses, and his dealings with Iran, the United States turned to Massoud almost by default. As Ahmed Rashid has written, "Masud was making a momentous transition from being a parochial local leader, often intolerant and sometimes ruthless, to becoming the most important national leader of the country."[70] In December 1999, Massoud offered to stage an attack against bin Laden's terrorist training camp at Drunta, but the U.S. government declined.[71] It may be that

Osama bin Laden learned of Massoud's offer; whether or not that is the case, bin Laden considered Massoud a threat to al Qaeda and himself.

On September 9, 2001, two members of al Qaeda posing as Belgian journalists were granted an interview with Massoud at his camp close to the border with Tajikistan. They set up their cameras, which, in fact, were filled with explosives. They started to ask questions, then shouting "*Allah Akbar*" detonated their explosives, killing themselves, the lion of Panjshir, one of his assistants, and the best hope for the future of Afghanistan.

September 11, 2001: Another Day That Will Live in Infamy

Americans who were old enough to understand what happened will never forget September 11, 2001, for it will live on in their memories, like the Japanese attack on Pearl Harbor for an earlier generation, as another "day that will live in infamy." Allow me to add a personal account. On September 9, 2001, I flew to Switzerland in order to attend the annual meeting of the International Institute of Strategic Studies (IISS) that was scheduled to meet in Geneva. The focus of the conference was to be economic factors of international security, and respected analysts of this topic were scheduled to speak. My wife accompanied me for several days of relaxing and hiking before the conference began. On September 11, we had gone for a long hike on a glacier outside the Swiss village of Wengen, and when we returned to our pension, I asked the desk clerk for the key to our room. She looked agitated and upset and asked me, "Aren't you American?" I replied that I was, and she said, "Something terrible has happened in your country." Having lived through the assassinations of John Kennedy, Martin Luther King, Jr., and Robert Kennedy in the 1960s, I immediately thought that the president had been killed. I asked the clerk what had happened, and she could only point to the television in the lounge and say, "You must see for yourself." My wife and I went to the lounge and watched a replay of the first airplane crashing into the first World Trade Center Tower. We were horrified and then doubly so as we watched in real time as the second plane crash into the second tower. A flood of questions came into my mind: Who would do this? Why? How many were killed? Would there be other attacks?

All commercial and general aviation flights in and out of the United States were grounded, approximately 4,500 flights; the United States had essentially declared an embargo of itself. My fellow IISS conferees and I were stranded in Geneva, but included among them were some of the foremost experts in the world on international security and terrorism. The conference organizers quickly and adeptly reorganized the conference to focus on "The Strategic Implications of Terror in the Information Age." The French chairman of the conference, Francois Heisbourg, quoted *Le Monde*'s headline of September 12: "We Are All Americans" and noted that the day after the attacks, the members of the North Atlantic Treaty Organization approved action under Article V of the NATO Treaty to come to the aid of a fellow member that has been attacked.[72] Heisbourg also noted that the attacks were not a crime, but rather an act of war, and that in war, the rules changed. James Rubin noted that the attacks did not represent a "clash of civilizations," but rather represented "a war of civilization versus the enemies of civilization." Prophetically, Lawrence Freedman noted that in Vietnam there was a tension between "winning hearts and minds," the acceptance and implementation of a counterinsurgency strategy, and "search and destroy," the execution of a classical military strategy of destroying the enemy. Former NSC staff members Daniel Benjamin and Steven Simon commented, "A great nation will never—must never—leave its dead unanswered."[73]

How had these tragic events come to pass? At 7:59 A.M., American Airlines flight 11 took off from Boston bound for Los Angeles, and twenty minutes later a flight attendant informed American Airlines that the plane had been hijacked.[74] At 8:46, the plane crashed into the North Tower of the World Trade Center in New York City. Seventeen minutes later United Airlines flight 175, also bound for Los Angeles, struck the South Tower of the Trade Center. At 9:37, American Airlines flight 77 crashed into the headquarters of the American military, the Pentagon, in Washington, DC, flying at an estimated speed of 530 miles per hour. At 8:42, United Airlines flight 93 took off from Newark, New Jersey, bound for San Francisco. It was hijacked forty-six minutes later at 9:28. Passengers and the flight crew began a series of calls on GTE airphones and cell phones, and at least ten of them shared information with family, friends, and officials on the ground. They learned of the attacks on the World Trade Center and decided to revolt against the hijackers. At the cost of their lives, the passengers stormed the cockpit and caused the hijackers to crash the plane outside of Shanksville, Pennsylvania. The 9/11 Commission concluded, "We are sure that the nation owes a debt to the passengers of United 93. Their actions saved the lives of countless others, and may have saved either the Capitol or the White House from destruction."[75]

At the time of the hijackings, President Bush was in Sarasota, Florida, visiting the Emma E. Booker Elementary School in order to talk with the children about education and to read to them. At 9:00 A.M., one of the president's advisers informed him that a small, two-engine plane had crashed into the World Trade Center. At 9:05, the president's chief of staff, Andrew Card, whispered to him, "A second plane hit the second tower. America is under attack." In the film footage of the president in the classroom, he looked stunned; he later told the 9/11 Commission that he wanted to project a calm demeanor. The president stayed with the children another five or six minutes and then went to a holding room where he watched the television coverage and was briefed by staff. The next day, he said, "The deliberate and deadly attacks which were carried out yesterday against our country were more than acts of terror. They were acts of war."[76] George W. Bush's appointment with history had tragically and devastatingly arrived. When Harry S. Truman learned that Franklin Delano Roosevelt had died on April 12, 1945, he told the press, "I felt like the moon, the stars, and all the planets had fallen on me." On September 11, 2001, George W. Bush probably had similar feelings.

The attacks had a deep and profound effect on Bush. On the night of the attacks, he dictated to his diary, "The Pearl Harbor of the 21st century took place today."[77] Soon after 9/11, Bush told his attorney general, John Ashcroft, "Don't ever let this happen again."[78] Concerning his response to 9/11, Bush told an associate, "This is what I was put on earth for."[79] Respected political scientist Robert Jervis has observed, "There is reason to believe that just as his coming to Christ gave meaning to his previously aimless and dissolute personal life, so the war on terrorism has become, not only the defining character of his foreign policy, but also his sacred mission."[80] Bush's sense of mission was consistently reflected in his statements throughout his presidency; for example, in his 2004 State of the Union address, he concluded, "The cause we serve is right, because it is the cause of all mankind. The momentum of freedom in our world is unmistakable—and it is not carried forward by our power alone. We can trust in that greater power who guides the unfolding of the years. And in all that is to come, we can know that His purposes are just and true."[81]

Key to that mission was the identifying and bringing to justice those who had perpetrated the attacks against the United States. To his credit, the president ordered that the available evidence be examined thoroughly and carefully, and this required time and effort. In addition, the president was anxious to make sure that Americans would not consider the conflict to be one between the West and Islam. While Bush urged toleration toward Muslims, he posed two stark alternatives: "Every nation in every region now has a decision to make. Either you are with us or you are with the terrorists."[82]

Part of the reason for this dichotomous view was Bush's conviction that the terrorists represented evil in the world, and the mission of the United States was, as President Bush asserted at a memorial service at the National Cathedral on September 14, 2001, "to answer these attacks and rid the world of evil."[83] Two days later, the president repeated this theme: "My administration has a job to do . . . . We will rid the world of the evildoers."[84] One week after the 9/11 attacks, the president returned to his theme of evil; in a news conference of September 16, he said, "This is a new kind of—a new kind of evil. And we understand. And the American people are beginning to understand. This crusade, this war on terrorism is going to take a while."[85] Bush's reference to a "crusade" was translated into Arabic as a "war of the cross" and resonated deeply and negatively throughout the Arab world, and the president had to amend his language quickly. The "crusade" against terrorism became the "war on terror," even though this was a declaration of war against a tactic rather than a tangible enemy, as a number of observers noted.

President Bush also realized that, contrary to the orientation of his administration during its first year in office, the war against terrorism could not be unilateral; it would require the support of as many other countries as possible. As CIA Director George Tenet noted, "[Y]ou cannot fight terrorism alone. There were clear limitations to what we could do without the help of like-minded governments."[86]

The traditional, like-minded allies of the United States were quick to offer their condolences and assistance. The North Atlantic Treaty Organization invoked Article V of the NATO Treaty for the first time in its history and committed seven airborne-warning aircraft to patrol the skies over the U.S. with European pilots and crews.

In this new age of terrorism, "like-minded" was redefined, and that became clear with the first call from a foreign leader to express his condolences and offer his nation's help; the call came from former Soviet KGB officer and Russian President Vladimir Putin. The help that Russia gave to the U.S. was valuable, tangible, and significant. No country had more knowledge of Afghanistan than Russia, which had waged a costly, nine-year campaign there. Russia provided the U.S. with valuable intelligence concerning the geography, culture, and social structure of Afghanistan. This provided a dramatic example of the ways that things had changed since the cold war and even the post–cold war period.

"Like-minded," as it turned out, was not restricted to Western allies or even recent competitors of the United States. In this new war on terrorism, the American government accepted help from whatever sources were judged to be valuable. One of the most dramatic collaborators was Syria, one of the seven countries that the U.S. government had officially identified as a state sponsor of terrorism.

After several weeks of collecting and analyzing the evidence, the U.S. government identified al Qaeda, the terrorist group founded and headed by Osama bin Laden, as responsible for the attacks on the United States and demanded that the Taliban government in Afghanistan close al Qaeda's terrorist training camps and hand over bin Laden to the U.S. When confronted with these demands, the Taliban leader of Afghanistan, Mullah Omar, refused, saying, "I will not hand over a Muslim to an infidel."[87] On October 7, 2001, almost exactly four weeks after the 9/11 attacks on the U.S., 426 Special Forces soldiers and CIA operatives in coordination with members of the Afghan Northern Alliance attacked and destroyed the al Qaeda training camps and overthrew the Taliban government within a matter of days. This remarkable feat indicated that the "revolution in military affairs" that incorporated high-tech advances was very real and not just a hypothetical idea in the mind of a visionary general or secretary of defense. To Rumsfeld, the U.S. success vindicated his ideas about the application of the revolution in military affairs.

The apparent American success in Afghanistan also demonstrated that in this new war on terror, the best defense was a good offense. To the Bush administration, the U.S. should not simply sit back and wait for a second major attack on the U.S. homeland; rather, it should take the war to the other side. But there were limits to success in this new type of war. Despite its success in destroying al Qaeda bases in Afghanistan and overthrowing the Taliban government, the United States failed to find or kill Osama bin Laden and Mullah Omar. The U.S. intensively bombed the Tora Bora area in the Afghan and Pakistani border region, but to no avail; the two most wanted fugitives in the world remained at large.

The war against terrorism could not, however, only be played as an "away game." The terrorists had already devastatingly struck the homeland of the United States, and measures had to be taken domestically as well as internationally to prevent another attack. Throughout the history of politics, there has been a tradeoff between freedom and security. Absolute freedom, as the Founding Fathers of the United States recognized, would be anarchy, and absolute security could represent safety, but not the kind of life anyone would choose. For example, a prisoner in solitary confinement in a maximum-security prison is about as close as someone can get to absolute security, but no one would choose to be in that position. In the post-9/11 world, the U.S. moved away from the pole of freedom toward the pole of greater security with greater surveillance and a lessening of rights of privacy, all in the name of "national security."

Even before 9/11, American officials recognized the threat posed by Osama bin Laden. In October 2001, Bill Clinton recalled, "You replay everything in your mind, and you ask, 'Was there anything else that could have been done?' I tried to take Mr. Bin Laden out of the picture for the last four years-plus I was in office . . . . I don't think I was either stupid or inattentive, so he is a formidable adversary."[88] Following the attacks of September 11, the full capabilities of the U.S. government were focused on capturing or killing bin Laden and his close associates, and yet, despite the awesome power of the United States, this goal was not achieved as of the writing of this book. The success of al Qaeda and the failure of the U.S. to hunt down bin Laden and Mullah Omar illustrated the challenges of dealing with a new kind of enemy in an unfamiliar environment.

6 The Bush Doctrine

The makers of American foreign policy can, broadly speaking, be characterized as primarily long-range conceptual thinkers or ad hoc problem solvers. Woodrow Wilson, the only president in American history to have earned a Ph.D., conceived of a new way of managing power in international relations, calling for the replacement of the balance of power system by a collective security system overseen by a new international organization, the League of Nations. Building in part on Wilson's grand design for world order, Franklin Roosevelt reintroduced the idea of collective security, but supported by the five victorious Allies of World War II on a permanent Security Council; each of these powers would have the right to veto any proposal coming before the Council.[1] In more recent decades, political scientists Henry Kissinger and Zbigniew Brzezinski attempted to introduce different conceptual frameworks for dealing with the international relations of the United States.[2]

In contrast to the attempt to develop and implement grand, conceptual designs for American foreign policy, other U.S. policymakers adopted an ad hoc approach to deal with problems as they arose. This approach was characteristic of a lawyer-like approach to dealing with problems, and can be seen in the way that attorneys who became secretaries of state—Dean Acheson, John Foster Dulles, Cyrus Vance, Warren Christopher, and Hillary Clinton—approached their job. This approach was task-oriented and designed to deal with problems on a case-by-case basis. Those who had served in the military or government often adopted this approach, as is evident in the way that Alexander Haig, Lawrence Eagleburger, and Colin Powell dealt with issues while serving as secretary of state.

Once confronted with the existential threat to the United States by terrorists on September 11, 2001, President George W. Bush and his advisers had to decide how best to deal with this new threat. Before discussing their approach, it is important to review their background and experience.

George W. Bush and the 2000 Presidential Election

George W. Bush was born to a political family; his grandfather was a U.S. senator from Connecticut, and his father served with distinction in a number of foreign policy positions, as vice president under Ronald Reagan for eight years, and then as the forty-first president of the United States. Journalist Jacob Weisberg contends, "Nearly everything he [George W. Bush] did in his youth represented an attempt to emulate his beloved, successful father—with unimpressive and sometimes farcical results."[3] During his education at Phillips Andover Academy and at Yale University, George W. Bush demonstrated little interest or even curiosity in academics.[4] Later interlocutors had similar impressions; after interviewing Bush several times, Weisberg noted, "I found him incurious and intellectually lazy."[5] In addition, his professors and fellow students at Yale recall little about any interest or involvement in the preeminent foreign policy issue of the sixties, the Vietnam War. Following graduation from college, Bush had little direction in his life. Facing the prospect of being drafted for military service, he joined the Texas Air National Guard with the help of his father's friends. This position meant that he never saw combat, and his record in the military was spotty; according to the records that exist, he missed a number of his reserve meetings and obligations.[6]

By his own admission, Bush developed a drinking problem, and in his memoirs, he recalled a dinner with his parents and family at their house in Kennebunkport, Maine, when after heavy drinking, he asked a female guest "So, what is sex like after fifty?"[7] Laura Bush encouraged her husband to give up alcohol, which he did following his fortieth birthday. With financial support from family members and friends, he entered the oil business, but he did not make the fortune for which he was hoping. With the $75 million investment of a number of personal and family friends, Bush then purchased the Texas Rangers baseball team using $600,000 of his own money. The city of Arlington, Texas, committed $135 million to building the Rangers a new stadium, which increased the value of the team significantly, and in 1998, Bush was able to sell his interest in the Rangers for $15 million, a profit of twenty-five times his initial investment.[8]

The only political office that George W. Bush held before becoming president was governor of Texas. In the early days of the American republic, service as secretary of state was common for American presidents; Thomas Jefferson, James Madison, James Monroe, John Quincy Adams, and Martin Van Buren all served in this capacity. In recent years, service as the governor of a state has become the most common road to the presidency: four of the past six presidents (Carter, Reagan, Clinton, and George W. Bush) served as governors prior to becoming president. However, in contrast to other recent governors-become-president, George W. Bush did not seem to have the interest in or knowledge of foreign policy that Carter, Clinton, or George H. W. Bush demonstrated. In terms of foreign policy interest and experience, ironically, the resume of Al Gore, the Democratic candidate in the 2000 presidential election, more closely resembled that of George H. W. Bush than did the resume of George W. Bush.

During the 2000 presidential campaign, Bush said that his priorities were "Laura Bush, Jesus Christ and working out"—that is, his spouse, his religion, and his health. While pundits had a field day with this quotation, it is revealing. Bush valued his health and regularly exercised, sometimes twice a day. In addition, Bush is very close to his wife and credits her with saving him from alcoholism. He is a devout, born-again Christian, and his religious beliefs contributed to a sense of mission and calling.[9] He told journalist Bob Woodward, "I'm here for a reason,"[10] and, "I get guidance from God in prayer."[11] In a meeting with Amish farmers in Lancaster County, Pennsylvania, Bush reportedly told them, "I trust God speaks through me."[12] Bush's religious views affected his policy preferences; for example, he noted, "I do believe there is an Almighty, and I believe a gift of that Almighty to all is freedom. And I will tell you that is a principle that no one can convince me that doesn't exist."[13] The president's policy of promoting democracy was, then, derived from his strongly held religious beliefs. According to Christian writer and editor Jim Wallis, "When I was first with Bush in Austin, what I saw was a self-help Methodist, very open, seeking . . . . What I started to see . . . [after the 9/11 attacks was] a messianic American Calvinist. He doesn't want to hear from anyone who doubts him."[14]

As in most presidential contests, foreign policy issues did not play a central role in the 2000 election. The Republican Party platform emphasized the "need to transform America's defense capabilities for the information age" and the need to develop defenses against a missile attack on the United States.[15] During the campaign, Bush noted, "The cold-war era is history. Our nation must recognize new threats, not fixate on old ones."[16] Included in these "new threats" were the threat of missile attacks against the U.S. and the emergence of China as a power to be reckoned with. Bush indicated that he would treat China more like a rival than a strategic partner and that he would give more support to Taiwan.[17]

George W. Bush chose a young political science professor, Condoleezza Rice, as his chief foreign policy adviser for the 2000 presidential campaign. Rice earned her undergraduate and doctoral degrees in political science at the University of Denver and a master's degree at Notre Dame. At Denver, she studied with Josef Korbel, a Czech émigré and the father of Madeleine Albright. After completing her doctorate, Rice won a postdoctoral fellowship at Stanford where she was appointed assistant professor. In 1984, General Brent Scowcroft, who at that time was the chairman of President Reagan's Commission on Strategic Forces, visited Stanford and presented a lecture on arms control. At the end of his talk, Rice directly challenged him on a number of fundamental points, and Scowcroft later recalled, "I thought, this is somebody I need to get to know. It's an intimidating subject. Here's this young girl, and she's not at all intimidated."[18] Scowcroft was so impressed that when he became national security adviser in George H. W. Bush's administration, he recruited Rice to be the principal adviser on the Soviet Union on the National Security Council (NSC), where she served for two years. In 1991, Rice returned to her professorship at Stanford and was appointed provost, the chief academic officer and the second most powerful position in the university.

In 1999, Rice resigned as provost and took a leave of absence from her professorship at Stanford and became the principal foreign policy adviser to George W. Bush's presidential campaign. She headed a group of experienced foreign policy advisers. In an important article published in the influential journal *Foreign Affairs* and written to indicate the projected contours of foreign policy under George W. Bush, Rice criticized the Clinton administration's efforts at "nation-building" among smaller, less influential countries such as Somalia, Haiti, and Kosovo, and indicated that a new Bush administration would focus on relations with great powers. Rice wrote, "To be sure, there is nothing wrong with doing something that benefits all humanity, but that is, in a sense, a second-order effect .... It is simply not possible to ignore and isolate other powerful states that do not share the values [of the United States].[19] In the same article, Rice called for the removal of Saddam Hussein not directly but by helping to support and encourage internal opposition to him and his Baath Party. Bush reiterated these themes during the campaign. At a debate with Al Gore at Wake Forest University in October 2000, Bush noted, "Our military is meant to fight and win war .... That's what it's meant to do. And when it gets overextended, morale drops. [I will be] judicious as to how to use the military. It needs to be in our vital interest, the mission needs to be clear, and the exit strategy obvious."[20]

The 2000 presidential election was one of the most contentious elections in American history and one of only four in which the candidate who received the most popular votes was not elected. Bush's electoral victory in Florida consisted of 537 votes out of 6,138,765 cast, and the election was so close that it took thirty-six days and a decision of the Supreme Court to resolve it. Once elected and inaugurated, George W. Bush embarked on a foreign policy which can best be described as "ABC unilateralism"; it was "Anything But Clinton" in that the new administration almost viscerally opposed anything that the Clinton administration had favored. If Clinton had supported something, George W. Bush was opposed to it, and vice versa. In addition, the new president and members of his administration believed that the United States as the world's sole remaining superpower was entitled to and, in fact, needed to act alone following its national interest and to cooperate internationally only when absolutely necessary. President Bush and the members of his administration entered office in January 2001 favoring the unilateral application of American military power and rejecting most of the foreign policy initiatives of the earlier Clinton administration. A new day and a new approach had arrived in Washington with the new administration.

In keeping with this approach, the new administration initiated a number of actions to reverse various Clinton administration initiatives. The administration opposed the Kyoto Protocol designed to reduce greenhouse gases in the atmosphere. Prior to leaving office, President Clinton had indicated that there were some problems that needed to be resolved but nevertheless signed the treaty establishing the International Criminal Court, even though there was almost no support in Congress for the agreement. Once in office, President Bush "unsigned" the treaty, the first time in American history that such an action had been taken. The administration refused to participate and sign a protocol to the 1972 Biological Weapons Convention establishing verification procedures for the agreement. In addition, Bush refused to reintroduce the Comprehensive Test Ban Treaty for ratification to the Senate, which had earlier rejected it, an action seen by many as the most significant rejection of a treaty since the rejection of the Treaty of Versailles at the end of World War I.[21] In the volatile Middle East, the administration retreated from the George H. W. Bush and Clinton administrations' efforts to support the peace process actively.[22] In another dangerous area of the world, the Korean Peninsula, the Bush administration did not support South Korea's efforts to engage and negotiate with its unpredictable neighbor to the north.

The strongest initiative of the new administration was to support the development, testing, and deployment of National Missile Defense (NMD). This seemed to be at the foundation of the administration's defense policy and necessitated the abrogation of the 1972 Anti-Ballistic Missile (ABM) Treaty, which had been negotiated and signed by an earlier Republican administration headed by President Nixon and Henry Kissinger. Most arms control advocates considered this treaty to be the foundation of modern strategic nuclear arms control.

In developing the foreign policy of the new administration, the president had a number of advisers, many of whom had served in the George H. W. Bush administration. Political scientists Ivo Daalder and James Lindsay have identified three different groups of advisers within the administration.[23] The first and least numerous consisted of pragmatic internationalists headed by Secretary of State Powell and his close advisers, including Richard Armitage and Richard Haass, and they were favorably inclined toward cooperation with allies and international organizations such as the United Nations whenever such cooperation furthered American national interests. The second group consisted of "assertive nationalists" Vice President Cheney and Secretary of Defense Donald Rumsfeld, who were "willing to use American military power to defeat threats to U.S. security but reluctant as a general rule to use American primacy to remake the world in its image."[24] In pursuit of this general objective, assertive nationalists favored smaller, more mobile military forces that would capitalize on the lead of the United States in technology. The third group consisted of neoconservatives, or "neocons" for short. Prominent in this group were a number of second-echelon officials, including Deputy Secretary of Defense Paul Wolfowitz, Under-Secretary of Defense for Policy Douglas Feith, foreign policy adviser to the vice president Lewis "Scooter" Libby, NSC staffer Elliott Abrams, and chairman of the Defense Policy Board, Richard Perle. The neocons within the administration were supported by a number of like-minded journalists and policy analysts outside of the government including Robert Kagan, Charles Krauthammer, William Kristol, Max Boot, and Joshua Muravchik. In contrast to the assertive nationalists who called for a "revolution in military affairs," the neocons favored strong, robust military forces to pressure rogue states such as Iran, Iraq, and North Korea either to reform or to face the overwhelming power of the United States. They also favored the spread of democracy, by force if necessary, to other countries.

Although the George W. Bush administration had a number of policymakers who had previously held offices in the executive branch, including Cheney, Powell, Rumsfeld, and Rice, Deputy Secretary of Defense Wolfowitz was the principal adviser who approached foreign policy with a focused, strategic perspective. Wolfowitz earned his doctorate in political science at the University of Chicago and taught for several years at Yale. He then entered government service, first in the Arms Control and Disarmament Agency and then the departments of State and Defense. Wolfowitz served in DOD during the first Gulf War in 1991 and was one of those who had recommended that Saddam Hussein be overthrown, a position that was overwhelmingly rejected by members of the George H. W. Bush administration.

Every two years the Department of Defense prepares a document called the Defense Planning Guidance that is designed to describe U.S. military strategy and to serve as the basis for determining the defense budget. The 1992 Defense Planning Guidance was viewed as particularly important, as it was the first prepared since the disintegration of the Soviet Union and end of the cold war in December 1991. Secretary of Defense Cheney assumed primary responsibility for preparing the document but delegated this to his deputy Paul Wolfowitz who, in turn, delegated the writing of the document to his aides Lewis "Scooter" Libby and Zalmay Khalilzad. Several consultants who were not in government, including Richard Perle and Wolfowitz's University of Chicago mentor, Albert Wohlstetter, were invited to contribute and comment on the planning document.[25]

The draft document's central thesis was that in the post–cold war world, the United States should work to prevent the emergence of any potential competitor to U.S. hegemony. Not surprisingly, Europeans and the Japanese criticized this approach. In the final draft of the document, Libby toned down the language and emphasized the need for the United States to maintain its "strategic depth," and Libby argued, if the U.S. achieved this, other countries would be dissuaded from challenging American dominance. The document also argued that the U.S. should be willing, if necessary, to use military force to prevent the spread of nuclear weapons, and that future coalitions should be based on ad hoc as opposed to permanent collections of allies.[26] In many ways, work on the Defense Planning Guidance of 1992 constituted the conceptual foundation for the neoconservative approach to foreign policy that was later implemented under George W. Bush. But that would have to wait until 2001.

Following the electoral victory of Bill Clinton in 1992, Wolfowitz left government and became the dean of the School of Advanced International Studies at Johns Hopkins University in Washington, DC. This provided him with a platform for continuing to participate in policy debates, albeit from outside the government. There are, in fact, a broad spectrum of academic institutions and think-tanks in Washington that provide out-of-office policymakers with platforms and bases of operation when their party is out of power. On the right, these include the Heritage Foundation and the American Enterprise Institute, and on the left, the Brookings Institution and the Center for American Progress.

Out of government, Wolfowitz continued to criticize the actions of the George H. W. Bush administration, which he had served; in 1993, he wrote: "With hindsight it does seem like a mistake to have announced, even before the war was over, that we would not go to Baghdad, or to give Saddam the reassurance of the dignified ceasefire ceremony at Safwan."[27] He went on to criticize "some U.S. government officials at the time" (that is, most of the other members of the George H. W. Bush administration) and the failure of the government to effectively protect the Kurds in the north and the Shia in the south. Without naming them, Wolfowitz criticized chairman of the Joint Chiefs of Staff Colin Powell and Iraq War commander Norman Schwarzkopf, who, in Wolfowitz's view, "in no small part reflected a miscalculation by some of our military commanders that a rapid disengagement was essential to preserve the luster of victory, and to avoid getting stuck with post war objectives that would prevent us from ever disengaging."[28]

In 1998, Wolfowitz signed the letter from the Project for a New American Century urging President Clinton to overthrow Saddam. In retrospect, it is clear that Clinton wanted to overthrow Saddam, but that he did not have support for doing this among U.S. allies or in the United Nations. In December 1998, following the unsuccessful attempt by Iraqi agents to assassinate George Herbert Walker Bush, who was visiting Kuwait, President Clinton ordered "Operation Desert Fox," a four-day bombing campaign targeted on Baghdad and military targets in Iraq. Critics of the Clinton administration dismissed the campaign as ineffectual, "pounding sand." Later in 1998, charging that the UN weapons inspection team included CIA intelligence agents (a charge that later proved to be accurate), Saddam kicked the team out of the country.

When George W. Bush decided to run for the presidency, he had his foreign policy adviser, Condoleezza Rice, assemble a group of foreign policy experts, many of whom had served in the previous Republican administrations of Ronald Reagan and George H. W. Bush. The group became known as "the Vulcans," named after the Roman god of iron.[29] There was a fifty-foot statue of Vulcan in Rice's hometown of Birmingham, Alabama, which had a significant steel industry at one time. The members of this group became many of the most important members of the George W. Bush administration, including Vice President Cheney, Secretary of State Colin Powell, Secretary of Defense Rumsfeld, Richard Armitage, Paul Wolfowitz, Scooter Libby, Stephen Hadley, Douglas Feith, and Paula Dobriansky.[30] During the presidential campaign, George W. Bush and the Vulcans pressed an "ABC" (Anything But Clinton) agenda and, once elected, vigorously pursued that objective.

September 11 and the U.S. Attack on Afghanistan

The first year of the George W. Bush administration ironically continued the basic contours of the Clinton administration's foreign policy. The attacks of September 11 dramatically changed that, and the Bush administration embarked on a new foreign policy in the aftermath of the attacks. But an overarching grand design or conceptual framework did not characterize this new foreign policy, and for good reason: the challenges that the United States faced were different from those it had ever previously faced. Terrorists, not states, had attacked the United States, and these terrorists, unlike states, controlled no territory of their own. The Bush administration's foreign policymakers consisted primarily of pragmatic problem solvers rather than strategic, conceptual thinkers; the exception to this orientation, however, was Wolfowitz, who had developed a conceptual strategy that called for the overthrow of Saddam.

In the aftermath of the attacks, American officials had to deal first with the immediate threats and problems posed by the attacks, and only after this could they turn to longer-term ways of dealing with a new era in international relations. Once the al Qaeda terrorist training camps were destroyed and the Taliban government was toppled in Afghanistan, policymakers could then turn their attention to the longer-term objectives for American foreign policy in this new world.

Strands of the new Bush approach to foreign policy emerged in the days, weeks, and months following 9/11. For example, in his State of the Union address of January 2002, Bush focused on the threat posed by terrorist groups such as Hamas, Hezbollah, and Islamic Jihad, but he also noted that the threat confronting the U.S. went beyond these groups to include state-supporters of terrorism. The president specifically identified the triumvirate of Iran, Iraq, and North Korea as the "axis of evil" in the modern world.[31] Beyond identifying the sources of threat to the U.S., however, the president did not describe how the United States was going to deal with this modern-day axis. Vice President Cheney indicated that dealing with the threat would depend primarily upon the U.S.: "America has friends and allies in this cause, but only we can lead it. Only we can rally the world in a task of this complexity, against an enemy so elusive and so resourceful. The United States, and only the United States, can see this effort through to victory."[32] Several members of the administration also called attention to the threat of chemical, biological, and nuclear weapons, "weapons of mass destruction" (WMD), falling into the hands of terrorists and state-supporters of terrorism.

The elements of the Bush strategy for dealing with terrorism were integrated in the commencement address that the president delivered at the U.S. Military Academy at West Point on June 1, 2002. Most graduation speeches repeat the same predictable themes and are eminently forgettable; however, on occasion American policymakers have used commencement addresses to announce important, memorable departures in U.S. foreign policy. Secretary of State George C. Marshall invited European countries to request aid to rebuild a war-torn continent in his Harvard commencement address of 1947, and the resulting program, one of the great successes of U.S. foreign policy, bears Marshall's name. Following the Cuban missile crisis of October 1962, President Kennedy "called for a reexamination of the cold war, a reexamination of our relations with the Soviet Union, and a reexamination of what kind of peace we truly wanted." According to JFK's adviser Ted Sorensen, the American University speech was an "unprecedented speech . . . combining eloquence, high principles, effective proposals, and idealism."[33]

Bush's speech at West Point followed in the tradition of hallmark presidential commencement addresses. Political scientist Edward Rhodes called Bush's speech at West Point "a masterpiece,"[34] and Jacob Weisberg called it "probably the most important of his presidency."[35] In this speech, the president presented an integrated policy for dealing with the terrorist threat confronting the United States.[36] In the speech, Bush emphasized terrorism, power, and peace; he mentioned terrorism fifteen times and power seventeen times in the speech. There were five principal themes. First, the president emphasized, "We face a threat with no precedent," in that the U.S. confronted not only state enemies, but also subnational enemies in the form of terrorist groups. Second, the president stipulated that "the gravest danger to freedom lies at the perilous crossroads of radicalism and technology. When the spread of chemical and biological and nuclear weapons, along with ballistic missile technology—when that occurs, even weak states and small groups could attain a catastrophic power to strike great nations." Third, Bush noted that in the past, the U.S. had depended upon the doctrines of deterrence and containment to provide for its defense. In the new world of terrorism, the president claimed deterrence "means nothing against shadowy terrorist networks with no nation or citizens to defend," and "containment is not possible when unbalanced dictators with weapons of mass destruction can deliver those weapons on missiles or secretly provide them to terrorist allies . . . . America has a greater objective than controlling threats and containing resentment." Fourth, Bush noted that "the war on terrorism cannot be won on the defensive. We must take the battle to the enemy." This could be accomplished by "transforming the military" and being "ready for preemptive action when necessary to defend our liberty and to defend our lives." International law provided for the possibility of preemption when a state was confronted by an imminent threat to its security; however, such threat had to be both significant and imminent. A number of observers noted that the president was really proposing the possibility of preventive war, rather than preemption.[37] Fifth, preventive war could be justified in the extraordinary circumstances of the war on terrorism because, the president claimed, "Moral truth is the same in every culture, in every time, and in every place . . . . We are in a conflict between good and evil, and America will call evil by its name." Throughout the speech, Bush emphasized the need for liberty, freedom, and democracy, saying, "We will extend the peace by encouraging free and open societies on every continent." Or, in other words, the U.S. would encourage and promote the spread of democracy throughout the world in a sort of a reversal of the cold war domino theory.

For many years, members of Congress have sought greater clarity and coherence in the elaboration of U.S. defense and foreign policy. In 1985, the Congress passed the landmark Goldwater-Nichols legislation that reformed the defense policymaking process. Attempting to apply the accomplishments of this legislation to foreign policy, the Congress mandated that an administration publish a document describing its national security strategy within six months of coming into office. The Clinton administration published a number of documents outlining its national security strategy.[38] The Bush administration failed to meet the congressionally imposed deadline, and published its first national security strategy report in September 2002.[39]

The national security strategy document repeated, elaborated, and extended the themes that President Bush had introduced in his West Point speech of two months before; in some cases, identical language was used. For example, in both cases the president noted, "The gravest danger our Nation faces lies at the crossroads of radicalism and technology," and that the U.S. could no longer depend upon the doctrines of deterrence and containment to provide for its security. He also noted that the U.S. would "extend the benefits of freedom across the globe." In several ways, the national security strategy extended the president's West Point speech. He argued that no competitor should be allowed to challenge the United States, in essence claiming the right of the United States to extend its hegemonic power in the world into the indefinite future. The document called for the creation of "coalitions of the willing" to augment the traditional international organizations and alliances including the United Nations, the World Trade Organization, and NATO. The gist of the new American strategy was summarized in this statement: "While the United States will constantly strive to enlist the support of the international community, we will not hesitate to act alone, if necessary, to exercise our right of self-defense by acting preemptively against such terrorists to prevent them from doing harm against our people and our country." The document addressed U.S. policies toward particular countries, international organizations, and issues such as economic development and HIV/AIDS, but the central thrust concerned how to deal with the new threat of global terrorism.

Reactions to the national security strategy document were quick and strong. The respected cold war historian and Yale professor John Lewis Gaddis called the report the most important document in U.S. foreign policy since the proclamation of the doctrine of containment in 1947.[40] Believing that the national security strategy was so important, political scientist Robert Kaufman included the entire document as an appendix in his book, *In Defense of the Bush Doctrine*.[41]

The report also stimulated a number of critics who contended that the strategy outlined in the president's West Point speech and his national security report "is significantly different from the one steered by his predecessors . . . . The president now makes the case that it is necessary to break with the past."[42] The critics argued that contemporary international problems, starting with terrorism but also including global health and economic development, were by definition multilateral and simply could not be effectively managed on a go-it-alone, unilateral basis. In addition, critics noted that the call for preemption posed a problem; namely, if the United States felt that it could engage in preemptive action, what would stop other countries from making similar claims?[43] Would the Bush administration's newly articulated national security strategy provide the rationale for a Chinese invasion of Taiwan or an Indian attack on Pakistan? There was also concern about the efficacy of the new, assertive American policy called for by the Bush administration. Throughout the post–World War II period, the United States had derived its power in international relations as much from its legitimacy and attraction as its military power, as the respected Harvard political scientist Joseph Nye noted in his work on "soft power."[44]

The New Approach

President Bush's commencement address at West Point and the 2002 *National Security Strategy* laid the groundwork for what became known as the Bush Doctrine, and subsequent speeches and reports built on this foundation. Some contend that the Bush Doctrine is a coherent, systematic description of a new American foreign and defense policy.[45] Others are critical of the Bush Doctrine.[46] When asked about the Bush Doctrine in an interview with journalist ABC anchor Charlie Gibson, 2008 Republican vice presidential candidate Sarah Palin could not describe it.[47] Perhaps part of the reason she could not was the amorphous character of the doctrine. Journalist and Bush biographer Jacob Weisberg contends that there have been, in fact, five Bush Doctrines: unipolar realism (3/7/99–9/10/01), with us or against us (9/11/01–5/31/02), preemption (6/1/02–11/5/03), democracy in the Middle East (11/6/03–1/19/05), and freedom everywhere (1/20/05–11/7/06).[48] Weisberg argues that from November 2006 on, there was "the absence of any functioning doctrine at all." In this section of the chapter, the principal elements of the Bush Doctrine as it evolved over time are examined.

1. *Preventive War*

In its 2002 *National Security Strategy*, the Bush administration noted, "For centuries, international law recognized that nations need not suffer an attack before they can lawfully take action to defend themselves against forces that present an imminent danger of attack." As the administration noted, there is a long history in international law justifying a preemptive attack if a state poses a direct, imminent threat to another. Members of the Bush administration noted with approval previous uses of preemption by the United States, including the Dominican Republic (1965), Grenada (1983), and Panama (1989). Both the president and his national security affairs adviser, Dr. Condoleezza Rice, claimed that John Kennedy's actions implementing the quarantine of Cuba during the 1962 missile crisis was also an application of preemption. Members of the Bush administration and their supporters generally used "preemption" and "preventive war" synonymously, glossing over the significant differences between the two concepts in international law. As noted, generally preemption can be justified in the face of a direct, imminent threat, but preventive war is not justified.

The American attempts to use preventive war have not been particularly successful. Rather than the Cuban missile crisis, political scientist Robert Jervis and historian Robert Dallek believe that the Bay of Pigs is a better example of preventive war, and the results of this case were disastrous: "Nearly 200 Cuban exiles died in the aborted attack, some 1,200 spent more than two years in Cuban prisons and the United States embarrassed itself before the world."[49]

Supporters of the Bush Doctrine cite a non-American case to establish the efficacy of preventive war: Israel's 1981 air raid to destroy Iraq's nuclear reactor at Osirak. Professor Robert Kaufman contends, "Israel was right. Otherwise, Saddam Hussein would have possessed a nuclear capability when he invaded Kuwait in the summer of 1990, which may have deterred the United States from responding decisively or raised exponentially the cost and risk of such a response."[50] Another foreign policy analyst, Robert Litwak, however, has pointed out that Israel's action was a short-term success but a long-term failure. Israel's attack caused Saddam to significantly increase his efforts to develop nuclear weapons; the budget for the nuclear program after 1981 went "from 400 scientists and $400 million to 7,000 specialists and a $10 billion budget."[51] Ironically, Saddam's increased effort to develop nuclear weapons became the principal reason for the United States to invade Iraq in 2003, which, in fact, "raised exponentially the cost and risk of such a response." Thus, Israel's action had the unintended consequence of both increasing Iraq's efforts to develop nuclear weapons and the expenditure of enormous human, military, and financial resources by the U.S.

Throughout history, preventive war has not been highly regarded. The great nineteenth-century British statesman Lord Salisbury once commented that it is rarely wise "to go to war against a nightmare."[52] Referring to preventive war, President Eisenhower once commented, "I don't believe there is such a thing, and frankly I wouldn't even listen to anyone seriously that came in and talked about such a thing."[53]

2. *Unilateralism*

Robert Jervis has noted, "The perceived need for preventive wars is linked to the fundamental unilateralism of the Bush doctrine."[54] The qualifier "fundamental" is important in this observation because members of the Bush administration and its supporters were quick to note that a number of other countries supported American counterterrorism efforts and U.S. policy toward Afghanistan and Iraq. For example, neoconservative and Bush administration supporter Kenneth Adelman noted, "It's ridiculous to say the United States is going to go it alone. When we go after Iraq, we're going to have Britain, Turkey, Qatar, Israel, Italy, and Spain with us."[55] However, when the U.S. invaded Iraq, only the combat troops of the United Kingdom, Australia, and the Czech Republic participated in the invasion. The UK's participation was particularly significant; at the high point of its involvement, one-third of the British army was deployed in Afghanistan or Iraq. President Bush claimed, however, that by the end of 2003, thirty-four countries had committed troops to Iraq.[56] However, taken together at the point of maximum commitment, the troop contributions of all of the coalition partners of the United States in Iraq equaled 24,000, and most of these were British forces.[57] This total represented about one-sixth of the number of American forces in Iraq.

Members of the Bush administration were clear concerning its unilateral approach. Vice President Cheney told the Council on Foreign Relations, "America has friends and allies in this cause, but only we can lead it."[58] In his State of the Union address of January 2004, President Bush was equally blunt: "America will never seek a permission slip to defend the security of our people."[59] For his part, Secretary of Defense Rumsfeld was publicly dismissive of the need for allies, even going as far as to dismiss the strongest, most reliable post–World War II Western European allies of the United States as "the old Europe," and praising the nations of the "new Europe," which consisted of the newly liberated, former Soviet allies of Eastern Europe. Despite Rumsfeld's comments, there was no comparison in the power represented by the "old" and "new" Europes.

European statesmen did not appreciate either the tone or the substance of the Bush administration's policies. The justice minister in German Chancellor Gerhard Schroeder's cabinet went as far as to compare President Bush's methods to those of Hitler, one of the strongest criticisms anyone, particularly a German, could make.[60] Respected American Ambassador Dennis Ross commented: "The Bush administration's failing has not been its instinct for unilateralism and its distain for multilateralism. Its failing too often has been how poorly it has practiced multilateralism."[61]

3. Regime Change and Democracy Promotion

As previously noted, political scientists Ivo Daalder and James Lindsay state that there were three different orientations to foreign policy within the Bush administration: the pragmatic internationalists, the neoconservatives, and the assertive nationalists. The neoconservatives, in particular, were similar to Woodrow Wilson in their zeal for promoting democracy. Their enthusiasm was catching, and President Bush reflected this view. In referring to the possibility of democratizing the Middle East, he told Bob Woodward, "I will seize the opportunity to achieve big goals." In his second inaugural address, the president said, "It is the policy of the United States to seek and support the growth of democratic movements and institutions in every nation and culture, with the ultimate goal of ending tyranny in our world."[62] Two years later, Bush returned to the same theme: "We also hear doubts that democracy is a realistic goal for the greater Middle East, where freedom is rare. Yet it is mistaken, and condescending, to assume that whole cultures and great religions are incompatible with liberty and self-government. I believe that God has planted in every heart the desire to live in freedom. And even when that desire is crushed by tyranny for decades, it will rise again."[63] Given these and numerous other strong statements in support of spreading democracy throughout the world, it is hard to take seriously Douglas Feith's claim that Bush "never argued, in public or private, that the United States should go to war *in order* to spread democracy."[64]

4. Use of Military Power

The members of the George W. Bush administration believed in the use and efficacy of military power. Neoconservatives both in and out of the administration were the most vociferous supporters of the use of military power; however, there was a general sense in the administration that the hegemonic position of the United States in the international system should be used to further its goals and objectives. What use, some in the administration asked, was military power if it was not used?

5. The Exercise of Presidential Power

Not only did members of the Bush administration believe that military power should be used; they also believed that the president had almost unlimited power when it came to using military force. Three second-level advisers were key in presenting the case for unfettered presidential power: David Addington in the vice president's office, John Yoo in the Justice Department's Office of Legal Counsel, and Timothy Flanigan in the White House Counsel's Office.[65] These three presented the theory of the "unitary executive"—the idea that the president exercising his role as commander-in-chief had the right to issue virtually any orders that he thought necessary in the pursuit of national security and that the Congress could not limit the president's power during wartime.[66]

On September 25, 2001, just two weeks after the al Qaeda attacks on the American homeland, Yoo sent a twenty-page memorandum to Flanigan in which he claimed that the Congress could "not place any limits on the President's determinations as to any terrorist threat, the amount of military force to be used in response, or the method, timing, and the nature of the response. These decisions, under our Constitution, are for the President alone to make."[67] Prominent members of the Bush administration were astounded by these claims. According to Jack Goldsmith, who served as assistant attorney general in the Office of Legal Counsel from October 2003 to June 2004, "On issue after issue, the administration had powerful legal arguments but ultimately made mistakes on important questions of policy. It got policies wrong, ironically, because it was excessively legalistic, because it often substituted legal analysis for political judgment, and because it was too committed to expanding the President's constitutional powers."[68] Commenting on Addington's views, Secretary of State Colin Powell was blunt: "He doesn't believe in the Constitution."[69]

6. Secrecy

Strongly influenced by the view that the power of the president was close to absolute, the Bush administration put a high priority on secrecy. The belief was that the president and his advisers could not expect free and candid advice unless secrecy could be assured. Commenting on Cheney's belief in secrecy to Larry King, Lewis "Scooter" Libby said: "And this is a case where he firmly believes—believes to the point where when he talks about it, his eyes get a little bluer—that for the presidency to operate properly, it needs to be able to have confidential communications."[70] An extreme example of the power of the small group that favored the exercise of unfettered executive power was the signing of a presidential directive authorizing warrantless wiretapping. Despite the opposition of the Justice Department, judicial decisions, and legislation prohibiting such action, President Bush, relying on his authority as commander-in-chief, signed an order drafted by Cheney's general counsel, David Addington, authorizing warrantless wiretapping. According to Pulitzer Prize–winning journalist Barton Gellman, "Addington's formula may have been the nearest thing to a claim of unlimited power ever made by an American president, all the more radical for having been issued in secret."[71]

George W. Bush won the most contested presidential election in American history and came into office promising to work with Democrats on both foreign and domestic policy. In foreign policy, he reversed many of the policies of the Clinton administration and emphasized the need for building and deploying a missile defense system and challenging China. The attacks on the United States of September 11, 2001, changed Bush's worldview and his policy priorities because the homeland of the United States had been attacked for the first time since 1812. Given the threat of terrorism, the Bush administration chose first to respond to those responsible for 9/11 and attacked al Qaeda bases and the Afghan Taliban government that provided sanctuary for Osama bin Laden and his followers. The administration then developed a new doctrine for dealing with terrorism that called for preventive war, and this new policy was applied in Iraq where the U.S. invaded and occupied the country. The invasions and occupations of Afghanistan and Iraq were based on a number of assumptions that will be examined in the next chapter.

Part II: Issues

U.S. soldiers standing under crossed swords in Baghdad. Source: U.S. Navy photo by Petty Officer 2nd class Todd Frantom, USN

Provincial Reconstruction Team at work. Source: U.S. Army photo by Specialist Russell Gilchrest, U.S. Army

7 Assumptions

Reporter Ron Suskind met with an unnamed senior advisor to President Bush (widely assumed to be Karl Rove) who told the reporter that people like him were "'in what we call the reality-based community,' which he defined as people who 'believe that solutions emerge from your judicious study of discernible reality.' I nodded and murmured something about enlightenment principles and empiricism. He cut me off. 'That's not the way the world really works anymore,' he continued. 'We're an empire now, and when we act, we create our own reality. And while you're studying that reality—judiciously, as you will—we'll act again, creating other new realities, which you can study too, and that's how things will sort out. We're history's actors . . . and you, all of you, will be left to just study what we do.'"[1]

The manufactured "realities" of the Bush administration sprang from certain fundamental assumptions, and as journalist Thomas Ricks has noted, "When assumptions are wrong, everything built on them is undermined."[2] Ambassador Dennis Ross has pointed out, "Get rid of Saddam, produce regime change, and everything would *fall into place, not fall apart.* That was the Bush administration's critical assumption, and it was based on a flawed assessment. Statecraft must start with assessments based on reality, and not on faith. If we are to understand the failures in Iraq, this is the starting point."[3]

This chapter will review the fundamental assumptions of the Bush administration concerning: (1) the effect of capturing the leaders of al Qaeda and Iraq, (2) linking 9/11 to Iraq, (3) military operations, (4) the reception of American soldiers, (5) the role of expatriate leaders, (6) the establishment of democracy, (7) the costs of the wars in Afghanistan and Iraq, and (8) assuming the best case. Assumptions concerning Iraq's possession of weapons of mass destruction will be covered in Chapter 8, concerning intelligence.

The Bush administration considered the evidence concerning those responsible for the 9/11 attacks on the United States and concluded that al Qaeda was to blame. Following this conclusion, the U.S. decided to proceed on the assumption that military operations with a "light footprint" would be better than a "heavy footprint."[4] American policymakers chose this approach because they believed in the efficacy of the revolution in military affairs and felt that a large, foreign army intervening in and occupying Afghanistan would meet a fate similar to the one the British and Soviets had previously met.

As a result of this assumption, the U.S. sent a small number of CIA paramilitary operatives and Special Forces soldiers to Afghanistan, where they met up with members of the Northern Alliance and anti-Taliban Pashtuns and then directed American air strikes on al Qaeda and Taliban targets.[5] This approach proved to be highly effective and successful and led a number of American policymakers to believe that a similar approach, relying on a relatively small number of forces and employing high tech weapons, would be successful against Iraq.

The Effect of Capturing Leaders of Al Qaeda and Iraq

Throughout history, one way of immobilizing an opponent has been to disable or kill the opponent's leadership. During the cold war, Soviet and American strategists worried about the possibility of a "decapitation" attack that would kill their leaders and paralyze the decision-making apparatus of their country. Indeed, al Qaeda sought to disable its Northern Alliance opponents by assassinating Ahmed Shah Massoud on September 9, 2001, just two days before the attacks on the United States.

In its invasions of both Afghanistan and Iraq, the United States initially sought to capture or kill the leaders of al Qaeda, the Taliban, and Iraq. The fundamental assumption was that if these leaders were captured or killed, the political movements they led would be significantly damaged, perhaps even beyond repair. As a result of this assumption, the U.S. invested enormous effort to locate and capture or kill Osama bin Laden and Taliban leader Mullah Omar after the initial invasion of Afghanistan. At the time, it was believed that these two leaders and their subordinates sought sanctuary in the border area between Afghanistan and Pakistan in the Tora Bora area. Later investigations have corroborated this belief. Yet, as of this writing, neither has been captured or killed.

Following the invasion of Iraq in March 2003, the United States placed high priority on capturing Saddam Hussein, and invested substantial resources in accomplishing this goal. In fact, a highly trained Special Forces unit under the command of General Stanley A. McChrystal was given the task of finding Saddam and bringing him to justice. On a tip from a local, the unit accomplished its task on December 13, 2003. Yet, the capture and subsequent trial and execution of Saddam did not result in the dissolution of the insurgency; in fact, some contended that Saddam's execution actually increased opposition to U.S. and coalition forces. Because bin Laden and Omar were not captured, the "decapitation" assumption was neither proved nor falsified.

Linking 9/11 to Iraq

The first and one of the most important of the Bush administration's fundamental assumptions was that the perpetrators of the 9/11 attacks and Iraq were linked. The day after the attacks, Bush told his chief counterterrorism analyst, "'See if Saddam did this. See if he's linked in any way.' The head of the counterterrorism group, Richard Clarke, replied, 'But, Mr. President, al-Qaeda did this.' And the president responded by saying, 'I know, I know but . . . see if Saddam was involved. Just look. I want to know any shred.'"[6] According to CIA Director Tenet, "During meetings at Camp David the weekend following the terrorist attacks, Paul Wolfowitz in particular was fixated on the question of including Saddam in any response."[7] Wolfowitz's boss, Secretary of Defense Donald Rumsfeld, also pointed to possible Iraqi involvement in the attacks, asking in a video teleconference with the principal decision-makers, "What if Iraq is involved?"[8] He then told CENTCOM commander General Franks, "What about Iran? . . . I want as much intel as we have on whoever we think was involved—whether it's Afghanistan, Iraq, Iran, or anyone else. Just because it was al-Qaeda doesn't mean they weren't working in conjunction with some state. I don't want to rule anything out until we know for sure."[9]

In the week following the attacks, the president repeatedly came back to the possible connection between Saddam and al Qaeda, mentioning it to chairman of the Joint Chiefs of Staff General Hugh Shelton and to National Security Council adviser Condoleezza Rice. Six days after the attacks, the president told his senior advisors, "I believe Iraq was involved."[10]

Two and a half months after the 9/11 attacks, Bush told Rumsfeld, "Let's get started on this. And get Tommy Franks looking at what it would take to protect America by removing Saddam Hussein if we have to."[11] By February

2002, Bush ordered Franks to begin moving troops to the Persian Gulf, and the next month, the president made his intentions explicitly clear to Rice and three senators: "Fuck Saddam. We're taking him out."[12] In June 2002, Bush declared, "[T]he reason that I keep insisting that there was a relationship between Iraq and Saddam and al Qaeda [is] because there was a relationship between Iraq and al Qaeda."[13] The president repeatedly stated that there was a connection between Iraq and 9/11 despite the fact that, according to George Tenet, the "CIA found absolutely no linkage between Saddam and 9/11."[14]

In July 2002, the head of British intelligence, Sir Richard Dearlove, visited Washington to meet with top American government officials. In his report to Prime Minister Blair, he wrote that he "believed that the crowd around the vice president was playing fast and loose with the evidence" and noted that Cheney's deputy, Scooter Libby, had tried to convince him that there was a link between Iraq and al Qaeda.[15] In October 2002, President Bush gave a speech in which he asserted, "Iraq has trained al-Qaeda members in bomb-making and poisons and deadly gas . . . . We know that Iraq and the al-Qaeda terrorist network share a common enemy: The United States of America."[16] There were a small number of Arabs who joined Ansar al-Islam, a terrorist group composed mostly of radical Kurds who operated on the border of Iraq and Iran, but al Qaeda did not have a significant presence in Iraq prior to the American invasion and occupation.[17]

Given these accounts and statements, it is hard to accept Douglas Feith's contention, "No one I know of believed Saddam was part of the 9/11 plot. We had no substantial reason to believe that he was."[18] In contrast to Feith's erroneous claim, most of those who have analyzed the U.S. decision to attack Iraq agree with former CIA official Paul Pillar who noted, "After 9/11, the administration was trying to hitch Iraq to the wagon of terror."[19]

Military Operations

Donald Rumsfeld, the man who had served as both the youngest (under Gerald Ford) and the oldest (under George W. Bush) secretary of defense, came into office believing that modern technology and communications provided the capability for a "revolution in military affairs," but the U.S. uniformed military was too conservative and tradition-bound to accept a radical, new approach. Rumsfeld planned to transform the American military by forcing it to accept and exploit the new technologies.[20]

Some, if not most, military officers were skeptical about the claims of Rumsfeld and his civilian aides; for example, chairman of the Joint Chiefs of Staff General Hugh Shelton retired in September 2001 in part because he was dubious about Rumsfeld's claims for the new approach.[21] Rumsfeld made a concerted effort to select military flag officers (generals and admirals) and civilian leaders of the services who supported his desire to "transform the military," going as far as to issue an order in 2003 that he personally approve all three- or four-star promotions. Retired lieutenant colonel and defense analyst Andrew Krepinevich observed, Rumsfeld "wanted people who believed in transformation so they could carry on after he was gone. But those decisions have typically been the prerogative of the military services. And if you really want to make someone angry, fool around with who is to have what job."[22]

In Operation Desert Storm of the first Gulf War, the U.S.-led coalition began with an air attack on Iraq on January 17, 1991, and followed this with a ground attack of 560,000 troops in fourteen divisions. Following the ground attack, coalition forces decisively defeated Iraq in 100 hours with fewer than 600 casualties. Following the first Gulf War, General Franks' predecessor at the Central Command, General Anthony Zinni, developed a contingency plan for invading Iraq, OPLAN 1003–98, which called for an invasion force of at least 300,000 and possibly up to 500,000 troops, a figure that was close to the total number deployed in the first Gulf War.[23] Zinni also noted that, were an invasion necessary, the subsequent U.S. occupation of Iraq could last ten years. When Bush and Rumsfeld asked General Franks to come up with an estimate of the number of troops an invasion would require, he initially responded with the estimates contained in OPLAN 1003–98. Rumsfeld was not pleased; surely, he reasoned, the revolution in military affairs reduced the need for numbers of troops. General Franks cut back his recommended number to 385,000, and still Rumsfeld and his deputy, Paul Wolfowitz, were not satisfied; they wanted an invasion force of 100,000 or less.[24] Whether it was due to pressure from his civilian superiors or a change in his assessment, General Franks became a supporter of the Rumsfeld-Wolfowitz approach, calling OPLAN 1003–98 "stale, conventional, predictable . . . . [It] is basically Desert Storm II."[25]

In December 2001, President Bush asked General Franks to visit him at his ranch in Texas where the conversation turned to a discussion of war plans for Iraq. According to Franks' deputy, Lieutenant General Michael DeLong, the conversation went as follows:.

"Show us what war plans you have on the shelf for Iraq today," Rumsfeld said from his video conference room in New Mexico.

Franks presented the plan—which called for the deployment of three to five hundred thousand troups.

They looked them over. Finally, Rumsfeld said, "This is old think."

"I agree," Franks said.[26]

In his memoirs, General Franks evaluated the "old think" war plan developed by his CENTCOM predecessor, General Anthony Zinni, and wrote: "The existing plan, OPLAN 1003, had last been updated after Desert Fox in 1998, but it was based on Desert Storm-era thinking. It was troop-heavy, involving a long buildup and a series of air strikes before boots hit the ground. It didn't account for our current troop dispositions, advances in Precision-Guided Munitions, or break-throughs in command-and-control technology—not to mention the lessons we were learning in Afghanistan."[27] Franks, like Rumsfeld, emphasized the importance of the pace of operations—speed—versus the importance of mass in military operations. According to Franks, "[T]he victory in Desert Storm proved that speed has a mass all its own" and "speed kills . . . the enemy."[28]

In October 2001, the United States attacked Afghanistan, destroyed al Qaeda training bases, and overthrew the Taliban government of Mullah Omar. This was accomplished with only 426 CIA paramilitary and U.S. military Special Forces officers calling in air strikes using extremely accurate weapons and coordinating with Northern Alliance forces on the ground. American forces in Afghanistan coupled twenty-first-century technology with ancient modes of warfare; they communicated with pilots over the battlefield and CIA headquarters in Virginia via satellite phones and traveled via horseback. According to one account, one of the first CIA operatives to enter Afghanistan to liaise with the Northern Alliance called CIA headquarters to let his superiors know that he had successfully met up with his Northern Alliance contacts and then made a special request for the first supply drop: a leather saddle. His Northern Alliance hosts had provided him with a wooden saddle like the ones they used.[29] Rumsfeld was particularly intrigued with the use of horses in Afghanistan and claimed this "innovation" as a modern application of military transformation.[30]

When the war in Afghanistan was won quickly and with few American casualties, it looked as if Rumsfeld was right and the skeptical generals were wrong. According to Thomas Ricks, "Rumsfeld had come out of the Afghan war believing that speed could be substituted for mass in military operations."[31] As in

Afghanistan, an attack on Iraq, Rumsfeld believed, would result in a rapid victory, and American forces would be able to withdraw from Iraq quickly. There were some who supported Rumsfeld's view, and General Franks was one of those; to him the revolution in military affairs "was no longer mere hyperbole. It would become the new reality of war."[32] Rumsfeld's former assistant, Ken Adelman, wrote in the *Washington Post* in February 2002, "I believe demolishing Hussein's military power and liberating Iraq would be a cakewalk."[33]

Many of the uniformed senior officers were not as enthusiastic about the efficacy of the revolution in military affairs as Rumsfeld and his military and civilian aides. For example, Army Corps of Engineers Brigadier General Steve Hawkins in February 2003 estimated that no fewer than 350,000 coalition troops would be needed to provide stability in the aftermath of a war to overthrow Saddam.[34] General Hawkins forwarded his estimate to Army Chief of Staff Eric Shinseki, who testified before the Senate Armed Services Committee on February 25, 2003. Senator Carl Levin, the senior ranking Democrat on the committee, asked, "Gen. Shinseki, could you give us some idea as to the magnitude of the Army's force requirement for an occupation of Iraq following a successful completion of the war?"

Shinseki replied, "In specific numbers, I would have to rely on the combatant commander's exact requirements. But I think . . ."

Levin interjected, "How about a range?"

"I would say," the general continued, "that what's been mobilized to this point, something on the order of several hundred thousand soldiers, are probably, you know, a figure that would be required . . . . [Iraq is a large country with competing ethnic groups,] so it takes significant ground forces to maintain a safe and secure environment to ensure that people are fed, that water is distributed, all the normal responsibilities that go along with administering a situation like this."[35] Shinseki's estimate of the number of troops required for an effective occupation was supported by a number of generals including Major General William Nash, General Barry McCaffrey, and others who had previously served in the postconflict environments of Bosnia and Kosovo.[36]

Despite the fact that those who had experience in occupations commonly held Shinseki's views, his comments created a firestorm within the Pentagon. The day after General Shinseki's testimony, Wolfowitz called Secretary of the Army Thomas White to complain about his estimate. The next day, Wolfowitz testified before the House Budget Committee and was asked about Shinseki's estimate. He replied, "Some of the higher end predictions that we have been hearing recently, such as the notion that it will take several hundred thousand U.S. troops to provide stability in post-Saddam Iraq, are wildly off the mark."[37] On the same day that Wolfowitz criticized Shinseki, Rumsfeld also did so in a press conference: "What is, I think, reasonably certain is the idea that it would take several hundred thousand U.S. force I think is far off the mark."[38]

In an "end of tour memorandum" to Rumsfeld, General Shinseki explained, "I didn't feel that there was a 'right' answer on the number of forces required to stabilize Iraq until the commander on the ground had the chance to conduct both his mission analysis and a troop to task assessment . . . . My estimate, based on past experiences, was provided in a way so as not to foreclose options for you or the Combatant Commander."[39] In his memoirs, Lieutenant General Ricardo Sanchez, the commander of U.S. military forces in Iraq, remarked, "Those critical remarks by Rumsfeld and Wolfowitz sent a chilling message to junior generals like me. They basically said the Army's generals had questionable credibility with senior civilian leadership of the Department of Defense."[40] Political scientist Dale Herspring has commented, "This was probably the worst public rebuke of a senior military leader by a civilian since President Truman fired Douglas MacArthur in 1951."[41] Shinseki's estimate was in keeping with his constitutional and legal duty, since all three- and four-star general officers must swear in writing as part of the confirmation process that they will render their best military opinion even if it conflicts with administration policy. In his case, General Shinseki acted honorably and in accordance with his legal obligations and was proved correct by ensuing events.

Those with experience in recent nation-building efforts agreed with Shinseki's estimate. Dr. Joseph Collins, the first deputy assistant secretary of defense for stability operations, did not accept the Rumsfeld-Wolfowitz view that a war with Iraq could be won with a relatively small number of troops.[42] Major General William Nash, who had commanded U.S. peacekeeping forces in Bosnia, advocated "going in hard" as the U.S. had done in Bosnia in order to assert and maintain control; such an approach would require a minimum of 200,000 troops for several years.[43] General Wesley Clark, who commanded military operations against Serbia during the Kosovo war, indicated that 200,000 to 250,000 troops would be required for multiple years. The consensus of opinion supported General Shinseki, but the secretary of defense and his deputy disagreed.

In the end, the U.S. attacked Iraq with a force of 145,000 troops in five divisions, compared with the 560,000 troops in fourteen divisions in the first

Gulf War.[44] As General Barry McCaffrey, one of the most aggressive generals in the first Gulf War, noted, the Bush administration "chose to go into battle with a ground combat capability that was inadequate, unless their assumptions proved out." Unfortunately, those assumptions were unrealistic, which contributed to postwar problems of reconstruction and nation-building.

The Reception of American Soldiers

A further assumption was that American soldiers in Iraq would be welcomed and greeted as liberators rather than as occupiers. The mental image was of Normandy in June 1944 following the D-Day landings to liberate German-occupied France. The month before the United States invaded Iraq, Paul Wolfowitz assured the Congress, "I am reasonably certain that they [the Iraqi people] will greet us as liberators, and they will help us keep the troop commitments down."[45] Three days before the start of the war, Vice President Cheney said on *Meet the Press*, "My belief is we will, in fact, be greeted as liberators."[46] Iraqi exiles in the United States assured members of the Bush administration that 25 million Iraqis "would rush to the side of a U.S.-supported opposition."[47]

The related assumption was that the ensuing occupation of Iraq would be similar to the post–World War II occupations. Several months before the invasion, Kanan Makiya, the author of an influential study of Saddam Hussein's Iraq, stated that Iraqis would greet American troops "with flowers and sweets."[48] Two days before the U.S. invasion of Iraq, an Army ground commander contacted the Army War College and requested copies of the manuals that had been used in the American occupation of Germany.[49] Marc Garlasco, a Department of Defense intelligence analyst noted, "[We] really thought it was Paris in the Second World War, where people are gonna be throwing flowers, and welcoming the U.S. Or at least that's what the policymakers thought."[50] Officials going to Iraq to work for the Coalition Provisional Authority (CPA) were reported to be reading books on the post–World War II occupations of Germany and Japan, and one of Ambassador Bremer's advisors, Hume Horan, told him, "'They're calling you the 'MacArthur of Baghdad,' Jerry."[51]

It is curious that CPA officials would turn to analyses of the post–World War II occupations of Germany and Japan—curious, because at least one of those studies, anthropologist Ruth Benedict's *The Chrysanthemum and the Sword: Patterns of Japanese Culture*, was written during the war at the request of the Department of War Information and became an important influence on American policymakers planning the occupation of Japan.[52] American policymakers in 1945 had the foresight to employ a respected social scientist to analyze the elements of Japanese culture and, importantly, based many of the ideas of the occupation on this analysis. In contrast to this, the key U.S. leaders making decisions on Iraq chose to ignore the most extensive study concerning postwar Iraq, the Future of Iraq Project.

There were some American policymakers who questioned both the assumption that the Iraqis would support the U.S. invasion and that the occupation of Iraq could be compared to World War II. Secretary of State Powell, for example, "thought that Wolfowitz was talking as if 25 million Iraqis would rush to the side of a U.S.-supported opposition. In his opinion, it was one of the most absurd, strategically unsound proposals he had ever heard."[53]

It is interesting that American officials consistently referred to the occupations of Germany and Japan as if they were similar or even the same, for there were significant differences between German and Japanese political cultures and the occupation strategies that the U.S. developed and implemented in each case. In Japan, General Douglas MacArthur assumed almost absolute control of Japan and gradually introduced democratic mechanisms into a society that had little previous direct experience with democracy. In contrast to Japan, Germany had some experience with democracy during the Weimar period preceding World War II; indeed, some political scientists consider the Weimar constitution to be a model democratic constitution.

Both Germany and Japan had surrendered unconditionally in World War II, so there was no question about who had won the war and who would make decisions after the war. In addition, both Germany and Japan were ethnically homogeneous compared with the ethnically mixed composition of Iraq, which was a very different case in these respects, but those who assumed that it would be like Germany and Japan did not recognize or adequately appreciate these significant differences. As George Tenet noted, "The assumption the U.S. government was working under was that this [occupation of Iraq] was going to be like the occupation of Germany, a supine country at our feet that we could remake in essentially whatever way we chose." Clearly, that was not to be.

Of course, the difference between the occupations of Germany and Japan and Iraq was, among other factors, the size of the occupation forces. At the end of World War II, the United States used a large occupation force for Germany and Japan, and the size of these forces contributed to the success of the occupation. The Rumsfeld war plans for Afghanistan and Iraq failed to provide the necessary number of forces for Phase IV of the two wars. In effect, the United States accomplished its immediate, military objectives but failed to achieve its longer-term strategic goals.

The Role of Expatriate Leaders

Rumsfeld and Wolfowitz may have believed that the U.S. needed only 100,000 troops for the invasion because they assumed that Iraqis would welcome American forces, and they believed this because they trusted expatriate leaders who assured them that this would be the case. In Afghanistan, the Bush administration depended on and supported Hamad Karzai to organize and lead the government founded after the fall of the Taliban.

In Iraq, the Bush administration depended on Ahmad Chalabi and the Iraqi National Congress. According to Under-Secretary of Defense for Policy Douglas Feith, there were five main anti-Saddam Iraqi opposition groups: (1) the Iraqi National Congress (INC) led by Chalabi, (2) the Iraqi National Accord led by Ayad Allawi, (3) the Kurdish Democratic Party led by Massoud Barzani, (4) the Patriotic Union of Kurdistan led by Jalal Talabani, and (5) the Supreme Council for the Islamic Revolution, a Shia group.[54]

Particular departments and bureaucracies within the U.S. government backed different groups. For example, the State Department provided millions of dollars in aid to Chalabi and the Iraqi National Congress, but then backed away from this support when it appeared that Chalabi and the INC were misusing funds. The CIA favored Ayad Allawi, and both Vice President Cheney and the Defense Department favored Chalabi. A Middle East expert who significantly influenced Cheney was Fouad Ajami, whom Chalabi's biographer has called "a cheerleader of Chalabi's."[55] Richard Perle, an influential neoconservative and the chairman of the Defense Policy Board in the Pentagon, was particularly enamored of Chalabi. Even after questions were raised about Chalabi, Perle came to his defense: "The arguments about Chalabi have been without substance . . . . He is far and away the most effective individual that we could have hoped would emerge in Iraq . . . . In my view, the person most likely to give us reliable advice is Ahmad Chalabi."[56] In addition to Perle, Wolfowitz also supported Chalabi; in fact, they had been in graduate school at the University of Chicago together.[57]

Not all American policymakers, even those within the Department of Defense, had the same high opinion of Chalabi as those in the vice president's and secretary of defense's offices. General Zinni characterized the members of INC as "Rolex wearing, silk-suited guys in London," and General Franks called Chalabi a "Gucci leader" who "would never be able to unite the ethnic and religious factions" of Iraq."[58] General Franks' Central Command deputy, Lieutenant General DeLong, was also critical of Chalabi: "Wolfowitz, I believe, put too much weight on the promises of Iraqi exiles, Ahmad Chalabi most of all . . . . Wolfowitz trusted him, which was unfortunate, because most of Chalabi's information has turned out to be suspect, and the CIA and State Department never thought highly of him."[59] Marc Garlasco, a former defense intelligence officer, had equally critical comments about the members of the Iraqi National Congress, who were "at best, I think, . . . they were liars. And at worst, they were provocateurs."[60]

For Chalabi, what intelligence and assurances he and the members of the INC gave American government officials was secondary to the objective that was achieved: "As far as we're concerned, we have been entirely successful. The tyrant Saddam is gone and the Americans are in Baghdad. What was said before is not important."[61]

Chalabi's importance should not be underestimated. According to Charles Ferguson, the author and filmmaker of *No End in Sight*, "The most important source of unrealistic optimism about postwar Iraq was Ahmad Chalabi, the Iraqi exile who exerted enormous influence upon the White House and Pentagon."[62] According to his biographer, "There are few foreigners who have had as much impact as Ahmad Chalabi has had on U.S. government policy and perhaps even on U.S. history."[63] American Ambassador Peter Galbraith has concluded, "If it were not for him, the United States military likely would not be in Iraq today."[64]

The Establishment of Democracy

If Iraq were going to be like Germany and Japan, then it was assumed that democracy would take hold in Iraq and would spread from there to the rest of the Middle East just as democracy took hold in Germany and Japan after World War II and then spread to neighboring countries. During the cold war, American policymakers feared that communism would spread from country to country and that once one country fell to communism, others would, like falling dominoes, also fall to communism. In his attempt to convince Congress to approve appropriations to provide aid to the Greek and Turkish governments in order to oppose communist movements, Dean Acheson used a similar, but different, analogy:

> No time was left for measured appraisal. In the past eighteen months, I said, Soviet pressure on the Straits, on Iran, and on northern Greece had brought the Balkans to the point where a highly possible Soviet break-through might open three continents to Soviet penetration. Like apples in a barrel infected by one rotten one, the corruption of Greece would infect Iran and all to the east. It would carry infection to Africa through Asia Minor and Egypt, and to Europe through Italy and France.[65]

The theory was that the attraction of democracy would cause it to spread across the Middle East, a kind of democratic domino theory. The empirical evidence for this assumption was weak if not nonexistent, but it became a powerful argument in favor of attacking Iraq and overthrowing Saddam Hussein.

In October 2002, Vice President Cheney told an interviewer that he expected the United States to shape an Iraq "that is democratic and pluralistic, a nation where the human rights of every ethnic and religious group are recognized and respected."[66] Reality, however, proved to be much different than Cheney's optimistic assumption. When the National Intelligence Council sponsored a study published in January 2003 entitled "Can Iraq Ever Become a Democracy?" it concluded: "Iraqi political culture is so imbued with norms alien to the democratic experience . . . that it may resist the most vigorous and prolonged democratic treatments."[67] By March 2003, even President Bush recognized the possibility that robust democracy might not result from the U.S. invasion and occupation of Iraq: "The important thing is to win the peace. I don't expect Thomas Jefferson to come out of this, but I believe people will be free."[68]

The Costs of the Wars

Of course, the spread of democracy was the political solution to Afghanistan's and Iraq's problems in the view of neoconservatives. What about the economic questions related to the wars in Afghanistan and Iraq, how much would the invasions and occupations cost, and how would Afghanistan and Iraq support themselves after the wars?

Members of the Bush administration assumed that the cost of the wars in Afghanistan and Iraq would be minimal. There was some basis for such a hope, since the first Gulf War cost a total of $55 billion and of this, American coalition partners, most prominently Saudi Arabia, Kuwait, and Japan, reimbursed the U.S. $50 billion. So, the first war against Iraq cost the U.S. a total of approximately $5 billion. After the war, the U.S. and its coalition partners imposed no-fly zones in northern and southern Iraq, and the cost of maintaining these was about $1 billion per year. Other American military operations such as exercises in Kuwait cost another $500 million per year, so the total for maintaining U.S. military operations in the 1991–2002 period was approximately $1.5 billion per year.[69]

As the Bush administration's plans for going to war against Iraq were considered, the potential costs of the war were raised. In September 2002, just as the administration was, according to former White House Press Secretary Scott McClellan, launching "its campaign to convince Americans that war with Iraq was inevitable and necessary," Lawrence Lindsay, one of Bush's chief economic advisers, told a *Wall Street Journal* reporter that the likely costs to the U.S. of a war with Iraq would be between $100 and $200 billion, and that even this amount would probably not have a significant effect on the American economy because it represented only 1 to 2 percent of U.S. gross domestic product.[70] When told about Lindsay's comments, Bush was angry and commented, "It's unacceptable . . . . He shouldn't be talking about that."[71] Lindsay was reprimanded and within four months had resigned under pressure and left the administration. Ironically, Lindsay's estimate was mistaken; it was off by at least an order of magnitude, since the total cost of the war was later estimated to be $3 trillion.[72]

Members of the Bush administration made another key economic assumption: that postwar reconstruction would be "self-financed" through the export of Iraqi oil. Colonel Paul Agoglia, who served as the Central Command's liaison to the Coalition Provisional Authority, recalled, "Now there were folks in Wolfowitz's office [who] said that it [sales of Iraqi oil] could pay for the whole thing [the reconstruction of Iraq]."[73] Wolfowitz assured Congress that Iraq was "a country that can really finance its own reconstruction, and relatively soon."[74] Following the invasion, however, American petroleum specialists found that the Iraqi oil industry was out of date and that much of the equipment needed extensive repair or replacement, so this assumption proved to be mistaken as well, as even Ambassador Bremer candidly recognized: "Reality on the ground made a fantasy of the rosy prewar scenario under which Iraq would be paying for its own reconstruction through oil exports within weeks or months of liberation. We were clearly involved in a long-term project of nation-building here, like it or not."[75]

Assuming the Best Case

In national security planning, the United States government consistently and prudently assumes the worst case; after all, if the worst case assumption proves false, the U.S. would have spent extra money, but its survival would not be threatened. This was the principle that was followed throughout the cold war and the planning assumption that resulted in high defense spending. When it came to Iraq, however, the Bush administration abandoned worst case planning assumptions and replaced them with best case assumptions that turned out to be wildly unrealistic. In particular, President Bush was consistently optimistic even when facts on the ground in Iraq challenged this view. As Thomas Ricks has noted, "[T]he Bush administration engaged in sustained self-deception over the threat presented by Iraq and the difficulties of occupying the country."[76] Ambassador Galbraith observed, "President Bush and his top advisors have consistently substituted wishful thinking for analysis and hope for strategy."[77] Of all the mistaken assumptions that the members of the Bush administration made about Iraq, their consistent tendency to assume the best case may be the most serious.

Charles Duelfer, the veteran U.S. government official whom President Bush appointed to evaluate the evidence related to suspected Iraqi weapons of mass destruction, has noted:

> Western thought is filled with assumptions, like the operating system of our computers, we have logic and assumptions that are virtually built in. We have been applying them successfully so long in our own frame of reference that we forget they are present and shape our thinking and conclusions.[78]

The Bush administration made a number of assumptions prior to invading and occupying Afghanistan and Iraq. Indeed, some of the assumptions that policymakers made about Iraq resulted from the American experience in Afghanistan, and several of these assumptions were deeply flawed. For example, only a small number of forces were used to destroy al Qaeda training bases and topple the Taliban government in Afghanistan, and consequently, American policymakers concluded that only a relatively small number of American forces were needed to topple Saddam Hussein. In addition, U.S. officials focused myopically on the acute, military phase of the wars, and in Afghanistan's case they assumed that the success of the kinetic phase of the war would be permanent. They were correct in a narrow, military sense; however, if victory in war includes a stable postwar environment following the kinetic phase, then surely they were shortsighted. Just as one operating system for one computer will not work on another computer, assumptions from one war cannot be applied to another; one size definitely does not fit all. When the assumptions from Afghanistan were applied to Iraq, they did not apply, and the results were disastrous.

The Bush administration assumed that 9/11 and Iraq were linked, that the revolution in military affairs would enable the U.S. to invade and defeat Iraq quickly and with relatively few costs, that the occupation would be similar to that in Germany and Japan, that democracy would take hold in Iraq and then spread throughout the Middle East, and that Iraq reconstruction would be financed by the sale of Iraqi oil. Observers noted that the Bush administration's foreign policy was "faith-based" rather than reality-based.[79] Plans built on faith and erroneous assumptions cannot succeed, and in the Iraq War the most basic assumptions were mistaken and doomed the American effort from the start. According to CIA Director Tenet, "We followed a policy built on hope rather than fact."[80]

8 Intelligence

In his *Instructions for His Generals* of 1747, Frederick the Great noted:

> Knowledge of the country is to a general what a musket is to an infantryman and what the rules of arithmetic are to a geometrician. If he does not know the country he will do nothing but make gross mistakes . . . . Therefore study the country where you are going to act.[1]

The process of gaining knowledge about "the country where you are going to act" involves the collection, analysis, and dissemination of information, and modern states devote substantial technical and human resources to this endeavor. Of course, the quality of the data collected is key to the entire intelligence process; if the information collected is irrelevant or erroneous, then no amount of sophisticated analysis will improve it, and such data can lead to costly mistakes and misguided policies. The importance of intelligence, particularly concerning terrorism, cannot be over-rated. In conventional interstate war, one generally knows where the enemy is, and it is difficult to kill him. With terrorism, it's the opposite problem: it is relatively easy to kill terrorists but difficult to find them. For this reason, intelligence enabling the U.S. to find terrorists is vital, and the United States government invests a substantial amount to obtain intelligence: an estimated $75 billion per year, an amount that is 250 percent of the amount prior to 9/11. In addition, 236 U.S. government agencies were created or reorganized in response to 9/11.[2]

The collection and analysis of data is difficult enough; it is made even more so by the deliberate attempt to influence or mislead actual or potential opponents. For example, in March 1917, President Woodrow Wilson made public the supposed secret "Zimmermann telegram," which was a pledge from German Foreign Minister Arthur Zimmermann to the German minister in Mexico promising that Germany would cede the southwestern United States to Mexico if it would enter the war on the Axis side. Although the British had intercepted and deciphered the telegram in January 1917, they waited until February 24 to present it to President Wilson. On March 1, the American press published accounts of the telegram, and six weeks later the U.S. declared war on Germany. According to intelligence expert David Kahn, author of *The Codebreakers*, "No other single cryptanalysis has had such enormous consequences."[3]

High quality, accurate intelligence is very desirable; however, it is rarely available because secrets are closely guarded, since they concern the security of states or other groups. In this chapter, the following topics are examined: (1) the nature and importance of intelligence, (2) past intelligence failures, (3) intelligence concerning al Qaeda, Afghanistan, and Pakistan, (4) intelligence leading up to the outbreak of the Iraq War, and (5) the issue of weapons of mass destruction (WMD).

The Nature and Importance of Intelligence

By definition, intelligence is a process fraught with uncertainty and ambiguity. As former U.S. and UN weapons inspector and intelligence official Charles Duelfer has noted, "'Intelligence' will always be incomplete. It is only a question of how, and to what degree. Some knowable facts may be missed. Incorrect meanings may be attached to known facts. Insufficient energy may be devoted to delving into the reasons for facts."[4] The difficulties of obtaining accurate intelligence are heightened when analyzing repressive, closed societies or organizations, such as Saddam Hussein's Iraq, al Qaeda, Mullah Omar's Taliban, or the Soviet Union and the People's Republic of China during the cold war, a point that Vice President Cheney recognized explicitly in 2002: "Intelligence is an uncertain business, even in the best of circumstances. This is especially the case when you are dealing with a totalitarian regime that has made a science out of deceiving the international community."[5] Those who studied the USSR had to infer conclusions based on a paucity of hard evidence. Thus, so-called Kremlinologists would study the arrangement of leaders standing on Lenin's Mausoleum at the annual May Day parade in Moscow in order to infer which Soviet leaders were the most powerful. Sinologists would comb through various issues of Chinese Communist Party and governmental publications and compare what articles were published and if there were any subtle or significant changes in the published versions of party leaders' speeches. The attempt to gain information and understanding about other countries became even more esoteric; for example, the Central Intelligence Agency had a group of analysts who specialized in determining what goods were carried in particular types of crates. These analysts were very busy in October 1962 analyzing the crates carried on Soviet ships to Cuba. Given the size and shape of the crates and based on photographs of other crates, the CIA analysts determined that the crates on the ships could be carrying offensive ballistic missiles.[6]

For the first century of its existence, the United States had no permanent intelligence collecting organization; instead, various governmental bureaucracies collected, analyzed, and disseminated intelligence concerning actual or potential enemies. In 1882, the first permanent intelligence organization in the U.S. government, the Office of Naval Intelligence, was founded, and during World War I, the Army established its own intelligence agency. In 1908, the attorney general appointed a group of Department of Justice agents to conduct investigations; one year later the Bureau of Investigations, the forerunner of the Federal Bureau of Investigations (FBI), was established. Over time, the organizational culture of the FBI became oriented to collecting evidence so that criminals could be successfully prosecuted in court. The FBI took on the added responsibility of a domestic intelligence organization, but this function was secondary within the organizational priorities and culture of the FBI. As former vice chairman of the National Intelligence Council, Gregory Treverton, has noted: "Understanding the Cold War FBI through its intelligence function, I realized after September 11, was like trying to understand the National Football League by interviewing the place-kickers. Intelligence may have been important, but it was not central."[7] In short, "[L]aw enforcement and intelligence are different worlds, with different missions, operating codes, and standards."[8]

In the Second World War, with the backing of President Franklin D. Roosevelt, Colonel William Donovan founded the Office of Strategic Services (OSS), which was responsible for collecting information and planning and implementing intelligence operations overseas. Donovan was able to recruit a diverse and talented group of people including the Marxist philosopher Herbert Marcuse, Julia Child, and Wall Street lawyer (and later CIA Director) William Casey. The OSS sponsored daring operations into Axis-occupied countries, and many agents paid for their participation with their lives. The reason that the United States and other governments went to extremes to collect, analyze, and store intelligence information is that it could make a great deal of difference in countries' interactions with one another, particularly during wartime. Historians now believe that the breaking of the German and Japanese codes by the

Allies in World War II made a significant difference in the war.[9] An interesting, successful counterpoint to this example was the use of the Native-American "code talkers" in the Pacific to thwart the Japanese breaking of U.S. military tactical communications.[10]

Reflecting Americans' traditional distrust of power in the hands of a central government and having witnessed the radical abuses of power of the Gestapo in Nazi Germany, the U.S. disbanded OSS at the end of the war. However, with the onset of the cold war in 1946–47, American policymakers realized that there was a vital need for foreign, as well as domestic, intelligence. In 1947, Congress passed the National Security Act establishing the Central Intelligence Agency (CIA), whose director was given the responsibility for heading both the CIA and all other activities of the U.S. government that focused on the collection and analysis of foreign intelligence. Over time, fourteen additional intelligence organizations were established within the U.S. government, including the National Security Agency (NSA), the Defense Intelligence Agency (DIA), the National Reconnaissance Office (NRO), the National Geospatial Intelligence Agency, and the Bureau of Intelligence and Research within the State Department. As of 2003, the intelligence agencies under the Department of Defense accounted for approximately 80 percent of U.S. spending for intelligence.[11] According to its charter, the CIA was prohibited from conducting operations within the United States. Thus, the FBI was given the responsibility of collecting domestic intelligence and the CIA foreign intelligence.

Throughout the cold war, intelligence activities were directed by states against other states, and most intelligence collection directly or indirectly concerned military activities. In contrast to the period that followed it, intelligence collection was straightforward. For example, CIA agents knew many of their opposing Soviet KGB agents and in some cases even communicated with them.[12] This was possible because they came from similar, albeit different, cultures and represented similar types of states—great powers. In addition, during the cold war, states posed the greatest threat to the United States. While other individuals and organizations may have posed some type of threat, it was only states that posed an existential threat to the U.S.

There are six principal means that organizations use to collect intelligence. Of course, the oldest way of gaining intelligence is through the use of spies, a technique that is documented at least back to Old Testament times, when God commanded Moses to send twelve spies into the land of Canaan; they returned to the Israelites and overestimated the strength of the Canaanites, perhaps the first recorded instance of intelligence being used to influence policy.[13] Ever since that time, spies have provided valuable information; for example, prior to and during the Cuban missile crisis, a Soviet colonel and member of the Soviet General Staff, Oleg Penkovskii, provided important information about Soviet war plans. He was the highest-ranking known Soviet spy for the U.S. throughout the cold war, although Polish Colonel Ryszard Kuklinski may have provided even more valuable information.[14] Julius and Ethel Rosenberg provided the USSR with information about the American nuclear weapons program, enabling the Soviet Union to develop nuclear weapons faster than it otherwise would have been able to do.[15]

The information provided by spies is called "human intelligence" or "HUMINT" within the intelligence community, and the Directorate of Operations within the CIA has been principally responsible for collecting this type of intelligence. It is relatively easy to place a spy in an open society such as the United States and more difficult to place a spy in a closed society or group. Another difficulty is identifying the important sectors of a particular society. Journalist Steve Coll has noted the problem that American intelligence faced in dealing with the post–cold war Middle East: "American Arabists had studied the Middle East for decades through a Cold War lens, their vision narrowed by continuous intimate contact with secular Arab elites. American spies and strategists rarely entered the lower-middle class mosques of Algiers, Tunis, Cairo, Karachi, or Jeddah."[16] In retrospect, it is hard to fault American intelligence officials because their principal goal in the Middle East was to prevent the expansion of Soviet power and influence in the region. In the case of Pakistan, American intelligence officials depended upon their counterparts in Pakistani intelligence agencies, the most important of which was the Inter-Services Intelligence (ISI) directorate. About 80 percent of the personnel in ISI are seconded from the military services. During the cold war, the U.S. depended upon ISI, the principal Pakistani intelligence agency for foreign intelligence, for information about topics of mutual interest and concern such as the USSR and China.[17]

One of the reasons that the United States intelligence agencies had such a difficult time obtaining reliable, accurate intelligence about al Qaeda is that Osama bin Laden relied only on trusted aides. Coll has noted, "Bin Laden practiced intensive operational security. He was wary of telephones. He allowed no Afghans into his personal bodyguard, only Arabs he had known and trusted for many years."[18] As author Lawrence Wright has noted, "The fact was that the CIA had no one inside al Qaeda or the Taliban security that surrounded bin

Laden."[19] Following the attacks on the U.S. on September 11, 2001, al Qaeda's intent was clear; however, the U.S. did not know its capability. During the cold war, the opposite was the case: the U.S. had a good idea of the Soviet Union's capabilities, but did not know its leaders' intent. Despite these difficulties, it was clear that intelligence was important in the war on terror; according to Richard Haass, "Intelligence, I predicted, would prove to be the most valuable tool against terrorists."[20]

Similarly, the U.S. had difficulty obtaining reliable intelligence about Saddam Hussein because he, for understandable reasons, was paranoid about threats to him and his regime and relied almost exclusively on long-time close associates and those from his tribe and hometown of Tikrit. As a result, it was almost impossible for the CIA or other Western intelligence agencies to obtain information about Saddam's inner circle, his intentions, or his whereabouts.

As technological capabilities developed during the cold war, the U.S. relied increasingly on a second type of intelligence, "signals intelligence" (SIGINT), consisting of the collection and analysis of electronic information. U.S. intelligence agencies pioneered the development of this form of intelligence and developed truly impressive capabilities. For example, for decades the National Security Agency has monitored international telephone calls and facsimile transmissions.[21] The magnitude of monitoring telephone, fax, and internet communications is daunting; in 2005 experts estimated that 9 trillion email messages were sent in the U.S. annually and that Americans make almost a billion cell phone calls and more than a billion land-line calls per day.[22] The collection capabilities of the National Security Agency, however, are mind-boggling; even prior to 9/11, NSA could collect (as opposed to analyze) the equivalent of the complete holdings of the Library of Congress in three hours.[23] In July 2010, Dana Priest and William Arkin of the *Washington Post* reported that NSA intercepts and stores 1.7 billion emails, calls, and other communications per day.[24]

A third type of intelligence consists of images and photographs collected by high-flying airplanes such as the U-2 or SR-71 or satellites. Such "image intelligence" (IMINT) played a key role in many of the conflicts of the cold war. For example, during the tense days of October 1962 when the USSR had tried secretly to deploy intermediate and medium-range ballistic missiles to Cuba, the U.S. representative to the United Nations, Adlai Stevenson, dramatically presented photographic evidence of Soviet troops and equipment in Cuba, evidence that strengthened the U.S. case and international support. Satellites were instrumental in providing the verification means for modern arms control agreements, a case of technology assisting with the control and limitation of weapons. Today, the reported resolution of satellite photographs is a six-inch square, and no longer are satellite photographs solely produced by countries; a number of commercial organizations, such as the French company SPOT, sell satellite photos. The internet source Google Earth provides satellite photos on the internet of many places in the world free of charge. Within the U.S. government, the National Geospatial Intelligence Agency is principally responsible for IMINT.

A fourth means of obtaining information is through open, unclassified sources such as published government reports, statistics, newspaper and magazine articles, radio and television broadcasts, and internet blogs and postings. In fact, much of the information that intelligence organizations rely on comes from open source intelligence (OSINT), and the job of analysts relying primarily on unclassified information is similar to that of academics who depend on similar sources. In a closed organization or country, however, open sources have a limited capability of providing valuable information, and some closed societies, such as the People's Republic of China, limit information both coming into and going out of their countries. Terrorist groups such as al Qaeda use the internet as a propaganda tool and as a means of communicating with its members, but such communication is often encrypted. Al Qaeda has used a sophisticated encryption technology known as steganography that allowed its leaders to hide messages within photographs on the internet.[25] Open sources did not prove to be very valuable in analyzing Iraq under Saddam Hussein, who used open sources as a means of propaganda and disinformation rather than as a means for conveying accurate information.

A fifth source of intelligence is technical intelligence (TECHINT), which refers to the information about the characteristics and capabilities of equipment and weapons used by the military forces of foreign countries. Such intelligence enables a country to develop countermeasures, to prevent technological surprise, and to evaluate foreign scientific and technical accomplishments.

A sixth source of intelligence is measurement and signature intelligence (MASINT), which enables countries to identify and describe targets through distinctive characteristics. MASINT and technical intelligence can be closely related. A technical intelligence analyst could draw conclusions from the examination of an actual piece of military equipment, whereas the MASINT analyst must draw conclusions from information that sensors collect remotely, including electro-optical, geophysical, composition of materials, radiation characteristics, radar, and radio frequencies.[26] In its review of intelligence capabilities of the U.S. regarding weapons of mass destruction, the Silberman-Robb commission on weapons of mass destruction concluded, "The collection of technologies known as MASINT, which includes a virtual grab bag of advanced collection and analytic methods, is not yet making a significant contribution to our intelligence efforts. In Iraq, MASINT played a negligible role."[27]

Intelligence Failures

Throughout history, states have suffered intelligence failures that were costly in both human and material resources, and these failures have often left an indelible impression on national memories and psyches. For example, in 1904, Japan launched a surprise attack against the Russian naval fleet at Port Arthur and wiped it out. This set the stage for Japan's defeat of Russia, the first defeat of a European power by an Asian power, and this event made a deep impression on Asians as well as Russians; for example, the former long-time head of the Soviet navy, Admiral Sergei Gorshkov, mentioned this event in nearly every speech he gave and every article he wrote.[28] Nazi Germany's successful surprise attack of the USSR in June 1941 underscored the Soviets' fear of surprise attack.[29]

Similarly traumatic for Americans was the Japanese surprise attack on Pearl Harbor of December 7, 1941, a day that according to President Franklin Roosevelt would "live in infamy." Within five years of the attack, there were four official investigations into the reasons for the intelligence failure leading to Pearl Harbor. These investigations blamed the military commanders in Hawaii, Admiral Husband Kimmel and General Walter Short, as those primarily responsible for the failure to anticipate the Japanese attack. In an exhaustive review and analysis of the investigations and data, however, Roberta Wohlstetter concluded that the local commanders were not primarily at fault, but that the "signals to noise ratio" and the compartmentalization of relevant information prior to the attack led to the intelligence failure.[30]

The Japanese surprise attacks on Port Arthur and Pearl Harbor and the German attack on the USSR of June 1941 caused Soviet and American policymakers to be fixated on the possibility and threat of surprise attack throughout the cold war. With the advent of nuclear weapons and the means to deliver them with ballistic missiles, the cost of and vulnerability to surprise attack became significantly greater than before, and policymakers and defense analysts in both countries sought ways to deal with this threat.[31] Over time, the doctrine of mutual assured destruction was developed, and it was based on the fundamental assumption that one country could absorb a first strike and respond with an effective counterattack. However, if a surprise attack proved to be devastatingly effective, then the fundamental assumption of American nuclear policy would be moot. Therefore, one of the principal reasons that the U.S. government established the CIA was to lessen the probability of a successful surprise attack.

The failure to anticipate surprise attack was not the only substantive intelligence failure that the U.S. has suffered. For example, none of the U.S. intelligence agencies predicted the fall of communism in Eastern Europe and the disintegration of the Soviet Union itself. These were failures of strategic intelligence and were particularly remarkable given the fact that the American intelligence community had devoted most of its resources and attention to the analysis of the USSR and its allies since the inception of the cold war.

The United States and Russia have not been the only countries that have suffered traumatic intelligence failures. For example, in October 1973, Egypt and Syria jointly attacked Israel on one of the holiest days of the Jewish calendar, Yom Kippur. Having decisively defeated Arab forces in 1948 and 1967, Israeli leaders were shocked when Egypt and Syria were able to stage a devastating and successful surprise attack against Israel. During the first week of the war, it appeared that Israel might lose the war; however, the tide of the war then turned, and after several weeks, Israel prevailed. But the human and material cost was high, and following the war, a former member of the Israeli Supreme Court conducted an official governmental inquiry.[32] The conclusion of the Agranat Commission was that the chief of staff of the Israeli Defense Forces, David Elazar, and the head of Israeli military intelligence, General Eli Zeira, were primarily responsible for the failure to anticipate the Arab attack, a conclusion similar to the one following investigations of Pearl Harbor in that military leaders were blamed for the intelligence failures.

The principal objective of the CIA since its founding was to avoid a surprise attack, yet, as one examines history it seems that intelligence failures and successful surprise attacks are inevitable, as Columbia University political scientist Richard Betts has shown.[33] This, however, should not be unexpected given the inherent uncertainties of the intelligence process.

Intelligence Concerning Afghanistan and Pakistan

In the 1980s, the U.S. government relied increasingly on satellite reconnaissance and the monitoring of electronic communications, which the intelligence community referred to as "national technical means of verification." CIA Director Stansfield Turner, in particular, emphasized this approach to intelligence collection by retiring or firing 820 CIA spies, an action that many bitterly criticized.[34] A number of Turner's successors as CIA director, such as John Deutsch, also emphasized technical means of obtaining intelligence; Deutsch described himself as "a technical guy, a satellite guy, a SIGINT guy."[35] Other intelligence officials, such as William Casey, resisted this orientation. According to Steve Coll, "The CIA in the 1990s was generally seen by intelligence specialists as strong on technology and mediocre at human intelligence operations against hard targets."[36] By the mid-1990s there were 800 case officers throughout the world, a reduction of 25 percent from the days of the cold war, and by 1995, the CIA was training only twelve new case officers per year at its training facility at Camp Peary outside of Williamsburg, Virginia.

During the Soviet-Afghan War, the CIA maintained an active HUMINT program with members of the *mujahideen*, providing them with supplies, weapons, and, starting in 1986, Stinger shoulder-fired, surface-to-air missiles. The CIA's and Saudi Arabia's assistance to the *mujahideen* was funneled through Pakistan's ISI, which had close relationships with the *mujahideen* because ISI had provided support for them for decades. There were several reasons for this support. Many of the ISI officers were religious fundamentalists and had similar beliefs, so there was a common religious orientation. As Charles Cogan, who was the chief of the Near East and South Asia Division of the CIA's Directorate of Operations from 1979 to 1984, has noted, "The Afghan resistance to the Soviet presence was propelled by Islamism, as well as by nationalism."[37] In addition, many ISI officers viewed the *mujahideen* as a means of pressuring India over Kashmir. And, of course, the *mujahideen* had been the principal opponents of the Soviet occupation of Afghanistan and provided, therefore, proxy forces for opposing the Soviet Union.

At the end of the war, however, American interest in Afghanistan waned, and the CIA substantially reduced its programs and activities in Afghanistan and its support of the ISI in Pakistan. As former CIA operative Gary Schroen noted, "The events in Afghanistan in the mid-1990s were back-page news at best, just another civil war among squabbling warlords in a country so devastated and backward that there was little or nothing to fight over."[38] Several CIA officers, however, maintained their ties to *mujahideen* leaders, and when the agency wanted to renew its activities in Afghanistan following the bombing of the American embassies in Kenya and Tanzania in August 1998, they were able to do so. In 1999, the National Security Council approved information collection activities in Afghanistan, and five CIA teams were sent into the Panjshir Valley in early 1999 to establish contacts and collect information from the Northern Alliance. In addition, the CIA attempted to recruit sources among various segments of Afghan society including tribal leaders, the Taliban, al Qaeda, businessmen, and soldiers. According to former CIA official Henry Crumpton, "This network ranged from fully vetted, reliable, well-trained, courageous foreign nationals to transient, unscrupulous mercenaries . . . . By September 2001, the CIA had more than one hundred sources and subsources throughout the country."[39]

After a thirty-five year career in the CIA at age fifty-nine, veteran operative Gary Schroen was getting ready to retire; however, on the morning of September 11, his plans changed dramatically. Schroen was one of the CIA agents who had maintained contact with members of the *mujahideen* following the Afghan War, and the agency called on its long-time operative to spearhead the agency's efforts to re-establish contact and work with the Northern Alliance, the group of Tajiks, Uzbeks, and others who opposed the Taliban. This group had good reason to increase its opposition to the Taliban, for on September 9, 2001, just two days before the attacks on the United States, al Qaeda terrorists had assassinated Ahmad Shah Massoud, the revered leader of the Northern Alliance. Schroen and his fellow CIA operatives worked in concert with American Special Forces soldiers, the Northern Alliance forces, anti-Pashtun tribes fighting under Hamid Karzai, and U.S. Air Force and Navy bombers to pinpoint and destroy enemy forces. By December 2001, these forces had destroyed the Taliban regime and al Qaeda training camps and killed an estimated 5,000 to 10,000 enemy forces. In addition, more than 5,000 prisoners were captured, and even though Osama bin Laden eluded capture or death, his deputy, Mohammed Atef, was killed. An estimated 25 percent of Taliban and al Qaeda leaders were either captured or killed.[40]

Human intelligence was key to U.S. operations in Afghanistan, and was supplemented by other forms of intelligence. SIGINT was used to track cell phone usage by known or suspected terrorists, and this information was used to locate them. For example, in June 2006, the U.S. military located al Qaeda leader Abu

Musab al-Zarqawi and used this information to attack and kill him.[41] Following this and other attacks, members of al Qaeda only rarely used cell phones and relied on couriers instead. As a result of U.S. actions, al Qaeda's command and control was significantly degraded. American policymakers had used image intelligence from satellites and U-2 aircraft (IMINT) to examine al Qaeda training camps and buildings, but it could not be used to identify individuals. Something with greater resolution and an ability to get closer to the target was needed. Since the early 1980s, CIA official Dewey Clarridge had supported a program to develop pilotless drones to search for American hostages in Lebanon.[42] The CIA also experimented with arming the drones with small rockets, but they were very inaccurate. Parallel to the CIA's drone program, the Advanced Research Projects Agency in the Department of Defense was also developing an unmanned drone called Amber. Over time, this program became the Predator, which was first deployed to a conflict in Bosnia in 1995. Predators were very slow-flying, about seventy miles per hour, but they had the ability to loiter over a target for up to twenty-four hours. In the Kosovo conflict of 1999, the Air Force equipped Predators with laser target finders and satellite links that would make highly accurate bombing operations possible, although Predators were not used for bombing in the Kosovo conflict. In the summer of 2000, Uzbekistan agreed to allow secret Predator flights into Afghanistan to search for bin Laden.

Over time, the Predator became one of the chief means that the United States employed for both gathering intelligence and for targeted killings, not only in Afghanistan but also in Pakistan. The Predator provided the United States the ability to hunt and kill terrorists who sought refuge in Pakistan without risking the capture or killing of American forces going into Pakistani territory and reducing political sensitivities for the Pakistani government. According to a senior Defense Department official, "The [unmanned aircraft] technology allows us to project power without vulnerability."[43] Another military official commented, "Predators and other unmanned aircraft have just revolutionized our ability to provide a constant stare against our enemy. The next sensors, mark my words, are going to be equally revolutionary."[44] Predators and their follow-ons were not particularly hi-tech; in fact, the Air Force initially was not very enthusiastic about the unmanned drone program; however, over time U.S. government officials, including Air Force officers, recognized the advantages of the drone program: it was a relatively low-tech platform equipped with high-tech sensors and weapons.

After several years of successfully employing Predators in Afghanistan, the U.S. developed and deployed a larger, high-flying unmanned aircraft, the MQ-9 Reaper, which has a maximum altitude of 50,000 feet and a top speed of 250 miles per hour compared with the Predator's maximum ceiling of 25,000 feet and 135 miles per hour. The United States carried out nine drone strikes in the period from 2004 through 2007, thirty-four in 2008, fifty-three in 2009, and 101 from January through mid-November 2010. An estimated 1,114 to 1,712 people were killed by these strikes, and of these between 803 and 1,182 were identified as militants in the press.[45] The capabilities of more recently deployed unmanned aircraft have also been improved so that they are able to intercept electronic communications from cell phones, radios, and other communication devices. Unmanned aircraft have proved their worth in Afghanistan; in 2006, the Air Force was able to fly six drones at a time, and by 2009 thirty-eight could be flown at a time. In February 2010, Secretary of Defense Gates during a visit to Pakistan disclosed that the U.S. would provide a dozen unarmed drones to the Pakistani government for reconnaissance and surveillance.[46] By 2011, the U.S. Air Force plans to be able to fly fifty at a time. Once in office, the Obama administration significantly increased its reliance on drones both to gain intelligence and to stage attacks on targets even inside of Pakistan. In fact, from 2004 through 2010, the U.S. staged more than 150 drone strikes in Pakistan.[47]

It is ironic that Afghanistan, one of the world's poorest, least developed countries, has been an area in which the United States and its allies have effectively deployed and utilized high-tech weapons systems: first the Stinger surface-to-air missile against Soviet aircraft and more recently unmanned aircraft against terrorist targets in both Afghanistan and Pakistan. The Stinger was a significant factor in the defeat of the Soviets. It remains to be seen if unmanned aircraft will play a similarly significant role in the war on terrorists.

Intelligence Concerning Iraq

By 2002 the CIA had only one spy inside Iraq. By the time Baghdad fell in 2003, the CIA station in Baghdad had only four case officers who were fluent in Arabic.[48] Given the shortage of case officers who were fluent in Arabic and able to fit into Iraqi society, it is not surprising that the CIA had a difficult time gaining accurate intelligence on Iraq. Ambassador Paul Bremer, the head of the Coalition Provisional Authority, noted, "[A] major concern was the lack of precise intelligence on the nature of the enemy."[49]

Central to the Bush Doctrine was preemption or, more accurately, preventive war; namely, that the United States would use military force against threats that it considered as imminent and substantial. One of the main requirements of preventive war is intelligence about the capabilities and intentions of potential enemies. Former Bush administration State Department official Richard Haass has noted, "[G]ood intelligence is central to the argument for preventive war,"[50] a sentiment echoed by General Wesley Clark: "It seems to me that the larger the scale of preemption, the greater the weight of evidence has to be."[51] Former U.S. weapons inspector David Kay has made a similar point even more strongly: "If you cannot rely on good accurate intelligence that is credible to the American people and to others abroad, you certainly cannot have a policy of preemption."[52]

The focus on Iraq was strengthened by the belief that Iraq possessed weapons of mass destruction (WMD), a belief that was held by United Nations inspectors and American and other governmental and nongovernmental analysts. As Professor Robert Jervis, a respected academic analyst of intelligence, has noted, "It appears that the belief that Iraq had active WMD programs was held by *all* intelligence services, even those of countries that opposed the war."[53] This belief increased the fear that al Qaeda could possibly obtain WMD from Saddam, and if this were done, the potential damage that al Qaeda could inflict would make the losses of 9/11 pale by comparison. Saddam actually encouraged the belief that Iraq possessed WMD in order to deter both the United States and Iran, with disastrous results for him and his country.[54] Jervis contends, "Perhaps the most studied intelligence failure since Pearl Harbor is the misjudgment of Iraq's programs for weapons of mass destruction."[55] The independent weapons of mass destruction (Silberman-Robb) commission "concluded that the intelligence community's failure on the Iraqi nuclear issue was perhaps the most damaging of any of its errors during the run-up to the Iraq War."[56]

On August 26, 2002, Vice President Cheney confidently announced, "Simply stated, there is no doubt that Saddam Hussein now has weapons of mass destruction .... There is no doubt that he is amassing them to use against our friends, against our allies and against us."[57] In October 2002, a National Intelligence Estimate (NIE), the formal assessment of the U.S. intelligence community, stated that Iraq "is reconstituting its nuclear program."[58] Lieutenant General Mike DeLong, the deputy commander of the Central Command from 2000 to 2003, noted in his memoirs, "We [in CENTCOM] were sure that Iraq had WMD."[59] In January 2003, Paul Wolfowitz stated, "There is incontrovertible evidence that the Iraqi regime still possesses such [nuclear] weapons."[60]

That same month, Arab allies of the U.S. also warned Central Command commander General Franks that Saddam had weapons of mass destruction. King Abdullah of Jordan claimed: "From reliable intelligence sources, I believe the Iraqis are hiding chemical and biological weapons," and President Hosni Mubarak of Egypt said Saddam Hussein "is a madman. He has WMD—biologicals, actually—and he will use them on your troops."[61] In the months following 9/11 both Jordan and Egypt had provided valuable intelligence to the U.S. As a consequence the warnings from Abdullah and Mubarak were taken seriously, and who, besides another Arab state, could have better intelligence about Iraq? Thus, by early 2003, the message was loud and clear: Saddam Hussein possessed weapons of mass destruction (certainly biological and chemical weapons) and was possibly several years away from developing and deploying nuclear weapons. These weapons posed a clear and present danger to the United States. What was the basis for these claims and to what extent were they simply a means that the Bush administration used to gain public support for invading Iraq? By 2003, U.S. intelligence agencies had concluded that Saddam had WMD, and this conclusion was a result of experience analyzing data from Iraq, inspections conducted by the United Nations, and Saddam's deceptions. There were, however, very few American intelligence agents in Iraq to confirm the U.S. government's conclusions.

Because of the paucity of agents in Iraq, the U.S. government came to rely on several Iraqi exiles for intelligence on Iraq. An Iraqi living in Germany, Rafid Ahmed Alwan, fled Iraq and went to Germany when he learned that an arrest warrant had been issued that charged him with stealing camera equipment. Once in Germany, he made contact with Germany's Federal Intelligence Service, known by its acronym in German as the BND, and told agents that he had intelligence on Iraqi weapons of mass destruction.[62] Alwan was given the codename "Curveball," and he reported that Iraq had mobile biological weapons laboratories that enabled the Iraqis to avoid detection by the United Nations weapons inspectors. This intelligence made its way into the October 2002 National Intelligence Estimate, which noted that Iraq has "transportable facilities for producing bacterial and toxin BW [biological weapons] agents."[63] Curveball's claim became an important part of Secretary of State Powell's presentation to the United Nations of February 2003, just weeks prior to the start of the war. Curveball remained in Germany where he has washed dishes in a Chinese restaurant, worked as a cook at McDonald's and Burger King, and baked pretzels in a bakery. But he did no more intelligence work.[64]

A second Iraqi exile on whom the Department of Defense and the vice president's office depended for intelligence was Ahmad Chalabi. He and his Shia family left Iraq in 1958, and he grew up in Britain and the United States. He earned a doctorate in mathematics from the University of Chicago and pursued a number of business ventures in the Middle East. In Jordan, Chalabi was convicted of wrongdoing in connection with the failure of Petra Bank. After the first Gulf War, he helped to found, with the CIA's assistance, the Iraqi National Congress. He claimed to have substantial support in Iraq, and Chalabi was successful in convincing the vice president's office and the Department of Defense of his bona fides. Among Chalabi's plans was one to create an "Iraqi Freedom Force" which he indicated would consist of 15,000 Iraqi exiles. DOD supported this and assigned 800 American military officers to train the Iraqi exile force. By the time the war started, there were a grand total of seventy-seven Iraqi exiles who constituted the entirety of the Iraqi Freedom Force.[65] Chalabi also provided intelligence that proved to be inaccurate or downright false concerning supposed Iraqi WMD. In retrospect, much, if not most, of Chalabi's "intelligence" proved to be inaccurate or self-serving.

Rumsfeld and his closest aides in the Department of Defense did not have high confidence in the intelligence assessments of the CIA and the State Department, and this distrust went back decades. In 1976, conservatives pressured President Ford to establish an independent group, referred to as "Team B," to provide an assessment of intelligence independent of the U.S. intelligence community. In 1998, a similar commission consisting of conservatives and chaired by Donald Rumsfeld was founded to assess the need for national missile defense, which the commission wound up recommending. Wolfowitz had been a member of both Team B and the Rumsfeld Commission. So, conservatives' distrust of the CIA was long-standing and deeply held. According to Richard Perle, "Let me be blunt about this: The level of competence on past performance of the Central Intelligence Agency, in this [WMD in Iraq] is appalling."[66] As a result of this distrust, some members of the Bush administration turned to sources other than the CIA for information and intelligence.

Four months after the 9/11 attacks, Wolfowitz sent a memo to Douglas Feith, the Under-Secretary of Defense for Policy, demanding that his office pull together intelligence linking al Qaeda and Iraq.[67] Several reporters, most notably Seymour Hersh, wrote articles that characterized the purpose of this new Office of Special Plans as being to compete with the CIA and State Department as a source of intelligence on Iraq.[68] However, the office was, in fact, the "Iraq shop" within Feith's office, and not the "mini-intelligence agency" that some journalists and politicians criticized.

The tension between the Department of Defense and the CIA was palpable. Tenet referred derisively to papers coming out of the office of the under-secretary for policy as "Feith-based" analysis.[69] Dr. Gregory Treverton, a former intelligence official and RAND analyst commenting on the tendency to "cherry pick" intelligence, noted: "[T]he cherries were not just picked, but also grown .... Some of the evidence supporting those cherries was rotten, provided by Ahmed Chalabi and the Iraqi National Congress, which had long been discredited in the eyes of the mainline intelligence agencies."[70] Feith's office was so controversial that the DOD Inspector General investigated the office and issued a report indicating that the establishment and operations of the office were, while not illegal, certainly highly unorthodox.[71]

The CIA, Iraqi exiles, and Feith's Office of Special Plans were not the only sources of intelligence for the U.S. government. The FBI also conducted intelligence-gathering operations within the United States and had a great deal of information on suspected terrorists and foreign agents. But there was a proverbial (and legal) wall that separated the FBI and the CIA. Later investigations would criticize the failure of the FBI and the CIA to share information as the problem of "stove-piping"; important information was simply not shared between the two organizations. This was not a strategic blunder; rather, the wall between domestic and foreign intelligence had been intentionally built when the CIA was founded in 1947, and it was maintained throughout the cold war. On 9/11 that wall failed to defend the United States and, in fact, contributed to the success of the attacks.

United Nations inspectors had been in Iraq from the end of the first Gulf War in 1991, and they shared intelligence information with American intelligence agencies, including the CIA.[72] In 1998 Saddam kicked the UN inspectors out of the country, and many were convinced that Iraq possessed WMD.[73] At a minimum, the inspectors who were part of the United Nations Special Commission (UNSCOM), the organization established to oversee and implement the disarmament of Iraq, concluded, "Iraq had not convincingly accounted for WMD programs."[74] American allies in the region thought that Saddam had weapons of mass destruction, and the warnings and the evidence that he saw led CENTCOM commander Franks to conclude, "I had no doubt WMD would be used against us in the days ahead."[75]

There were two indicators of a possible Iraqi nuclear program that became important in the debate over the possible Iraqi development and possession of nuclear weapons: uranium from Niger and aluminum tubes used for reprocessing uranium and producing weapons grade fissile material. In September 2002, just one week before the anniversary of the 9/11 attacks, *New York Times* journalists Judith Miller and Michael Gordon published a report that Iraq was trying to purchase aluminum tubes to be used in centrifuges.[76] Members of the Bush administration appeared on the major Sunday television news programs to underscore the importance of this development. Condoleezza Rice warned, "There will always be some uncertainty about how quickly [Saddam] can acquire nuclear weapons. But we don't want the smoking gun to be a mushroom cloud."[77] Donald Rumsfeld's warning was no less frightening: "Imagine a September eleventh with weapons of mass destruction. It's not three thousand [killed]—it's tens of thousands of innocent men, women, and children."[78] The American government scientists in the Department of Energy who knew the most about the technical aspects of reprocessing did not believe that the tubes could be used for reprocessing. They believed, instead, that they were designed to be used in artillery rockets, which later analysis proved to be the case.[79]

In January 2002, Cheney's office received documents via British and Italian intelligence agencies indicating that Iraq was trying to purchase "yellow cake" (uranium oxide, a precursor of fissile material) from Niger. The documents were passed on to the CIA, which enlisted a retired diplomat, Joseph Wilson, who had previously served as U.S. ambassador to three different African countries.[80] The CIA commissioned Wilson to go to Niger in February 2002, and he concluded that the documents were forgeries and without merit, the same conclusion that Mohammed ElBaradei, the head of the International Atomic Energy Agency, had reached.[81] Despite Wilson's report, the British government released a report in September that mentioned the Iraqi purchase of uranium from Niger. When he presented his evidence indicating that Iraq was developing weapons of mass destruction to the United Nations in February 2003, Secretary of State Powell presented the story of uranium from Niger. Ambassador Wilson later went public and published an article in the *New York Times*, "What I Didn't Find in Africa."[82] Members of the Bush administration were furious with Wilson—so angry, in fact, that they revealed to several journalists that Wilson's wife, Valerie Plame, was a covert CIA operative, who worked on nonproliferation issues, a disclosure that was against the law. The FBI opened a case in order to determine who leaked this classified information, and eventually the vice president's principal aide, Lewis "Scooter" Libby, was convicted of lying to the FBI.

The most dramatic moment of the entire debate over weapons of mass destruction occurred when Colin Powell went to the United Nations to present the evidence on which the United States was basing its case against Iraq. Powell and his staff worked very hard on the presentation and removed much of the material suggested by DOD and Vice President Cheney's office. Depending heavily on information provided by the Iraqi exile codenamed Curveball, Secretary Powell contended that Iraq possessed mobile biological weapons laboratories and showed photos of what he contended were these labs. "There can be no doubt," Powell told the Security Council, "that Saddam Hussein has biological weapons and the capacity to produce more, many more."[83] In the end, much of what Powell presented was false, and this episode became the low point of his otherwise distinguished career.

In historical retrospect, it is interesting to consider the reason that the Bush administration focused so intently on the WMD issue. An obvious reason was the substantial threat weapons of mass destruction in the hands of terrorists posed to the security of the U.S. Terrorists had definitively and devastatingly demonstrated that they had the ability to attack the U.S. successfully on 9/11, and the administration was determined to do all that it could to prevent a much worse attack on the U.S. The American public would not support going to war simply to remove a given leader or to establish democracy in another country. Therefore, the imminent threat to the security of the United States had to be front and center as the rationale for going to war. In addition, Wolfowitz pointed out another reason: "The truth is that for reasons that have a lot to do with the U.S. government bureaucracy, we settled on the one issue that everyone could agree on, which was weapons of mass destruction."[84] Or in other words, WMD was the least common denominator when considering the threat posed by Iraq. Although some critics charged that the Bush administration "manufactured" the WMD threat, there is little evidence of this. As former State Department official and adviser to Colin Powell, Richard Haass, recalled, "I know of no attempt to falsify intelligence by anyone in the U.S. government. It was more a case of people selecting ('cherry picking') reports that supported a certain position and going with them despite questions about their accuracy."[85]

In addition to the WMD issue, members of the Bush administration sought to use intelligence in order to prove the assumption that al Qaeda and Iraq were linked. Following the 9/11 attacks on the U.S., the Bush administration enlisted former CIA Director James Woolsey to investigate the possible links between Iraq and the attacks. Woolsey's principal evidence for such a link was a meeting that supposedly took place in Prague in April 2001 between the chief 9/11 hijacker, Mohammed Atta, and an Iraqi intelligence official, Ahmad Khalil Ibrahim Samir al Ani. Once this was investigated, Czech officials found no evidence for the meeting, and subsequent investigation uncovered evidence (receipts and travel documents) that, in fact, Atta was in the U.S. at the time of the supposed meeting. The 9/11 Commission concluded, "The available evidence does not support the original Czech report of an Atta-Ani meeting."[86] The CIA looked into the Prague meeting and concluded there was "no evidence that Iraq has engaged in terrorist operations against the United States in nearly a decade, and the agency is also convinced that President Saddam Hussein has not provided chemical or biological weapons to Al Qaeda or related terrorist groups."[87] On October 7, 2002, President Bush claimed, "Iraq has trained al Qaeda members in bomb-making and poisons and deadly gas." He also asserted, "We know that Iraq and the al Qaeda terrorist network share a common enemy: The United States of America."[88] After he retired from the CIA, Dr. Paul Pillar, the national intelligence officer for the Near East and South Asia, commented, "Intelligence was misused publicly to justify decisions that had already been made."[89] In the end, the United States did not find WMD in Iraq, and, with the exception of a small number of Arabs in the al Qaeda–affiliated Ansar al-Islam group on the Iran-Iraq border, al Qaeda did not have much of a presence in Iraq before the war.[90]

Why did the administration focus on the issue of WMD, almost to the exclusion of all other issues? First, members of the administration and their critics believed that Iraq possessed WMD, which posed an imminent threat to the United States. Second, members of the Bush administration linked al Qaeda and Iraq and warned of the threat of terrorists obtaining WMD. Third, important members of the Bush administration, most significantly the Department of Defense and Vice President Cheney and his office, relied on what turned out to be inaccurate intelligence reports from Iraqis including the agent codenamed Curveball and Ahmed Chalabi. The fourth reason was a political argument: WMD was the "least common denominator," and among American political leaders there was a solid, bipartisan consensus on the need to confront Iraq, enforce the disarmament of Iraq, and remove Saddam from office. The possibility that Saddam possessed weapons of mass destruction was a terrifying prospect to Republicans and Democrats alike.

In the end, the two intelligence chiefs of the two principal members of the coalition were very critical of the use of intelligence by their governments. Sir Richard Dearlove, according to George Tenet, "believed that the crowd around the vice president was playing fast and loose with the intelligence" and that Scooter Libby had tried to convince Dearlove that there was a connection between Iraq and al Qaeda.[91] For his part, in his memoirs, Tenet acknowledged the shortcomings of the CIA and also repeatedly noted a central problem of intelligence in the Bush administration: "Policy makers have a right to their own opinions, but not their own set of facts."[92]

Investigating the 9/11 and Iraq Intelligence Failures

Professor Robert Jervis has noted that 9/11 and WMD in Iraq were two of the greatest intelligence failures in U.S. history.[93] If intelligence failures leading to successful surprise attacks are inevitable, as Richard Betts contends, then just as inevitable are the inquiries, fact-finding commissions, and parliamentary or congressional hearings called to investigate the causes for the failure and to present recommendations on how such failures could be avoided in the future.

Fourteen months after the attacks on the United States of September 11, 2001, the president and the Congress established a commission to investigate the causes of the attacks. The commission was co-chaired by former Republican New Jersey Governor Thomas Kean and long-time Democratic Congressman Lee Hamilton.[94] In addition, there were four Republican and four Democratic members on the commission, which interviewed more than 1,200 individuals in ten countries and reviewed more than 2.5 million pages of documents. The final report of the commission was hailed as one of the most comprehensive, incisive governmental reports ever written. Parts of the report read like a novel, although sadly, this was nonfiction and not a Hollywood thriller. The commission presented forty-two recommendations focusing on terrorists and their organizations, preventing the growth of Islamist terrorism, protecting and preparing for terrorist attacks, organizing the government to deal with the terrorist threat, improving intelligence, and improving congressional oversight.[95] In broad terms, the commission recommended the creation of a new organization, the Department of Homeland Security, and the establishment of a new director of national intelligence who would be responsible for overseeing the activities of the existing fifteen intelligence agencies of the U.S. government concerned with intelligence. More specifically, the 9/11 Commission recommended:

- Establishing a National Counterterrorism Center responsible for both joint operational planning and joint intelligence collection;
- Establishing other national intelligence centers modeled on the National Counterterrorism Center but focusing on different issues;
- Maintaining the director of the CIA as primarily responsible for improving the espionage capability of the U.S.;
- Rethinking and revising the "wall" that existed between the FBI (responsible for domestic intelligence) and the CIA (responsible for foreign intelligence);
- Retaining the FBI as the principal U.S. domestic intelligence agency and rejecting the establishment of a separate domestic intelligence organization along the lines of the United Kingdom's MI-5.

These recommendations were adopted, resulting in the most widespread reform of defense and intelligence organizations since the passage of the National Security Act of 1947. Once established, the Department of Homeland Security brought together 180,000 employees from twenty-two disparate federal agencies.

At about the same time that the 9/11 Commission presented its report, the Bush administration was planning an attack on Iraq which was based on two fundamental assumptions: that Saddam Hussein was linked to al Qaeda and 9/11 and that Iraq possessed weapons of mass destruction (WMD). The United States government was not the only international actor concerned about Iraq's possible development of weapons of mass destruction. In 1968 Iraq had signed the Nuclear Non-Proliferation Treaty, which obligated it not to attempt to develop nuclear weapons. The International Atomic Energy Agency was responsible for monitoring Iraqi nuclear research and development to assure that these activities were not designed to develop nuclear weapons. Iraq's observance of IAEA rules was spotty and intermittent, and due to this, the IAEA reports on Iraq were inconclusive. In fact, following the first Gulf War, American inspectors "discovered an advanced nuclear weapons program that inspectors from the International Atomic Energy Agency had previously failed to notice."[96]

From 1991 to 1997, Swedish diplomat Rolf Ekeus led UNSCOM, and he was succeeded by Australian diplomat Richard Butler.[97] Reports surfaced that UNSCOM was cooperating with Western intelligence agencies including the CIA and MI-6; for example, in March 1998, a CIA agent posing as a UN inspector installed an eavesdropping system to pick up the conversations of high-ranking Iraqi officials in Baghdad.[98] Following President Clinton's signing of the Iraq Liberation Act in October 1998, Saddam Hussein ejected the members of UNSCOM from Iraq. A year later the United Nations passed a new resolution that called for the lifting of sanctions on Iraq once it accepted new inspections. A new organization, the UN Monitoring, Verification and Inspection Commission (UNMOVIC), was established under the direction of Dr. Hans Blix, a former head of the International Atomic Energy Agency.[99] Even though UNMOVIC was established in 1999 and had a staff in place in New York at UN headquarters, it did not go to work until late 2002 when Saddam, under duress, admitted the inspectors into Iraq. Although UNMOVIC stayed in business until the American invasion of Iraq in March 2003, it did not uncover significant evidence of the existence of stockpiles of Iraqi weapons of mass destruction.

Following the U.S. invasion of Iraq of March 2003, American forces made substantial efforts to locate WMD. When the military found no such weapons, the Iraq Study Group led by Dr. David Kay was established in June 2003 to search for WMD. When it was fully up and running, this organization had 1,400 CIA and Pentagon analysts working for it. After eight months, Kay abruptly resigned from his position on January 23, 2004, and told reporters that WMD stockpiles did not exist.[100] The next day, Kay told the Senate Armed Services Committee, "It turns out we were all wrong," an assertion that challenged one of the fundamental reasons that the Bush administration had presented for going to war.

The publicity engendered by Kay's assertions caused President Bush in February 2004 to appoint another bipartisan governmental commission to review the evidence concerning WMD and to study how intelligence on newly emerging threats could be improved. Former Acting Attorney General and Federal Appeals Court Judge Laurence Silberman and former Virginia Senator and Governor Charles Robb chaired the WMD commission, which made a number of significant recommendations, including suggestions concerning the organization of the FBI and CIA to collect and share information more effectively. As the commission concluded, "The intelligence failure in Iraq did not begin with faulty analysis. It began with a sweeping collection failure."[101]

As the Silberman-Robb WMD commission embarked on its work, a number of other organizations studied the WMD issue and coincidentally presented their conclusions in July 2004. CIA Director George Tenet had tasked Richard Kerr, the former deputy director of the agency, to conduct an in-house investigation concerning what had gone wrong with the CIA's estimate of WMD in Iraq. Initially, the study was classified, although it was publicly released after two years. The study concluded that the CIA, born in the first days of the cold war, had not adapted to the fall of the Soviet Union, which had an impact on the agency "analogous to the effect of the meteor strikes on the dinosaurs."[102] The same month Kerr's report was completed, the Senate Select Committee on Intelligence also published a report on WMD in Iraq.[103]

Allied governments conducted their own reviews of the Iraqi intelligence failure. The British House of Commons conducted several investigations and issued reports; the most comprehensive of these was a report of a committee of privy counselors chaired by Lord Butler.[104] The Butler report was not as scathing as the U.S. reports but was nevertheless critical of the process that led to the erroneous conclusions concerning WMD in Iraq, noting that part of the reason for erroneous conclusions stemmed from the paucity of human intelligence on Iraq WMD programs.[105] The Australian government conducted a parliamentary investigation headed by former Australian intelligence official Philip Flood and published its report in July 2004, concluding, like the Butler Report, that there were few reliable sources on Iraqi weapons of mass destruction.[106] In 2009, the Dutch government established a special committee chaired by Wilibrord Davids to investigate the events leading to the invasion, concluding that there was no basis in international law justifying the invasion.[107] In June 2009, the British Prime Minister announced the establishment of an official inquiry to "identify the lessons that can be learned from the Iraq conflict."[108] Sir John Chilcot chaired the inquiry, and there were four other members: Sir Lawrence Freedman, Sir Martin Gilbert, Sir Roderic Lyne, and Baroness Usha Prashar. The inquiry held a number of hearings, beginning in the fall of 2009 and continuing through most of 2010. A final report was expected to be published in late 2010 or early 2011.

Consistent with past investigations of intelligence failures in both the United States and other countries, attention was focused on individual culpability. Respected *Washington Post* journalist and author Thomas Ricks concluded, "Responsibility for this low point in the history of U.S. intelligence must rest on the shoulders of George Tenet."[109] Tenet had served as CIA director for seven years during a period that was consistently intense and demanding; as he pointed out in his memoirs, "Few understand the palpable sense of uncertainty and even fear that gripped those in the immediate aftermath of 9/11."[110] On July 8, 2004, Tenet resigned. It was not coincidental that he resigned the same month that saw the release and publication of a cascade of critical studies and reports.

As a result of the furor created by the Bush administration's claims that Iraq possessed WMD and the findings of various UN, U.S., and other governmental agencies that Iraq did not have such weapons, President Bush appointed Charles Duelfer to succeed David Kay and commissioned him to study and reach definitive conclusions about the WMD issue. Duelfer began his work in January 2004 and had 1,200 military and civilian personnel to support the work of his organization.[111] President Bush saw Duelfer's work as providing the last word on WMD; when asked in June 2004 whether he thought that Saddam had possessed WMD, the president responded that he would "wait until Charlie gets back with the final report."[112] Based on exhaustive investigations of Iraq and extensive interviews with former Iraqi officials, including Saddam Hussein, Duelfer issued his 1,000-page report on September 30, 2004.[113] (When Duelfer appeared before a Senate committee to present the report, one senator commented, "Mister Duelfer . . . your report . . . your report . . . . Your report has well, it has a lot of words in it.")[114] The report concluded that Iraq had ended its program to develop nuclear weapons in 1991 following the first Gulf War and had no plans to restart it. Iraq's last program to develop and produce biological weapons was destroyed in 1996, and Duelfer's group found no evidence that Iraq was going to restart this program. Stockpiles of chemical weapons were destroyed in 1991, and there was evidence that Iraq had plans to resurrect this program once UN sanctions were lifted, which appeared to be Saddam's principal objective. After exhaustive investigations and searches throughout Iraq, no actual weapons of mass destruction were found.

At the beginning of this chapter, I quoted Frederick the Great, who advised that knowledge of "the country where you are going to act" is essential for successful military operations. A contemporary analyst, Ahmed Hashim, has defined strategic intelligence as "our knowledge based on thorough education and language training of a general 'area of responsibility' (AOR), and of a particular country and its mores, culture, strengths and vulnerabilities, peculiarities, and idiosyncrasies."[115] So what knowledge did American leaders have about Iraq? As noted in this chapter, there were a number of views within the U.S. intelligence community concerning Iraq's capabilities and intentions, particularly as they related to WMD and al Qaeda. Some U.S. intelligence officials argued that Iraq did not have WMD and that there was no al Qaeda–Iraq link, but officials in the Department of Defense and the vice president's office held different views and were able to gain the support of President Bush.

Charles Duelfer commented, "President Bush was making critical decisions based on no direct knowledge of the Iraqis in Iraq."[116] Duelfer was equally critical of the Pentagon's leadership: "The OSD [Office of the Secretary of Defense] pursued its objective with a theological zeal that did not admit contrary indicators. The disaster of Iraq did not stem from miscalculations of WMD; it stemmed from complete ignorance of what dynamics existed in Iraq. This was a miscalculation of Saddam-like proportions."[117] To be fair, however, American policymakers had a very difficult time knowing what was going on in Iraq given its closed, secretive nature and the disinformation propagated by the government. Two academic experts on intelligence, Robert Jervis and Richard Betts, concluded that given the evidence that was available and given Saddam's previous pattern of behavior, the conclusion that Iraq was developing and hiding WMD programs was a plausible conclusion even though it was wrong.[118]

9 War Plans

> Once the fight starts, the one sure thing you can be sure of is that you cannot be sure of anything.
>
> —Gen. Dwight David Eisenhower

By the turn of the millennium, the United States possessed the most technologically advanced and most powerful military forces in the world, and Yale historian Paul Kennedy claimed that the U.S. was the most powerful hegemon in world history. And yet, America's power did not prevent the audacious attacks on the U.S. of September 11, 2001, which were perpetrated not by the hitherto predominant actors of international relations—states—but rather by a non-state terrorist group. Among the many vexing questions that the 9/11 attacks posed, one of the most immediate and important was how the United States should respond to the first major attack on its homeland in almost two centuries. This chapter will describe the various military options for Afghanistan and Iraq that policymakers in the U.S. government considered, which plans they chose and implemented, and finally will assess the effectiveness of these plans.

Dealing with Osama bin Laden and Saddam Hussein

From the fall of the Berlin Wall in November 1989 and the disintegration of the Soviet Union in December 1991, the international situation had been characterized by what it was not: not the cold war, that is, but the "post–cold war" era. When terrorists forcibly took over and used four commercial airliners as manned missiles on September 11, 2001, the post–cold war era ended and a new era of international relations—the age of terror—began.

As noted in Chapter 6, George W. Bush's commencement address at West Point in June 2002 and the release of the *National Security Strategy* in September 2002 had the function of both laying out the administration's foreign policy and making the case for war against Iraq. How did the administration move toward war, and when was the decision made to go to war?

By analyzing the evidence, it is now clear that the decision to attack Iraq was made in June or July 2002. Bush delivered the West Point address on June 1, laying the conceptual justification for attacking Iraq. On July 7, Richard Haass, the director of policy planning in the State Department, went to see Condoleezza Rice to make the case against going to war. Dr. Rice told him to save his breath, that the "decisions were made" and that unless Iraq capitulated to U.S. demands, war was inevitable.[1] In July, the head of British intelligence, Sir Richard Dearlove, visited Washington for consultations with his counterparts and other top Bush administration officials. His impressions were recorded in several memos to Prime Minister Tony Blair, which were later leaked to the press and came to be known as the "Downing Street memos."[2] Based on his conversations, Sir Richard concluded that the U.S. was going to attack Iraq.

In this chapter, I will examine the different strategies that the Bush administration considered for dealing with Osama bin Laden and Saddam Hussein and Iraq, and the way that the Bush administration's plan played out.[3] Broadly speaking, dating back to the first Gulf War, six different strategies were considered: (1) contain and deter Iraq, (2) assassination or coup d'état, (3) employ limited, highly mobile Special Forces, (4) implement a counterinsurgency strategy, (5) adopt a conventional strategy employing overwhelming military force, and (6) utilize a small armored force and exploit the advantages offered by the revolution in military affairs.

1. Contain and Deter

In January 1991, the United States and thirty-eight other countries attacked Iraqi forces to force them to withdraw from Kuwait, an action supported by thirteen different UN resolutions. But these resolutions did not support the overthrow of Saddam Hussein or the taking of Baghdad. There were understandable reasons why the United States did not favor eliminating Saddam, for doing so could have enabled the Shia in Iraq to come to power and ally with Iran. Or, if the Iraqi government were eliminated, then a power vacuum in a vital region containing a majority of the world's oil reserves would have been created. As a result, the George H. W. Bush administration was unwilling to go beyond the mandate provided by the United Nations. In their coauthored book published in 1998, George H. W. Bush and Brent Scowcroft recalled:

> While we hoped that a popular revolt or coup would topple Saddam, neither the United States nor the countries of the region wished to see the breakup of the Iraqi state . . . . Going in and occupying Iraq, thus unilaterally exceeding the United Nations mandate, would have destroyed the precedent of international response to aggression that we hoped to establish. Had we gone the invasion route, the United States could conceivably still [in 1998] be an occupying power in a bitterly hostile land.[4]

General Norman Schwarzkopf, the overall commander of U.S. and coalition forces in the first Gulf War, indicated the reasons why the objectives were limited:

> Had the United States and the United Kingdom gone on alone to capture Baghdad . . . we would have been considered occupying powers and therefore would have been responsible for *all* the costs of maintaining or restoring government, education, and other services for the people of Iraq. From the brief time we did spend occupying Iraqi territory after the war, I am certain that had we taken all of Iraq, we would have been like the dinosaur in the tar pit—we would still be there, and we, not the United Nations, would be bearing the costs of that occupation. This is a burden I am sure the beleaguered American taxpayer would not have been happy to take on.[5]

According to Richard Haass, "The truth is there was no interest in going to Baghdad. I do not recall any dissent on this point . . . . We would have become an occupying power in a hostile land with no exit strategy."[6] However, there were some in the administration, most notably Paul Wolfowitz, who favored removing Saddam from power, but the administration's policy was to contain and deter Iraq from expanding its territory or influence. Once in office, the Clinton administration essentially continued the contain-and-deter policy of the George H. W. Bush administration, although the administration applied the policy to Iran as well as Iraq in a policy it referred to as "dual containment."[7]

2. Assassination or Coup d'État

Following the 1998 attacks on the American embassies in Tanzania and Kenya, U.S. government officials considered ordering assassination attempts on bin Laden.[8] In his memoir, President Clinton wrote that his goal was "to wipe out much of the al Qaeda leadership,"[9] and in her memoir, Secretary of State Madeleine Albright recalled that Clinton explicitly authorized the use of force to capture or kill bin Laden and his subordinates.[10] In addition, there were reports that the CIA hired the private security contractor Blackwater to locate and assassinate top leaders of al Qaeda.[11] Soon after the 9/11 attacks, 60 percent of Americans supported the assassination of foreign leaders, presumably including Saddam, in order to achieve victory. By contrast, in 1981, a Gallup poll had found that 82 percent of Americans opposed political assassinations under all circumstances.[12]

Following the first Gulf War, George H. W. Bush called on the Iraqi people to rise up against Saddam, and in response, the Kurds in the north and the Shia in the south demonstrated against Saddam and the Baathist controlled government. Saddam reacted immediately and brutally and repressed the fledgling revolt within seven weeks. Reformists would not be in a position for several years to stage another revolt.

During and at the end of the 1991 Iraq War, leading members of the coalition openly expressed their hope for a new Iraqi leader; in January 1991, former British Prime Minister John Major told the House of Commons: "I very strongly suspect that he [Saddam] may yet become a target of his own people . . . . It is perfectly clear that this man is amoral. He takes hostages. He attacks population centres. He threatens prisoners. He is a man without pity and, whatever his fate may be, I for one, will not weep for him."[13] President George H. W. Bush commented that it would "be a heck of a lot easier if he and that [Baathist] leadership were not in power in Iraq."[14]

One possible way to get rid of Saddam was to assassinate him; in fact, during the 1980s there had been at least four different assassination attempts. In July 1982 Saddam's motorcade was attacked; in 1985 in Tikrit, Saddam's native city, a car packed with explosives was parked along Saddam's motorcade but detonated before Saddam entered the city. In addition, there were assassination attempts in 1984 and 1987.[15] These were all attempts, presumably, by Iraqis. U.S. law formally prohibited such action. In response to revelations that the CIA had planned several assassination plots against Fidel Castro, President Gerald R. Ford issued Executive Order 11905, which banned assassinations in 1976, a prohibition that was reinforced by President Reagan with Executive Order 12333 in 1981. In the mid-1990s, there were reports that a CIA agent, Robert Baer, had initiated an assassination plot against Saddam, which was blocked by Clinton's national security affairs adviser, Anthony Lake.[16]

By 1995, three options for overthrowing Saddam were being prepared.[17] In November 1994, an Iraqi major general who had served as an adviser to Saddam defected to the Kurdish area of Iraq and began to plan for the overthrow of Saddam. His plan called for three experienced combat units—the 76th Brigade, the 15th Infantry Division, and the 5th Mechanized Division—to attack Saddam's forces and to foment dissention.

Jalal Talabani, the head of the Patriotic Union of Kurdistan (PUK), had a second plan for getting rid of Saddam, focusing on an attack on Iraq's V Corps, which was the main Iraqi military force confronting Kurdish forces. According to Talabani, "Entire companies, even divisions, will surrender at the first shot."[18] The only problem was that Talabani's forces consisted of only 2,000 lightly armed Kurdish fighters called *peshmerga.*

Several Iraqi exiles were also working on plans; they wanted to re-enter Iraq and form a force to overthrow Saddam. Ahmed Chalabi, a Shia Iraqi whose family left Iraq when he was thirteen years old, was elected president of the Iraqi National Congress in 1992 and was well connected in Washington, particularly in the Pentagon and Vice President Cheney's office. Following the Kurdish and Shia revolt of early 1991, Chalabi had written a paper entitled "End Game," calling for Kurdish forces under Talabani and Masoud Barzani, the leader of the Kurdish Democratic Party (KDP), to attack from the north and Shia forces to attack from the south. The problem was that Talabani and Barzani had not agreed to the plan, and Chalabi had little support in Iraq. Chalabi believed, according to his biographer, Aram Roston, "The Iraqi army would not fight but would simply shift its allegiance, unit by unit. Iraq, he said, was like a junkyard full of gasoline cans, and all one needed to do was throw in a match to get the fire started."[19]

Ayad Allawi, a Baathist and a rival of Chalabi's, was also working on a plan to stage a coup d'état. Allawi convinced the CIA to support his plan, codenamed Panther. The attempted coup took place in 1996 and was "an unmitigated disaster."[20] Within two months Saddam had arrested 120 conspirators, an action which ended the hopes for a coup. These failures, however, did not diminish Wolfowitz's support for overthrowing Saddam; in December 1998, he wrote, "Toppling Saddam is the only outcome that can satisfy the vital U.S. interest in a stable and secure Gulf region."[21] The former Central Command commander, General Anthony Zinni, referred to plans calling for the support of Iraqi exiles as the "Bay of Goats," comparing them to the disastrous Bay of Pigs invasion of Cuba in 1961, and a group of three respected foreign policy experts publicly criticized Wolfowitz's plan in the respected journal *Foreign Affairs.*[22]

3. Attack by Special Forces

Buoyed by the impressive military victory of the United States in Afghanistan, some favored the use of a similar military strategy in Iraq; indeed, Secretary of Defense Rumsfeld thought that the Afghanistan campaign validated his support for light, mobile, Special Forces employing high technology weapons and unconventional forces.[23] In Afghanistan, slightly more than 400 Special Forces and CIA operators had worked closely with Northern Alliance forces. The Americans called in air strikes and the Northern Alliance provided the ground forces, a combination that proved to be successful in overthrowing the Taliban government and destroying al Qaeda training camps. Despite the achievement of these objectives, however, Osama bin Laden and Mullah Omar remained at large, a fact that blemished the otherwise successful performance of the United States in Afghanistan.

The problem in applying the Afghan strategy to Iraq was that there was no organized force similar to the Northern Alliance with the exception of Kurdish rebels in northern Iraq. Saddam had acted forcefully and brutally following the first Gulf War to eliminate any possible opponents. In addition, the most likely and most capable opposition came from the Kurds in the north, but they were divided between the two leading groups, the Kurdish Democratic Party (KDP) and the Patriotic Union of Kurdistan (PUK). As a result, there was only a limited possibility of applying the Afghan strategy to Iraq, and in all likelihood, it could only be applied in northern Iraq.[24]

4. Implement a Counterinsurgency Strategy

According to the current U.S. Army and Marine Corps relevant field manual, an insurgency is "an organized movement aimed at the overthrow of a constituted government through the use of subversion and armed conflict. . . . [An] insurgency is an organized, protracted politico-military struggle designed to weaken the control and legitimacy of an established government, occupying power, or other political authority while increasing insurgent control."[25] The strategic objectives of conventional and counterinsurgent military operations are radically different. In the conventional or counterterrorist approach, the aim is to destroy enemy forces, and the metrics of success consist of the number of enemy killed, amount of equipment destroyed, territory captured, and so on. In contrast, according to insurgency expert David Kilcullen, "In counterinsurgency the population is the prize, and protecting and controlling it is the key activity."[26]

Prior to the wars in Afghanistan and Iraq, the largest scale U.S. counterinsurgency campaign was waged in Vietnam; however, the counterinsurgency approach was at odds with and in competition with the conventional military approach. During the early years of American involvement in Vietnam, the U.S. adopted a counterinsurgency approach; in later years, the U.S. adopted a conventional military approach, and one of the main measurements used to evaluate the military's success was the "body count" of enemy killed.

Vietnam was the first war that the United States had lost. Because of this, it had a deep and profound effect on the U.S. military, many of whose members blamed either politicians for not supporting the American effort sufficiently or the mistaken U.S. strategy of counterinsurgency.

5. Adopt a Conventional Strategy Employing Overwhelming Military Force

Planning for a possible war in Iraq began soon after the first Iraq War ended in 1991. A standard practice of the military is to plan for various contingencies, and given the bellicose actions of Saddam Hussein even after his country had been decisively defeated in 1991, there was ample cause for the U.S. military to plan for eventual war against Iraq. While he was commander of Central Command, General Anthony Zinni developed OPLAN (Operational Plan) 1003–98, a contingency plan that called for up to 500,000 troops and a possible postwar occupation of Iraq for up to ten years.[27]

When Lieutenant General Greg Newbold, in charge of the J-3 Operations Directorate of the Joint Chiefs of Staff, briefed Secretary Rumsfeld, JCS Chairman Myers, and other top military leaders, it was clear that Rumsfeld was unhappy with the plan, which in his view required too many troops and supplies and would take too long to implement. Instead, Rumsfeld wanted to get in, defeat Saddam's forces quickly, and get out of Iraq as quickly as possible. But was that feasible?

In the first Gulf War, the United States and its thirty coalition partners deployed 560,000 military personnel to the region to fight and defeat Iraq. Rumsfeld believed that general officers tended to plan for the future based on the past, that a revolution in military affairs had occurred, and that the United States needed to exploit these changes in the conduct of war. The war in Afghanistan provided the first test case of the application of these new technologies and had been a great success. Why then, Rumsfeld asked, could they not be applied with equal success to Iraq?

General Erik Shinseki publicly expressed his doubts about the level of forces that Rumsfeld and Wolfowitz approved for the invasion of Iraq. For his part, Colin Powell was also concerned about the unrealistic assumptions for the invasion and occupation. Powell had been the chairman of the Joint Chiefs of Staff during the first Gulf War and was, therefore, very familiar with the issues involved concerning a war with Iraq. Having served in Vietnam, Powell, like many of his fellow officers of that cohort, wanted the United States to go to war only if certain conditions were met: vital national interests were at stake, there was substantial public, congressional, and international support, the use of military force was a last resort, and there was an exit plan from the war. In the discussions leading to the war, Powell raised criticisms concerning the assumptions that Cheney, Rumsfeld, and Wolfowitz were making. In his memoirs, General Franks dismissed Powell's concerns in a condescending manner: "Colin had concerns. He was from a generation of generals who believed that overwhelming military force was found in troop strength—sheer numbers of soldiers and tanks on the ground. As Chairman of the Joint Chiefs of Staff during Desert Storm, General Colin Powell had seen the number of coalition ground forces rise to more than five hundred thousand. Indeed, this principle of overwhelming force was often referred to as the 'Powell Doctrine.'"[28] Interestingly, Franks did not address or even recognize the other two elements of the Powell Doctrine—the need for public support and an exit plan from the war—which would prove to be critical.

6. Utilize a Small Armored Force and the Revolution of Military Affairs

During the 2000 presidential campaign, George W. Bush called for a significant transformation of the United States military forces from "industrial age operations" toward "information age battles" of the new century.[29] Once elected and soon after his inauguration, Bush signed Presidential Directive 3, which stipulated: "The secretary of defense is hereby given a broad mandate to challenge the status quo and establish new and innovative practices and processes for acquiring U.S. defense capabilities for decades to come."[30]

Rumsfeld came into office committed to transforming the U.S. military by taking advantage of the revolution in military affairs, including advanced technology, mobility, and speed. He believed that modern improvements in information processing and highly accurate weapons to some extent obviated the need for large numbers of troops. The problem in reaping the benefits of the advantages offered by these technological developments was bureaucratic resistance. On September 10, 2001, the day before the attacks on the United States, Rumsfeld told Pentagon employees:

> The topic today is an adversary that poses a threat, a serious threat, to the security of the United States of America. From a single capital, it attempts to impose its demands across time zones, continents, oceans and beyond. With brutal inconsistency, it stifles free thought and crushes new ideas. It disrupts the defense of the United States and places the lives of men and women in uniform at risk . . . . You may think I am describing one of the last decrepit dictators of the world. But their day, too, is almost past, and they cannot match the strength and size of this adversary. The adversary's closer to home. It's the Pentagon bureaucracy.[31]

Following the 9/11 attacks, Rumsfeld pressed his plan for transforming the U.S. military; in his annual report to the president of 2002, Rumsfeld wrote: "[S]ome believe that, with the U.S. in the midst of a difficult and dangerous war on terrorism, now is not the time to transform our Armed Forces. The opposite is true. Now is precisely the time to make changes."[32] Ever sensitive to the need to gain public acceptance of his ideas, Rumsfeld wrote an article in *Foreign Affairs* describing his vision of transforming the military.[33]

What transformation actually meant in operational terms was never very clear. Early in his tenure, Rumsfeld convened the Pentagon's senior civilian and military staffs to define transformation and how it could be achieved. This group developed a definition: Transformation is "a process that shapes the changing nature of military competition and cooperation through new combinations of concepts, capabilities, people, processes, and organizations that exploit our nation's advantages and protect against our asymmetric vulnerabilities to sustain our strategic position, contributing to peace and stability in the world."[34] The problem with this definition is that it could include almost anything, and it did. Following the Afghanistan campaign, Rumsfeld was fond of claiming that Special Forces soldiers riding horses with the Northern Alliance forces in Afghanistan were an example of military transformation.[35] This, however, did not represent the utilization of speed, firepower, and technology; rather, it represented the adaptation to the circumstances of battle, something that successful military commanders have done throughout history.

After a consideration of these approaches for dealing with Saddam Hussein and Iraq, the United States went to war, but curiously, even high-ranking members of the George W. Bush administration either were not consulted or did not know of a firm decision for war.[36] Bob Woodward reported, "Both Powell and Rice knew that Powell had never made an overall recommendation on war to the president since he had never been asked."[37] CIA Director George Tenet recalled, "In none of the meetings [concerning Iraq] can anyone remember a discussion of the central questions. Was it wise to go to war? Was it the right thing to do? The agenda focused solely on what actions would need to be taken if a decision to attack were later made."[38] Richard Haass, concluded, "The fundamental decision to go to war against Saddam's Iraq had effectively been made by a president and an administration with virtually no systematic, rigorous, in-house debate."[39]

U.S. Military Operations in Iraq: A "Catastrophic Success"

Official U.S. doctrine divides military activities into the following four phases, which General Franks used in designing the U.S. war plan for Iraq:[40]

Phase I—preparations for a possible invasion
Phase II—"Shaping the battle space," beginning with the start of air operations
Phase III: decisive offensive operations and major combat operations, including "complete regime removal
Phase IV—post-hostilities stabilization and reconstruction

In November 2001, Secretary Rumsfeld tasked General Franks, the commander of CENTCOM, with the responsibility of updating and refining the previous war plan for Iraq that Franks' predecessor, General Tony Zinni, had developed. In other words, Rumsfeld wanted Franks to develop a war plan that reflected the revolution in military affairs and to move away from the conventional U.S. approach of employing overwhelming military force.

On March 20, 2003, U.S. forces attacked Iraq; major combat operations lasted twenty-three days, and by April 9 American forces had reached Baghdad and toppled the iconic statue of Saddam at Firdos Square. On May 1, President Bush landed on the USS *Abraham Lincoln* with a banner proclaiming "Mission Accomplished." But was it? The fall of Baghdad marked the end of Phase III, the acute military combat part of the war, but Phase IV—reconstruction—remained. Those, such as Kenneth Adelman, who believed that the war against Saddam would be a "cakewalk" were largely correct concerning the first three phases of the war; however, they made a costly mistake in assuming that American forces would be welcomed as liberators and that Phase IV would proceed as smoothly as the acute, kinetic phases of the war.

Members of the Bush administration were ecstatic about the results of the war and the way that it was fought. On the day that Baghdad fell, Vice President Cheney said that the success of the United States was "proof positive of the success of our efforts to transform the military."[41] Rumsfeld triumphantly noted that the coalition's success was not a result of "overwhelming force," as the U.S. had used in the first Gulf War, but rather resulted from the use of speed, mobility, firepower, and technology. One of Rumsfeld's principal deputies, Steven Cambone, remarked, "What you see in Iraq in its embryonic form is the kind of warfare that is animating our desire to transform the force."[42]

Ultimately, the United States invaded and defeated the Iraqi military with a force of 145,000, which was less than half the number of forces called for in General Zinni's OPLAN 1003–98. As it turned out, even though the United States deployed a maximum number of troops, between 140,000 to 175,000, to Iraq at various times during the war, General Shinseki's estimate proved to be, in fact, the number of forces that were required for the occupation of Iraq. Unwilling to admit its disastrous underdeployment of troops to Iraq, the Bush administration made up for the shortfall by hiring civilian contractors to do many of the jobs that in previous conflicts would have been performed by members of the military. By mid-2007, the number of civilian contractors in Iraq equaled 130,000.[43] Added to the 150,000 soldiers and marines, this totaled 280,000, which was close to the 300,000 troops called for in OPLAN 1003–98 and as General Shinseki had predicted. In Afghanistan, contractors made up 57 percent of the Department of Defense's force as of March 2009.[44] As of this same date, the combined U.S. military forces in Iraq and Afghanistan equaled 282,000 troops and the number of contractors equaled 242,657.

CIA Director George Tenet summarized the acute combat phase of the war and the "peace" that followed: "On a scale of one to ten, the plan to capture the country scored at least an eight. Unfortunately, the plan for 'the day after' charitably was a two. The war, in short, went great, but peace was hell."[45] Tenet was not alone in his judgment. Counterinsurgency expert Ahmed Hashim concluded, "The reconstruction of Iraq has been a tragic failure."[46] Journalist Nir Rosen commented, "[T]he Americans lost the war when they won it."[47] Tragically, this result had not been unforeseen; in the run-up to the war, General Franks recalled, "Washington needed to get ready for the occupation and reconstruction—because combat operations might be over sooner than anyone could imagine. At NSC briefings, Rumsfeld and I referred to that possibility as a 'catastrophic success.'"[48] An Army War College study had warned: "The possibility of the United States winning the war and losing the peace in Iraq is real and serious."[49]

The faulty assumption and mistakes of the postwar "Phase IV" operations of the Coalition Provisional Authority have been well documented by both observers and participants.[50] Suffice it to note that the U.S. came close to losing the war in 2005, and by 2006, according to Ambassador Ryan Crocker, Iraq "came pretty close to just unraveling."[51] The question by that time was what could be done to snatch victory from the jaws of defeat.

The Counterrevolution

For much of its history, the United States fought small wars as both insurgents and counterinsurgents. During the Revolutionary War, some Americans fighting for independence waged an insurgent war against a conventional European army, the British "redcoats." Francis Marion, known as the "swamp fox," staged hit-and-run raids against the British in South Carolina. Having gained its independence and expanding its territory to the west, the U.S. Army fought a series of battles against Native-American tribes and nations. Once the frontier closed, Americans turned their attention to foreign parts. In 1805, the U.S. Navy and Marines engaged the Barbary pirates—what contemporary international relations analysts would call nonstate actors—off the coast of North Africa.

The Civil War marked the first large-scale war in which the U.S. fought, and in many ways, it was one of the first truly modern wars in which advanced technologies such as machine guns, railroads, and even balloons were used. In part due to modern technologies and in part due to the ideological character of the Civil War, the losses were horrific—approximately 620,000 were killed. Even in the Civil War, however, some forces, particularly on the Confederate side, engaged in hit-and-run attacks characteristic of an insurgency.

Toward the end of the nineteenth century, U.S. forces fought insurgent forces in a number of "small wars" in places around the world including Panama, Samoa, the Philippines, China, Haiti, the Dominican Republic, Nicaragua, and Mexico. In confronting these insurgencies, the U.S. developed tactics and strategies for doing so.[52]

In the twentieth century the United States moved from fighting small wars to fighting big wars. Reflecting a traditional isolationist approach to international involvement, the U.S. entered World War I only after the war had been raging for more than three years. As in the Civil War, modern technologies, including the first use of tanks, airplanes, submarines, and poison gas, resulted in high casualties for the combatants. In World War I, the U.S. lost almost 117,000, and the Second World War resulted in even more losses—405,000 Americans killed.

Although it would be an exaggeration and an affront to the enormous losses of the Allies to claim that U.S. forces "won the war," they certainly were essential to the Allied victory. American military leaders learned a number of lessons from the war, including the value of firepower and technological superiority, and these were seen as the quintessential elements of a modern, successful military. The development and use of *Blitzkrieg* (lightning war) military tactics by Nazi Germany removed any doubt that modern technologies provided distinct advantages to strengthening military capabilities.

Many of the generals who fought the Korean War had previously served in World War II, and fortunately for the U.S., the North Korean and Chinese forces opposing the U.S. chose to fight the type of conventional war that the U.S. had experience fighting. In the mid-1950s, however, a new kind of conflict became evident, "wars of national liberation" fought by indigenous insurgents. Many thought that the Eisenhower administration's policy of "massive retaliation," threatening a possible nuclear response to local aggression, was simply not credible. Former Secretary of State Dean Acheson, retired Army chief of staff General Maxwell Taylor, strategist Bernard Brodie, Professor Henry Kissinger, and then-Senator John F. Kennedy all criticized Eisenhower's strategy.[53]

According to Roger Hilsman, a close aide of Kennedy and a veteran of the insurgency fighting in Burma in World War II, Kennedy's first question after his inauguration was "What are we going to do about guerilla warfare?"[54] Kennedy and his closest advisers had served as junior officers rather than general officers during World War II, and they recognized that a shift in the character and conduct of war had occurred. In his address to the West Point class of 1961, Kennedy noted the existence of "another type of war, new in its intensity, ancient in its origin—war by guerillas, subversives, insurgents, assassins, war by ambush instead of by combat, by infiltration instead of aggression, seeking victory by evading and exhausting the enemy instead of engaging him."[55]

To meet these new challenges, President Kennedy strongly supported and expanded the Special Forces, which had been first established in the 1950s despite the strong resistance of the Army. As Colonel David Hackworth, one of the most highly decorated military officers in U.S. history, noted in his memoir, "Counterinsurgency was *the* thing in the early sixties. It was endorsed enthusiastically by Kennedy and his brain trust."[56]

When Kennedy became president, he was confronted with what to do in Vietnam. His preference was to send U.S. military personnel to advise Vietnamese units in counterinsurgency tactics and strategy, but the top U.S. military leadership at the time neither was trained in counterinsurgency nor did it have much respect for it. Characteristic of this view is that of General Harold K. Johnson, Army chief of staff from 1964 to 1968:

> Well, the Special Forces that were available at the time President Kennedy latched on to them as a new gimmick, were what I would describe as consisting primarily of fugitives from responsibility. These were people that somehow or other tended to be nonconformist, couldn't quite get along in a straight military system, and found a haven where their actions were not scrutinized too carefully, and where they came under only sporadic or intermittent observation from the regular chain of command . . . . Perhaps there is a desirability for this highly specialized effort, but I continue to really question it as such.[57]

There was neither an understanding nor an appreciation for what counterinsurgency was. As a consequence, when the U.S. military in Vietnam embarked on what it considered a counterinsurgency approach, it did not reflect the thinking or lessons learned of the foremost theorists, such as Sir Robert Thompson. The U.S. military remained focused on destroying the enemy rather than protecting the indigenous population, as called for in classical counterinsurgency doctrine. According to Colonel Hackworth, "The outspoken Green Berets . . . warned that the counterinsurgency training we were receiving wasn't counterinsurgency at all, but conventional tactics with increased mobility by helicopters."[58] A junior Army officer recalled, "I can personally vouch that much Army counterinsurgency training was not counterinsurgency training at all. I was amazed after my basic course in July 1970 to see what the Army had recorded as counterinsurgency subjects. I remember all our UCMJ [Uniform Code of Military Justice] instruction was considered to be a counterinsurgency subject. Whole lotta lip service there!"[59] Thompson, one of the most respected counterinsurgency experts in the world in the early 1960s, noted, "[T]he helicopter . . . exaggerated two great weaknesses of the American character—impatience and aggressiveness . . . . It is probable that without the helicopter 'search and destroy' would not have been possible, and, in this sense, the helicopter was one of the major contributions to the failure in strategy."[60]

According to Army officer and scholar H. R. McMaster, "Vietnam was a test case for defeating communist insurgencies."[61] General Westmoreland, a veteran of World War II and the Korean War, sought to fight the war in Vietnam along conventional lines, but, of course, the problem was that the Vietcong and North Vietnamese, much like Americans in the Revolutionary War and later insurgents in Afghanistan and Iraq, chose not to fight in this fashion. They chose instead to fight an asymmetrical war. By the time that a new American commander in Vietnam, General Creighton Abrams, sought to revise the way that the U.S. was fighting the war, it was too late. As former Army officer John Nagl has concluded, "The army that General Westmoreland commanded was a firepower army, one broadly inappropriate to the demands of counterinsurgency warfare in South Vietnam. . . . By failing to learn the lessons of Vietnam, the U.S. Army continued to prepare itself to fight the wrong war."[62]

In the traumatic period following the defeat of the United States in Vietnam, a number of scholars, military officers, and government officials sought to explain "America's longest war" (up to that point in time), and notable among these were the members of the post-Vietnam generation, including H. R. McMaster, John Nagl, and David Petraeus, who wrote his doctoral dissertation at Princeton on the lessons of Vietnam.[63] In his assessment Petraeus concluded, "The lessons taken from Vietnam would indicate that, in general, involvement in a counterinsurgency should be avoided."[64] Ironically, when President George W. Bush appointed General Petraeus commander of U.S. forces in Iraq, Petraeus implemented a counterinsurgency strategy.

When George W. Bush and his advisers were discussing various military strategies for dealing with Saddam Hussein and Iraq, no high-ranking adviser advocated a counterinsurgency strategy. There was, to be sure, significant disagreement about the strategy to be employed, but there were only two principal strategies suggested. The first was the Rumsfeld-Franks transformational strategy emphasizing speed, mobility, technology, and precision weapons. In contrast, many of the top military officers—General Shinseki, General Zinni, and General Shelton—favored a large number of forces to overwhelm the enemy. Secretary of State Colin Powell had expanded and elaborated on his "doctrine," really guidelines, for the United States to follow before using force in international relations, and supported his former Army colleagues. At the end of the day, the Rumsfeld-Franks "transformers" won the debate on the military strategy for the Iraq War, due in part to the fact that prior to and at the beginning of the war, there was no influential institutional or individual advocate of a counterinsurgency strategy at the higher levels of the U.S. government.

Members of the Bush administration were hesitant to acknowledge the existence of an insurgency in Iraq. In May 2005, Vice President Cheney said of the insurgents, "I think they are in the last throes, if you will, of the insurgency."[65] Rumsfeld initially referred to the insurgents as "dead enders" and predicted their eminent demise. As soon as he was appointed commander of Central Command, General John Abizaid contradicted Rumsfeld and labeled what was going on in Iraq "a classical insurgency," thus paving the way for rethinking U.S. strategy.

By 2005, U.S. strategy focused on training Iraqi security forces so that they could take over from American forces; according to President Bush, "[As] the Iraqi forces stand up, coalition forces can stand down."[66] This was the strategy that was presented in a special White House document, *National Strategy for Victory in Iraq*.[67] However, several events called the viability of this strategy into serious question. Just several weeks after the publication of the White House strategy paper, John Murtha, a Democratic congressman from Pennsylvania with a reputation for being strong on defense issues, declared, "Our military has accomplished its mission and done its duty," and that it was time to bring the troops home as soon as possible but no later than six months.[68] In February 2006, al Qaeda terrorists blew up the Golden Dome mosque in Samarra, Iraq, which catalyzed bloody sectarian conflict between Sunnis and Shia. There were several instances in which Iraqi forces simply failed to show up for the fight. At this point, it appeared that rather than a "strategy for victory," U.S. policy was a strategy for defeat, and as Peter Feaver, one of the authors of the strategy, noted, "Over the course of 2006, the National Strategy for Victory in Iraq collapsed."[69]

Only when Iraq seemed to be on the verge of collapse because of the insurgency did President Bush and his advisers begin to consider seriously an alternative military strategy to the conventional, enemy-centric approach employed from the beginning of the war until 2007. A new strategy did not come from the traditional military chain of command; rather, the new approach was initially suggested to President Bush by a retired general, Jack Keane, who had been impressed with the thinking and career of a young general, David Petraeus.[70] Retired General Barry McCaffrey had described Petraeus as the brightest of his cohort of generals.[71] After his first tour of duty in northern Iraq and a second tour in charge of Iraqi military training, Petraeus served as commander of the Combined Arms Center at Fort Leavenworth, Kansas, where he recruited a bright staff including Marine Lieutenant General James Mattis and lieutenant colonels John Nagl and Conrad Crane to rewrite the Army and Marine Corps counterinsurgency manual.[72] Building on classic works of counterinsurgency by T. E. Lawrence, Robert Thompson, and David Galula, the drafters emphasized the "paradoxes of counterinsurgency." "Principles" or "paradoxes" such as these were well and good for war college journal articles or doctoral dissertations, but how and under what circumstances could they be applied to real-world situations?

By the end of 2006, the situation in Iraq was dire, and the American people recognized it as such. In the congressional elections of 2006, the Democrats won control of both the House and the Senate, for the first time since 1994. The day following the election, President Bush accepted Donald Rumsfeld's resignation, a clear signal that the president was moving away from Rumsfeld's policies. The president decided to change U.S. strategy and to send an additional 30,000 American troops to Iraq. Bush's action, however, represented much more than simply sending more troops; rather, it represented the implementation of a true counterinsurgency strategy. What was going on, according to Dr. David Kilcullen, a counterinsurgency expert and an adviser to General Petraeus, was "a counterrevolution in military affairs."[73] Whether or not this counterrevolution will be successful is still not clear; however, it is clear that it has met with greater success than the transformational strategy of Rumsfeld and Franks.

Assessment and Prospects

In his 1987 doctoral dissertation, David Petraeus quoted Army General John Vessey, "We don't learn new lessons. We relearn old lessons that we haven't paid attention to."[74] Donald Rumsfeld wanted to transform the U.S. military by taking advantage of the revolution in military affairs, but the enemy in both Afghanistan and Iraq learned that they could not effectively take on the U.S. military using a conventional military strategy. Thus, they adopted their own revolution in military affairs, insurgency, and in response the U.S. recognized this, adapted to it, and implemented its own counterinsurgency strategy.

Some recent analysts have concluded that Rumsfeld placed higher priority on transformation than U.S. operations in Iraq; according to Bush's chief of staff, Andrew Card, "It's my belief that he [Rumsfeld] had an expectation of what his job would be as secretary of defense, and it probably centered around transformation. . . . And then a war got in the way. Transformation had been a labor of love for him. The war became a labor of responsibility. It was the beautiful siren of transformation that had attracted him to the job, but the shoals ended up being the shoals of war."[75]

But Rumsfeld should not be held primarily responsible for the failure of the strategy he supported in Iraq; that responsibility is shared by George W. Bush, who, after all, as commander-in-chief was Rumsfeld's boss. In addition, it is clear from published memoirs and analyses that Vice President Cheney and his office played a central role in influencing the strategy and tactics of the wars in Afghanistan and Iraq, particularly U.S. policy on detainees and torture.

The British military strategist Basil Liddell Hart defined strategy as "the art of distributing and applying military means to fulfill ends of policy."[76] Another respected international relations expert, Hedley Bull, defined strategy as "exploiting military force so as to attain given objects of policy."[77] The problem with the Bush administration's strategy for the Iraq War is that the "ends of policy" were either not specified or were unattainable, e.g. the establishment of a democratic Iraq and Middle East. T. E. Lawrence defined tactics as "the means toward the strategic goal, the steps of the staircase."[78] The Bush administration's strategic goal was unclear, so it is hardly surprising that the means for achieving that goal, tactics, were also confused.

General Wesley Clark has pointed out that the "U.S. military is as sharp as a diamond-pointed drill bit but as brittle as glass." The U.S. military's sustained operations in Afghanistan and Iraq have increased that brittleness, and these campaigns may, ironically, have a similar effect on the U.S. military as Vietnam. The weakening of the Army is precisely what many post-Vietnam officers sought to avoid, and ironically, the wars in Afghanistan and Iraq may have moved the Army in that direction.

In his memoirs, General Tommy Franks noted, "It's a military axiom that no plan survives initial contact with the enemy."[79] The Bush administration's war plan survived the initial contact with the enemy, but not the postwar operations, and the failure to realistically plan for the occupation and rebuilding of Iraq was a costly mistake for both Americans and Iraqis. It is a mistake that will affect Americans and Iraqis for many years.

10 Postwar Reconstruction

Military strategists consider acute combat to be only one part of war; postwar operations are vital to the execution of a successful campaign. As Richard Haass has noted, "[It] is not enough to have a military that can fight modern wars. It is also essential to have a military that can consolidate peace."[1] In the cases of Afghanistan and Iraq, postwar reconstruction of the countries was both vital and difficult. As previously described in Chapter 9, in any war plan there are four phases, from preparing for conflict to postwar stabilization and reconstruction. In this chapter, I will describe reconstruction planning and operations and then analyze U.S. Phase IV actions toward Afghanistan and Iraq.

Planning for Postwar Reconstruction

During the twentieth century, the United States gained substantial experience in helping other countries to establish postwar stability and reconstruction. Of course, the principal efforts of the United States were in Western Europe and Japan following the conclusion of World War II. In Europe, the U.S. invited both the victorious and vanquished countries to submit plans for their reconstruction to the U.S. through the Marshall Plan, one of the great successes of American foreign policy. Ultimately, the U.S. granted $13 billion of aid to the European states, which enabled them to rebuild their societies. In any reconstruction effort, providing security is the essential prerequisite for other reconstruction tasks. In Europe, the establishment of the North Atlantic Treaty Organization (NATO) provided for the defense of Western Europe and therefore complemented the Marshall Plan.

While the Marshall Plan represented the reconstruction of an entire region, the United States has also assisted with the postwar reconstruction of individual, developing countries, a task that differed significantly in scale from larger scale efforts; however, in both endeavors, providing security was a necessary antecedent to other tasks. Once basic security was assured, four other basics are needed: sewage and trash disposal, water, electricity, and communications capability.[2] It would be impossible for American forces to provide all of these social services; they would have to be provided by locals, but the U.S. could help to provide the basic security and funding for these services to be delivered.

The RAND Corporation, one of the oldest and most respected think tanks in the United States, sponsored a study of seven previous cases of nation-building undertaken by the U.S. government: West Germany (1945–52), Japan (1945–52), Somalia (1992–94), Haiti (1994–96), Bosnia (1995–present), Kosovo (1999–present), and Afghanistan (2001–present).[3] Overall, the RAND study found that successful occupations required enormous investments of resources for a period of five years at a minimum. A key conclusion of the study was: "There appears to be an inverse correlation between the size of the stabilization force and the level of risk. The higher the proportion of stabilizing troops, the lower the number of casualties suffered and inflicted."[4] The study claimed that more rather than fewer peacekeeping forces were desirable and based this conclusion on the analysis of ratios of peacekeepers to civilians in the cases that it examined. In Bosnia and Kosovo, there was one peacekeeper per fifty civilians. If this ratio were to be applied in Afghanistan, then approximately 500,000 peacekeepers would be required, and if applied to Iraq, another 500,000 would be required. As desirable as this commitment might be to establish stability, it clearly was not feasible. What then was the alternative?

Postwar Operations in Afghanistan

The initial objective of the United States in Afghanistan was to get in and get out quickly. As then Deputy Secretary of Defense Paul Wolfowitz noted in November 2001: "In fact, one of the lessons of Afghanistan's history, which we have tried to apply in this campaign, is if you're a foreigner, try not to go in. If you go in, don't stay too long, because they don't tend to like any foreigners who stay too long."[5] At the time that Wolfowitz said this, he was supporting an invasion of Iraq, and that may have been part of the reason that he did not want to "stay too long" in Afghanistan.

The U.S. opted for a "light footprint" deployment of troops on the ground, which necessitated heavy reliance on airpower.[6] According to RAND Corporation analyst Seth Jones, the light footprint approach "was based on the assumption that a heavy footprint would lead to a Soviet- or British-style quagmire."[7] This light footprint approach resulted in the deployment of only 9,000 American and 1,200 coalition troops in Afghanistan within a year of the initial invasion.[8] These troops focused on a narrow counterterrorism mission: to hunt down, capture, or kill members of al Qaeda and remnants of the Taliban. Beyond this objective, there was no strategic plan for Afghanistan's postwar reconstruction and development, a shortsighted failure for which the United States and its allies would have to pay within several years.

Between 2002 and 2005, U.S. troop levels grew modestly from 9,000 to 19,000, a force that paled in comparison to the 145,000 American troops who invaded Iraq in March 2003. Because of the demand for troops in Iraq, the U.S. did not have sufficient forces in Afghanistan to provide for the essential prerequisite of any stabilization force: security of the population. Gary Schroen, the CIA officer who had directed the CIA's effort in Afghanistan after 9/11, recalled, "[As] early as March 2002, the U.S. military began to withdraw many of the key [Special Forces] units involved in this [counterterrorism] effort, in order to allow them to regroup and train in preparation for the coming war with Iraq."[9] Schroen also noted that the "focus on Iraq . . . became a magnet that drew away personnel and resources, making it increasingly difficult to staff the CIA teams in Afghanistan with experienced paramilitary officers."[10] The overall effect of Iraq on the war effort in Afghanistan was crippling; as then Deputy Secretary of State Richard Armitage concluded, "The war in Iraq drained resources from Afghanistan before things were under control. And we never recovered. We never looked back."[11]

Postwar Operations in Iraq

The Rumsfeld-Franks war plan for Iraq failed to accurately predict the nature of the postwar phase of military operations and to adequately plan for what was needed.[12] Phase IV of the Iraq War was designed to be short, and American forces were supposed to begin withdrawing from Iraq within ninety days of the end of the war and to reduce the American presence to 25,000 to 30,000 troops by late summer of 2003.[13] But the political, economic, religious, and ethnic realities in Iraq made the achievement of this plan impossible, and the war dragged on, leading journalist Thomas Ricks to conclude: "It now seems . . . likely that history's judgment will be that the U.S. invasion of Iraq in the spring of 2003 was based on perhaps the worst war plan in American history."[14] What went wrong with postwar operations?

In February 2003, the month before the invasion, Douglas Feith from DOD and Marc Grossman from the State Department briefed members of the Senate Foreign Relations Committee about the administration's postwar plans for Iraq. Grossman noted that the U.S. would "stay as long as necessary in Iraq, but not one day more," and Feith noted, "A lot depends on what the nature of the war is, how much destruction there is, how much cooperation one gets, how many Iraqi units defect. The most you can do in planning is develop concepts on how you would proceed, not rigid plans based on some inflexible assumptions about how future events are going to unfold." Senator Joseph Biden was not satisfied with the vague, general presentations from the two administration officials and commented, "One of the things [we] are worried about is that you don't have a plan."[15] In fact, Biden was correct; if the administration's assumptions concerning the short duration of the occupation were incorrect, there was no systematic back-up plan.

Plan A: Get In and Get Out Quickly

As the United States moved toward war, both the U.S. government and various think tanks and policy organizations focused their attention on the requirements for postwar operations in Iraq. The State Department, RAND Corporation, Council on Foreign Relations, Center for International and Strategic Studies, Army War College, U.S. Institute of Peace, National Defense University, Washington Institute for Near East Policy, and Atlantic Council of the United States all produced studies of what was needed in postwar Iraq.[16] The historical record is clear: there was no shortage of thinking about postwar Iraq; in fact, there was a great deal of thinking about the issues. What were the conclusions of these studies, and was there any consensus?

In April 2002, the State Department organized the Future of Iraq Project, which involved seventeen U.S. federal agencies, was headed by a veteran State Department official, Tom Warrick, and ultimately cost $5 million. It involved 240 Iraqis and produced a thirteen-volume study focusing on a number of diverse issues including the generation of electricity, the running of ports, and social and economic issues in Iraq.[17] The group's report did not present an operational plan for postwar Iraq, but it did address many of the issues that would confront those responsible for postwar Iraq. Warrick pressed hard for the State

Department to be in charge of postwar operations, but DOD and the vice president's office opposed him and his boss, Colin Powell. So postwar planning became a bureaucratic battle within Washington. On January 20, 2003, Rumsfeld was successful in getting President Bush to sign National Security Presidential Directive number 24, giving the Department of Defense complete control over postwar planning and operations in Iraq.[18] Two months before the war began, retired Army Lieutenant General Jay Garner was appointed to be in charge of postwar operations in Iraq, to be called the Office for Reconstruction and Humanitarian Assistance (ORHA). Garner's contact in the Pentagon, Douglas Feith, told him he would be in Iraq for only ninety days. The decision for DOD to run postwar operations in Iraq was significant because it was the first time since World War II that the State Department was not given the responsibility for taking charge of a postwar situation.[19] As Ambassador James Dobbins noted, "The decision to transfer civilian aspects of reconstruction from the State Department to the Pentagon imposed immense costs as Defense had not handled anything like it [Iraqi reconstruction] for at least 50 years, while State garnered considerable experience over the previous decade."[20] Yet, much of this experience had been lost. The U.S. Agency for International Development (AID) had shrunk from 13,000 staff members during the Vietnam War to only 2,300 by 2001. At the height of the Vietnam War, one of every twenty-five AID employees was in Vietnam; during the occupation of Iraq, only one of every 333 AID employees was in Iraq.[21] The amount of money committed to economic and military assistance had also declined dramatically; during Vietnam, the United States spent 2 percent of its gross domestic product on assistance to Vietnam; in Iraq, the U.S. spent less than one-fifth of 1 percent.[22]

Before he left for Iraq, Garner held a series of meetings with experts and he recalled, "There was this one guy who knew everything, everybody," and that was Tom Warrick.[23] When Garner asked him how he knew so much, Warrick told him about the Future of Iraq Project, and Garner then asked him to come to work for him. Warrick worked briefly for Garner and then was fired, reportedly on orders from Rumsfeld and Cheney.[24] So, one of the most knowledgeable people about postwar Iraq within the U.S. government was excluded from working on the topic about which he was an expert. The firing of Warrick illustrated the serious interagency problems that existed.

The original U.S. postwar plan for Iraq was to "get in and get out" quickly; in short, the Iraqis were to be put in charge as soon as possible, and President Bush had approved this plan. Three regional conferences were held in February and April 2003 to discuss and plan for the turnover of power to the Iraqis. General Garner and Zalmay Khalilzad had wanted to hold a nationwide meeting of influential Iraqis in May 2003, but Bremer canceled the planned meeting and the quick turnover of the government to the Iraqis. Bremer not only replaced Garner; he also asked Bush to terminate Khalilzad's status as a presidential envoy, thus ending his involvement with postwar planning for Iraq. Rumsfeld, Powell, Rice, and Khalilzad were all surprised by the president's action, which cleared the decks for Bremer to determine the direction of postwar Iraq.[25]

Key to the future of Iraq was the issue of security. If the ratio of peacekeepers to civilians that the RAND Corporation had concluded was needed were applied to Iraq, a peacekeeping force of almost 500,000 would be required, but that clearly went far beyond what DOD was willing to commit. Soon after, Paul Bremer was appointed to replace Garner as the head of the American occupation of Iraq. Although he was an experienced diplomat, Bremer had never been posted in the Middle East, did not speak Arabic, and was ideologically a neoconservative. According to author and filmmaker Charles Ferguson, "Nobody I interviewed ever questioned Bremer's work ethic, his dedication, or his courage. . . . At the same time, the overwhelming majority of those with whom I spoke also felt that Bremer was rigid, authoritarian, ideological, arrogant, and unwilling to listen to ideas contrary to his own."[26] James Dobbins, the principal author of the RAND study on reconstruction and nation-building, visited Bremer in his Pentagon office and gave him a draft copy of the report. Bremer read the study and recalled in his memoirs, "Although I was not a military expert, I found the conclusions persuasive. And troubling."[27] Bremer gave a copy of the report to Rumsfeld but never received a response to it. Rumsfeld and his aides had a plan for Iraq and would not allow it to be derailed by the "reality-based community."

Plan B: The American Occupation under Ambassador Bremer

The failure to provide security became obvious for the world to see in the days following the entry of the U.S. Army into Baghdad when many Iraqis took to the streets and for a three-week period looted government ministries, office buildings, Saddam's palaces, and other targets of opportunity. Tom Warrick, the director of the State Department's Future of Iraq Project, had provided the ORHA a list of the vulnerable sites to be secured after the invasion, but either this list was not passed on to the military field commanders, or it was ignored.[28]

Even the Iraqi National Museum was pillaged; one of the few sites that ORHA protected from looting was the oil ministry, which, of course, led many Iraqis to conclude that the U.S. had invaded and occupied Iraq for only one reason: oil. The U.S. government's response to the looting exacerbated the problems. Bremer favored changing the military's rules of engagement to authorize American soldiers to shoot looters. When this proposal was leaked to the press, it caused such a furor that this change was not adopted.[29] When Rumsfeld was asked about the looting, he responded, "Think what's happened in our cities when we've had riots and problems and looting. Stuff happens. . . . Freedom's untidy, and free people are free to make mistakes and commit crimes and do bad things."[30]

There were significant costs to the failure of the U.S. to respond to looting effectively. Seventeen of the twenty-three ministries in Baghdad were looted, which crippled them from acting effectively following the liberation of Iraq. The economic cost was estimated to be $12 billion.[31] Images of the looters contrasted with the images of Saddam's statues being pulled down and destroyed and raised questions about the effectiveness of the U.S. occupation. Bremer himself later admitted, "We paid a big price for not stopping [the looting] because it established an atmosphere of lawlessness."[32]

What could have been done to prevent or reduce the looting? Changing the rules of engagement could have reduced the looting, but could also have increased Iraqi antipathy toward American forces more quickly. A more effective means of reducing the looting would have been to increase the number of troops patrolling the streets. As Major General Paul Eaton, who was in charge of rebuilding Iraqi military forces in 2003–4, noted, "There is no way that the number of soldiers that we had on the ground could have prevented that looting. . . . There was just no where near enough soldiers to provide the security coverage of that nation."[33] When asked what could have been done to stop the looting, Deputy Secretary of State Richard Armitage replied, "It could have been done if you had a sufficient number of troops. But I don't think, given the number of troops that were used in the initial attack, there was sufficient force to prevent the looting."[34] Because there were not enough U.S. troops to provide security, and because the Iraqi army was disbanded, errors compounded, and the situation in Iraq worsened.

The shortage of troops affected not only the domestic situation in Iraq; it also had an impact on insurgents coming into Iraq. General Garner noted, "We did not seal the borders because we did not have enough troops to do that, and that brought in terrorists."[35] Because of the porous Iraqi borders, Iraq became a kind of advanced training ground for members of al Qaeda and other Islamic, radical terrorist groups, and they viewed it as such. Members of the coalition captured terrorists from countries around the world who came to Iraq to engage in *jihad* against the Americans and their allies.

Ambassador Bremer arrived in Baghdad on May 11, 2003, and within two months recognized that there were not enough troops in the country. On a trip to Washington, Bremer told NSC advisor Condoleezza Rice, "In my view, the Coalition's got about *half* the number of soldiers we need here and we run a real risk of having this thing go south on us."[36] Despite the conclusions of General Shinseki, the RAND Corporation, and the two principal American decision-makers in Iraq, the Pentagon resisted sending more troops; it had a plan, and it was not going to divert from it even in the face of tangible evidence that more troops were needed. As journalist Michael Gordon and retired Marine General Bernard Trainor concluded, "The violent chaos that followed Saddam's defeat was not a matter of not having a plan but of adhering too rigidly to the wrong one."[37]

The failure of the United States to send enough troops to Iraq was exacerbated by the first two orders that Bremer promulgated soon after his arrival in Iraq. The Baath Party had approximately 1.5 million members under Saddam Hussein, but of these only about 25,000 were active party members. On May 16, 2003, just four days after his arrival in Baghdad, Bremer issued Coalition Provisional Authority (CPA) Order Number 1 calling for the "de-Baathification" of Iraq.[38] At the time that this order was issued, unemployment in Iraq was more than 50 percent. Disqualifying, in effect firing, members of the Baath Party increased unemployment and alienation significantly and contributed to the growing insurgency movement within Iraq. Like so many of the issues concerning Iraq, the de-Baathification order reflected the bureaucratic battle in Washington. For its part, the State Department had favored a "de-Saddamification," a policy that would have prohibited two classes of Baathists from participating in the government: those who had committed crimes and those who were at the top of the leadership structure. Vice President Cheney, Secretary of Defense Rumsfeld, and their staffs favored comprehensive de-Baathification, and the order was implemented on the president's guidance, according to Bremer.[39]

Ahmed Chalabi, the Iraqi Shia exile leader favored by DOD, was put in charge of de-Baathification and broadened the scope of the order from its original relatively narrow scope to include, for example, teachers who had joined the party in order to keep their jobs. In his memoirs, Bremer admits that this was a significant error: "Clearly I had been wrong to give a political body like the Governing Council responsibility for overseeing the de-Baathification policy."[40] Likewise, the Iraq Study Group acknowledged the error of de-Baathification when it noted, "Political reconciliation requires the reintegration of Baathists and Arab nationalists into national life, with the leading figures of Saddam Hussein's regime excluded."[41] The former commander of American military forces in Iraq, General Ricardo Sanchez, concluded, "[T]he whole de-Baathification order became a catastrophic failure."[42] Political scientist and former State Department official Dale Herspring has noted, "[D]e-Baathification probably did more to disrupt efforts to get the country running smoothly than anything al-Qaeda could have done."[43]

On May 23, eleven days after arriving in Baghdad, Bremer issued CPA Order Number 2 calling for the dissolution of the Iraqi army, the defense ministry, and Iraq's intelligence agencies.[44] In Bremer's view, the Iraqi military had "self-demobilized," members of the military had simply left their units and bases and gone home.[45] In fact, this is precisely what the U.S. military had requested of Iraqi military units. Other reasons were presented for disbanding the Iraqi military. Some noted that the Iraqi military infrastructure and bases had been either destroyed in the war or looted following the U.S. victory. Shia complained that Sunnis had dominated and controlled Saddam's military and that the officer corps was corrupt, ineffective, and politicized. In addition, Shia leaders, particularly the Grand Ayatollah Sistani, were opposed to the reconstitution of the Iraqi military.

CPA Order Number 2 fired the 385,000 members of the armed forces, 285,000 interior ministry forces, and 50,000 presidential security personnel for a total of 720,000 people.[46] Despite the significance of this order, the top foreign policy officials of the Bush administration, including Secretary of State Colin Powell, national security adviser Condoleezza Rice, and her deputy Stephen Hadley, vice chairman of the Joint Chiefs of Staff, General Peter Pace, and General Jay Garner, Bremer's predecessor, did not know about the order until it was issued.[47] This order had profound economic and security implications for Iraqi society and the American occupation. The average Iraqi family contains six people, so CPA Order Number 2 affected the lives of more than 4 million Iraqis, about 17 percent of Iraq's total population.[48] In his report to Rumsfeld of July 2003, president of the Center for Security and International

Studies John Hamre concluded, "Iraq is a completely failed economy. The CPA is confronting the equivalent of both a defeated Germany in 1945 and a failed Soviet Union in 1989."[49]

When Garner heard about the impending disbanding of Iraqi security forces, he went to Bremer with the CIA Baghdad station chief and strongly objected. Garner recalled, "I thought it [CPA Order #2] was a poor idea. I thought we needed to bring them [Iraqi military and security forces] back."[50] The CIA officer who accompanied Garner told Bremer that the order would only "give oxygen to the rejectionists."[51] Military leaders including General Franks and his successor, General Abizaid, and General McKiernan, the commander of U.S. forces in Iraq, were all opposed to disbanding the Iraqi military.[52] Those military officers on the ground responsible for providing security in Iraq were also critical of this order; former U.S. Army brigade commander Colonel Peter Mansoor noted, "When Ambassador Bremer disbanded the Iraqi army, the immediate Iraqi capability to provide security disappeared."[53] The order was issued without discussing it with CIA Director Tenet, and there is some evidence that the order may have been issued without President Bush's advance knowledge.[54] Bush told journalist Robert Draper that disbanding the Iraqi military was not his policy and that he was not sure why it occurred.[55] In response to this claim, Bremer published a letter that he sent to President Bush on May 22, 2003, that stated, "I will parallel this step [dismissal of public servants] with an even more robust measure dissolving Saddam's military and intelligence structures to emphasize that we mean business."[56] In addition, Bremer claimed that he sent a draft copy of the order to disband the Iraqi security forces to Rumsfeld, Wolfowitz, Feith, and Lieutenant General David McKiernan on May 9 and that he and Rumsfeld's adviser in Baghdad, Walter Slocombe, had discussed the order in detail.[57]

With the promulgation of CPA Orders 1 and 2, the United States disqualified former Baathists and members of Iraqi defense forces from participating with the Coalition Provisional Authority in the rebuilding of their country. Rumsfeld's decision not to send enough American troops to Iraq and Bremer's decision to disband the Iraqi military had a multiplicative, negative effect and made it difficult to provide for the absolute necessity of any successful postwar occupation, security. According to Michael Gordon and Bernard Trainor, "In their own way, Rumsfeld and Bremer each contributed to the security problem. Rumsfeld limited the number of troops in Iraq, and Bremer limited the number of Iraqi forces that were immediately available. The two decisions combined to produce a much larger security vacuum."[58] In an interview that he gave after leaving Iraq, General Garner recalled, "The force levels weren't high enough at the end of the war. They were more than high enough to win the war, but not high enough at the end of the war."[59] Charles Duelfer, the U.S. official who was in charge of a comprehensive study of the weapons of mass destruction issue, characterized the first and second CPA directives succinctly: "With these two decisions, the United States had committed irreversible damage."[60]

The CPA: "Can't Provide Anything"

The shortage of troops to provide security was critical; however, innovative, creative civilian leadership could have made up part of this deficit. Having disqualified former Baathists from participating in the government, the Coalition Provisional Authority had to rely on its own resources for establishing the new government. Despite the large numbers of Americans going to Iraq at the end of combat operations, the CPA was chronically understaffed, and there were several causes and effects of this.[61] First, many Iraqis were denied the opportunity to gain experience in running a government during the transitional period of the occupation, and these exclusions added to the demands on the CPA. Second, many jobs simply did not get done, or done well, given the pressures on staff members. Third, the CPA relied heavily on exiled Iraqis, such as Ahmed Chalabi, Nuri al Maliki, Ayad Allawi, and Ali Allawi, who had been out of the country for decades and only returned with the end of military operations. Some of these were competent, but others were marginally qualified. General Franks, for example, referred to Chalabi as "a 'Gucci leader' who would never be able to unite the ethnic and religious factions."[62] Noah Feldman, a CPA adviser, referring to the overly ambitious character with a shady past in F. Scott Fitzgerald's novel, called Chalabi "the Jay Gatsby of the Iraq War."[63] Fourth, given the shortage of qualified Iraqis, the CPA relied on a number of young, inexperienced advisers. Jay Hallen, a twenty-four-year-old recent graduate of Yale who had majored in political science and who had never studied economics or finance, was put in charge of establishing the Iraqi stock exchange.[64] Another twenty-five-year-old helped write Iraq's interim constitution while he was completing his law school application.[65] A recent Georgetown graduate was assigned to develop a traffic plan for Baghdad despite the fact that he had no previous experience in city planning. One CIA officer in Baghdad sent his impressions to Tenet one month after the CPA had taken over: "Boss, that place [the CPA] runs like a graduate school seminar, none of them speaks Arabic, almost nobody's ever been to an Arab country, and no one makes a decision but Bremer."[66] A former member of the CPA, Heather Coyne, admitted that the CPA represented "amateur hour in Iraq."[67]

In retrospect, an obvious question is why were such ill-prepared people assigned such important jobs? Colonel Paul Hughes, who worked for both Garner's Office of Reconstruction and Humanitarian Assistance and Bremer's CPA, recalled, "We were getting new people in, after Bremer showed up. Kids right out of college. . . . They'd have a baccalaureate degree; just got it in the fall, the previous spring. Daddy made a contribution to the campaign, so the kid gets a chance to go over and experience some fun travel and adventure. Pretty boys, that's what I called 'em."[68] So, political connections helped get one a job in the CPA. Religion helped too. Jacob Weisberg has pointed out that the head of the White House Office of Personnel, Kay Coles James, had previously served as dean at evangelical Pat Robertson's Regent University and as vice president of conservative Christian Gary Bauer's Family Research Council. According to Weisberg, she ordered the placement of evangelical Christians in important positions at the departments of Justice, Interior, State, Health and Human Services, the FDA, NASA, and the CDC. Reportedly, applicants to the Coalition Provisional Authority in Iraq "were vetted for evangelical status—not because it mattered to their work, but on the straight-forward principle of patronage."[69]

Three months after the successful U.S. invasion, only three or four CPA officials spoke Arabic fluently, and at the time that the Iraq Study Group prepared its report, it noted that the situation with regard to linguists had not changed much: of the 1,000 Americans at its embassy in Baghdad, there were thirty-three Arabic speakers, and of these only six were fluent.[70] The problems caused by the shortage of personnel, inexperience, and downright incompetence of the coalition authority were exacerbated by short tours of duty; as General Eaton noted, "[As] soon as somebody [in the CPA] would develop the appropriate relationships with the Iraqis, in ninety days, a hundred days, a hundred and twenty days, they'd go home."[71]

The obvious inexperience, clear incompetence, and resulting ineffectiveness of some Coalition Provisional Authority officials caused some in the military to quip that CPA stood for "Can't Provide Anything." Paul Bremer arrived in Baghdad on May 11, 2003, and stayed until June 28, 2004. During that time, three fateful strategic decisions were made: (1) to prohibit former members of the Baath Party from participating in the new Iraqi government, (2) to disband Iraqi military and security forces, and (3) to delay the return of sovereignty to Iraqi officials. Bremer's three decisions changed the role of the United States in Iraq from that of liberator to that of occupier with significant, long-term, costly implications.

Plan C: Sovereignty Turned over to Iraq

The ultimate U.S. objective of all of the postwar plans for Iraq was to turn over sovereign control of their country to Iraqi leaders, and everyone involved believed that security was the prerequisite for such action. When the Bush administration decided not to send the number of troops requested by the military to Iraq and when Ambassador Bremer decided to disband Iraqi military and security forces, security proved to be impossible to achieve. As former CIA official Paul Pillar noted, "Reconstruction has fared poorly above all, because of the security situation."[72] Security, then, was a prerequisite for turning over sovereignty to the new Iraqi government.

The most effective way to provide security, short of sending more American forces to Iraq or reconstituting the Iraqi army and security forces, was to train new Iraqi security forces. This proved to be problematic for several reasons. Gerald Burke, an adviser to the Iraqi police with fifteen years of experience training law enforcement officers in Haiti, Bosnia, and elsewhere, estimated—based on the population and geography of Iraq—that a police force of 20,000 would be needed. Burke and his fellow advisers realized that this was an unreasonable number and decided to provide training for 6,000.[73] When the insurgency was just developing, there were a total of fifty trained police advisers in Iraq trying to train a planned force of 150,000 to 200,000 officers. This was simply not feasible.[74] T. X. Hammes, a Marine colonel who specialized in the study of guerilla warfare, commented, "It is clear that the only way you get out of Iraq is to train Iraqi security forces. . . . This administration failed to do that."[75]

The shortage of police trainers was not the only reason that it proved impossible to provide security with Iraqi forces. The insurgents realized that American-trained security forces were key to the success of the U.S. occupation, and they, therefore, targeted Iraqi soldiers and police. From the beginning of the occupation in May 2003 through late 2007, more than 7,500 Iraqi soldiers and police officers had been killed, and many of these were killed execution-style to deter other Iraqis from volunteering for the army or police.[76] Ambassador Bremer admitted, "The biggest obstacle has been the failure to provide adequate security for the Iraqi people."[77]

In April 2003, Dr. Larry Diamond, whom Condoleezza Rice asked to go to Iraq to advise the CPA, wrote a prophetic memo to Bremer: "The road to democracy in postconflict situations is littered with the corpses of transitions that failed because they could not establish this most basic condition [security] of a viable state."[78] On May 16, 2003, Bremer announced that the establishment of an interim government with sovereign authority would be indefinitely postponed. Ultimately, the U.S. turned over sovereign control to the Iraqi government on June 28, 2004, and even supporters of the war were critical of this decision. Under-Secretary of Defense for Policy Douglas Feith commented, "All in all, the fourteen-month occupation of Iraq was a self-inflicted wound. It was the product of a handful of thoughts that turned out to be wrong. . . . The occupation was long and, in my view, unnecessary."[79]

Other Postwar Plans

As the occupation wore on and as the insurgency grew, other plans were considered. Senator Joseph Biden, Dr. Leslie Gelb (former president of the Council on Foreign Relations), diplomat Peter Galbraith, and some Kurds favored the partition or decentralization of Iraq into Shia, Sunni, and Kurdish states or regions.[80] Biden and Gelb favored dividing Iraq into three "autonomous regions" with a central government in Baghdad that would be responsible for border defense, foreign policy, and collecting and distributing oil revenues. Ambassador Galbraith favored the establishment of three independent states.

The principal problem with the partition/decentralization plan is that about 40 percent of the Iraqi population lives in mixed areas, particularly in Baghdad. Determining which areas belonged to which ethnic group was very difficult to do. In addition, countries neighboring Iraq did not favor a formal partition. Lastly, if politics is "who gets what, how and when," as political scientist Harold Lasswell famously observed, then the collection and distribution of Iraq's significant oil revenues could become very contentious. As a result of these potential problems, the Bush administration dismissed the idea of partition as a "nonstarter," and many Sunnis and Shia opposed the idea believing that they might get less than they deserve.

Provincial Reconstruction Teams

Once the kinetic phase of war ends, postwar operations begin, and a key requirement in this phase is to improve stability in the host nation so that it can deliver basic services and begin the process of economic and political reconstruction. Several months after the invasion of Afghanistan, "Coalition Humanitarian Liaison Cells," consisting of ten to twelve military personnel, were created to assess humanitarian and reconstruction needs.[81] In late 2002, this function was taken over with the creation of the first Provincial Reconstruction Team (PRT) that was established at Gardez; seven more were created in 2003. These units were staffed primarily by military personnel and were commanded by a military officer with the rank of lieutenant colonel.

The establishment of PRTs reflected the past history of the United States in counterinsurgency and reconstruction. For example, in its campaign to defeat the Philippine insurgency from 1899 to 1902, the U.S. established more than 500 small garrisons throughout the country.[82] Many years later, the United States established the Civil Operations and Rural Development Support (CORDS) program in Vietnam to provide development assistance in Vietnam. Civilian government officials primarily staffed CORDS; for example, in the I Corps area, only 750 of 2,000 CORDS personnel were military, and these officials had received four to six months of Vietnamese language training prior to their eighteen- to twenty-four-month assignments.

In contrast to the CORDS program, PRTs in Afghanistan were primarily staffed by military personnel including a commanding officer, two Army civil affairs teams, a military police unit, a psychological operations unit, an explosive ordnance/demining team, an intelligence unit, medics, a force protection unit, and administrative and support personnel. Civilian departments and agencies—primarily the Department of State and the Agency for International Development—had a difficult time providing personnel to staff the PRTs. In the early years, the Provincial Reconstruction Teams often only had one junior-level civilian official who was often on a ninety-day assignment, hardly enough time to develop situational awareness or personal relationships with local leaders.[83] In June 2005, the State Department had only thirteen Foreign Service Officers serving in PRTs, and even by 2008, out of a total of 1,055 personnel assigned to PRTs in Afghanistan, there were only thirty-four civilians from State, USAID and the Department of Agriculture.[84]

TABLE 10.1
Provisional Reconstruction Teams (PRT) in Afghanistan and Iraq

Year	Afghanistan	Iraq
2002	First PRT established	
2003	8	
2004	14	
2005	22	First PRT established
2006	23	10
2007	25	25
2008	26	31
2009	26	22
2010	27	16

Source: Compiled by the author from various sources.

The mission of the PRTs was threefold: to enhance security, to strengthen the reach of the central Afghan government, and to facilitate reconstruction.[85] At times, these goals conflicted with military missions. For example, the PRTs would attempt to improve relationships with local leaders only to have U.S. military units raid and/or arrest the very leaders with whom they were trying to develop improved relationships. Despite problems, when he took over in Afghanistan in November 2003, Lieutenant General David Barno almost doubled the number of PRTs from eight to fourteen in less than a year. By 2005, there were twenty-two PRTs in Afghanistan, and they were viewed as "one of the few efforts in Afghanistan to approach military S&R [stabilization and reconstruction] tasks in a coordinated fashion at the tactical level."[86] By 2010 there were 27 PRTs in Afghanistan, and the number of civilians relative to military staff had increased significantly.

On November 11, 2005, Secretary of State Condoleezza Rice announced the founding of the first Provincial Reconstruction Team for Iraq, and Table 10.1 summarizes the number of PRTs in both Afghanistan and Iraq. But the Iraqi PRTs differed significantly from those in Afghanistan. In Iraq, a State Department official, not a military officer, was in charge, and the PRTs were staffed mostly by civilians. By the end of 2006, there were ten PRTs in Iraq, followed by twenty-five in 2007, and thirty-one in 2008. According to President Bush, the teams helped "local Iraqi communities pursue reconciliation, strengthen the moderates, and speed the transition to self-reliance."[87] Some of those in Iraq, however, disagreed that these objectives were being achieved. Colonel Peter Mansoor, the commander of the 1st Combat Brigade, 1st Armored Division, in Baghdad from 2003 to 2004 and later the executive officer to General

David Petraeus, noted, "Only in 2007 were provincial reconstruction teams embedded with combat teams across Iraq, thereby providing a powerful tool to assist brigade commanders in accomplishing their mission. Regrettably, the change came four years too late."[88] There were two main stumbling blocks in deploying the teams in a timely fashion: the State Department wanted assurance that security would be provided for their personnel, and Rumsfeld was unenthusiastic about committing military forces to provide security. According to a State Department official interviewed by Tom Ricks, "The president would say, 'Get this done,' and leave the room. . . . And then Rumsfeld would start squabbling with Condi—'We're not gonna secure your PRTs!' "[89] The debate concerning these issues caused a delay in fully deploying the teams and embedding them with combat units.[90]

There were other problems as well.[91] One was the ongoing staffing problem. As of July 2008, State had 230 personnel deployed to PRTs in Iraq, USAID had ninety-five, and DOD had only ninety personnel in PRTs in Iraq. In some cases, military personnel were assigned to PRTs outside of their training and specializations. For example, RAND analyst Seth Jones describes meeting and interviewing a PRT leader, Commander Larry Legere, in landlocked Afghanistan; he was a nuclear-trained naval surface warfare officer who had previously served on an aircraft carrier, a destroyer, and an amphibious landing ship. According to Commander Legere, "The four and a half months I spent at Fort Bragg in North Carolina before deploying to Afghanistan was about the only preparation I had. I learned how to wear body armor and shoot, move, and communicate, but didn't learn any real fundamentals about counter-insurgency."[92]

The United States was decisively and rapidly successful in defeating the forces of al Qaeda and the Taliban in Afghanistan and the Iraqi army. It was far less successful in capturing or killing the leaders of al Qaeda and the Afghan Taliban and in dealing with postwar reconstruction in both countries. Many of the assumptions that the U.S. made—such as the reception of American soldiers—proved not to be the case, and U.S. forces paid for these mistaken assumptions in blood and lives. The disbanding of Iraqi security forces and the Baath Party contributed to the failure to provide security in postwar Iraq, and the withdrawal of U.S. soldiers, particularly Special Forces, from Afghanistan to Iraq lessened the effectiveness of the U.S. there. As Ahmed Rashid has pointed out, "In Iraq, the United States committed too much money for reconstruction when stability had not been established. In Afghanistan, the United States committed too little money for reconstruction."[93] In both countries, the United States attempted to restore order and stability with a combination of military and civilian efforts, most notably the Provincial Reconstruction Teams, but these were often marked by a lack of coordination, amateurish efforts, and an ad hoc approach.

11 Policymaking

Making sense of policymaking in supposedly open societies can sometimes be as hard as penetrating the mysteries of closed societies.[1]

—Sir Lawrence Freedman

The Constitution of the United States delineates the powers and responsibilities of the government for making and implementing American foreign policy; Article I grants the Congress some specific powers, and Article II grants the executive branch the principal responsibility for foreign policymaking. But the references to foreign policymaking are general and brief, and because of this, one scholar characterized constitutional provisions concerning foreign policy as "an invitation to struggle" between the congressional and executive branches. Because of the ambiguity of constitutional provisions related to foreign policy, various presidential administrations have developed differing conceptions of presidential control over foreign policy. In addition, foreign policymaking within the executive branch is often contentious. In this chapter, I will describe: (1) the approach of the George W. Bush administration to foreign policymaking, (2) congressional-executive relations concerning U.S. policy toward Afghanistan, Pakistan, and Iraq, and (3) the divisions within the executive branch.

Foreign Policymaking in the George W. Bush Administration

Although the Constitution is vague about the particulars of foreign policymaking, the Constitution set general responsibilities: the president and the executive branch would develop and implement foreign policy, and the congressional branch would oversee it. Over time, the Department of State became the lead department in making and implementing foreign policy.

The National Security Act of 1947 established the National Security Council (NSC) as an advisory body in the executive branch and as the principal body to advise the president about foreign and national defense issues. In terms of organizational theory, the NSC had a "staff" advisory function rather than a "line" or implementing function. Different presidents and their NSC advisers, however, interpreted the functions of the NSC very differently. For example, the Nixon National Security Council under Henry Kissinger often operated as a line agency, contrasting with the NSC of the George H. W. Bush administration under General Brent Scowcroft that operated as a classic staff advisory agency.[2] The principal function of the NSC was to present options to the president and to provide coherence in an administration's foreign policy.

When members of the Bush administration entered office in January 2001, as noted previously in Chapter 6, many members of the new administration's foreign and national security officials had worked together before and had substantial policymaking experience. Both international relations specialists and members of the public assumed that this group would work together as a team and that U.S. foreign policy was in competent hands.

Other than the president, Vice President Dick Cheney was the most powerful influence on foreign policy in the administration. As Michael Gordon and Bernard Trainor have noted, "Cheney was, by common consent, the most powerful vice president in history," a view seconded by Bob Woodward, Jane Mayer, and others.[3] Among Bush's advisers, Cheney was clearly *primus inter pares*; Cheney himself told his biographer, "I'm not a staffer, I'm the vice president, a constitutional officer, *elected same as he* [the president] *is*."[4] Because the vice president was elected, he did not serve at the pleasure of the president and could not be fired. This gave him a degree of independence and leeway that other advisers did not have, and he exercised his power in several principal ways. First, he promoted an expansive view of executive power, and according to this view, the presidential power was virtually unlimited. Second, Cheney supported the appointment of government officials who supported this view of presidential power. Perhaps the most important of these officials was Cheney's mentor and good friend, Donald Rumsfeld, as secretary of defense. Third, Cheney and his staff took an active role in the policymaking process. Fourth, because he lacked experience and background in international relations, President Bush essentially handed the administration's foreign policy portfolio to Cheney, who had both substantial background and interest in these issues.

Members of the Bush administration had an expansive view of presidential power and relied heavily on those advisers who held this view. A number of those who served in the George W. Bush administration had previously served in the Nixon administration and believed that the Watergate scandal had badly skewed the balance of power between the congressional and executive branches. Furthermore, many of the same people were bothered by the conclusions of the majority report that investigated the Iran-Contra scandal of the Reagan administration. At the time of the scandal, Cheney was a member of the House of Representatives and the ranking minority Republican member on the committee investigating Iran-Contra. When the majority issued its report, which was critical of the Reagan administration, Cheney and the other minority members with the contributions of David Addington and others issued their own report, which argued that President Reagan had been motivated to act by "a legitimate frustration with abuses of power and irresolution by the legislative branch."[5]

Frustrated and concerned by increasing congressional involvement in foreign policy and wanting to defend the Reagan administration against congressional attacks, a number of legal scholars such as Samuel Alito and Steven Calabresi, a founder of the conservative Federalist Society, developed a theory of the "unitary executive." Alito argued that the president should not just exercise "some executive powers—but *the* executive power—the whole thing."[6] Cheney and Addington strongly supported the "unitary executive" view that Congress could not unduly limit presidential power during wartime, and there were a number of other supporters of this view in the Bush administration. For example, John C. Yoo, a third tier official, a deputy assistant attorney general in the Department of Justice, had previously written that the president has "plenary powers" as commander-in-chief that belonged exclusively to the president. Yoo argued that the president is the "sole organ of the nation in its foreign relations" and that the president may "violate international law and treaties, if he so chooses."[7] As journalist and Cheney biographer Barton Gellman noted, "Yoo never rose above deputy assistant attorney general, but he was the fulcrum of the lever that Cheney pulled to move the world."[8] President Bush came to accept the expansive view of presidential power. In an exit interview with former Justice Department official James Comey, President Bush commented, "I decide what the law is for the executive branch."[9] Apparently, President Bush, who called himself "the Decider," could determine whether the U.S. government would observe the prohibition of torture as mandated by international legal treaties and agreements. Those in the Office of Legal Counsel (OLC) in the Justice Department argued, "[T]he President could argue that torture was legal because he authorized it. The commander in chief, according to the OLC, had inherent powers to order any interrogation technique he chose."[10] According to this view, the president could also decide that the U.S. government should not abide by the provisions of the internationally recognized Geneva Accords concerning the treatment of prisoners of war, and following the American attack on Afghanistan in October 2001, at the recommendation of John Yoo, President Bush announced that the United States would not observe the Geneva Accords. The president had made his decision without consulting Secretary of State Powell, a former chairman of the Joint Chiefs of Staff, or the top American military leaders, the chairman and vice chairman of the JCS, generals Myers and Pace, all of whom strongly objected to the president's decision. Later, at the recommendation of Cheney and his staff, the government announced that to try detainees it would establish military commissions, which had not been used since World War II.[11]

Vice President Cheney and his staff strongly influenced many of the key foreign policy decisions in the Bush administration. A master of bureaucratic politics and behind the scenes policy machinations, Cheney was often able to manipulate the interagency system to produce the recommendations that he favored and that carried the day with Bush. Once policy was determined, the president and vice president often gave the Department of Defense responsibility for implementing it. In many ways Cheney was the architect for the Bush administration's foreign policy, and Rumsfeld was the contractor, the policymaker responsible for translating Cheney's decisions into actual programs and policies. Because of the trust that both Bush and Cheney placed in Rumsfeld, his previous service as secretary, and his force of personality, Rumsfeld became the most powerful secretary of defense since Robert McNamara.

Having previously served in government for many years, Cheney and Rumsfeld understood the importance of making personnel appointments that reflected their policy views, and they worked hard to make sure that the views of those appointed to the Bush administration were close to their own. For example, they insisted that the secretary of state appoint hard-line, neoconservative John Bolton as the State Department official in charge of arms control. Not only would Bolton slow down or block arms control initiatives, he could also report back to Cheney and Rumsfeld about what was happening in the State Department. Cheney's and Rumsfeld's interest in appointments extended down the bureaucratic pecking order to include second or third tier officials. When Jay Garner appointed Tom Warrick, the director of the Future of Iraq

Project, and Meghan O'Sullivan to be on his staff, Rumsfeld called Garner and told him that they would be unacceptable and that he could not appoint them. Garner later noted that everyone thought that the order not to hire Warrick and O'Sullivan came from Cheney's office.[12] Rumsfeld was also proactive in the appointment of senior officers who led the military. In late August 2001, President Bush announced the appointment of Air Force General Richard Myers as chairman of the Joint Chiefs of Staff (JCS), the first Air Force officer to hold this position in more than two decades.[13] Myers was sympathetic to Rumsfeld's ideas of military transformation and had a reputation for being unfailingly loyal, an important attribute to Rumsfeld.[14] As vice chairman of the JCS, Rumsfeld selected Marine General Peter Pace, who had a reputation for being "pliable," "a consummate team player," and someone who "would not stand up to Rumsfeld."[15] But Rumsfeld was not satisfied only selecting the top military officers; after becoming secretary of defense, he insisted on approving all three- and four-star general officers. This enabled him to assure that the top ranking officers in the military would reflect his views and preferences on military issues such as the military transformation. It also meant that top ranking officers took positions that differed from Rumsfeld only at their professional peril. General Eric Shinseki gave his honest estimate in testimony to the Senate Armed Services Committee of the number of troops that would be required for the invasion of Iraq, and Rumsfeld and Wolfowitz strongly criticized him for doing so. Later in the Iraq War, a number of general officers, who had served in command positions in Afghanistan and Iraq, took the very unusual action of publicly criticizing Rumsfeld and his running of the Pentagon and the Iraq War.[16] In an after action report on his visit to Iraq and Kuwait in December 2007, General Barry McCaffrey wrote, "Mr. Rumsfeld was an American patriot, of great personal talent, energy, experience, bureaucratic cleverness, and charisma—who operated with personal arrogance, intimidation and disrespect for the military, lack of forthright candor, avoidance of personal responsibility, and fundamental bad judgment."[17]

Part of the reason that Rumsfeld ultimately was unsuccessful and ineffective was his arrogance and the lack of respect he showed for people, particularly high-ranking military officers. For example, several months before the start of the war in Iraq, Army General John Abizaid, who at the time was the director of the Joint Staff of the Joint Chiefs of Staff and later the commander of Central Command, was barred from a planning meeting in the Pentagon to discuss possible military operations in Iraq by DOD civilian officials.[18] Bush's chief of staff, Andrew Card, recalled, "Sometimes Don would fall into the trap of saying, 'I'm smart, you're not.'"[19] General Wayne Downing, a four-star general and former commander of the Special Operations command, recalled, "He [Rumsfeld] was toxic to the interagency process because there was little cooperation. It was Rumsfeld's way or no way."[20] A long-time, trusted adviser to Rumsfeld, Steve Herbits, resigned in July 2004 and wrote a seven-page memo to his boss characterizing his "style of operation" as the "Haldeman model, arrogant," referring to Nixon's White House chief of staff H. R. Haldeman. Herbits also portrayed Rumsfeld as "indecisive, contrary to popular image. . . . Would not accept that some people in some areas were smarter than he. . . . Trusts very few people. Very, very cautious. Rubber glove syndrome," meaning that he did not want to leave his fingerprints on decisions.[21]

Rumsfeld was willing, even enthusiastic, about "leaving his fingerprints" on the public presentation of progress in the war effort. In previous conflicts, most often military leaders presented information about the course of the war. For the wars in Afghanistan and Iraq, it was Rumsfeld who conducted the almost daily Pentagon press briefings. While Rumsfeld was often witty, intelligent, and humorous, his arrogance and impatience sometimes tripped him up. At a town hall meeting with soldiers in Kuwait, one soldier asked the secretary why troops had to scavenge for scrap metal and bullet-proof glass—what soldiers called "hillbilly armor"—to bolt onto their Humvees and trucks in order to provide protection against improvised explosive devices (IEDs). Rumsfeld responded, "As you know, you go to war with the Army you have. They're not the Army you might want or wish to have at a later time."[22] In April 2004, a reporter asked Rumsfeld why he was ordering the extension of the tours of duty for 20,000 troops in Iraq for three months, and he replied impatiently, "Come on, people are fungible. You can have them here or there. We have announced the judgment. It is clear. You understand it. Everyone in the room understands that we needed additional—the commander decided he'd like to retain in-country an additional plus or minus 20,000 people and that is what we are doing."[23] Former Army brigade commander Colonel Peter Mansoor described the reaction to Rumsfeld's comment in Baghdad: "Watching the news conference in the brigade tactical operations center, a young soldier turned to Major Mike Shrout and asked, 'Sir, what does *fungible* mean?' For the record, it means replaceable or exchangeable. Try telling that to our families."[24]

Cheney, Rumsfeld, and their subordinates took a very active role in making policy, particularly in foreign policy and national security. Cheney established a kind of mini-NSC within his office headed by his chief of staff, Lewis "Scooter" Libby. After he resigned as secretary of state, Colin Powell was asked whether a different NSC with more effective leadership would have had an effect on foreign policymaking in the Bush administration, and he responded, "I don't know. Probably not." The interviewer asked why not, and Powell responded succinctly with one word, "Cheney."[25] After leaving office, Powell's long-time aide and chief of staff at the State Department from 2002 to 2005, Larry Wilkerson, was even blunter: "In President Bush's first term, some of the most important decisions about U.S. national security—including vital decisions about postwar Iraq—were made by a secretive, little-known cabal. It was made up of a very small group of people led by Vice President Dick Cheney and Defense Secretary Donald Rumsfeld."[26] The result, according to Wilkerson, was the "ruinous foreign policy of George W. Bush. . . . It's a disaster. Given the choice, I'd choose a frustrating bureaucracy over an efficient cabal every time." One of the other ironies of the division between the State and Defense departments in the Bush administration is that the State Department had more top civilian officials who were military combat veterans than the Defense Department or the vice president's office. At State, Colin Powell, his deputy Richard Armitage, and Larry Wilkerson had all served multiple combat tours of duty in Vietnam; of the top civilian officials at DOD, only Rumsfeld had served in the military, and the vice president had received five deferments from the draft which allowed him to avoid military service. Yet, it was the vice president's office and the senior civilians in DOD who were the most hawkish on the war.

Interagency Differences: "Cats in a Sack"

Scholars who have studied the Bush administration have noted the divisions among those responsible for making foreign policy. Ivo Daalder and James Lindsay identified three distinct groups within the Bush administration: assertive nationalists (Dick Cheney, Donald Rumsfeld), neoconservatives (Paul Wolfowitz, John Bolton, Richard Perle), and pragmatic internationalists (Colin Powell, Richard Haass). Each of these three groups had a distinctive worldview and preferred means of dealing with international relations in general and Afghanistan and Iraq in particular. The attacks of September 11 reduced the significance of these differences as the nation rallied to defend itself against the clear and present danger of terrorism, and when the United States attacked Afghanistan in October 2001, there was substantial bipartisan support. However, as the Bush administration moved toward a decision to attack Iraq, these differences became more important and pronounced. In January 2003, Rumsfeld went to the White House and requested authority for the Department of Defense to oversee postwar reconstruction in Iraq. President Bush responded to Rumsfeld's request by signing National Security Presidential Directive 24, giving formal responsibility for postwar planning in Iraq to the Department of Defense.[27] This action was taken despite the fact that DOD had not been primarily responsible for postwar reconstruction since the end of World War II, more than half a century before.

Dov Zakheim, a member of the "Vulcans," the small number of foreign policy experts who advised George W. Bush in the 2000 presidential campaign, and who later served in the Bush administration as the Pentagon's comptroller, noted the extent of the interagency differences: "State and Defense were at war—don't let anyone tell you different. Within policy circles, it was knee-jerk venom, on both sides. Neither side was prepared to give the other a break. It began in 2001, got exacerbated during the buildup to Iraq, and stayed on." Zakheim noted that these differences did not just exist at the top, but affected the "working level" as well and that "people who had to work with, and trust, each other—and they didn't."[28] *Washington Post* journalist Karen DeYoung noted that the bureaucratic differences "extended far beyond specific policy disagreements. It was institutional, ideological and even personal."[29] Commenting on the State and Defense departments, CIA official Charles Duelfer noted, "It was Sunnis and Shias, but in Washington. They could never agree on a shared set of facts or strategy."[30] General Tommy Franks was blunter, "On far too many occasions the Washington bureaucracy fought like cats in a sack."[31]

Over time major differences developed between the vice president's office and the Department of Defense on one side and the State Department and the Central Intelligence Agency on the other.[32] The events leading to the war in Iraq heightened the disagreements. Cheney and Rumsfeld focused on intelligence that led them to reach conclusions different from those of the State Department and the CIA. For example, Cheney and Rumsfeld believed that there was a link between al Qaeda and Iraq. Representing DOD and the vice president's office, Paul Wolfowitz and Scooter Libby repeatedly pressured the CIA to change its conclusion, as did the deputy director of the NSC, Steve Hadley. The CIA's chief analyst, Jami Miscik, refused to change the agency's conclusions. CIA Director Tenet called Hadley and said, "Knock this off. The paper is done. It is finished. We are not changing it. And Jami is not coming down there to discuss it anymore."[33] Several days later, President Bush met with Miscik and asked if "his guys" had "stepped over the line."[34] She told the president that the agency could deal with the pressure; however, this episode revealed the depth of division within executive branch agencies.

There were other issues that underscored the depth of differences among the various executive branch agencies. In his 2003 State of the Union address, President Bush referred to reports that Iraq was attempting to buy uranium ("yellow cake") from the African country of Niger, and that this showed that Saddam Hussein was trying to develop nuclear weapons.[35] Upon closer investigation, the intelligence reports on which this conclusion was reached turned out to be forgeries, yet the damage had been done: the president had used erroneous information on which to base his case. NSC adviser Rice and CIA rirector Tenet debated over who was responsible for this error, and it provided another example of the negative effect of interagency dissention.

The divisions between State/CIA and Defense/vice president's office were not atypical within the executive branch, for relations among offices in other parts of the executive branch were not cordial. CENTCOM commander Franks needed to work closely with the designated action officer for Iraq within the Pentagon, Douglas Feith, but General Franks had little or no confidence in Feith. In his memoirs, Franks recalled a comment he made to a colleague concerning Feith, "I have to deal with the fucking stupidest guy on the face of the earth almost every day."[36] In Iraq, both Jay Garner and later Paul Bremer reported to Secretary of Defense Rumsfeld, and General Franks, General Abizaid, and General Sanchez reported to Rumsfeld. This arrangement violated the hallowed military organizational principle of "unity of command." No single official in Iraq was superior, and the consequences were both clearly evident and negative. General Abizaid complained that he could not even talk with Bremer.[37] According to journalist George Packer, "Bremer and Sanchez literally hated each other. . . . Jerry [Bremer] thought Sanchez was an idiot, and Sanchez thought Jerry was a civilian micromanaging son of a bitch."[38] In his memoirs, General Sanchez expressed his frustration with the dysfunctional organizational arrangements in Iraq: "The Department of State was reluctant to deal with the CPA, which was now under control of the National Security Council. The CPA was reluctant to deal with the Department of State or the Department of Defense. There was no indication that the NSC was making any effort to synchronize all governmental agencies to achieve unity of effort in Iraq."[39]

The interagency battles in Washington had a direct influence on the plans for governing postwar Iraq. Journalists and historians believe that the decisions to disband the Iraqi military and security forces, to ban former members of the Baath Party from participating in the postwar government, and to postpone the formation of an interim government were three of, if not the single most significant decision, influencing the future of postwar Iraq. The evidence indicates that Rumsfeld, Wolfowitz, Paul Bremer, Douglas Feith, and Walter Slocombe did not consult with the State Department, the CIA, or the NSC on these three momentous decisions.[40]

A further indicator of the interagency split concerned the leadership of Iraq. Each powerful department or agency in Washington had its own preferred postwar leader. The Department of Defense favored Ahmed Chalabi—that is, until there were indicators that he was passing U.S. intelligence information to Iran. The CIA favored Ayad Allawi, and the State Department favored Adnan Pachachi.[41]

In the interagency battles, Colin Powell and the State Department were on the losing side time after time. Finally, Powell had enough and went to the Oval Office in January 2005 for his last meeting with President Bush. Powell told the president, according to journalist Karen DeYoung, "[S]enior officials in Rumsfeld's office at the Pentagon were actively and dangerously undermining the president's diplomacy, he said, mentioning several by name. Bush replied that every administration had similar problems and recalled the legendary battles between Secretary of State George Shultz and Defense Secretary Caspar Weinberger in President Reagan's administration. Powell assured him that he had been there as Weinberger's chief military aide and later as Reagan's national security adviser, and that what was happening now was something altogether different."[42] In short, Powell told the president that the interagency process was broken, a conclusion that was later seconded by veteran American diplomat Dennis Ross, who wrote, "[D]ivisions within the administration were never resolved."[43] Even Rumsfeld himself recognized this problem; in January 2005, Rumsfeld told NSC deputy Steve Hadley, "You know, the interagency's broken."[44] Other participants agreed with this critical assessment. In his memoirs, General Franks remarked, "I wish some things had been done differently. I wish Don Rumsfeld and Colin Powell had forced the Defense and State Departments to work more closely together."[45] Of course, the only person who had the authority to order such cooperation was President Bush, and he chose not to do so.

So what if the interagency process was, as Powell put it, "broken"; what difference did that make? The principal result of this broken process was that the president, the American government official responsible for making decisions of import, was not presented with options. According to CIA Director Tenet, "In none of the meetings [concerning Iraq] can anyone remember a discussion of the central questions. Was it wise to go to war? Was it the right thing to do? The agenda focused solely on what actions would need to be taken if a decision to attack were made."[46] Based on his interviews, Bob Woodward reported, "Both Powell and Rice knew that Powell had never made an overall recommendation on war [against Iraq] to the president since he had never been asked."[47] Why did the United States go to war against Iraq? Not even those closest to the policymakers know the answer.

Former government official Gregory Treverton has written, "In general, the federal government achieves interagency coordination in two ways: either designating a lead agency or passing the coordinating responsibility to the White House—for instance, to the NSC. If an agency leads, it then constructs its own means of achieving interagency coordination."[48] Traditionally, the State Department is the "lead agency" in foreign policy; however, the George W. Bush administration gave the Department of Defense this responsibility prior to and during the Iraq War because the president deferred to Cheney and Rumsfeld. Only after the dissention between the two principal departments responsible for foreign and defense policy became debilitating and dysfunctional, did President Bush on May 14, 2004, sign National Security Presidential Directive 36, reversing his earlier directive and giving responsibility for postwar reconstruction in Iraq to the State Department.[49]

The National Security Council

When dissention and conflict developed among various executive branch departments and agencies, the National Security Council could and should have taken responsibility for coordination. The National Security Act of 1947 created the NSC as the organization responsible for coordinating policy and making recommendations to the president for issues related to foreign and defense policy of the United States. The president's assistant for national security affairs is responsible for coordinating the interagency process and making recommendations to the president. During the first term of the Bush administration, Condoleezza Rice held this position and in the view of most observers did not do a good job. Richard Armitage of the State Department thought that the NSC under Rice was "dysfunctional."[50] Another State Department official, David Kay, thought that Rice "was probably the worst national security adviser in modern times since the office was created."[51] According to a member of Rice's NSC staff, "Condi was a very, very weak national security advisor."[52] In his memoirs, George Tenet wrote, "Quite simply, the NSC did not do its job,"[53] and another CIA official was even more critical, saying, "I think Rice didn't really manage anything, and will go down as probably the worst national security advisor in history."[54]

In the absence of Rice asserting the prerogatives of her office, the Department of Defense and the Office of the Vice President became the principal sources of national security policy direction in the Bush administration. Rumsfeld principally determined U.S. policy in the Afghan War. Cheney provided overall guidance for the Iraq War, and Rumsfeld conveyed his wishes to the civilian and military leaders in the field. The result was what Ambassador Dennis Ross called "bureaucratic dysfunction."[55] Another experienced policymaker and former close adviser to Colin Powell, Richard Haass, commented, "Presidents tend to get the NSC they want, and this [the Bush administration] was no exception. What this president didn't get was the NSC he needed."[56] Jacob Weisberg concluded that Condoleezza Rice primarily fed "the president's need to feel that he was doing the right thing once he made up his mind," and that this was "an abdication of her fundamental responsibility."[57]

In the second Bush administration, Stephen J. Hadley, who had served as Rice's deputy during the first term, replaced Rice as national security adviser. Hadley graduated from Yale Law School in 1972 and worked in both the private and public sectors. He worked on the National Security Council under Brent Scowcroft in the Ford administration, on the commission to investigate Iran-Contra (Tower Commission) in the Reagan administration, and as assistant secretary of defense in the George H. W. Bush administration. In this position, Hadley worked for Secretary of Defense Dick Cheney, Paul Wolfowitz, and Lewis "Scooter" Libby. When Bush ran for the presidency in 2000, Hadley was one of the "Vulcans" and worked closely with Condoleezza Rice in the campaign and after.

In contrast to Rice and some other previous national security advisers, Hadley was considered low-key and even-keeled and preferred to remain in the background rather than in the public spotlight; he was rarely on the Sunday morning news shows and did not give many interviews. Given his previous association with Cheney and Rumsfeld, there were persistent rumors that Hadley was "Cheney's mole"[58] and that he would provide Rumsfeld with advance information as a "heads up."[59]

He was willing to take responsibility for his statements and actions, even when mistaken. In his State of the Union address of January 28, 2003, President Bush said, "The British government has learned that Saddam Hussein recently sought significant quantities of uranium from Africa."[60] Bush's claim was based on a report that Iraq had attempted to buy uranium ore ("yellow cake") from Niger as part of its plan to develop nuclear weapons. CIA Director Tenet had earlier told Hadley that this claim could not be substantiated, and yet it appeared in Bush's speech.[61] Following the disclosure that the "yellow cake" charge was false, the White House and CIA debated who would take responsibility for the mistake. After Tenet disclosed the memos that the CIA had sent to the White House challenging the claim, Hadley admitted that Tenet had told him this and that he had forgotten it prior to the speech and said, "Signing off on these facts is my responsibility. . . . And in this case, I blew it. I think the only solution is for me to resign."[62] The president did not accept Hadley's offer to resign, and he remained the deputy NSC adviser.

As deputy national security adviser, Hadley chaired the Deputies Committee, which included Richard Armitage from State, either Wolfowitz or Feith from DOD, John McLaughlin from CIA, and Libby from the vice president's office. NSC member Richard Clarke recalled that Hadley had a "methodical, lawyerly style," and that "[it] was his idea to slowly build a consensus that action was required, 'to educate the Deputies.'"[63] Given the strong personalities and policy differences represented on the Deputies Committee, building consensus was a difficult process.

Once he became national security adviser, Hadley modeled his behavior on his old NSC boss, Brent Scowcroft, who sought to present options to the president rather than serve as the president's chief defender, as Condoleezza Rice had done. Hadley was also willing to acknowledge realities; for example, in February 2005, Hadley told a colleague regarding U.S. policy in Iraq, "I give us a B-minus for policy development and a D-minus for policy execution."[64] Due to his concern about the course of the war, on December 11, 2006, Hadley invited several outside advisers including retired General Jack Keane, Stephen Biddle, and Professor Eliot Cohen to come to the White House and share their views of the state of the Iraq War with the president and the vice president.[65] This meeting began a series of meetings that would culminate in the development and acceptance of the surge, the plan to send an additional 30,000 American troops to Iraq. In the discussions reviewing Iraq policy, Hadley "wanted to remain a neutral broker of alternatives in the traditional mold of his office. All options were examined, including the resources required to implement each one."[66] The low-key, Scowcroft "honest broker" model of national security policymaking adopted by Hadley served President Bush much better than the more adversarial Rice approach.

Congress: Hawks, Doves, and Lambs

Political scientists have demonstrated many times a trend in public and congressional support for American foreign policy; namely, in the immediate wake of a crisis, the American people and members of Congress will "rally round the flag" and support the president, at least for a limited amount of time. This characteristic was clearly evident in the aftermath of the 9/11 attacks on the United States. In early September 2001, polls showed that President Bush's public approval rating stood at 51 percent—an historic low for a president in his first eight months of office—but soon after the 9/11 attacks his approval rating soared to 90 percent, a figure that was only surpassed in recent American political history by the president's father following the first Gulf War.

On September 14, the Congress, with only one dissenting vote, passed a resolution empowering the president to "use all necessary and appropriate force against those nations, organizations, or persons he determines planned, authorized, committed, or aided the terrorist attacks that occurred on September 11, 2001, or harbored such organizations or persons."[67] The atmosphere created by 9/11 influenced the way in which Congress acted. The homeland of the United States had been attacked for the first time in almost two centuries, and Congress generally approved whatever the president requested to respond to the attacks and to provide for the security of the United States. Soon after 9/11, President Bush requested an additional $9.8 billion for homeland security, and in February 2003, he requested and the Congress approved $37.7 billion for homeland security, an amount that was more than double what he had requested when he became president.

On the foreign policy front, Congress supported President Bush's actions in Afghanistan against the Taliban government and al Qaeda sanctuaries. Because the U.S. was responding to a direct attack on its homeland, there was little controversy regarding the responses to the attacks, which were strongly supported by a cross-section of Republicans and Democrats, liberals and conservatives. When the U.S. attack on Afghanistan began, polls indicated that 88 percent of Americans and 65 percent of Britons supported military action.[68]

Congressional and public opinion concerning Afghanistan's neighbor, Pakistan, was more complicated. As noted in Chapter 3, the United States and Pakistan were close allies during the cold war. For example, Pakistan was a member of both the Southeast Asian Treaty Organization (SEATO) and the Central Treaty Organization (CENTO, also known as the Baghdad Pact). In addition, Pakistan allowed the U.S. to base its U-2 spy planes in Pakistan to conduct missions over the USSR, and in the early 1970s Pakistan served as a go-between for the United States and the People's Republic of China in their effort to normalize their relations. Following the Soviet invasion and occupation of Afghanistan in December 1979, Pakistan served as the conduit for money and arms to the *mujahideen*. However, after the defeat of the USSR, the U.S. significantly decreased its support of Pakistan. Following the end of the Soviet-Afghan war, a number of members of Congress became concerned about Pakistan's effort to develop nuclear weapons, and in 1985 Congress passed the Pressler Amendment, which prohibits U.S. foreign and/or military assistance unless the president certifies that Pakistan did not possess a nuclear weapon. In 1990, President George H. W. Bush would not issue such a certification, and as a result, American aid virtually ceased, and this included support for military-to-military exchanges. According to former chairman of the Joint Chiefs of Staff General Myers, "The Pakistani military no longer knew the American military and we didn't know them. For many Pakistani officers, their view of the Americans was often based upon the shrill rhetoric of extremists, since they no longer were able to come to the United States for training and have the chance to see our country firsthand."[69] As a result of the sanctions imposed by the Pressler Amendment, U.S. officials had not had direct contact with Pakistani officials for more than a decade at the time of the 9/11 attacks.

George W. Bush entered office as the first Republican president in almost eight decades at the same time that both houses of Congress were in control of his party. This meant that Republicans chaired all of the principal committees in Congress, and this enabled them to exert major control over the congressional agenda, appropriations, and, significantly, hearings. In a time of war, few members of Congress—Republican or Democrat—were willing to question or challenge the commander-in-chief, and this hesitance applied particularly to holding hearings to examine the administration's war plan. This behavior was eerily reminiscent of the role that Congress had played in the Vietnam War. In August 1964, when reports reached Washington that two American naval vessels had been attacked by North Vietnamese patrol boats, the Congress passed the Gulf of Tonkin Resolution empowering President Johnson to take "all necessary measures to repel any armed attacks against the forces of the United States and to prevent further aggression." Senator J. William Fulbright served as the floor manager of the resolution, which passed with only two dissenting votes. As U.S. commitments and casualties increased in Vietnam, the Congress became more assertive, and it was Senator Fulbright, the chairman of the Senate Foreign Relations Committee, who held the first significant hearings on the war. Three and a half decades later there was no Republican analogue to Fulbright; the Republicans in Congress were not willing to question the Republican president, and Democrats were not willing to question the president's policies in wartime. In looking back on this period, Senator Chuck Hagel has written, "One of the questions that future historians will consider is: 'What was and what should have been the role of Congress in the lead up to and entry into war with Iraq?'"[70]

As the Bush administration moved toward war with Iraq, Congress was not very active. As journalist Thomas Ricks pointed out, "In previous wars, Congress had been populated by hawks and doves. But as the war in Iraq loomed, it seemed to consist mainly of lambs who hardly made a peep."[71] There were several reasons for this. First, several leading Democrats had publicly opposed going to war in 1990–91, prior to the first Gulf War, and they had been proved wrong in their dire predictions of costs and casualties. Second, Democrats are often viewed as soft on defense, and, therefore, they want to underscore their commitment to and support of a robust national security policy. Third, the United States had been attacked and was at war, and in this environment, it was even more difficult for Democrats to oppose action against Iraq.

On October 10, 2002, the House voted 296–133 to authorize the president to use military force against Iraq, and shortly after midnight the Senate voted 77–23 to authorize such action. A number of Democratic senators who would later run for their party's presidential nomination, including John Kerry, John Edwards, Joseph Biden, and Hillary Clinton, voted in favor of the resolution, votes that would later prove embarrassing.

Once the U.S. invaded and occupied Iraq, the Congress acquiesced in the president's decision. The quietude on Capitol Hill lasted until the spring of 2004, when shocking photos of American soldiers abusing prisoners at Abu

Ghraib prison were published. The Senate Armed Services Committee held hearings on the scandal, and the members, particularly Democrats, were scathing in their criticism. When Paul Wolfowitz appeared before the committee, Senator Clinton forcefully attacked him, saying, "You come before this committee . . . having seriously undermined your credibility over a number of years now. When it comes to making estimates or predictions about what will occur in Iraq, and what will be the costs in lives and money, . . . you have made numerous predictions, time and time again, that have turned out to be untrue and were based on faulty assumptions."[72] Wolfowitz faced a similar reception when he appeared before the House Armed Services Committee. Representative Ike Skelton, one of the most respected members of Congress for his interest in and understanding of military affairs, told Wolfowitz, "I see two Iraqs. One is the optimistic Iraq that you describe . . . . And the other Iraq is the one that I see every morning, with the violence, the deaths of soldiers and Marines."[73] These hearings did not command much attention and did not mark the beginning of systematic and careful oversight and assessment of the U.S. war effort in Iraq. As Thomas Ricks concluded, "There was little follow up or oversight. There were, for example, no hearings with returning division commanders. In retrospect, the hearings of May and June 2004 were a spasm before the election season."[74]

Former CENTCOM commander Marine General Anthony Zinni was also scathing in his criticism: "In the lead up to the Iraq war and its later conduct, I saw, at a minimum, true dereliction, negligence, and irresponsibility; at worst, lying, incompetence, and corruption. False rationales presented as a justification; a flawed strategy; lack of planning; the unnecessary alienation of our allies; the underestimation of the task; the unnecessary distraction from real threats; and the unbearable strain dumped on our overstretched military."[75]

Scott McClellan, who served as White House press secretary from 2003 to 2006, concluded, "The first grave mistake of Bush's presidency was rushing toward military confrontation with Iraq. It took his presidency off course and greatly damaged his standing with the public. His second grave mistake was his virtual blindness about his first mistake, and his unwillingness to sustain a bipartisan spirit during a time of war and change course when events demanded it."[76]

The results of the 2006 congressional midterm elections sent a shockwave throughout the U.S. government. In the Senate, six incumbent senators were defeated, and the Democrats (with the support of two independents who caucused with the Democrats) gained a 51–49 majority. In the House, Democrats gained thirty-one seats and gained control for the first time since 1994. In both houses of Congress, Democrats assumed majority control of committees and subcommittees, enabling Democrats to call hearings and to call witnesses to question the Bush administration's policies.

12 Allies

> Tis our true policy to steer clear of permanent alliances with any portion of the foreign world.
>
> —George Washington, Farewell Address

> Peace, commerce, and honest friendship with all nations—entangling alliances with none.
>
> —Thomas Jefferson, Inaugural Address

> We are a strong nation. But we cannot live to ourselves and remain strong.
>
> —General George C. Marshall, January 22, 1948

These three quotations illustrate two tendencies that have been at odds with one another since the founding of the American republic: isolationism and internationalism. Washington, Jefferson, and other founding fathers wanted to remain separate from European politics, which they considered to be amoral, if not evil. Making this assumption, they wanted to remain separate and uninvolved with Europe and the rest of the world. Beginning in the eighteenth century, three major international trends increasingly challenged the viability of isolationism. First, the industrial revolution depended upon access to the components of industrialization: iron ore, coal, and petroleum, and few states had indigenous supplies of these resources. Second, involvement in two world wars and numerous smaller wars in the twentieth century caused many Americans to change their view, as expressed by General George C. Marshall in the above quotation. Third, globalization increased international interdependence and made it impossible for a great power state to isolate itself from international involvement, and as the United States increasingly depended upon imported oil to fuel its society and industry, the U.S. had to be concerned and involved with Middle Eastern politics.

Alliances in History

Allies and alliances have existed as long as politics. There are, for example, numerous references to alliances throughout the Old Testament of the Bible.[1] The eminent British historian Sir Michael Howard has defined alliances as "the coming together of independent states, potentially hostile, with divergent interests in an atmosphere of distrust."[2] This definition underscores a significant attribute of most alliances; namely, they are temporary agreements among states that compete, as well as cooperate, with one another. Alliances have played a vital role in world politics for centuries. Following the emergence of nation-states after the conclusion of the Thirty Years War in 1648, the balance of power became the system for managing power within international relations, and alliances were an important means of balancing power within the system. In many cases, alliances were temporary and short-lived; today's ally could be tomorrow's enemy. In a nonideological, less nationalistic age, it was possible for leaders to shift a state's allegiance from one state to another. Over time, with the growth in importance of ideology and nationalism, such shifts became less feasible.

The twentieth century witnessed the most destructive wars in human history, World Wars I and II, and in both of them alliances proved key to victory; indeed, the name of the collection of victorious states in both wars was the "Allied Powers." In World War II, the "Grand Alliance" consisted of the opponents to the Axis Powers of Germany, Japan and Italy. The "Big Three" of the Grand Alliance consisted of the United States, Great Britain, and the Soviet Union. Because of their cultural similarities, same language, and common history, relations between the U.S. and the UK were characterized as the "special relationship," and ever since World War II, British and American leaders have recognized and respected this. As with any alliance, however, there have been ups and downs; for example, when Britain joined France and Israel in attacking Egypt to take over the Suez Canal in 1957, President Eisenhower strongly criticized the erstwhile allies of the United States and pressured them to withdraw and to return control of the Suez to Egypt. But time and again throughout the cold war, the U.S. supported the United Kingdom and vice versa.

One of the most important and successful alliances in history is the North Atlantic Treaty Organization (NATO), founded in 1949 in order to deter an attack on its members by the Soviet Union and its Warsaw Pact allies. NATO was what is called in international law a "self-executing treaty," meaning that if one member was attacked, the other members would automatically come to the aid of the attacked member. The crux of the NATO treaty is contained in Article V, which stipulates: "The Parties agree that an armed attack against one or more of them in Europe or North America shall be considered an attack against them all." The principal assumption throughout the more than four decades of the cold war was that it might become necessary for the United States to come to the aid of the Western European states as it had done on two previous occasions in the twentieth century. The 9/11 attacks on the U.S. were to prove that assumption wrong.

On November 11, 1989, the unexpected, unpredicted occurred: the Berlin Wall, the iconic symbol of the cold war and the division of East and West, came down and people crossed the hitherto impermeable barrier freely.[3] This was followed by another unexpected, unpredicted event a little more than two years later in December 1991 when the Soviet Union disintegrated. With these two events, the raison d'etre of NATO had disappeared; the USSR and its alliance, the Warsaw Pact, no longer existed, so what was the purpose of NATO in the post cold war world?

In the decade between the disintegration of the Soviet Union and the 9/11 attacks on the U.S., NATO explored a number of new functions and objectives. It sought to assist the former Soviet bloc countries integrate into the Western-oriented international system and in 1994 established the "Partnership for Peace" in furtherance of this objective. In March 1999, NATO accepted the Czech Republic, Hungary, and Poland as members of NATO.

Conflict erupted among the three principal ethnic groups in former Yugoslavia in the late 1990s, and an estimated 200,000 Muslim Bosnians were killed between 1992 and 1995. When conflict broke out in Kosovo, which was also a part of Yugoslavia, many feared that a similar genocide would follow. When UN intervention proved to be ineffectual, NATO approved a military mission—the bombing of Yugoslavian forces—from March 24, 1999, through June 10, 1999. Significantly, this was NATO's first "out of area" military operation since its founding. According to most observers, this action stopped a potential genocide from developing in Kosovo, a worthy and remarkable accomplishment when compared to the tragic events in Bosnia.

The War on Terror and U.S. Allies

Soon after the hijacked commercial airliners crashed into the Twin Towers of the World Trade Center, the Pentagon, and a field in Pennsylvania, world leaders responded immediately and sympathetically. The first condolence call and offer of help came not from a long-time American ally, but rather from Vladimir Putin, the leader of the former cold war competitor of the United States, Russia. Putin pledged to assist the U.S. to find those responsible for the attacks. Twelve days after the attacks, Putin told the president, "We are going to support you in the war on terror."[4] Later, Putin encouraged the former Soviet republic of Uzbekistan to allow the U.S. to establish a base in order to be able to supply its forces in Afghanistan and to be able to launch search and rescue teams for any downed pilots or lost soldiers. Two months after 9/11, Putin met with a delegation from the Department of Defense, and according to one of the American participants, Douglas Feith, he "was in a mood to share. He offered his opinion of key players in the country [Afghanistan], his military observations, and his take on Afghanistan's neighbors. He touted Russian weapons for the Northern Alliance as far better than other weapons, because its commanders knew the Russian equipment so well."[5] Putin's reaction and offer of assistance and information indicated that this was a new kind of war in which former competitors had become de facto allies literally overnight. Of course, Russia's interests were also at stake because Russia had a significant number of Muslim citizens and did not want militant Islamist states on its borders.

Long-time, close allies of the United States responded immediately and courageously. On September 11, there were about 4,500 commercial and general aviation planes in American airspace.[6] Any of these could have been used for further attacks on U.S. cities; no one knew the extent of the threat. The government of Canada allowed 239 airplanes to divert to Canada from U.S. airspace. In doing this, the Canadian government may very well have invited attacks on Canadian cities; such was the commitment of Canada to assisting the United States in its time of need.

American allies in the Middle East expressed strong support for the United States in the aftermath of the 9/11 attacks. Fifteen of the nineteen hijackers were Saudi, and 9/11 served as a dramatic wake-up call for the Saudi government about the implications of its laissez-faire policy toward anti-Western, Islamic radicals within the kingdom and allowing "charitable" organizations to raise money in Saudi Arabia to send to *jihadists*. During the Afghan-Soviet War, this was not only allowed but actively encouraged by both the Saudi and American governments; 9/11 changed that. Of course, the Saudi government had to try and satisfy both the U.S. government and the conservative, Wahhabi religious elements within Saudi society who were sympathetic and supportive of Islamist groups such as al Qaeda. Just one month after 9/11, Sheikh Saleh bin Luheidan, the chairman of the Supreme Judicial Council and a member of the senior council of religious scholars (*ulema*), issued a statement strongly criticizing Osama bin Laden and his followers for their call to holy war against the U.S., saying, "*Jihad* refers to the struggle to hold high His word; he who struggles in the way of God is the one who adheres to religious rites, avoids aggression and injustice, abides by *Shariah* and never becomes a cause for bloodshed and destruction to his people and country."[7] In essence, Sheikh bin Luheidan was challenging the *salafis'* authority to declare a *jihad*.

A country that often disagreed with its Arab neighbors, Israel, along with the Saudi government strongly condemned the attacks on the U.S. Two weeks after 9/11, former Israeli Prime Minister Binyamin Netanyahu spoke to a committee of the U.S. House of Representatives and said, "Today we are all Americans. In grief, as in defiance. In grief, because my people have faced the agonizing horrors of terror for many decades, and we feel an instant kinship with both the victims of this tragedy and the great nation that mourns its fallen brothers and sisters."[8]

As previously noted, the U.S. and UK share a "special relationship" dating back at least to World War II. Following the 9/11 attacks, British Prime Minister Tony Blair flew to Washington, DC, to express his condolences and support personally. In his speech to the American people of September 21, President Bush noted, "America has no greater friend than Great Britain."[9] In his speech to the Labour Party in October 2001, just three weeks after the attacks on the U.S., Blair said, "[In] retrospect, the millennium marked a moment in time, but it was the events of the 11th of September that marked a turning point in history, where we confront the dangers of the future and assess the choices facing humankind. It was a tragedy, an act of evil. And from this nation goes our deepest sympathy and prayers for the victims and our profound solidarity for the American people. We were with you at the first, we will stay with you to the last."[10]

In the ensuing wars in Afghanistan and Iraq, Great Britain and Blair were the strongest supporters of the United States, and President Bush publicly acknowledged the on-going "special relationship" between the U.S. and UK. During a visit to London in November 2003, the president said, "More than an alliance of security and commerce, the British and American peoples have an alliance of values. And today this old and tested alliance is very strong."[11] Because of the importance of British support, President Bush acted in ways to address concerns of Blair and the British public. For example, prior to invading Iraq, Blair insisted that the U.S. attempt to obtain UN approval of military action. Cheney, Rumsfeld, and others were opposed to going to the UN, but because Blair insisted on this, the U.S. did so.

Both Canada and Great Britain are members of NATO, which acted quickly to invoke Article V of the NATO Treaty. In his speech to the nation, President Bush referred to this: "Perhaps the NATO charter reflects best the attitude of the world: an attack on one is an attack on all."[12] NATO backed up its words with tangible action and military forces. In the days and weeks following the 9/11 attacks, NATO aircraft patrolled the skies over American cities. The U.S. did not have the capability to provide for the number of combat air patrols that were required, and NATO committed seven Airborne Warning and Control System (AWACS) aircraft from September 2001 through May 2002. More than 830 crewmen from thirteen NATO members flew 4,300 hours and 360 operational sorties during their deployment in the U.S.[13] This was the first time that Americans in the continental U.S. had been protected in their homeland by foreign military forces.

In addition to Russia, there were some surprising, new de facto allies of the United States in its war on terror. Syria, which was on the U.S. State Department's list of state sponsors of terrorism, provided American intelligence agencies with information about al Qaeda and other terrorist groups such as the Muslim Brotherhood, which had influenced a number of al Qaeda members. Syria is a secular state run by the Alawites, a branch of Sunni Islam, and as a secular state, al Qaeda represents an existential threat to Syria. This helps to explain Syria's support of American counterterrorism efforts and its hostility toward al Qaeda. In a controversial process known as "rendition," the CIA sent prisoners to Syria and Egypt, where they were interrogated and tortured.[14] In addition to Syria and Egypt, Libya and even Iran, which had had a hostile relationship with the U.S. since the hostage crisis of 1979, pursued al Qaeda persistently and aggressively following the 9/11 attacks on the U.S.

Other Arab countries also assisted the United States. Jordan had long had a complicated relationship with the U.S.; at least 30 percent of its population consisted of Palestinians who were hostile toward the foremost American ally in the Middle East, Israel. The long-time ruler of Jordan, King Hussein, attempted to placate his Palestinian constituency while maintaining a friendship with the U.S. At times, this proved difficult or impossible. For example, during the first Gulf War, King Hussein and Jordan supported Iraq, an action that caused tension between his country and the U.S. But the split between the U.S. and Jordan was not irreparable, and in the aftermath of the 9/11 attacks on the U.S., Jordan—and in particular its intelligence service, the General Intelligence Directorate—provided valuable information on suspected and actual terrorists to the U.S. This cooperation came to light prominently in January 2010 when a Jordanian intelligence official took a double agent, Humam Khalil Abu-Mulal al-Balawi, to a CIA base in Khost, Afghanistan.[15] Al-Balawi supposedly had information on the location of Ayman al-Zawahiri, the second most important leader of al Qaeda after Osama bin Laden. Al-Balawi and his Jordanian handler were admitted to the CIA's Forward Operating Base Chapman, where al-Balawi detonated explosives that were hidden on his body, killing himself, seven CIA officers, and the Jordanian intelligence officer. In addition, six more CIA officers were critically wounded. This incident demonstrated the inherent dangers in intelligence cooperation even among close allies.

The War in Afghanistan and U.S. Allies

Most American policymakers recognized the value and importance of having allies in its war against terrorists. In his memoirs, George Tenet wrote, "[Y]ou cannot fight terrorism alone. There were clear limitations on what we could do without the help of like-minded governments."[16] Former General and NATO commander Wesley Clark observed, "Without public support abroad, we cannot defeat al Qaeda."[17] Others in the Bush administration, most importantly Vice President Cheney and Secretary of Defense Rumsfeld, did not agree with this view. Shortly after the 9/11 attacks, Rumsfeld wrote, "The war [on terrorism] will not be waged by a grand alliance united for the single purpose of defeating an axis of hostile powers. Instead, it will involve floating coalitions of countries, which may change and evolve."[18] Cheney remarked on *Meet the Press,* "The fact of the matter is for most of the others who are engaged in this debate, they don't have the capability to do anything about it anyway."[19] Cheney expressed the view that "a good part of the world, especially our allies, will come around to our way of thinking."[20] So, Cheney believed that American allies did not have the capabilities to help and that they would support the U.S. in any event; there was no need for allies. Besides, they were often difficult to work with and could place restrictions on the exercise of American power, and this was simply unacceptable to Cheney, Rumsfeld, and other hardliners in the administration.

Several long-standing American allies—most notably the United Kingdom, Australia, Canada, and Germany—sent special operations forces to Afghanistan and helped to overthrow the Taliban and destroy al Qaeda training camps working with a new American ally, the Northern Alliance. When the U.S. turned its attention to and invaded Iraq in March 2003, American officials recognized the need for allies despite whatever misgivings they had, and in August 2003, NATO took control of the International Security Force Afghanistan (ISAF).

The War in Iraq and the Coalition of the Willing

In March 2003, when the United States invaded Iraq, American military forces equaled 145,000 and British forces equaled 46,000. Other countries that sent forces for the invasion included Australia (2,000) and Poland (200). Table 12.1 lists the maximum number of troops that the thirty-nine members of the U.S.-led coalition sent to Iraq during the war. These contributions to the war effort varied from the significant British commitment to the three soldiers sent by Iceland. Although some critics of the Iraq War contended that it represented a "unilateral intervention" by the United States, such a statement ignores the substantial British commitment; at one point in the war, one-third of the British Army was deployed to Iraq, a higher percentage than the U.S. Army.

President Bush was fond of pointing out that the Iraq War was a multinational effort involving forty-nine allies of the U.S.[21] In fact, ten members of the "Coalition of the Willing" never committed troops; they only gave permission to have their names be placed on the list of countries supporting the U.S. The nature of the Iraq War coalition differed both quantitatively and qualitatively from previous American alliances. Noticeably missing from the list of participants in the war were long-time U.S. allies such as Germany and France, both of which had participated in the first Gulf War and the bombing of Kosovo in 1999. Secretary of Defense Rumsfeld dismissed the charges that long-time allies were missing from the coalition by noting that they were members of "old Europe" and that they had been replaced by members of the "new Europe." The problem, of course, was that the "new Europe" consisted of smaller, poorer, less militarily capable countries than the "old Europe." Also noticeably missing in President Bush's "Coalition of the Willing" were any Islamic countries, which could have provided valuable services such as translators and trainers for the Iraqi security forces. Not one Muslim country provided forces, a marked

TABLE 12.1

U.S. and Coalition Troop Deployments in Iraq, 2003–9

Country	Maximum number deployed	Date deployed	Date withdrawn
Albania	240	4/03	12/08
Armenia	46	1/05	10/08
Australia	2,000	3/03	7/09
Azerbaijan	250	8/03	12/08
Bosnia and Herzegovina	85	6/05	11/08
Bulgaria	485	5/03	12/08
Czech Republic	300	12/03	12/08
Denmark	545	4/03	12/08
Dominican Republic	302	8/03	5/04
El Salvador	380	8/03	1/09
Estonia	40	6/05	2/09
Georgia	2,000	8/03	10/08
Honduras	368	8/03	5/04
Hungary	300	8/03	3/05
Iceland	3	5/03	?
Italy	3,200	7/03	11/06
Japan	600	1/04	12/08
Kazakhstan	29	9/03	10/08
Latvia	136	5/03	11/08
Lithuania	120	6/03	12/08
Macedonia	77	7/03	11/08
Moldova	24	9/03	12/08
Mongolia	180	8/03	10/08
Netherlands	1,345	7/03	3/05
New Zealand	61	9/03	9/04
Nicaragua	230	9/03	2/04
Norway	150	7/03	8/06
Philippines	51	7/03	7/04
Poland	200	3/03	10/08
Portugal	128	11/03	2/05
Romania	730	7/03	7/09
Singapore	175 (offshore)	12/03	12/08
Slovakia	110	8/03	12/07
South Korea	3,600	5/03	12/08
Spain	1,300	4/03	4/04
Thailand	423	8/03	8/04
Tonga	55	7/04	12/08
United Kingdom	46,000	3/03	7/09
Ukraine	1,650	8/03	12/08
Total of non-U.S. Coalition	67,918		
Total of non-U.S./UK	21,918		

Source: Author's calculations from various sources.

contrast to the first Gulf War, in which a number of Muslim countries participated.

Quantitatively, only one member of the coalition, the United Kingdom, sent tens of thousands of troops; seven (Australia, Georgia, Italy, the Netherlands, South Korea, Spain, and Ukraine) sent more than a thousand; twenty-one sent more than a hundred; and ten sent fewer than a hundred. The maximum number of forces deployed for the entire non-U.S. coalition equals 67,918; of course, because these troops were deployed at different times, there were never this many allied forces in Iraq, but this figure gives an idea of the magnitude of commitment. If one subtracts the 46,000 British troops from this figure, the total number of non-American-Anglo forces equals 21,918.

Many of the national forces sent to Iraq did not have a significant enough number to perform operational tasks effectively. In addition, there were problems of restrictive rules of engagement, communicating in different languages, and equipment interoperability. One Coalition Provisional Authority official told journalist Tom Ricks, "Except for the Brits, they [allied forces] weren't there to fight. The Dutch did good patrols, on foot. The Italians patrolled by vehicle. . . . The Japanese didn't patrol at all," and the Thais' rules of engagement did not allow them to leave the camp near Karbala at all.[22] One soldier who was deployed next to a unit of soldiers from Georgia, who were equipped with Kalashnikov assault rifles, told the author that the Georgians were frequently caught stealing American weapons.[23]

The Sometimes Allies: Turkey and Pakistan

Some of the strongest allies of the United States during the cold war, including Turkey and Pakistan, were hesitant to support the U.S. in its wars in Afghanistan and Iraq. Turkey had been a strong, reliable ally of the U.S. During the first Gulf War, Turkish President Turgut Ozal strongly supported the international coalition opposing Saddam Hussein, unlike the leaders of some other Islamic countries such as Jordan. The Kurdish issue influenced Turkey's relationship with Iraq. There are an estimated 15 to 20 million Kurds in Turkey, and many would like independence from Turkey. Several radical groups including the PKK and PUK have engaged in terrorist activities against targets in Turkey, and Turkish authorities, according to the U.S. Department of State, have responded by committing serious human rights violations against Kurdish individuals and groups including "torture, beatings, and extrajudicial killings."[24]

Following the end of the first Gulf War, the United Nations imposed sanctions on Iraq, and Turkey formally participated in the sanctions, but also turned a blind eye toward smugglers and sanction-busters operating from Turkish territory. According to Ali Allawi, "These parallel tracks—formal support for the policy of containing Iraq and exploiting the trade and other opportunities afforded it by the Iraqi regime's isolation—were a recognized and accepted feature of Turkey's Iraq policy in the 1990s."[25]

Turkey faced the threat of terrorism not only from its indigenous Kurds, but also from other groups. For example, in a plot that in some ways presaged the 9/11 attacks, in November 1998, Turkish authorities discovered and broke up a plot by a radical Islamist extremist group to fly an airplane loaded with explosives into the tomb of modern Turkey's founder, Ataturk.[26] Two years later, CIA Director George Tenet sent a memo to President Clinton concerning the threat of al Qaeda: "Our most credible information on bin Laden activity suggests his organization is looking at US facilities in the Middle East especially the Arabian Peninsula, in Turkey and Western Europe."[27]

When the United States attacked Afghanistan, Turkey was supportive and participated in the training of members of the Afghan National Army in 2002. As the war dragged on, two tiers of NATO countries developed: those that severely restricted the actions of their troops, including refusing to provide troops for counterinsurgency operations.[28] These reluctant allies included France, Germany, Italy, Spain, Greece, and Turkey. The coalition forces engaged in ground combat operations, included forces from the United States, United Kingdom, Canada, Germany, and the Netherlands. Rumsfeld grew frustrated with the reluctance of U.S. allies to engage in combat and at one point commented that it was like "having a basketball team, and they practice and practice for six months. When it comes to game time, one or two say, 'We're not going to play.'"[29]

Turkey was even less willing "to play" in Iraq than Afghanistan. The initial war plan for the invasion of Iraq called for a two-pronged attack by the Third Infantry Division and a Marine Expeditionary Force coming from the south from Kuwait, and 92,000 troops of the Fourth Infantry Division from the north from Turkey. This deployment would have to be approved by the Turkish Parliament, which was problematic because 94 percent of the Turkish population did not want American troops in Turkey, and 50 percent saw U.S. policies as the greatest threat to Turkish security.[30] The vote was scheduled for mid-February and postponed until March 1. In this interim period, the Turkish foreign minister, Yasar Yakis, traveled to Washington to negotiate the terms for Turkey to allow U.S. troops to transit Turkey into Iraq. Initially, Yakis requested an astounding $92 billion, which amounted to $1 million for each of the American troops transiting through Turkey. In addition, the foreign minister demanded that an equal number of Turkish troops be permitted to enter northern Iraq ostensibly to control the border, with the unspoken objective of controlling the Kurdish population in this area. Secretary of State Powell rejected both demands and following negotiations, the U.S. agreed to a total aid package of $26 billion. On March 1, the Turkish Parliament refused to approve the transit of American troops, an action that had major repercussions for both the U.S. and Turkey. For the U.S., it meant that the soldiers and equipment of the Fourth Infantry Division, which were on twenty-four ships waiting off the coast of Turkey, would have to transit to Kuwait; in short, the entire war plan would have to be revised on the fly. By the time the Fourth Infantry Division reached Kuwait and offloaded its soldiers and equipment, the main combat phase of the war was over. However, the threat that the Fourth Infantry Division would attack from the north caused the Iraqi general staff to send Iraqi divisions to the north that could have been used in the south. Therefore, even though the Fourth Infantry Division missed the kinetic phase of the war, it accomplished a valuable goal: to tie up several Iraqi divisions. The Turkish Parliament's action had a dramatic effect on the Turkish stock market, which fell 12.5 percent within forty-eight hours of the parliament's decision on fears that the U.S. would withdraw its aid.

On March 19, 2003, the U.S. attack on Iraq began, and on the same day Turkey reluctantly approved overflight rights for American aircraft, the last member of NATO to do so. On March 20, the day after the start of the invasion, the Turkish government repeated its demand to be allowed to intervene into northern Iraq. Secretary Powell was furious and rejected the Turkish demand. A senior U.S. official commented, "It feels like the Turks have taken a hot poker and stuck it in my eye. Don't they watch CNN? Don't they know that the war has already started?"[31] Despite the rejection of Turkish demands, Turkish forces massed on its border with Iraq, an action that gave the Turks the capability to intervene, if they so chose. And if they did, they would confront not only Iraqi forces, but also those of another NATO ally, the United States. Although Turkish forces did not intervene en masse, American forces captured a group of Turkish special forces in July who claimed that they were operating against a Kurdish terrorist group.[32]

Turkey was not the only reluctant ally of the United States. Pakistan was also hesitant to support the U.S. in its wars on terror and in Afghanistan and Iraq. In 1998, Pakistan detonated six nuclear explosions, and the United States imposed sanctions on Pakistan in response. A year later, General Pervez Musharraf led a bloodless coup to overthrow the civilian government. In addition, the Pakistani government through its Inter-Services Intelligence (ISI) directorate, which the late Pakistani Prime Minister Benazir Bhutto had called "a state within a state," had provided support and funds to the Taliban and other Islamic radical groups. As President Clinton recalled in his memoir, "Although we were trying to work with Pakistan to defuse tensions on the Indian subcontinent, and our two nations had been allies during the cold war, Pakistan supported the Taliban and, by extension, al Qaeda."[33] As a result of this history, relations between the U.S. and Pakistan as of September 11, 2001, were shaky at best.

Secretary of State Powell and his principal deputy, Richard Armitage, had worked closely with the Pakistanis during the 1980s and 1990s. Armitage had worked with the *mujahideen* during the final throes of the Soviet-Afghan War, and Powell, as chairman of the Joint Chiefs of Staff, had worked with the Pakistani military during the first Gulf War. Both men, however, had been out of government during the Carter years when relations between the U.S. and Pakistan became strained. Faced with the crisis catalyzed by 9/11, Powell and Armitage made a list of seven non-negotiable demands for Pakistan: "[S]top al Qaeda operatives at your border; . . . provide the U.S. with blanket overflight and landing rights; . . . provide as needed territorial access to U.S. and allied military intelligence and other personnel; . . . provide the U.S. immediately with intelligence; continue to publicly condemn the terrorist acts of September 11; . . . cut off all shipments of fuel to the Taliban; . . . [and] should the evidence strongly implicate Usama bin-Laden and the al Qaeda network in Afghanistan and should Afghanistan and the Taliban continue to harbor him and this network, Pakistan will break diplomatic relations."[34] Just hours after the 9/11 attacks, Armitage met with the head of ISI, Lieutenant General Mahmoud Ahmed, who coincidentally was visiting Washington, presented the seven U.S. demands, and told him, "No American will want to have anything to do with Pakistan in our moment of peril if you're not with us."[35] The next day, the U.S. ambassador to Pakistan, Wendy Chamberlain, met with President Musharraf in Islamabad and "bluntly" told him "that the September 11 attacks had changed the fundamentals of the [Afghanistan-Pakistan] debate. There was absolutely no inclination in Washington to enter into a dialogue with the Taliban. The time for dialog was finished as of September 11. There was only one response to the terrible events: preventing the terrorists from ever repeating such actions again." [36] When Musharraf was initially noncommittal about supporting the United States, Chamberlain told him, "Frankly, General Musharraf, you are not giving me the answer I need to give my president." Musharraf then quickly responded, "We'll support you unstintingly."[37]

Despite Musharraf's assurances, however, during the ensuing years of the war in Afghanistan, Pakistan's support of the United States was spotty. For example, the Pakistani government had followed a hands-off policy toward the tribal areas on the border between their country and Afghanistan, a policy that the British had previously followed. In 1920, Lord Curzon, the British Viceroy of India, established the North-West Frontier Province as a buffer zone and recommended "respect for the independence and sentiment of the tribes."[38] American soldiers stationed on the border could see that Pakistani military outposts would allow Taliban and al Qaeda members to move about freely on the Pakistani side of the border.[39] In his memoir, Army captain and infantry platoon leader Craig Mullaney recalled that on one patrol along the border, a Pakistani military outpost began firing on his soldiers: "Plumes of smoke trailed from the Pakistani observation post as grenades screamed toward McGurk [a soldier in the platoon] below. Action steadied my nerves. I raised the radio handset to my mouth and called the artillery battery. I read off the grid coordinates . . . enough to level our ally's observation post. I understood now what it meant to kill or be killed."[40] In this case as well as others, the reluctant ally of the United States became its opponent.

Allies' Public Opinion and the Coalition of the Willing

The relationship of terrorism, the war in Iraq, and allied cooperation was brought home in March 2004 when members of al Qaeda simultaneously detonated bombs in Madrid, Spain, killing 192 and wounding 1,600. In response to the bombings, Spanish Prime Minister Jose Luis Rodriquez Zapatero announced that his government was ordering the withdrawal of all Spanish forces from Iraq. This action was clearly taken to placate public opinion, which was restive in other countries as well.

The public opinion of American allies is an important aspect of the relations of the United States with other countries. The Pew Global Attitudes Pro-

TABLE 12.2
Percentage of Respondents Who View the U.S. Positively, September 2003

Country	Summer 2002	Summer 2003	Change %
Brazil	52	34	–18
Britain	75	70	–5
Canada	72	63	–9
France	62	63	+1
Germany	61	45	–16
Indonesia	61	15	–46
Italy	70	60	–10
Nigeria	77	61	–16
Pakistan	10	13	+3
Russia	61	36	–25
South Korea	53	46	–7
Turkey	30	15	–15

Source: Pew Global Attitudes Project, *New York Times*, September 11, 2003, p. A18.

ject regularly measures public opinion concerning positive views of the United States. Table 12.2 indicates the percentage of respondents from selected countries in three different surveys who viewed the U.S. favorably.

Public opinion experts recognize that there are many variables that affect people's beliefs and attitudes, and it is difficult to isolate one or even several variables that definitively influence public opinion; however, the timing of the surveys in Table 12.2 is significant. The surveys in the first column were taken less than a year following 9/11, and the surveys in the second column were taken several months following the invasion of Iraq by the U.S. and its coalition. One can correlate that event with the public opinion results without concluding that the invasion caused the results. With that caveat, what is the significance of these figures?

Of the dozen countries listed, only two showed a small, statistically insignificant increase in positive views of the U.S.: France (+1%) and Pakistan (+3%). The French figure is so small that it essentially indicates no change, and the Pakistani change does not represent a very significant positive change: from 10 to 13 percent positive ratings for the U.S. Ten of the thirteen countries listed have negative changes from the summer of 2002 to the summer of 2003, and some of these changes are impressive. The greatest change occurred in the largest Muslim country in the world, Indonesia (–46%), followed by Russia (–25%), Brazil (–18%), Germany (–16%), Nigeria (–16%), and Turkey (–15%).

Beyond these survey results, the outpouring of international goodwill toward the United States following 9/11 contrasts markedly with the precipitous decline of positive views of the U.S. following the invasion of Iraq. American actions in Iraq and the drawn-out war in Afghanistan contributed to the creation of a coalition of the unwilling even among those countries that had supported the United States in both Afghanistan and Iraq. The government of Canada announced that it would remove its 2,800 soldiers from Afghanistan by the end of 2011. In February 2010, the Dutch government fell after it attempted to keep its 2,000 troops in Afghanistan, and there were predictions that the Netherlands would withdraw all of its troops by the end of 2010. Professor Julian Lindley-French of the Netherlands Defense Academy predicted, "If the Dutch go, . . . that could open the flood gates for other Europeans to say, 'The Dutch are going, we can go, too.'"[41] If Dutch and other European forces withdraw, there will be increased pressure on the already-stretched American forces.

In the U.S. encounters with terrorism and Islamic radicalism in Afghanistan, Pakistan, and Iraq, the views of allies were significant. Following the attack on the U.S. on September 11, 2001, there was almost universal support for the United States, even from countries and people that were traditionally either not friendly or downright hostile toward the U.S. *Le Monde*'s headline of September 12, "We Are All Americans," was hardly characteristic of that French newspaper's usual editorial positions. Most countries recognized the clear and present danger that al Qaeda, for which the Taliban provided sanctuary, posed to the United States and supported American military efforts to destroy al Qaeda training camps and to overthrow the Taliban government. Support of the U.S. was still strong. It was the U.S. invasion of Iraq that caused strong allies of the U.S. to waver and in many cases to go from being part of the "coalition of the willing" to becoming reluctant allies or even opponents of American policy. And this transition occurred in a matter of several years.

The loss of allies was very significant. One of the main problems of the U.S. in Iraq was the shortage of troops, a problem that was accentuated with the disbanding of the Iraqi military but could have been ameliorated with an increase in the number of allied forces in Iraq. But U.S. allies, with the most notable exception of Great Britain, were lukewarm about the Iraq War at the beginning of the war and became less and less supportive as the war dragged on. The loss of support for the U.S. and the resulting loss of allies was a major cost of the war in Iraq for the United States.

Table 12.3 shows U.S. and NATO forces deployed to Afghanistan as part of the International Security Assistance Force (ISAF), which took over operations

TABLE 12.3

International Security Assistance Force (ISAF) Deployments to Afghanistan, January 2007, February 2010, and November 2010

Country	Number of troops deployed		
	January 2007	February 2010 (Pre-surge)	November 2010 (Post-surge)
Albania	30	255	258
Armenia	0	0	40
Australia	5	1,550	1,550
Austria	0	3	
Azerbaijan	20	90	94
Belgium	300	575	491
Bosnia and Herzegovina	0	10	45
Bulgaria	100	540	516
Canada	2,500	2,830	2,922
Croatia	130	295	299
Czech Republic	150	440	468
Denmark	400	750	750
Estonia	90	150	140
Finland	70	95	150
France	1,000	3,750	3,850
Former Yugoslav Republic of Macedonia	120	165	163
Georgia	0	175	924
Germany	3,000	4,415	4,341
Greece	170	15	80
Hungary	180	315	502
Iceland	5	3	4
Ireland	10	8	7
Italy	1,950	3,150	3,688
Jordan	0	0	0
Latvia	35	175	189
Lithuania	130	165	219
Luxemburg	10	9	9
Malaysia	0	30	
Mongolia	0	47	
Netherlands	2,200	1,940	242
New Zealand	100	220	234
Norway	350	500	353
Poland	160	1,955	2,519
Portugal	150	105	95
Romania	750	945	1,648
Singapore	0	40	38
Slovakia	60	240	250
Slovenia	50	70	78
Spain	550	1,070	1,576
Sweden	180	410	500
Turkey	800	1,755	1,790
Ukraine	0	8	16
United Arab Emirates	0	25	35
United Kingdom	5,200	9,500	9,500
United States	14,000	47,085	90,000
Total	34,955	85,793	130,573

Source: International Security Assistance Force (ISAF) http://www.isaf.nato.int.

in Afghanistan in January 2007, at which time there were thirty-seven countries contributing forces with a total strength of 33,955. Following the surge of forces into Afghanistan, the total number of ISAF forces from forty-three countries by February 2010 equaled 85,793. Table 12.3 indicates the number of forces from each of the contributing countries.

Table 12.1 shows U.S. and non-U.S. deployments to Iraq from 2003 through 2009. As the table demonstrates, by August 2009, all non-U.S. members of the coalition had withdrawn from Iraq, and as of January 1, 2010, the Multi-National Force-Iraq had become the United States Force-Iraq, thus ending allied cooperation in Iraq.

The dearest cost that any country pays for a war is the loss of its citizens. As of September 2010, there were a total of 2,086 fatalities in Afghanistan: 61 percent of these were American; 16 percent were British; and 22 percent were other nationalities. There were 4,739 coalition fatalities in Iraq: 93 percent of these were American; 4 percent were British; and 3 percent were other nationalities.

13 Strategy

In February 2005, Vice President Cheney claimed that the insurgency in Iraq was in its "last throes," and ten months later, he told an interviewer, "I do believe that when we look back on this period of time, 2005 will have been the turning point when, in fact, we made sufficient progress both on the political front and the security front, so that we'll see that as the watershed year."[1] In fact, 2005 was indeed "a watershed year": the U.S. war in Iraq was in deep trouble.

According to *Washington Post* journalist Thomas Ricks, "In 2005 the United States came close to losing the war in Iraq."[2] The situation continued to worsen throughout 2005 and into 2006. In testimony to the U.S. Congress, Ambassador Ryan Crocker, one of the State Department's most experienced and respected diplomats with extensive service in the Middle East, commented, "[The year] 2006 was a bad year in Iraq. The country came close to unraveling politically, economically, and in security terms."[3] A former U.S. Army brigade commander observed, "In 2006, the war was almost lost; Iraq was in shambles."[4] The year had been marked by a number of significant events. In February, the Al-Askari ("Golden Dome") Mosque in Samarra was bombed; in March, polls indicated that a majority of Americans no longer supported the U.S. presence in Iraq; and in August, General John Abizaid, the commander of U.S. forces in the Middle East, warned of the possibility of civil war in Iraq. According to journalist Linda Robinson, "By the summer of 2006, Baghdad was on fire. Sectarian violence was spilling over into all-out war, and it swept up hundreds of thousands of Iraqis."[5] On the U.S. domestic front, congressional elections were to be held in November. By the end of 2006, twelve of the thirty-nine members of the allied coalition, including three of the biggest contributors of forces—Italy, the Netherlands, and Spain—had withdrawn their troops from Iraq. Given these disturbing indicators, what was the Bush administration to do about Iraq? And, of course, conflict continued in Afghanistan and on the Afghan-Pakistani border.

What to Do about Iraq?

Members of the Bush administration were concerned about the indicators and trend lines for Iraq in 2006. Gone was the neoconservative inspired talk of democratizing Iraq and the Middle East; by 2006, policymakers were talking about ways simply to avoid defeat—nothing more grandiose. In March, President Bush and the Congress appointed the Iraq Study Group co-chaired by former Secretary of State James A. Baker III and former long-time Representative Lee H. Hamilton, one a Republican and the other a Democrat. They were joined by eight other distinguished Americans with previous extensive government service. The first sentence of the final report bluntly stated the starting assumption of the commission: "The situation in Iraq is grave and deteriorating."[6] In their transmittal letter in their final report, the co-chairs commented not only on the situation in Iraq, but also on the situation in the United States: "Many Americans are dissatisfied, not just with the situation in Iraq but with the state of our political debate regarding Iraq."[7] The study group created four different working groups with forty-four foreign policy analysts and specialists on Iraq. In addition, the commission held nine plenary sessions and consulted with officials and representatives from the U.S. executive and congressional branches of government, the Iraqi government, foreign officials, former U.S. policymakers, and foreign policy specialists. After almost nine months of study, the commission issued its final report in December 2006, which contained seventy-nine recommendations. The commission recommended that the U.S. launch a diplomatic offensive throughout the Middle East including engaging directly with Iran and Syria, two countries with which the U.S. did not have good relations. In addition, the commission recommended that the U.S. deal directly with the Arab-Israeli conflict. In dealing with Iraq, the commission recommended specific benchmarks for the Iraqi government to meet in order to continue to receive American assistance. There were also recommendations that reversed earlier U.S. actions such as the "de-Baathification" program instituted by the Coalition Provisional Authority in May 2003. The commission recommended, "The United States should encourage the return of qualified Iraqi professionals—Sunni or Shia, nationalist or ex-Baathist, Kurd, Turkmen or Christian or Arab—into the government."[8] In regard to security and military strategy, the commission "considered proposals to make a substantial increase (100,000 to 200,000) in the number of U.S. troops in Iraq. We rejected this course because we do not believe that the needed levels are available for a sustained deployment."[9] The commission also addressed personnel, economic aid, and other issues in its recommendations.

The Iraq Study Group was not the only group considering "the way forward" for the U.S. in Iraq. The Army and Marine Corps had borne the brunt of the U.S. fighting and dying in Iraq, and its members knew better than any others the dire situation in Iraq. As described in Chapter 9, the U.S. had chosen a military strategy in Iraq that relied on conventional forces employing significant firepower and primarily focused on destroying the enemy. By 2006, it was clear that despite the heroic efforts of the members of the military, this strategy was not working.

Beginning in 2005 and continuing into 2006, several significant efforts began that would dramatically alter the U.S. strategy in Iraq. First, those in charge of Iraq policy in the White House recognized that the "strategy for victory in Iraq" was eroding and, according to NSC adviser on Iraq, Peter Feaver, "[T]he situation in Iraq had eroded beyond the point envisioned by the Baker-Hamilton report; under the horrific conditions now at play, we concluded, Iraq's security forces were far more likely to crack under the strain than to 'stand up.' And those forces were the essential glue of a stable, unified future. If they went the way of Humpty Dumpty, neither they nor the new Iraq could ever be put back together again."[10] As a result of this assessment, the NSC began to consider other options. Second, in September 2006, Rumsfeld met with a retired general, Jack Keane, who had been the frontrunner to become chief of staff of the Army, but had to withdraw his name from consideration because of his wife's health. Keane recommended an increase in forces in Iraq. Third, in the Department of Defense, the new chairman of the Joint Chiefs of Staff, General Peter Pace, convened a small group of Army and Marine officers to "think outside the box" about alternative strategies; this group became known as the "council of colonels." These efforts resulted in the reassessment of strategy that culminated in the surge of forces to Iraq.

General Keane was retired, but nevertheless remained interested and concerned about the war in Iraq. Many retired flag officers maintain close contact with other active duty and retired officers, which stands to reason since they have spent most of their adult lives in the military and have been focused on providing for the security of the United States. General Keane was a member of an informal, elite group: retired four-star generals. Since his retirement, he had stayed in contact with Secretary of Defense Rumsfeld, and in mid-September, Keane made an appointment to see his old boss to discuss his concern and thinking about the Iraq War.

Keane had been impressed with the thinking and career of a young general, David Petraeus, who focused on the lessons of counterinsurgency in his Princeton doctoral dissertation, claiming: "The painful experience of Vietnam is indelibly etched in their [military leaders'] minds, and from it they have taken three general impressions that influence their advice on the use of force. First, they have become very sensitive to the finite limits of public support for protracted military operations. Second, they have developed a nagging doubt about the efficacy of American military force in solving certain international problems. And third, they have carried from Vietnam a greater disillusionment with, and heightened wariness of, civilian officials."

Petraeus noted that characteristics of military involvements that were particularly disliked by the military included "a relatively 'fuzzy' objective, ambivalent public support, and little prospect for quick resolution of the situation." In short, time was of the essence; "Recognizing the perishability of public support for military action abroad, the post-Vietnam military have come to regard time as the principal limit in limited wars." In his thesis, Petraeus noted that Vietnam contributed to the distrust of civilian leadership: "There was from the beginning of the McNamara era a belief that the civilians who 'took over' the Pentagon did not understand the complexities and difficulties of military operations." Of course, many of the officers in Rumsfeld's Pentagon had precisely the same feeling. The curious thing in both Vietnam and Iraq was the rarity of resignations in protest. As Petraeus asked, "If things were so screwed up in Vietnam, why didn't admirals and generals resign?" In his dissertation, Petraeus was skeptical about the United States military's ability to conduct successful counterinsurgency operations: "The lessons taken from Vietnam would indicate that, in general, involvement in a counterinsurgency should be avoided."

There was a close, personal bond between Keane and Petraeus. Following the completion of his doctorate at Princeton, Petraeus returned to his alma mater, West Point, to teach for several years. In 1991, Petraeus was a lieutenant colonel in the 101st Airborne Division stationed at Fort Campbell, Kentucky. As he and the division's assistant commander, General Keane, were observing an exercise in which live ammunition was used to increase the realism of the training, a soldier tripped and accidentally discharged his M-16 rifle, and the bullet hit Petraeus in the chest. Keane called a medical evacuation helicopter that took the wounded officer first to the post hospital and then on to a hospital in Nashville that was better staffed and equipped to deal with his serious injury. The doctor who operated on Petraeus for five hours was a cardiologist, Dr. Bill Frist, who would subsequently become a U.S. Senator and majority leader. Within a month, Petraeus was back with his unit leading his battalion on training exercises, and the bond between Keane and Petraeus was cemented.

Petraeus had served as the commander of the famed 101st Airborne Division in Operation Iraqi Freedom in the first Gulf War, and retired General Barry McCaffrey had described him as the brightest of his cohort of generals and claimed that he was "the most talented person he had ever met."[11] General Petraeus served more than fifteen months as the first Commander of the Multi-National Security Transition Command-Iraq and the NATO Training Mission-Iraq. Following these two assignments in Iraq, he served as commander of the Combined Arms Center at Fort Leavenworth, Kansas, where he recruited a staff of bright, young officers who had excelled as both soldiers and scholars, something that Petraeus would continue to do throughout his career. The staff at Fort Leavenworth included Marine Lieutenant General James Mattis, who was Petraeus' Marine counterpart, and lieutenant colonels John Nagl and Conrad Crane, to rewrite the Army and Marine Corps counterinsurgency manual.[12] Nagl had been a Rhodes Scholar and had written a book on counterinsurgency for which he borrowed a phrase from T. E. Lawrence for the title: *Learning to Eat Soup with a Knife: Counterinsurgency Lessons from Malaya and Vietnam.*[13] Crane had been a classmate of Petraeus' at West Point and, like Petraeus, earned a doctorate in history from Stanford University while in the Army. When he retired, he became a professor at the Army War College in Carlisle, Pennsylvania, and, among other things, wrote a study focusing on the difficulties of occupying Iraq.[14]

Building on classic works of counterinsurgency by T. E. Lawrence, Sir Robert Thompson, and David Galula, the drafters of the new counterinsurgency manual reviewed the experience of the United States with counterinsurgency, paying particular attention to Vietnam. In a foreword to the edition of the manual published by the University of Chicago Press, John Nagl wrote, "The story of how the Army found itself less than ready to fight an insurgency goes back to the Army's unwillingness to internalize and build upon the lessons of Vietnam."[15] The manual emphasized the following "paradoxes of counterinsurgency":

- Sometimes, the more you protect your force, the less secure you may be.
- Sometimes, the more force is used, the less effective it is.
- The more successful the counterinsurgency is, the less force can be used and the more risk must be accepted.

- Sometimes doing nothing is the best reaction.
- Some of the best weapons for counterinsurgents do not shoot.
- The host nation doing something tolerably is normally better than us doing it well.
- If a tactic works this week, it might not work next week; if it works in this province, it might not work in the next.
- Tactical success guarantees nothing.
- Many important decisions are not made by generals.[16]

"Principles" or "paradoxes" such as these were well and good for war college journal articles or doctoral dissertations, but how and under what circumstances could they be applied to real-world situations?

General Keane not only met with Rumsfeld in order to recommend a new strategy for Iraq; he also met with chairman of the Joint Chiefs of Staff, Marine General Peter Pace, who appointed a group of sixteen colonels and assigned them to review U.S. policy in Iraq. This group soon came to be known as the "council of colonels," and it included some of the brightest officers in the Army; in fact, several had doctorates. H. R. McMaster had written a doctoral dissertation, later published as a book, criticizing senior Army officers during Vietnam for not challenging and questioning civilian leadership during the war.[17] This view stood in stark contrast to the view of the Army's most popular historian, Colonel Harry Summers, who assigned principal responsibility for the Vietnam disaster to the civilian leaders whom Summers claimed made the main mistakes.[18] McMaster, like the other members of the council of colonels, had served in Iraq; in his case, he served in Tal Afar and implemented a large-scale, successful counterinsurgency campaign.[19] Another soldier-scholar member of the council was Peter Mansoor, who graduated first in his class from West Point, earned a doctorate in history from Ohio State University, served as a brigade commander in 2003–4, and then wrote an account of his service in Iraq.[20]

After weeks of discussion and debate, the council of colonels presented four options to the Joint Chiefs of Staff: Go Big, Go Home, Go Long, and an amalgam of the third and fourth options. "Go Big" called for a substantial increase in the number of troops in Iraq, which the colonels ultimately judged was infeasible given the manpower demands for such an alternative to be implemented. "Go Home" was considered to be unacceptable because the colonels concluded that if the U.S. withdrew from Iraq precipitously, the result would be all-out civil war. "Go Long" called for a long-term advisory presence for U.S. troops, and the fourth, "hybrid" option called for a short-term increase in the number of American troops followed by a reduction from 140,000 to approximately 60,000.[21]

In addition to the Iraq Study Group, the council of colonels, and General Keane, there were several other individuals outside of government who influenced the decision of what to do about Iraq. Stephen Biddle was an academic who had written an award-winning book on military power and a senior fellow at the Council on Foreign Relations.[22] Biddle also wrote analyses for the U.S. Army War College and was an adviser to General Petraeus. Eliot Cohen was a professor of international security at the Johns Hopkins Nitze School of Advanced International Studies in Washington, DC, and had close ties to a number of civilian and military leaders in the Bush administration. He also served as counselor in the Department of State. In addition, Frederick Kagan, an analyst at the American Enterprise Institute (AEI), also had close ties to the Bush administration and was a strong supporter of the surge. Andrew Krepinevich was a career Army officer when he went to Harvard and wrote a doctoral dissertation with the controversial thesis that the U.S. Army, rather than the media or the civilian politicians, was primarily responsible for losing the Vietnam War by failing to adopt and implement a counterinsurgency strategy.[23] In September 2005, Krepinevich published an article in *Foreign Affairs* in which he argued that the U.S. needed to adopt what he called an "oil spot" strategy in Iraq which would focus primarily on protecting the Iraqi population rather than killing the insurgents.[24]

Because the Army and the Marines were the services that were most directly impacted by a troop surge in Iraq, top-ranking Army officers discussed the advantages and disadvantages of this option.[25] Although after his first tour in Iraq, Lieutenant General Peter Chiarelli coauthored an article in the influential Army journal *Military Review* in which he advocated a counterinsurgency strategy for Iraq,[26] most top-ranking Army officers were opposed to increasing the number of troops in Iraq, and these included chief of staff General Peter Schoomaker, CENTCOM commander General John Abizaid, U.S. Iraq commander George Casey, and the chief of the joint staff Lieutenant General Douglas Lute.[27] Retired Colonel Bob Killebrew asked an important question: "Why did the American military establishment so fail to come up with a war-winning strategy that it was up to a retired general [Keane] and a civilian think tank, AEI, to do their job? This is a stunning indictment of the American military's top leadership."[28] Criticism of the Army's leadership came from within the Army itself. For example, in May 2007 Lieutenant Colonel Paul Yingling published an essay entitled "A Failure in Generalship" in *Armed Forces Journal* and in it he charged, "America's generals failed to prepare their forces for counterinsurgency."[29] Another officer, Colonel J. B. Burton, the commanding officer of the Dagger Brigade Combat Team in Iraq, wrote a memo to senior Army officers warning of a potential retention crisis in the junior officer ranks: "This is a very tough crowd of warriors. They have been ridden hard. Some have been involuntarily extended on their first duty assignment to their fourth year on active duty and are now serving on their 2nd or 3rd combat deployment. They see no end in sight, so our offerings should acknowledge this group specifically that has been caught up fully in the deployment cycle."[30] Another officer had earlier analyzed the effects of Vietnam on the Army; Petraeus wrote in his doctoral dissertation: "Vietnam cost the military dearly. It left America's military leaders confounded, dismayed, and discouraged. Even worse, it devastated the armed forces, robbing them of dignity, money, and qualified people for a decade." By 2006, it looked as if the wars in Afghanistan and Iraq were having a similar, destructive effect.

The Counterrevolution in Military Affairs

The analyses produced by David Petraeus, Andrew Krepinevich, H. R. McMaster, John Nagl, and others were not simply of academic interest; they had direct application in Iraq and Afghanistan. Vietnam was the shadow that hovered over these studies like a threatening thundercloud, and the authors drew very different conclusions than other soldiers, such as Colin Powell and Harry Summers, who had served in Vietnam. To many of those who had served in Vietnam, the principal lessons of that tragic conflict was that the United States should only enter into war when there was strong public support, it was ready to employ overwhelming force, and there was an exit strategy. To many post-Vietnam soldiers, the U.S. needed to adopt the strategy of counterinsurgency in order to avoid repeating the mistakes of Vietnam and defeat on the battlefield.

Following the U.S. invasion of Iraq in March 2003, two distinctive strategies were evident. In Falluja and Ramadi, Major General Charles Swannack, the commander of the 82nd Airborne Division, primarily emphasized the traditional military objective of capturing or killing the enemy, and in the area around Saddam's hometown, Tikrit, General Ray Odierno, the commanding officer of the 4th Infantry Division, ordered aggressive patrols—kicking down doors in the middle of the night and taking prisoners without highly reliable intelligence. American soldiers who were not in Odierno's division thought of those in the 4th Infantry Division as "cowboys," that is, undisciplined, aggressive soldiers "who shot first and asked questions later."[31] Contrasting to generals Generals Swannack and Odierno was General David Petraeus, who commanded the 101st Airborne Division in Mosul in northern Iraq. If Swannack's and Odierno's approach was characterized by a closed fist, Petraeus' was the open hand.[32] Many of those who worked with Petraeus said that he had been deeply influenced by his doctoral studies and that he sought to apply in Mosul what he had studied at Princeton and seen first-hand in Central America, Haiti, and the Balkans. In contrast to many other military commanders and consistent with classical counterinsurgency doctrine, Petraeus viewed the protection of the population and the reestablishment of government and the economy, rather than strictly military operations, as the top priority. Marine Colonel T. X. Hammes, who served in Iraq in 2004 and who later wrote a book on strategy,[33] commented on the contrasting approaches of different military commanders, "Each division was operating so differently, right next to the other—absolutely hard-ass here, and hearts-and-minds there."[34]

According to William Hickman, Petraeus' operations officer, his central message to the soldiers in his division was, "What have you done for Iraqis today?"[35] By simply asking this question, Petraeus was reflecting the conclusion of classical counterinsurgency campaigns that in this type of warfare 20 percent is military and 80 percent is political.[36] In keeping with these objectives, Petraeus obtained approval from the Coalition Provisional Authority head, Ambassador Paul Bremer, to sell Iraqi oil to Syria in order to finance projects to rebuild local schools, medical clinics, and other basic reconstruction projects known in the Army as "SWET": sewage, water, electricity, trash disposal. By the time that his tour of duty in Mosul was done, Petraeus' division had spent more than $57 million on 5,026 projects, about one-third of the total amount spent in all of Iraq. This approach was so successful that it was formally established as the Commander's Emergency Response Program (CERP) throughout Iraq. The 101st Airborne Division with 17,000 troops was replaced in February 2004 by a Stryker brigade with 10,000 troops, and as things began to unravel throughout Iraq in late 2004, the gains made by Petraeus and his division in Mosul proved to be unsustainable. Nevertheless, the division's experience showed that an approach other than kicking down doors and shooting people could work.

When the United States reduced its presence in Mosul, the insurgents moved back into the city. Similarly, when the U.S. reduced its presence in other cities, the insurgents would move back in. In Tal Afar, a town of 200,000 close to the Syrian border, as the U.S. reduced its presence in 2004, insurgents moved back in and asserted their control. In the spring of 2005, one of the other post-Vietnam scholar-soldiers, Colonel H. R. McMaster, took command of the 3rd Cavalry Regiment in Tal Afar. Influenced by his study and thinking about Vietnam, McMaster decided to adopt a counterinsurgency approach. He told journalist George Packer, "When we came to Iraq, we didn't understand the complexity—what it meant for a society to live under a brutal dictatorship, with ethnic and sectarian divisions. When we first got here, we made a lot of mistakes. We were like a blind man, trying to do the right thing but breaking a lot of things. You gotta come in with your ears open. You can't come in and start talking. You have to really *listen* to people."[37] For starters, McMaster ordered his soldiers not to swear at Iraqis or to call them "*Hajjis*," the pejorative term many soldiers applied to all local people. The colonel told his troops, "Every time you treat an Iraqi disrespectfully, you are working for the enemy."[38] Like Petraeus in Mosul, McMaster recognized that the main objective was to win over the local people. To do that, American soldiers had to be closer to the people, so McMaster ordered his soldiers to move into the city from the outskirts and to patrol on foot rather than in armored vehicles. In contrast, General Abizaid had said that U.S. forces in cities were like a virus, that they needed to be concentrated on large bases. Building on the analyses of Krepinovich and Nagl, McMaster came to summarize his strategy as "clear, hold, and build": clear the city of insurgents, hold control of the city, and build the infrastructure necessary for a city to function. Secretary of State Rice picked up the phrase and used it in congressional testimony and passed it on to President Bush, who in March 2006, extolled the success in Tal Afar: "In this city, we see the outlines of the Iraq that we and the Iraqi people have been fighting for. . . . A free and secure people are getting back on their feet . . . are participating in government and civic life."[39] Tal Afar was one of the first large-scale, sustainable counterinsurgency operations in Iraq, and yet, despite that fact, top military commanders either ignored it or dismissed it as irrelevant.[40]

Colonel Sean MacFarland's Army unit was initially assigned to replace the 3rd Armored Cavalry Division in Tal Afar, and its members spent several months there and observed the different approach and modus operandi that the division had adopted. MacFarland's brigade was ordered south to Ramadi in Anbar Province, a desert area about the size of Arkansas where al Qaeda's presence and influence were strong and growing. Like other U.S. commanders in Iraq, Colonel MacFarland was confronted with a stark choice: either pursue a narrow, military objective focusing on capturing or killing the enemy or a broader counterinsurgency strategy of protecting the local population and building the infrastructure. Influenced by his time in Tal Afar and what he had observed there, MacFarland opted for the latter approach.

In Anbar as well as in other parts of Iraq, members of al Qaeda were ruthless and brutal toward any locals who did not support them; for example, beheading the children whose parents cooperated with the Americans or cutting off fingers of those who smoked.[41] MacFarland and his subordinates studied the local society and concluded that it was the *sheikhs*, the local tribal leaders, who exercised real influence and power locally, and they began meeting with the *sheikhs* to convince them that the U.S. was in Iraq to stay for the long haul and that the *sheikhs* had more to gain from cooperating with the U.S. than al Qaeda. Of course, a major problem was that many of the *sheikhs* and their men had been insurgents opposed to and at war with the U.S.

Al Qaeda had killed several *sheikhs'* family and tribal members, and one *sheikh* in particular, Sittar Abu Risha, was particularly angry at al Qaeda, which had attacked his relatives and had encroached on his smuggling profits. In response, during the summer of 2006, Sittar ordered counterattacks on members of al Qaeda and had their bodies dumped in the streets of Ramadi with signs identifying them as associated with al Qaeda.[42] In September 2006, Sittar called a meeting with group of fifty *sheikhs* to meet with MacFarland and his fellow officers. The *sheikhs* proposed the creation of what they called the "Awakening Council," which would be responsible for recruiting local police and security. The U.S. took the risky step of arming the Awakening groups with captured weapons and ammunition in order to be able to effectively engage and defeat al Qaeda members. As counterinsurgency specialist David Kilcullen noted, "In Anbar, we've got the tribal vengeance structure working in our favor."[43] Eventually, more than 200 contracts between the U.S. government and Iraqi tribes were signed, and they stipulated that the members of the Awakening movement called the "Sons of Iraq" would: (1) not fire at American forces, (2) stay in their areas, (3) wear distinctive clothes, and (4) provide biometric data (fingerprints, retina scans) so that anyone who violated these rules and was captured could be definitively identified. If there was a violation of any of these rules and the perpetrator was identified through the use of biometric data, the U.S.

brigade commander would go to the *sheikh* and tell him that if the *sheikh* did not deliver him, then he would be arrested. American authorities sent anyone who violated the agreements and was caught to Camp Bucca in southern Iraq. For its part, the U.S. agreed not to raid the houses of the Sons or Iraq, not to shoot them, and to pay them $300 per month. The program grew quickly and by April 2008 approximately 100,000 "Sons of Iraq" were being paid by the U.S. for a total cost of $30 million per month or $360 million per year. The U.S. government agreed to continue to pay the Sons of Iraq until the government of Iraq either hired them or took over the payments to them.

Ethnic conflicts influenced the development of security. During Saddam's rule, Sunnis had held most of the powerful positions in the military, security, and policy organizations. With the overthrow of Saddam and the election of the Shia Nuri al-Maliki, Shia controlled the security agencies. The U.S. demanded that Maliki integrate some of the Sunni Sons of Iraq into government security forces, but this remained a contentious issue.

There were, of course, dangers associated with the Awakening approach. First, there was some question about whether the Sunni Anbar tribes would ever be effectively integrated into Iraqi governmental security units. Second, the long-term aspirations of the Sons of Iraq were unclear, and some seemed to harbor the desire to take over the government. Third, following the Sunni Awakening, some of the Anbar *sheikhs* bragged about how they had taken care of al Qaeda and expressed the desire to go after "the Persians," that is, the Shia. Fourth, some American officers objected to empowering the local *sheikhs* since this, in essence, marked a backward step toward the feudalistic organization of traditional Iraq. These goals hardly constituted the foundation for a stable future.

McFarland's successful efforts in Anbar were recognized and praised by his superiors. Major General Peter Chiarelli, the second-ranking commander in Iraq in 2006, commented that MacFarland's "operation marked the first time in the Iraq war that a counterinsurgency campaign had been conducted and then had been sustained by the succeeding unit. 'Sean was the first guy who did it and it stuck for the guy who followed.'"[44] General Petraeus noted, "Sean had obviously done something extraordinarily important. . . . What you had there was the first really significant example of the concept of reconcilables and irreconcilables."[45] In a move that was as unusual as the Secretary of Defense demanding to approve all three- and four-star general officers during his tenure, General Petraeus in November 2008 returned to Washington from Iraq in order to chair a promotion board to select new Army brigadier generals; two of the forty new generals were H. R. McMaster and Sean MacFarland, who were undoubtedly selected in part because of their successful tours in Tal Afar and Anbar.

Enter the Surge

By the end of 2006, the situation in Iraq was dire, and the American people recognized it as such. In the congressional elections of 2006, the Democrats won control of both the House and the Senate, for the first time since 1994. Many considered the elections the turning point of the Iraq War. The day following the election, President Bush accepted Donald Rumsfeld's resignation, a clear signal that the president was moving away from Rumsfeld's policies. On December 19, Bush said for the first time, "We're not winning, we're not losing in Iraq," his most candid admission to that date that the situation in Iraq was not going well. At this point, the president faced three broad options: withdraw from Iraq, increase the number of American forces, or adopt a significantly different strategy. Faced with a clear and present crisis in Iraq, President Bush and Vice President Cheney chose to ignore the advice of the senior leadership of the Army and the bipartisan, congressionally established Iraq Study Group and to accept the recommendation of an eclectic group of ad hoc advisers.

On January 5, 2007, President Bush appointed General David Petraeus as the commander of all U.S. forces in Iraq, and five days later, the president announced that he would send an additional 28,000 U.S. troops to Iraq to support the new American strategy, widely known as the "surge." As Thomas Ricks noted, "Bush effectively had turned over the fate of his presidency to Petraeus and Odierno. Over the next six months, he would mention Petraeus in speeches and press conferences at least 150 times."[46]

When he was nominated to be the overall military commander in Iraq, General Petraeus went before the Senate to seek confirmation. He supported the "surge" of troops which was not popular in the Congress. Despite this, the Senate confirmed him unanimously. Reflecting his academic study of the lessons of Vietnam, his two tours of duty in Iraq, and his work on revising the Army and Marine Corps counterinsurgency manual, Petraeus emphasized the need to protect the Iraqi population. In a letter that he sent to all military personnel in Iraq, the general recognized, "The environment in Iraq is the most challenging that I have seen in over 32 years of service. . . . Improving security for

Iraq's population is, of course, the overriding objective of our strategy."[47] Petraeus went on to acknowledge that securing the population would mean that many military personnel would have to live in local neighborhoods and that this would pose increased risks for coalition forces. He also described the three essential elements of the new strategy: "[We] will not just 'clear' their neighborhoods of the enemy, we will also stay and help 'hold' the neighborhoods so that the 'build' phase that many of their communities need can go forward."

Three months after President Bush named General Petraeus the commander of U.S. forces in Iraq, he appointed the distinguished American diplomat Ryan Crocker to replace Zalmay Khalilzad as ambassador to Iraq. Crocker was fluent in Arabic and had previously served as ambassador to Lebanon, Kuwait, Syria, Afghanistan, and Pakistan. In December 2002, Crocker served as Assistant Secretary of State William Burns' deputy, and at the request of Secretary of State Powell the two of them drafted "a memo on everything that could go wrong" following a military victory in Iraq.[48] In their twelve-page memo, they concluded that the forces unleashed by a war could result in "The Perfect Storm." The memo proved to be remarkably prescient. Announcing Crocker's appointment, President Bush called him "America's Lawrence of Arabia" and said that his understanding of the Middle East region was unmatched. *Washington Post* writer David Ignatius wrote, "Journalists probably shouldn't have heroes, but Crocker is one of mine. . . . "[He] took on the toughest challenges in the Foreign Service and became a superstar diplomat without ever losing his mordant sense of humor or his determination to speak truth to power."[49] Sometimes personal characteristics and habits can affect policy. Crocker was a runner, as was General Petraeus, who ran eight to ten miles a day when stateside and five to six miles when deployed overseas. Petraeus and Crocker would take daily runs of five miles and while on these would discuss the issues that confronted them.

In a conflict in which political and military actions must be planned and coordinated, the relationship between the military commander and the political chief is vitally important. Unfortunately, at the beginning of the occupation of Iraq, the head of the CPA, Ambassador Paul Bremer, and the military commander in Iraq, General Ricardo Sanchez, did not get along and barely spoke to each other. This poisonous relationship may, in fact, have contributed to the problems that developed in postwar Iraq. Petraeus and Crocker were undoubtedly aware of the dysfunctional relationship that existed between their predecessors, and both believed in working together. Petraeus was committed to operating on the principle of "one team, one mission," and at his swearing in ceremony, Crocker promised to work for "unity of effort" with the military.[50] Fortunately, the general and the ambassador seemed to genuinely like and respect each other and that showed. For example, whenever one had a meeting with Prime Minister Maliki, the other would join the meeting as well so that there would be no misunderstandings between the two Americans regarding who was in charge of U.S. policies and programs in Iraq. In addition, the two men thought about Iraq in similar terms, which were decidedly more modest than the neoconservative ideas that had propelled the U.S. into invading. As Petraeus put it in testimony to Congress, "Ambassador Crocker and I, for what it's worth, have typically seen ourselves as minimalists. We're not after the holy grail in Iraq; we're not after Jeffersonian democracy. We're after conditions that would allow our soldiers to disengage."[51]

General Petraeus and Ambassador Crocker were not the only personnel changes in the United States team dealing with Iraq. In June, Secretary of Defense Gates chose not to reappoint chairman of the Joint Chiefs of Staff General Peter Pace to a second term, the first chairman in more than forty years to have such a short term of service. He was replaced by Admiral Mike Mullen. These personnel changes were not the only conflicting indicators both in the U.S. and Iraq concerning the course of the war. In July, the National Intelligence Council issued a report indicating that al Qaeda was the greatest threat to U.S. security and that al Qaeda was centered in the Federally Administered Tribal Areas of Pakistan. In December, Benazir Bhutto, the former Pakistani prime minister who was campaigning to regain her previous office, was assassinated. Following demonstrations and protests, President Musharraf stepped down in August 2008. These developments indicated both the importance and fragility of Pakistani politics.

In Iraq, it appeared that the surge was having a positive effect. At the end of August 2007, militant Shia leader Moqtada al-Sadr ordered a ceasefire for the forces under his control, and he then extended his ceasefire order for another six months in February 2008. Despite these positive signs, Ambassador Crocker noted in January 2008, "There is a chance of this [increased stability in Iraq] breaking down at a whole range of points."[52] In April, Petraeus and Crocker testified before the U.S. Congress, and Crocker referred to the possible "Lebanonization" of Iraq, referring to the possibility that conflicting ethnic and religious groups could destabilize the country as had occurred in Lebanon years before.

By mid-2008, there were positive indicators that the surge was having intended effects. For example, Admiral William J. Fallon, former CENTCOM commander, noted in July 2008, "The number of incidents of violence nationwide in Iraq is less than a tenth of what we were experiencing in the spring of 2007."[53] After a visit to Kuwait and Afghanistan in October/November of 2008, General Barry McCaffrey noted specific indicators of progress: daily attacks went from 180+ per day in July 2007 to 20+ per day in November 2008; civilian deaths went from 3,700 per month in December 2006 to 400+ per month in October 2008; U.S. military deaths went from 110 in May 2007 to 10 in October 2008; and Iraqi security forces killed in action went from 310 in June 2007 to 50 in October 2008.[54]

The surge of troops in Iraq represented much more than simply sending more troops to Iraq; rather, it represented the implementation of a true counterinsurgency strategy. What was going on, according to David Kilcullen, was "a counterrevolution in military affairs."[55] Or as Thomas Ricks put it, "With the advent of the surge, the Army effectively tuned the war over to its internal dissidents."[56] Whether or not this counterrevolution would be successful was still not clear; the future of Iraq is still uncertain, but as Vali Nasr observed, the surge enabled Iraq to go from being a failed state to a fragile state.[57] In his news briefing at the Pentagon, General Petraeus noted the "operational environment in Iraq is the most complex and challenging I have ever seen—much more complex than it was when I left last in September 2005, and vastly more complex than what I recall in Central America, Haiti and the Balkans in previous tours in these locations." Despite the uncertainties, one thing was clear: the surge was far more successful than the Rumsfeld transformational strategy.

At the same time that the United States government sought to deal with the simultaneous challenges in Afghanistan, Pakistan, and Iraq, the American people were confronted with the need to select a new president in 2008. The Republicans nominated senator and former prisoner of war John McCain, and the Democrats nominated Senator Barack Obama. McCain favored sending more troops to the wars, and Obama was in favor of troop reductions. In a hard fought election, Obama won and was inaugurated as the first African-American president in U.S. history on January 20, 2009.

What to Do about Afghanistan?

Once inaugurated, Barack Obama faced more domestic and foreign challenges than any incoming president since Franklin D. Roosevelt. Among the most significant of those challenges was the daunting task of deciding what to do about Afghanistan, where things were not going well; the Taliban was resurgent and gaining in power, and terrorists continued to enjoy a safe haven in the tribal areas on the border between Afghanistan and Pakistan. The Obama administration put substantial pressure on the Pakistani government to move against the terrorists in the border areas, and toward the end of 2009, the Pakistani military moved against these forces. In Afghanistan, elections were held in November 2009, and there were charges that the Afghan leader, Hamad Karzai, and his followers had rigged the elections. The charges were substantial enough that the election results were not validated for six weeks.

President Obama took six weeks to consider what strategy to pursue regarding Afghanistan, and according to journalist Bob Woodward, the review was contentious among Obama's advisers, with the military pushing for an increase of 40,000 troops and Obama's advisers advocating a lesser number.[58] At the end of his deliberations, the president announced an increase of 30,000 in the number troops to be sent to Afghanistan, the appointment of General Stanley McChrystal as the commander of American forces, and the implementation of a counterinsurgency strategy. McChrystal had substantial experience in dealing with Afghanistan and Iraq, for he had been the commander of the Joint Special Operations Command (JSOP) from 2003 to 2008. Under his command, JSOP captured Saddam Hussein in December 2003 and killed Abu Musab al-Zarqawi, the leader of al Qaeda in Iraq, in June 2006. Like General Petraeus, McChrystal believed in the goals of the counterinsurgency approach; namely, to protect the population and not simply kill enemy insurgents. To do this, McChrystal claimed, "[P]ersonnel must be seen as guests of the Afghan people and their government, not an occupying army . . . [and they] must spend as much time as possible with the people and as little time as possible in armored vehicles or behind walls of forward operating bases."[59] In his initial assessment of conditions in Afghanistan that General McChrystal prepared for Secretary of Defense Gates, he soberly concluded, "The situation in Afghanistan is serious; neither success nor failure can be taken for granted. . . . This is a different kind of fight. We must conduct classic counterinsurgency operations in an environment that is uniquely complex."[60]

Under McChrystal, JSOP implemented an effective counterinsurgency campaign; however, his tenure as commander and career as an officer ended surprisingly and abruptly in June 2010 when McChrystal and members of his staff made a number of comments to a free-lance journalist from *Rolling Stone* magazine criticizing President Obama and members of his administration.[61] McChrystal told the reporter that Obama appeared to be "uncomfortable and intimidated" in his first meeting with the general. Members of McChrystal's staff said that national security adviser was "a clown" and also criticized Vice President Biden. The disrespectful comments created a firestorm, and General McChrystal tendered his resignation, which President Obama accepted. The controversy illustrated the concept of "friction" that the great military strategist Carl von Clausewitz had described: "Everything is very simple in War, but the simplest thing is difficult. These difficulties accumulate and produce a friction which no man can imagine exactly who has not seen War. . . . [In] War, through the influence of an infinity of petty circumstances, which cannot properly be described on paper, things disappoint us, and we fall short of the mark."[62]

General Petraeus stepped down as CENTCOM commander and replaced General McChrystal in the job he previously held providing continuity and stability to a potentially destabilizing situation. General James Mattis replaced Petraeus at Central Command. The newly appointed military commanders continued to emphasize the counterinsurgency approach. By August 19, 2010, U.S. combat troops withdrew from Iraq. In Afghanistan, the U.S. was challenged to differentiate between Muslim groups and leaders who were irreconcilably opposed to the U.S. and its allies and those who could be co-opted to support the U.S. In essence, the United States was attempting to implement a similar policy in Afghanistan to that it had previously implemented in Iraq.

As correspondent Dexter Filkins wrote, "The Afghan reconstruction plan is intended to duplicate the Awakening movement in Iraq, where Sunni tribal leaders, many of them insurgents, agreed to stop fighting and in many cases were paid to do so."[63] The problem with exporting the Sunni Awakening approach to Afghanistan is that there was no analogous group excepting the Taliban, which demanded that all foreign troops leave Afghanistan before reconciliation talks begin. The United States insisted that the Afghan Taliban renounce its ties to al Qaeda and that it support the Afghan constitution, which, among other things called for equal rights for men and women.[64] Thus, the two sides seemed to hold irreconcilable positions.

In his 1987 doctoral dissertation, David Petraeus quoted Army General John Vessey, "We don't learn new lessons. We relearn old lessons that we haven't paid attention to."[65] That is the story of how Petraeus turned Rumsfeld's "revolution of military affairs" into the counterrevolution of the surge and counterinsurgency. In one sense the surges in both Iraq and Afghanistan were underrated in terms of the number of forces who were sent to each country because in both cases, U.S. military forces were supplemented with tens of thousands of civilian contractors. Once the surge was implemented in Iraq in 2007, there were 180,000 American military personnel in Iraq, and these were supported by somewhere between 130,000 and 160,000 contractors.[66] As of July 2007, approximately 1,000 contactors had been killed and 13,000 injured.[67] Once President Obama ordered a surge of 30,000 additional troops into Afghanistan, the Congressional Research Service estimated that an additional 26,000 to 56,000 contractors would also be sent to Afghanistan. This would bring the total number of civilian contractors in Afghanistan to 130,000 to 160,000. Although most of these contractors performed service jobs to support the troops, there were reports that some contractors accompanied CIA officers on raids to gather intelligence and even killed suspected terrorists.[68]

Part III: Conclusion

General David Petraeus briefing leaders of the International Security Assistance Force (ISAF) and NATO in Kabul, Afghanistan

14 Lessons and Legacies: Twenty-Six Articles

In his doctoral dissertation, David Petraeus wrote, "Lessons of history in general and the lessons of Vietnam in particular . . . have much to offer those confronting contemporary problems—but only if used with care and not pushed too far."[1] The objective of this concluding chapter is draw lessons for the United States from its experience in the wars on terror and in Afghanistan and Iraq, but not to push those lessons too far.

Carl von Clausewitz, the great German strategist, wrote, "The first, the supreme, the most far-reaching act of judgment that the statesman and commander have to make is the kind of war on which they are embarking, neither mistaking it for, nor trying to turn it into something that is alien to its nature. This is the first of all strategic questions and the most comprehensive."[2] Following the 9/11 attacks on the United States, the respected British military historian John Keegan commented, "The world changed on September 11. Now the nature of war must change to keep up with it."[3] The U.S. government has struggled to develop and implement the right tactics and strategies for the conflicts in which it is now engaged; some of those tactics and strategies have worked relatively well and others have not. In this conclusion, I will focus on the legacies and lessons to be learned from the period since 9/11.

In 1917, T. E. Lawrence published "Twenty-seven Articles" in which he summarized his tactical advice for members of the British government's Arab Bureau working with tribal insurgents fighting the Ottoman Turks.[4] Almost nine decades later, counterinsurgency theorist and practitioner David Kilcullen following in Lawrence's footsteps wrote his "Twenty-eight Articles" offering tactical advice for captains involved in insurgency campaigns.[5] In this chapter, I will shift Lawrence's and Kilcullen's focus from the tactical to the strategic and point out twenty-six lessons and legacies of the conflicts analyzed in this book.

1. *Wars have unintended consequences, and these should be expected, however unpredictable*

The wars in Afghanistan and Iraq have had a number of unintended consequences. As noted in the early chapters of this book, the primary purpose of the war on terror and the invasions and occupations of Afghanistan and Iraq was to decrease the terrorist threat against the United States. In fact, a number of informed analysts, including the National Intelligence Council, have concluded, "[T]he Iraq war made the overall terrorism problem worse."[6]

States go to war in pursuit of their own national interests, and the wars in Afghanistan and Iraq were no exception to this generalization; the U.S. has both achieved some of its objectives and fallen short of achieving others. The fact that there has been no second major terrorist attack on the homeland of the U.S. since 9/11 is a major achievement and due, at least in part, to the effectiveness of American policies. An unintended consequence of U.S. policies in the region has been to increase the power and influence of Iran, hardly a friend to the United States. In fact, one of the reasons that the George H. W. Bush administration left Saddam in power was to provide a counterweight to Iran. Once the U.S. defeated Saddam, Iran's power in the region significantly increased. In addition, with the emergence of the Shia in post-Saddam Iraq, Shia Iran had more influence domestically in Iraq.

2. *Expect war to be costly in both human and material terms*

There were significant costs of the war on terror and the wars in Afghanistan and Iraq. Of course, the dearest cost that any country pays for war are its citizens who are killed or wounded. As of November 2010, the U.S. and its coalition partners have lost 2,220 in Afghanistan and 4,745 in Iraq. In addition, another 35,000 Americans have been grievously injured in these two wars, and they will pay a heavy price for their service for the rest of their lives.

The economic cost of the wars is momentous. Nobel prize winning economist Joseph Stiglitz has estimated that the eventual cost of the wars will surpass $3 trillion. When one compares the economic state of the U.S. in 2010 with 2001, it is astounding. George W. Bush entered office with a projected $5.6 trillion surplus over the next decade. The Congressional Budget Office reported that U.S. debt held by the public equaled $7.5 trillion (53 percent of GDP) by the end of 2009 and that is projected to grow to $15 trillion (67 percent of GDP) by 2020.

3. *There are opportunity costs in war, and to the extent possible, these should be factored into the calculation of a war's ultimate costs*

With the resources—military, material, and economic—that the U.S. expended on the tripartite wars on terrorism, Afghanistan, and Iraq, the U.S. experienced some significant opportunity costs. First, with its military forces tied down on two principal fronts, the U.S. could not respond to crises elsewhere, specifically in Iran and North Korea. In retrospect, it is clear that North Korea and Iran were both further along in developing weapons of mass destruction than Iraq, but the idée fixe of the Bush administration was on Saddam Hussein's Iraq. The U.S. found no WMD in Iraq, but North Korea has now tested and deployed a handful of nuclear weapons, and Iran is moving in that direction.

In Iraq, the U.S. missed various opportunities. As an aide to UN representative Brahimi told journalist Rajiv Chandrasekaran, "[T]he story of Americans in Iraq [is one of] missed opportunities."[7] Opportunities were missed not only in Iraq, but also in the greater Middle East. In the spring of 2009, public opinion polls conducted annually by the the University of Maryland, the Brookings Institution, and Zogby International found that 45 percent of Arabs had a positive view of President Obama, and this fell to 20 percent by August 2010. Asked which of Obama's policies influenced their negative views, 63 percent cited the Israeli-Paliestinian relations, and 27 percent indicated the policy of the United States toward Iraq.[8]

4. *An understanding of the history, geography, and demographics of a country and region is essential before going to war*

Political scientists have clearly demonstrated in many studies that most Americans do not care about foreign policy most of the time, unless they perceive their interests as threatened. As a result, the level of knowledge about international relations issues in the United States is abysmal, and there is not a strong knowledge base. This is not a new problem in U.S. foreign policy.

When Franklin Delano Roosevelt met with Chinese nationalist leader Chiang Kai-shek toward the end of World War II, he offered control of Vietnam to Chiang, who responded incredulously by saying, "Why would we want Vietnam; they are not Chinese."[9] At the beginning of the Vietnam War, there were only a handful of experts on Southeast Asia in the U.S., and at the beginning of the wars in Afghanistan and Iraq, there were few experts on that region.

There is a need for the U.S. government to continue its support of area study programs and to provide support, such as the Boren scholarship program, to individuals and educational institutionsto develop an expertise and understanding of non-European languages and cultures. If the U.S. government can support poets, dancers, and artists via the National Endowment for the Arts, then surely it can support strong area studies programs.

5. *Obtain the best possible intelligence utilizing the sources that are most likely to be the most reliable in a given situation*

Intelligence about one's actual and potential enemies has always been important in international relations, and it is even more so today. For the United States at the present time, collecting information is not the major problem; rather, identifying the important from the insignificant is a major challenge. As of 2010, each day the National Security Agency intercepts and stores 1.7 billion emails, calls, and other types of communications.[10]

Intelligence must be tailored to the target. Although signals intelligence provided useful information in the early days of the war on terror, the leaders of al Qaeda and other terrorist groups became aware of American capabilities and changed their behavior to reduce the possibility of disclosing valuable information to the U.S. Advances in technology provided new types and capabilities of intelligence. According to journalist Bob Woodward, the National Security Agency has developed the ability to intercept and process communications rapidly and reliably; according to former director of national intelligence Mike McConnell, the insurgents "talk, we listen. They move, we observe. Given the opportunity, we react operationally."[11]

Despite new capabilities, the oldest form of intelligence collection—by human beings—is likely to remain important in dealing with threats from subnational actors such as terrorist groups in the foreseeable future, and this development will raise important questions and issues. Throughout its history, the United States has generally supported the rule of law and human rights, yet, in the war on terror, the U.S. has had to depend on and deal with some notorious violators of American ideals. This dilemma—whether to observe human rights or deal with nefarious characters in order to obtain valuable intelligence—is likely to increase in the future. Intelligence concerning Afghanistan, Pakistan, and Iraq is important and will remain so for the foreseeable future.

Accurate intelligence is crucial. The primary rationale for the United States to attack Iraq was the assumption that Iraq possessed weapons of mass destruction, and virtually everyone—Americans and non-Americans, liberals and conservatives, Republicans and Democrats—believed this to be the case. In fact, after the invasion and the inspections of several different U.S. and international organizations, it is clear that Saddam Hussein was bluffing and that Iraq, as of March 2003, possessed no weapons of mass destruction. An interesting counterfactual question is whether the United States would have invaded had its leaders known that Iraq did not possess WMD. The invasion of Iraq as a preventive war to eliminate WMD underscores the importance of accurate intelligence, which is also likely to be increasingly difficult to obtain. Even though the United States at the time of the invasion of Iraq had the most sophisticated means to collect, store, process, and distribute intelligence information, its intelligence agencies nevertheless reached the wrong conclusion. It is striking that despite its sophisticated technologies and means of collecting intelligence information, despite its considerable expenditure of effort and resources (the intelligence budget in 2009 was estimated to be $75 billion), the United States has been unable to locate and capture or kill former Afghan Taliban leader Mullah Omar and al Qaeda leader Osama bin Laden. As it has throughout its history, the United States has sought a solution to this problem through the use of technology, and the utilization of unmanned drone aircraft in Afghanistan, Pakistan, and Iraq has provided new forms of intelligence information and a new means of attacking and killing enemy forces; however, whether this technology is a "game changer" is still an open question.

6. *Never underestimate the enemy*

Like some other nationalities, Americans tend to be ethnocentric, if not arrogant, concerning the capabilities of the United States relative to other states. In 1957 when the Soviet Union, which most Americans at the time considered backward, launched *Sputnik*, the world's first satellite orbiting the earth, Americans were shocked, surprised, and alarmed. President Lyndon Johnson dismissed North Vietnamese guerillas as "little men in black pajamas" and was shocked and surprised when they were able to defeat U.S. forces.

Underestimating the enemy is not unique to the United States; during the Soviet Union's war in Afghanistan, Soviet leaders and military commanders underestimated the courage, determination, and commitment of the *mujahideen*. It took more than nine years and a new Soviet leader—Mikhail Gorbachev—to recognize that the Soviet "great game" was a losing proposition.

The quick, decisive victory of American forces over Iraqi forces in both January 1991 and March 2003 led some Americans to conclude that Iraqi forces were comparatively weak and ineffective; however, once defeated on the conventional battlefield, many of those forces adopted a different approach for challenging U.S. control of their country. They adopted an asymmetrical approach, which proved to be relatively effective against the military forces of the most powerful country in the world until the U.S. modified its strategy for fighting the insurgents.

7. *Develop a realistic set of objectives for military operations*

American objectives in Afghanistan were limited to overthrowing the Taliban government, destroying al Qaeda training camps, and capturing Osama bin Laden and Mullah Omar. The U.S. succeeded in achieving the first two objectives and failed in achieving the last objective. The invasion of Iraq diverted resources from the war in Afghanistan and decreased the probability of capturing or killing bin Laden, Omar, and their followers. In this more permissive environment, the Taliban regrouped and grew in strength and influence.

American objectives in Iraq were far more grandiose: to overthrow Saddam Hussein, to find and destroy weapons of mass destruction, to establish a democratic government in Iraq and other Middle Eastern states, and to promote human rights. These goals proved to be impossible to achieve even with the expenditure of substantial human and economic resources.

8. *Make assumptions about the enemy and military operations that are based on facts and not wishful thinking*

The assumptions underlying the invasion of Iraq were based on wishful thinking rather than facts and hard analysis. American soldiers were welcomed in the initial days of the invasion, but soon thereafter, most Iraqis wanted the Americans to leave. They stayed, and the insurgency developed.

In Afghanistan and Iraq, American policymakers made best-case as opposed to worst-case assumptions. This was a curious reversal of the practice throughout the cold war, when U.S. leaders assumed the worst case with regard to the Soviet Union and its military capabilities. In fact, it was worst case planning that led to the building of the enormous arsenals of American and Soviet nuclear weapons that reached its high point of 69,000 weapons in 1986.[12]

It is essential that American leaders make realistic, plausible assumptions prior to going to war. In Afghanistan, policymakers assumed that advanced technologies would give the United States advantages in conducting war against the Taliban and al Qaeda, and these assumptions proved to be correct; however, American policymakers' assumptions concerning war in Iraq proved to be wildly off the mark. For example, key U.S. decision-makers assumed that expatriate Iraqi leaders such as Ahmad Chalabi and Ali Allawi would be accepted and even welcomed by Iraqis. This assumption grossly simplified the complex reality of Iraqi politics, which was based on complex connections among families, clans, and tribes, in addition to the fundamental split between Sunnis and Shia. In addition, accepting the facile assurances of neoconservatives, American policymakers assumed that once Saddam Hussein was overthrown, democracy and the rule of law would take hold in Iraq and then spread throughout the Middle East. In retrospect, such an assumption is completely unrealistic given the lack of democratic processes, institutions, or traditions in the Middle East, and yet, this was a central assumption of United States policy.

9. *Obtain the support of other states, nongovernmental organizations, and intergovernmental organizations*

Many contemporary international problems can only be dealt with effectively through international cooperation. For example, it is impossible for one country—even if the most powerful in the world, the United States—to solve some problems alone. Global climate change, HIV/AIDS, and reducing global poverty are a few of such problems. Terrorism is another.[13]

In the days and weeks following the 9/11 attacks on the U.S., there was substantial international support for and cooperation with the United States in identifying and taking down individual terrorists and their networks. Such cooperation came from former U.S. adversaries such as Russia and even one publicly identified state sponsor of terrorism, Syria.

States interact with one another not only bilaterally, but also multilaterally through intergovernmental organizations at the regional and global levels. Different presidential administrations place differing priorities on the U.S. level of commitment and involvement with such organizations, and this is not a partisan political issue. For example, George H. W. Bush placed a high priority on cooperation with U.S. allies, and this paid off during the first Gulf War. It is crucial that the United States work closely with its long-time allies. The contrast between the first and second Gulf wars is instructive. In the first Gulf War, President George Herbert Walker Bush worked tirelessly to convince close American allies to support the coalition in opposing and reversing Iraq's takeover and occupation of Kuwait. In the end, more than thirty countries supported the coalition with both military and economic support. Although the first Gulf War cost a total of $55 billion, American allies—principally Kuwait, Saudi Arabia, and Japan—reimbursed the U.S. $50 billion. As a result, the first Gulf War cost the U.S. a total of $5 billion, which is equivalent to the cost of the wars in Afghanistan and Iraq for two weeks in 2009. As of 2010, it costs $1 million per year to support one U.S. soldier in Afghanistan. Such a level of spending is unsustainable over the long term. The United States needs the support of allies, and even with that support, the U.S. will be taxed, literally and figuratively, to support a long-term presence of American forces in Afghanistan and/or Iraq.

Faced with a new and unknown threat following 9/11, George W. Bush chose to almost "go it alone" in Afghanistan and with only the United Kingdom and several other close allies in Iraq. This almost unilateral approach was costly to the U.S. in both human and economic terms. It is worth remembering that in those cases in which the United States had a legitimate cause and genuine coalition (World War II, Korea, Afghanistan), it was successful. When the U.S. went it alone or had a weak coalition (Iraq), it had serious problems or it failed (Vietnam).

Classic international relations theory focused on three levels of analysis: individuals, the state, and the international system.[14] A distinguishing feature of contemporary international relations is the rise and increasing prominence of transnational and nonstate actors, which vary from the beneficent (International Red Cross, CARE, Amnesty International) to the malevolent (drug cartels, terrorist groups). In thinking about future conflict, U.S. leaders should consider the possible roles of nonstate actors. The United States Institute of Peace has sponsored a number of studies and programs focusing on the need for cooperation and coordination of governmental and nongovernmental actors, the need for which will likely only increase in the future.

10. *Concentrate on the development and training of local security and military forces*

Security is the essential prerequisite for rebuilding a war-torn society, and local security forces most effectively and most economically can provide security. Therefore, it is essential to develop and implement training programs, to recruit personnel, and to deploy local security forces as soon as possible.

In both Afghanistan and Iraq, the United States has confronted the challenge of providing security for the local population, and this has proved difficult and costly. In Iraq, the U.S. exacerbated the problem by disbanding Iraqi security forces and disqualifying any Iraqi who had belonged to the Baath Party. These two decisions resulted in significant costs for U.S. forces to provide security and delays in standing up Iraqi security forces.

Without security postwar reconstruction plans and programs either cannot proceed or can only proceed at great human and financial cost. Once a basic level of security is assured, other basic functions of society can be provided, including sewage disposal and treatment, providing potable water, and providing assured access to electricity, transportation, and communications. A common Iraqi criticism of the United States following its invasion and occupation of Iraq was that after the first Gulf War, Saddam Hussein had restored access to electrical power faster than the U.S. after its invasion and occupation of 2003.

In planning for security, absolute security is impossible to achieve. As Kenneth Waltz noted, "States, like people, are insecure in proportion to the extent of their freedom. If freedom is wanted, insecurity must be accepted."[15] This is not to say that there is a choice between security and freedom; rather, there is a spectrum, and the cost of greater security may be at the expense of freedom.

11. *Develop plans for postwar reconstruction and development before the war begins and make adjustments as the war develops*

Official U.S. military plans call for commanders to plan military operations focusing on four phases of war from kinetic to postwar operations. Historian Russell Weigley has demonstrated that "the American way of war" is to use massive force in order to overwhelm the enemy, and that approach worked well in World War II and the first Gulf War.[16] The effectiveness of the application of U.S. military force in both of these cases eclipsed the effectiveness of postwar operations. Following the cessation of hostilities at the end of World War II, the U.S. invited the European states—victors and vanquished alike—to submit plans for reconstruction; the Marshall Plan, which provided the funds to assist European states to rebuild, stands as one of the greatest successes of American foreign policy. At the end of the first Gulf War, the U.S. and the international community agreed that, despite his act of blatant aggression against Kuwait, Saddam Hussein should remain in power. This had the advantage of maintaining a stable government in Iraq and counterbalancing Iran in the region.

Following the defeat of the Soviet Union in Afghanistan by the *mujahideen*, the U.S. withdrew its support from Afghanistan, an action that contributed to the ability of the retrogressive Taliban to take over the country and to allow al Qaeda a sanctuary. Following 9/11 and the finding that al Qaeda's leadership was in Afghanistan, the U.S. military plan was to get in and get out as quickly as possible. Consequently, working with the Northern Alliance, the U.S. accomplished two of its three strategic objectives in Afghanistan quickly.

The invasion of Iraq in March 2003 placed increased demands on American resources, particularly the need for special operations forces, which were moved from Afghanistan to Iraq. This action degraded the effort to rebuild in Afghanistan. In Iraq, there were a number of studies on postwar issues and problems, most notably the "Future of Iraq" project.[17] Clausewitz was correct in noting that a key requirement in war is "not to take the first step without considering the last,"[18] something the United States failed to do in both Afghanistan and Iraq.

12. *Develop a plan for local, regional, and international strategic communications*

Tactical communications are essential to conducting effective military operations; if a unit cannot communicate with another, combat effectiveness is significantly eroded. Likewise, strategic communication is also vital, and contemporary military commanders recognize its importance. In his formal initial assessment after assuming command of the International Security Assistance Force (ISAF) in Afghanistan, General Stanley McChrystal wrote: "The information domain is a battlespace, and it is one in which ISAF must take aggressive actions to win the important battle of perception. Strategic Communication (StratCom) makes a vital contribution to the overall effort, and more specifically, to the operational center of gravity: the continued support of the Afghan population."[19]

Strategic communication cannot always be managed and controlled. For example, the release of the photographs of American soldiers abusing Iraqi prisoners at Abu Ghraib had an enormous effect on attitudes toward the United States in Iraq, the Middle East, and the rest of the world, and it was hard to counter the negative effects.

Maintaining effective strategic communication, even for those who are aware of its importance, can be difficult, as the indiscrete comments of General McChrystal and his staff to a *Rolling Stone* reporter illustrate.

13. *Inform and involve members of Congress in war planning from the beginning to the end of the conflict*

Reflecting the "checks and balances" approach of Montesquieu, the Constitution grants the executive branch the power to make foreign policy; however, it also delegates the congressional branch certain specific responsibilities and grants Congress oversight functions. During foreign policy crises and particularly during war, the Congress tends to "rally round the flag" to support the president's policy.[20] At other times, the relationship between the congressional and executive branches can be contentious.

An administration ignores or snubs the Congress only at its peril; the Congress controls appropriations and the ratification of treaties, reviews senior governmental appointments, holds hearings, and conducts investigations. Taken together, these can be formidable powers. By including members of Congress in war planning, an administration can head off opposition to its policy, but such a policy must genuinely involve members of Congress and not be window dressing.

There was little congressional involvement in the attack on Afghanistan in October 2001; the American homeland had been attacked, and members of Congress wanted the perpetrators to pay for their misdeed. Consequently, Congress allowed the executive branch significant leeway in responding to the 9/11 attacks.

When the George W. Bush administration decided to attack Iraq, the vote in the House was 296 to 133, and a majority of Democrats voted for the war. In the Senate, the vote was 77 to 21 with twenty-one Democrats voting in favor of going to war, including a number of those Democrats who would subsequently run for their party's presidential nomination. With congressional support, the Bush administration went to war. As journalist Thomas Ricks has noted, "In previous wars, Congress had been populated by hawks and doves. But as war in Iraq loomed it seemed to consist mainly of lambs. There are many failures in the American system that led to the war, but the failures in Congress were at once perhaps the most important and the least noticed."[21] During the Vietnam War, a turning point came when Senator J. William Fulbright, the chairman of the Senate Foreign Relations Committee, held hearings on the war. There was no analogue to Fulbright prior to and during the Afghanistan and Iraq wars, although individual senators such as Robert Byrd strongly criticized the move toward war in Iraq.

For its part, the Bush administration chose by and large not to consult with Congress on the war. This was in keeping with the theory of the "unitary executive" that key members of the administration held. Over time, ignoring Congress had negative effects on the administration's policies, and it would have been in a stronger position if it had involved and consulted on a bipartisan basis with members of Congress.

14. *Coordinate policy within the executive branch*

Congressional-executive relations are not the only problem of policy coordination in the U.S. government; coordination within the executive branch itself can be problematic and even debilitating. Disagreements between or among individual policymakers, agencies, and departments have negatively affected presidential administrations in both parties. For example, the contrasting, if not contradictory, policy views of Secretary of State Cyrus Vance and National Security Affairs Adviser Zbigniew Brzezinski contributed to the inconsistent Soviet policy of the Carter administration. Or the debates between Secretary of State George Shultz and Secretary of Defense Caspar Weinberger negatively impacted the Reagan administration's foreign policymaking.

The George W. Bush administration was marked by deep differences in international relations perspectives, and Vice President Cheney and his office had unprecedented influence on American foreign policy, particularly concerning detainee issues following 9/11. Because of their past appointments and common worldviews, the vice president and Secretary of Defense Donald Rumsfeld worked together closely and saw eye to eye on most foreign policy issues. Opposing Cheney and Rumsfeld on a number of important issues were Secretary of State Colin Powell and his staff, and standing in the wings was national security adviser Condoleezza Rice, who failed to manage and take charge of the internecine debates within the executive branch. She, however, does not bear primary responsibility for the split within the executive branch; after all, the president is the commander-in-chief and, as Clinton Rossiter pointed out many years ago, is the chief executive officer of the U.S. government.[22] To the detriment of his administration and the country, George W. Bush chose not to get involved in developing a coherent, consistent foreign policy toward Afghanistan, Pakistan, and Iraq.

15. *Do not ask too much from the members of the military and their families compared to the rest of American society*

In the aftermath of 9/11, Americans experienced a wave of patriotic feeling, and many responded to defend their country that had been attacked. I had a student, for example, who had graduated from college in 1998 and then entered investment banking. By the time of 9/11, he was making a six-figure income. The day after the attacks on the U.S., he went to a recruitment office and volunteered for the military. The recruiter apologized and said that there were no openings for college graduates like him in officer candidate school, and my former student asked, "What about signing up as an enlisted man?" Surprised, the recruiter said there were plenty of openings for soldiers, and my former student signed up. Because of his intelligence, motivation, and physical fitness, he was accepted for Special Forces training, and following that he was deployed all over the world chasing suspected terrorists. After six years and deployments to Afghanistan, the Philippines, and other places he could not disclose, he had had enough. He got out of the Army and went back to graduate school—for a year until he was called to active duty from the reserves.

Young people like my former student are an inspiration and a challenge to Tom Brokaw's contention that World War II veterans constitute "the greatest generation." I'm not sure of that, but I am sure that people in the military today have paid a grossly disproportionate price for the wars in Afghanistan and Iraq. Almost all members of the Army or the Marines during their first four-year enlistment have been deployed to Afghanistan or Iraq for one tour of duty; many have been deployed for two tours; and some for three tours. In contrast, civilians are not directly involved or affected by the wars unless they have a loved one overseas. Of course, all Americans, civilian and military alike, will be paying for these wars for several generations, given the deficits that have been run up in order to pay for them. And, of course, those who have lost loved ones will never fully recover.

16. *Return real control of the government to locals as soon as possible*

From the early days of the republic, Americans have believed in and supported independence and self-determination. During and following World War I, Woodrow Wilson incorporated the principle of self-determination as a foundation of the new system for managing power in international relations that he supported, collective security.

The goal of conflicts and wars in which the U.S. is engaged should be to return control of the government to locals as soon as possible following hostilities. Local people will have a better situational awareness than foreigners, and they will be more likely to obtain the support of the local populace. Of course, the danger is that local leaders may not conform to American ideas of how a leader should act. In Afghanistan, the U.S. supported the *mujahideen* during the Soviet-Afghan war despite the fact that some were engaged in drug trafficking and violated human rights. In Iraq, Ambassador Bremer decided to postpone for more than a year returning control of the government to Iraqis, with disastrous results.

Based on the Afghan and Iraq wars, U.S. officials in the future need to recognize that it is essential to work with local political leaders and to return power and control to them as quickly as possible. For a short time after they invaded Iraq and toppled Saddam Hussein and the Baath Party from power, American and coalition forces were welcomed by Iraqis; however, the longer they stayed, the less popular they became. After Ambassador Paul Bremer canceled the turnover of power to Iraqis and announced a year-long occupation, U.S. popularity declined significantly, and when he ordered that no member of the Baath Party could serve in the new Iraqi government and the disbanding of Iraqi security forces, both anti-American feelings and support for the insurgency increased. Bremer's decision and actions had the unintended consequences of stimulating the insurgency.

17. *Allow sufficient time to achieve mission goals*

There are a number of ways in which military force is used, including a quick, decisive use of force (*Blitzkrieg*), a drawn-out war of attrition (World War I), the simultaneous pursuit of political and military objectives (coercive diplomacy), and counterinsurgency.[23] There are many differences among these various uses of force, and one of the most important is the amount of time required for the successful application of a particular strategy. Counterinsurgency is the most demanding in terms of time. In September 2005 in testimony to the Senate Armed Services Committee, General George Casey, the U.S. commander in Iraq at the time, noted, "The average counterinsurgency in the twentieth century lasted nine years. Fighting insurgencies is a long-term proposition, and there's no reason that we should believe that the insurgency in Iraq will take any less time to deal with."[24] The findings of RAND Corporation analyst Seth Jones were even more sobering; he found that since 1945 "successful counterinsurgency campaigns last for an average of fourteen years, and unsuccessful ones last for an average of eleven years. . . . "[M]ore than a third of all insurgencies last more than twenty years."[25] The message is clear: if a country chooses a counterinsurgency strategy, it should be prepared to wage it for a long period of time—a least a decade.

The conflicts that the United States will face in the future will most likely not resemble those of the past. The epic tank battles of the past—El Alamein, Kursk, the first Gulf War—are likely just that: of the past, and the United States is far more probable to face insurgencies in the future. In these cases, as the developments of the wars in Afghanistan and Iraq have demonstrated, a counterinsurgency strategy focusing on the protection of the local population is more likely to be successful than one employing large numbers of troops focused on killing the enemy.

18. *Encourage close cooperation between military and civilian officials*

It is vital that future U.S. military strategies be appropriate for the conflicts that the United States is likely to face, and it is unlikely that those conflicts will be similar to those confronted by the U.S. during the cold war. Rather, it is likely that future conflicts will be similar to those of the 1980s and 1990s: Rwanda, Bosnia, Haiti, Somalia, Kosovo, Macedonia, East Timor, Democratic Republic of Congo, Burma, and Darfur. The first task of the future is to assess what type of conflict is presented: Is it an ethnically based conflict? Is it caused by outside insurgents? Is it a civil war? What is the likelihood that peacekeeping forces can keep the conflict from escalating? In many of these conflicts, a traditional "big Army" strategy is less likely to be successful than a peacekeeping or a counter-insurgency approach. Of course, traditional capabilities must be maintained for possible large-scale conflicts, but capabilities for counterinsurgency, nation-building, and peacekeeping must also be more fully developed and retained.

In this regard, military and civilian capabilities for nation-building should be supported. George W. Bush and his advisers entered office disdainful of nation-building only to find themselves facing the most comprehensive, demanding cases of nation-building since the end of World War II; however, the U.S. government's nation-building capabilities had eroded since the end of the Vietnam War, and the U.S. had to depend upon the Department of Defense to provide the personnel and training for nation-building in both Afghanistan and Iraq. This situation was necessary but not ideal. Basic security is a prerequisite for nation-building, and military forces are best able to provide for security; however, civilians are better suited to develop and implement the processes and organizations of civil society. Several years into the wars in Afghanistan and Iraq, the U.S. government established Provincial Reconstruction Teams (PRT) headed by American officials who were charged with overseeing the establishment and implementation of civil society. Following the invasion of Afghanistan, military personnel were the ones who implemented postwar reconstruction and nation-building programs; however, historically, civilians in the State Department and the Agency for International Development have had the most experience running such programs. In the future, it will be important to rely on civilian officials and agencies that have the experience of implementing such programs; in fact, in Iraq, civilians were given primary responsibility. In order to do this, however, programs will have to be vastly expanded. For example, as of 2008, twenty-six Provincial Reconstruction Teams (PRT) were established in each Afghan provincial capital, and they were formally responsible for the U.S. government's local development efforts. In Iraq, thirty-one PRTs were established by 2008, and in both Afghanistan and Iraq, an increased number of civilian experts in development have been assigned, marking a kind of "civilian surge" policy.

19. *As commander-in-chief, the president must be actively involved and knowledgeable about the conflict*

American presidents must assume central responsibility for the making and implementation of U.S. foreign policy concerning conflict and war. In retrospect, it seems clear that George W. Bush ceded his constitutional responsibility for making foreign policy to others in his administration. In many ways and for the first six years of the George W. Bush administration, it appears that Vice President Dick Cheney and Secretary of Defense Donald Rumsfeld and their subordinates made a number of the important decisions concerning U.S. policy toward Afghanistan, Pakistan, Iraq, and the war on terror. The "unitary executive" theory of presidential preeminence in foreign policymaking came from the vice president's office and was supported by like-minded officials in DOD and the Department of Justice. In addition, the U.S. government's policy supporting the use of torture to obtain information from suspected terrorists was also supported by a similar group within the administration. In his memoirs, President Bush noted that he supported "enhanced interrogation techniques," including waterboarding, which he contends "did not constitute torture."[26] The goal for future administrations should be Harry S. Truman's adage: "The buck stops here," rather than the more typical presidential practice of passing the buck.

20. *Sustain economic development programs over the long term*

Sustained, substantial economic and military aid from the United States and the international community is required to maintain stability in Afghanistan, Pakistan, and Iraq, and without such aid economic and political stability is unlikely. As wealthy and as powerful as it is, the United States does not have the resources unilaterally to provide the aid that these states and their populations need; international cooperation is a necessity.

21. *Be willing to modify or change the battle plan if it is not achieving the strategic goals of the military campaign*

Throughout history successful military commanders have been able to recognize when the tide of battle was turning against them and have been able to adapt and change their tactics and strategy. In 2006 when it looked as if Iraq was unraveling, U.S. leaders, led by President Bush, dramatically changed a conventional strategy focused on killing the enemy to a counterinsurgency strategy focused on providing security for the population. Without this change in policy, it is likely that the United States would have been defeated in Iraq.

22. *Be willing to compromise with hostile forces that will work with you*

Immediately after 9/11, George W. Bush sought to divide the world into two camps: those who supported the United States and those who supported terrorism. There was little leeway in this dichotomous division. It was reminiscent of the cold war division of the world into the Free World and the communist bloc. The key to understanding international relations was simple and straightforward: communists were bad, and anticommunists were good. One of the most significant errors of the cold war was the failure to recognize differences among communists. For example, the founder of the North Vietnamese communist party was Ho Chi Minh, and when he proclaimed independence from France, he quoted the U.S. Declaration of Independence. Despite this tip of the hat to American ideals, Americans dismissed Ho because he was a communist. Unquestionably, some communists would never have compromised with the Untied States, and undoubtedly, some terrorists in the contemporary era would never compromise with the U.S. However, the U.S. learned in Iraq that some terrorist sympathizers or actual terrorists could be convinced to work with, rather than against, the Americans. This was the lesson of the Sunni Awakening, and it is a valuable lesson to keep in mind for the future.

23. *In fighting the enemy, maintain and observe fundamental ideals*

Soon after the al Qaeda attacks on the United States of September 11, 2001, a number of Americans worried that the fear engendered by the attacks would cause the United States to weaken its traditional support for and observance of fundamental individual and human rights. The George W. Bush administration's response to the attacks in some significant ways confirmed these fears by weakening rights of privacy with warrantless wiretaps and the passage of the Patriot Act. In addition, the long-standing prohibition on torture was violated by different government agencies, most dramatically at Abu Ghraib prison in Iraq. The weakening of the U.S. observance of international and domestic laws regarding privacy and the prohibition of torture underscores the need to observe American values and ideals assiduously so that these values do not appear hypocritical or even meaningless. The United States owes the courageous members of the military no less, for they are the ones who have paid for the wars in Afghanistan and Pakistan disproportionately compared to the rest of American society.

24. *Try to prevent attacks on the homeland, but prepare physically and mentally for the worst*

Following 9/11, many experts on terrorism believed that a second major attack on the U.S. was all but inevitable. As of the writing of this book, such an attack has not occurred; however, experts remain concerned that such an attack is possible, if not probable. It is important to think about a possible future terrorist attack in two ways. First, many years ago, David Fromkin noted, "Terrorism wins only if you respond to it in the way the terrorists want you to; which means that its fate is in your hands and not theirs."[27] Americans' greatest fear of terrorism, of course, is of a nuclear attack. But even if this were to occur and as damaging as it could be, it still would cause only a small percentage of the damage that would have resulted during an all-out war between the United States and the USSR during the cold war. The reality of the contemporary era is that the probability of a nuclear weapon being detonated is higher than during the cold war, but the probability of a global conflagration is less.

If a major terrorist attack were to occur, it would be vital for Americans to respond with determination to rebuild and carry on their lives. In this regard, the response of Londoners to the bombing of the subway in July 2005 is instructive; the day after the attack, Londoners got back on the trains and carried on. Resiliency is the key.[28]

25. *Pay close attention to Pakistan*

During the initial years of war and conflict, from 2001 to 2006, Pakistan remained largely on the sidelines, mostly uninvolved in a central way in the war on terrorism and the war in Afghanistan. There are three major reasons for American policymakers to pay close attention to Pakistan. First, Pakistan is the only Islamic state and one of only nine countries in the world to possess nuclear weapons. If the government of Pakistan were to become unstable or taken over by Islamic radicals, the control of nuclear weapons could be degraded and under such circumstances, U.S. policymakers' nightmare could come true: "the world's most destructive weapons could fall into the hands of the world's most dangerous terrorists." Second, the Afghan-Pakistani border area, particularly around Tora Bora and several Pakistani cities such as Quetta, is a sanctuary for radical Muslims who could destabilize the Pakistani government. Third, Pakistan is key to the future of Afghanistan. The two countries are integrally related. Former Under Secretary of Defense Douglas Feith has written, "No country in the world was of greater importance to our military operations in Afghanistan than Pakistan."[29] When he was the commanding officer of the International Security Force, Afghanistan (ISAF), General Karl Eikenberry testified to Congress in February 2007: "NATO could not win in Afghanistan without addressing the sanctuaries the Taliban enjoyed in Pakistan."[30] General McChrystal echoed this point: "Stability in Pakistan is essential, not only in its own right, but also to enable progress in Afghanistan."[31]

26. *Relearn the lessons of the past*

At the end of the first Gulf War, a number of commentators, including President George H. W. Bush, indicated that the United States had at long last kicked the "Vietnam syndrome" and had shown that the "U.S. was back." It had taken a decade for the U.S. military to recover from Vietnam, and by 1990, it was clear that the U.S. military had recovered, and its impressive performance in the first Gulf War clearly proved this. The generation of military leaders who had served as junior officers in Vietnam came into prominence in the 1990s, and, having experienced the trauma of Vietnam, they worked assiduously to avoid the mistakes that the earlier military leaders had made. First, they supported the creation and the building of the all-volunteer force consisting of those who wanted to be in the military rather than those who, many against their will, were drafted into service. Second, they believed in the massive application of military force. Third, they criticized the limited application of force such as counterinsurgency and believed that the purpose of war was, first and foremost, to defeat the enemy. Lost in pursuing this objective, of course, was winning the support of the local people.

The irony of the wars in Afghanistan and Iraq from the military's perspective is that the effect was similar to Vietnam; namely, the war in Afghanistan supplanted Vietnam as "America's longest war" and imposed such demands on the military that it was at the breaking point by the end of 2010.

In the preface of this book, I recounted the haunting question that a friend of mine who is a military officer and who spent a year in Iraq asked me, "Why are we in Iraq?" I also recalled seeing a young Marine on the beach in San Clemente who had lost both legs below his knees. A number of students of mine have asked me why we are in Afghanistan and Iraq, and what the United States should do about Pakistan. I hope that this book provides at least a partial explanation for my friend, my students, and that young Marine on the beach. And I hope that it provides an explanation, if not solace, for the families of those who have served in Afghanistan and/or Iraq, those who have been seriously wounded or those who have given "their last full measure of devotion."

Appendixes

Appendix A: Maps

The maps of Afghanistan, Iraq, and Pakistan are based on maps at the CIA web site, https://www.cia.gov/library/publications/the-world-factbook/geos/af.html. The map of the Middle East region is from the United Nations, Department of Peacekeeping Operations, Cartographic Section, August 2004.

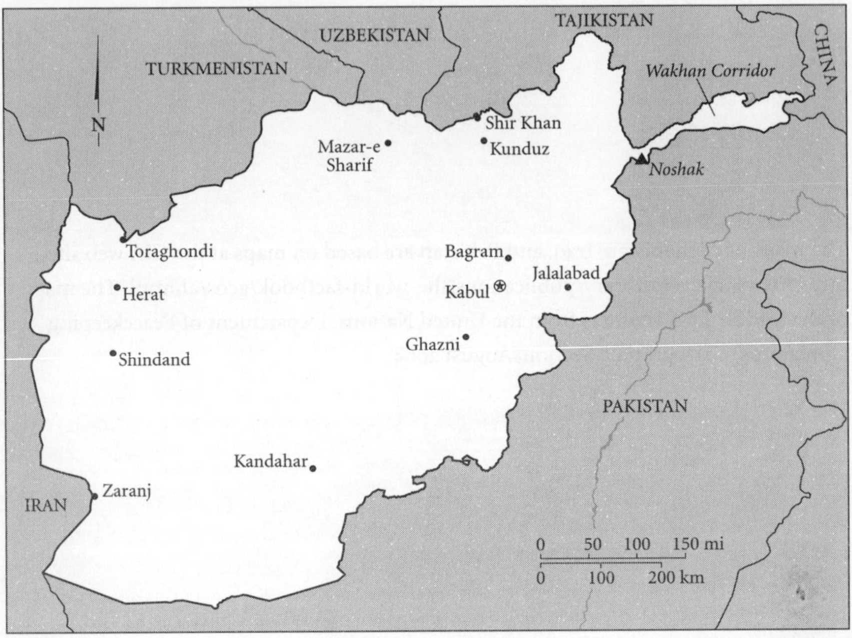

Afghanistan

TURKEY
SYRIA
IRAN
JORDAN
SAUDI ARABIA
KUWAIT
N
Dahùk
Mosul
Irbil
Kirkuk
Sulaymaniyah
Samarra
Rutbah
Ramadi
Baghdad
Tigris R.
Karbala
Kut
Najaf
Euphrates R.
Nasiriyah
Basra
Umm Qasr
0 50 100 mi
0 50 100 150 km

Iraq

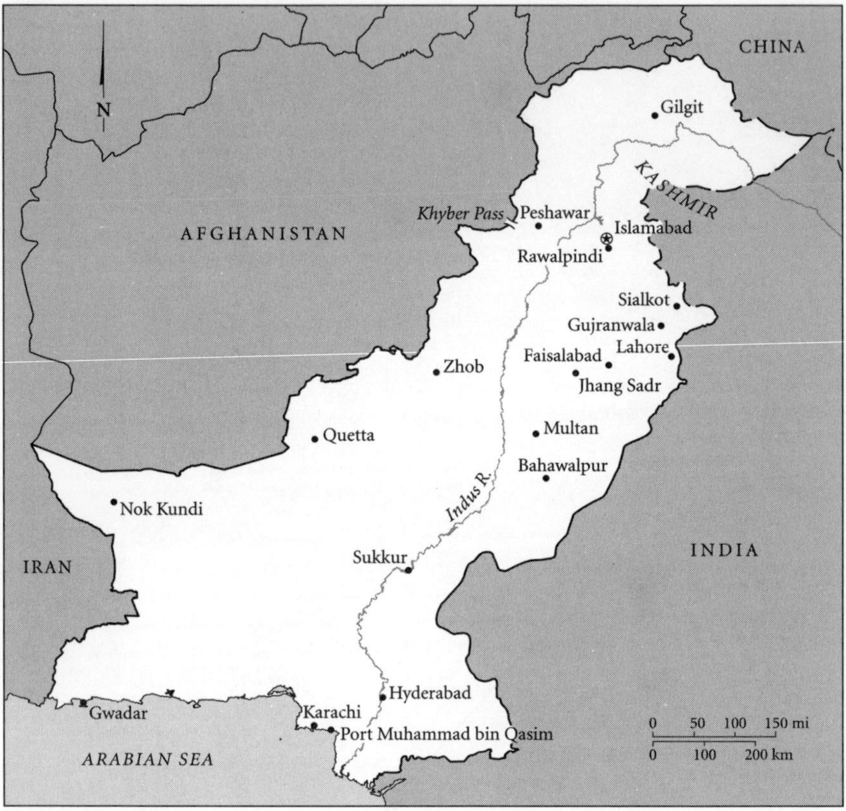
CHINA
N
Gilgit
KASHMIR
Khyber Pass
Peshawar
Islamabad
Rawalpindi
AFGHANISTAN
Sialkot
Gujranwala
Lahore
Faisalabad
Zhob
Jhang Sadr
Quetta
Multan
Bahawalpur
Indus R.
Nok Kundi
INDIA
Sukkur
IRAN
Hyderabad
Gwadar
Karachi
Port Muhammad bin Qasim
ARABIAN SEA
0 50 100 150 mi
0 100 200 km

Pakistan

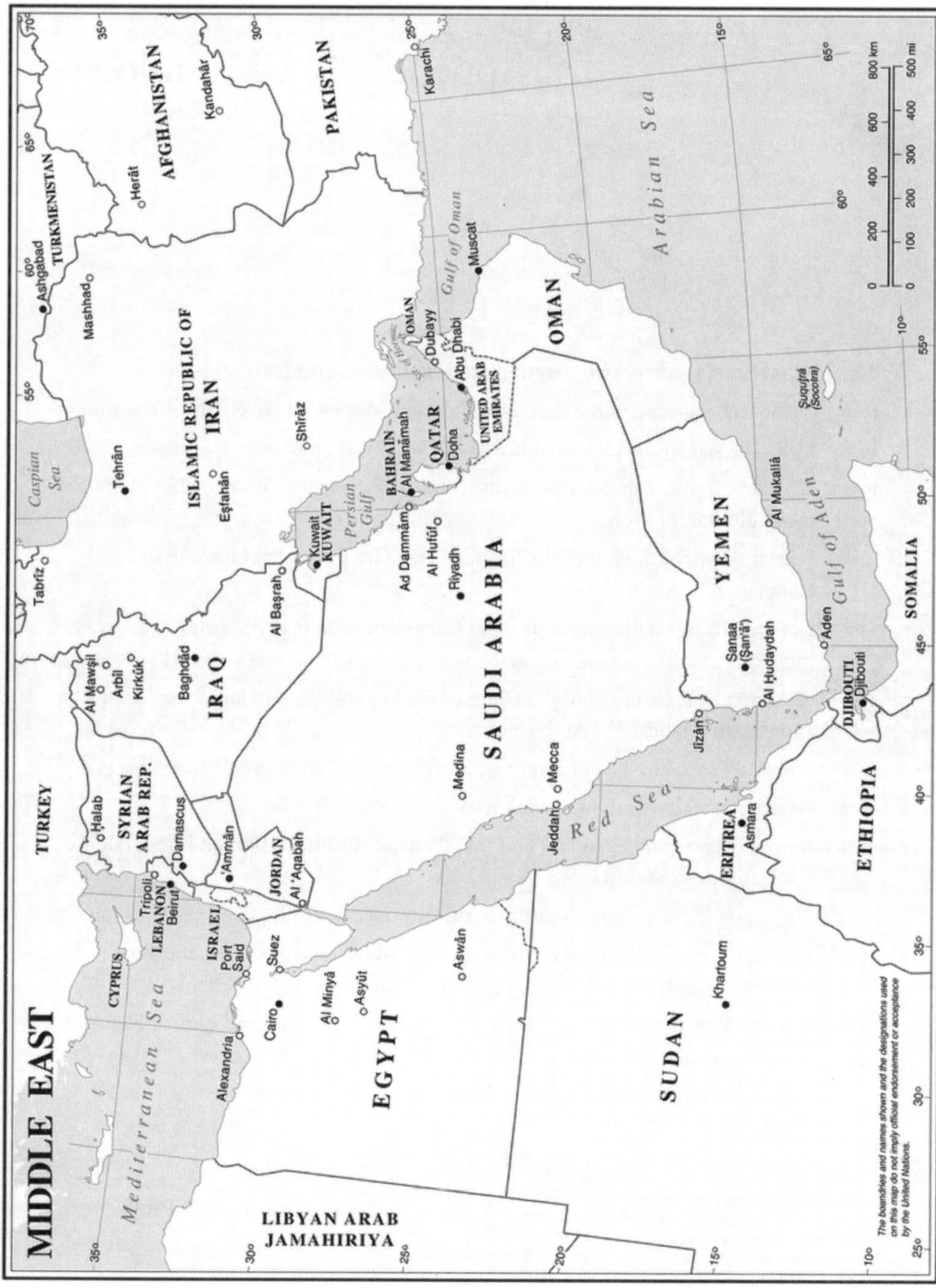
MIDDLE EAST
TURKEY
CYPRUS
SYRIAN ARAB REP.
LEBANON
ISRAEL
JORDAN
IRAQ
KUWAIT
ISLAMIC REPUBLIC OF IRAN
TURKMENISTAN
AFGHANISTAN
PAKISTAN
SAUDI ARABIA
BAHRAIN
QATAR
UNITED ARAB EMIRATES
OMAN
YEMEN
EGYPT
LIBYAN ARAB JAMAHIRIYA
SUDAN
ERITREA
ETHIOPIA
DJIBOUTI
SOMALIA
Mediterranean Sea
Caspian Sea
Persian Gulf
Gulf of Oman
Arabian Sea
Red Sea
Gulf of Aden
Halab
Damascus
Tripoli
Beirut
'Ammān
Al 'Aqabah
Al Mawşil
Arbil
Kirkūk
Baghdād
Al Başrah
Kuwait
Tabrīz
Tehrān
Eşfahān
Shīrāz
Mashhad
Ashgabad
Herāt
Kandahār
Karachi
Muscat
Dubayy
Abu Dhabi
Doha
Al Manāmah
Ad Dammām
Al Hufūf
Riyadh
Medina
Mecca
Jeddah
Jīzān
Sanaa (Şan'ā')
Al Ḩudaydah
Aden
Al Mukallā
Suquţrá (Socotra)
Asmara
Djibouti
Khartoum
Alexandria
Port Said
Suez
Cairo
Al Minyā
Asyūt
Aswān
0 200 400 600 800 km
0 100 200 300 400 500 mi
The boundaries and names shown and the designations used on this map do not imply official endorsement or acceptance by the United Nations.

Appendix B: Chronology

The United States, Terrorism, Afghanistan, Pakistan, and Iraq

1947 October: Beginning of the first Indo-Pakistani War over sovereignty of Kashmir

1948 May: The state of Israel is established and war breaks out

1952 February: Iraq concludes agreement with Iraq Petroleum Company calling for a 50–50 division of profits

1955 February: Establishment of the Baghdad Pact (Iraq, Iran, Pakistan, Turkey, and Britain)

1956 October: Nasser nationalizes the Suez Canal and Britain, France, and Israel invade Egypt to take over the canal

1958 February: Establishment of the United Arab Republic (Egypt and Syria); Iraq and Jordan establish the Arab Union

July: Military coup d'état in Iraq; General Qasim becomes prime minister

1959 December: Iraq withdraws from the Baghdad Pact

1961 Kuwait becomes independent and Iraq demands its integration into Iraq; UK sends troops to Kuwait

1965 Beginning of the second Indo-Pakistani War over Kashmir

1967 June: Six Day War between Egypt and Israel, which occupies Gaza, the Sinai Peninsula, Old Jerusalem, the Golan Heights, and Jordan's West Bank

1968 July 17: Military coup in Iraq; Baath Party takes over in Iraq and Ahmad Hasan al-Bakr becomes president

July 22: George Habash's Popular Front for the Liberation of Palestine (PFLP) hijacks El Al airliner

1971 December 3: Pakistan attacks India pre-emptively; war begins

1972 April: Iraq and the Soviet Union sign a Treaty of Friendship and Cooperation

June: Iraq nationalizes the Iraq Petroleum Company

1973 October 6: Egypt and Syria attack Israel on Yom Kippur

1977 July: Pakistani General Mohammed Zia-ul-Haq seizes power from Zulfikar Ali Bhutto and subsequently orders his execution

1979 January: Shah of Iran deposed

February 14: U.S. embassy in Tehran attacked and staff is trapped; later freed by Khomeini forces

February 14: A Tajik, anti-Pashtun separatist group, the Setam-i-Milli, kidnaps U.S. ambassador to Afghanistan, Adolph Dubs, who is later killed

March 26: Israel and Egypt sign peace treaty

July 16: Saddam Hussein becomes president of Iraq

November 4: Iranians take over the U.S. embassy in Tehran; 66 American hostages

November 20: Terrorists seize the Grand Mosque in Mecca

November 21: Pakistani mob burns down U.S. embassy in Islamabad and two American cultural centers in Rawalpindi and Lahore, Pakistan; four killed

December 24: Soviet invasion of Afghanistan

1980 April 25: Failed secret rescue attempt of American hostages in Iraq

September 21: Iraq invades Iran; beginning of the eight-year war

1981 January 20: U.S. hostages in Iran are released; Ronald Reagan inaugurated

May: Gulf Cooperation Council formed

June: Israel destroys an Iraqi nuclear reactor at Osirak

1982 October 6: President Anwar Sadat assassinated

1983 April 18: U.S. embassy in Beirut bombed; 63 killed

October 23: U.S. Marine barracks in Beirut bombed; 298 killed including 241 U.S. Marines

December: As President Reagan's special envoy, Donald Rumsfeld meets Saddam

U.S. embassy in Kuwait City bombed; 6 killed

1984 Kuwait Airways flight bound for Pakistan hijacked; two Americans killed after landing at Tehran airport

September 20: Bombing of U.S. embassy annex in Beirut; 14 killed

1985 March: President Reagan signs National Security Decision Directive 166, authorizing U.S. covert activities in Afghanistan

May 17: Iraq fires Exocet missile at USS *Stark*; killed 37 sailors

June 14: TWA plane hijacked; U.S. sailor killed

1986 February 1: CIA established the Counter Terrorism Center

April 14: U.S. airstrike on Libya

September 26: *Mujahideen* in Afghanistan use the first U.S.-supplied Stinger missiles against Soviet aircraft

1987 December: Palestinian refugees demonstrate, marking the beginning of the *intifada*

1988 February–December: Saddam's Anfal campaign against the Iraqi Kurds

March: Iraqi attack on Halabja; an estimated 5,000 Kurds killed

April 18: Geneva Accords formalize the Soviet withdrawal from Afghanistan

July 3: USS *Vincennes* shot down an Iranian civilian airplane; 290 killed

August: Iraq-Iran War ends

August: Al Qaeda founded in Peshawar, Pakistan

December 21: PanAm flight 103 blown up over Lockerbie, Scotland; 259 killed

1989 February 15: Last remaining Soviet units in Afghanistan withdraw

November 9: Berlin Wall falls

1990 July 25: U.S. Ambassador April Glaspie meets with Saddam

August 2: Iraq attacks and occupies Kuwait

October: President George H. W. Bush imposes sanctions on Pakistan for its nuclear program

November: UN Security Council passes Resolution 678, demanding Iraq's withdrawal from Kuwait by January 15, 1991

1991 January: U.S. Senate votes (52–47) to authorize the use of force against Iraq

January 16: U.S. and coalition airstrikes on Iraq begin

January–March: Operation Desert Storm; U.S. and its coalition force Iraq to withdraw from Kuwait

February 28: Ceasefire agreement signed between Iraq and the coalition

March: Iraq crushes rebellions in the Kurdish north and Shia south

April: UN Security Resolution 687, demanding the destruction of Iraq's conventional weapons, is passed, and 688 establishes a no-fly zone north of the 36th parallel

May: First inspection of UN Special Commission on Disarmament (UNSCOM)

December 24: USSR disintegrates

1992 Osama bin Laden moves to Khartoum, Sudan

April: Communist regime in Kabul is overthrown

December 29: Bombs exploded at two Western hotels in Aden, Yemen; two killed

1993 January: U.S. attacks suspected nuclear facility and missile sites south of Baghdad

February 26: World Trade Center in NY bombed; 6 killed, 1,000 wounded

April: Assassination attempt on President George H. W. Bush uncovered by Kuwait

October 3–4: Eighteen U.S. soldiers killed in Mogadishu, Somalia, with the assistance of al Qaeda

1994 March: Saudi government strips Osama bin Laden of his citizenship

October: Iraq moves troops toward Kuwait; U.S. deploys carrier battle group and 54,000 troops to the region in response

October–November: Taliban forces take control of Spin Boldak and Kandahar

1995 June: President Clinton signs Presidential Decision Directive 39, "US Policy on Counter Terrorism"

June: Unsuccessful assassination attempt on Egyptian President Hosni Mubarak during visit to Addis Ababa, Ethiopia

August: Saddam's sons-in-law defect to Jordan and provide evidence on WMD

November 13: Al Qaeda bombs Saudi National Guard building in Riyadh; 7 killed, 60 wounded

November 19: Al Qaeda bombs Egyptian embassy in Islamabad, Pakistan; 16 killed, 60 wounded

1996 May–June: Osama bin Laden and Ayman al-Zawahiri leave Sudan and move operations to Afghanistan

June: Al Khobar Towers in Dhahran, Saudi Arabia, bombed; 19 U.S. military personnel killed, 515 wounded

August: Iraq sends forces into northern Iraq and U.S. fires 27 cruise missiles and extends no-fly zone

August 23: Osama bin Laden declares war on the U.S.

September 26: Taliban take over Kabul; execute former Afghan ruler, Najibullah

1997 May 25: Pakistan recognizes the Taliban government of Afghanistan

October: Iraq accuses U.S. members of UNSCOM of spying and expels them from Iraq

November 17: Al Qaeda attack on tourists in Luxor, Egypt; 58 killed, 26 wounded

1998 January 16: Project for a New American Century recommends the removal of Saddam in a letter to President Clinton

February 23: Bin Laden issues *fatwa* against "Jews and Crusaders"

May 12: India tests nuclear bomb

May 28: Pakistan tests five nuclear weapons followed by a sixth on May 30

August 7: Bombings of the U.S. embassies in Dar es Salaam, Tanzania, and Nairobi, Kenya; 224 killed, 5,000 wounded

August 20: U.S. launches cruise missiles against al Qaeda training camps in Afghanistan and pharmaceutical factory in Sudan

October 31: Iraq stops cooperating with UNSCOM inspectors

October 31: President Clinton signs the Iraq Liberation Act

November 5: UN Security Council passes resolution charging Iraq with flagrantly violating UN resolutions

December 16–19: Operation Desert Fox: U.S. and UK air strikes against Iraq

1999 February 18: Assassination of Iraqi Grand Ayatollah Muhummad Sadiq al-Sadr and two sons

March 24–June 10: NATO bombing of Yugoslavia

October: UN Security Council unanimously adopts Resolution 1267, demanding that the Taliban turn over Osama bin Laden and imposing sanctions

October 12: Nonviolent coup ousts Pakistani Prime Minister Nawaz Sharif; replaced by General Pervez Musharraf

December 17: UN Resolution 1284 passes, establishing the UN Monitoring, Verification and Inspection commission (UNMOVIC) to replace UNSCOM

December 31, 1999: Ahmed Ressam fails in his attempt to detonate a bomb at Los Angeles International Airport

2000 January 3: Abortive attack on the USS *The Sullivans* in Aden, Yemen

June: Final report of the U.S. National Commission on Terrorism released

September 7: Predator unmanned drone flies over Afghanistan for the first time

October 12: Bombing of the USS *Cole* in Aden, Yemen; 17 U.S. sailors killed, 40 wounded

November 7: U.S. presidential election; due to the closeness of the vote, George W. Bush is not officially elected until December 12, following a Supreme Court ruling.

2001 February 16: U.S. and UK bomb Iraq air defense sites

March: Taliban destroy the statues of Buddha at Bamiyan, Afghanistan

May–July: U.S. and UK try to get UN to adopt "smart sanctions" against Iraq

July 27: Rumsfeld sends memo to Powell, Rice, and Cheney outlining U.S. options in Iraq

August 6: CIA delivers Presidential Daily Briefing to President Bush, warning of a possible al Qaeda attack

September 9: Agents of al Qaeda assassinate Northern Alliance leader Ahmed Shah Massoud

September 11: Al Qaeda attacks on New York and Washington; almost 3,000 killed

September 13: U.S. presents demands to Pakistan; President Musharraf agrees to join U.S. coalition in the "war on terror"

September 15–16: Bush meets at Camp David with principal advisers

September 20: President Bush addresses Congress; identifies Osama and al Qaeda as responsible for 9/11 attacks

September 26: CIA team lands in Panjshir Valley to work with Northern Alliance

October 7: Operation Enduring Freedom: U.S. attacks the Taliban and al Qaeda bases in Afghanistan

November 13: Kabul falls

December: Bombing of Tora Bora

December 5: Afghan leaders sign the Bonn Agreement, calling for a timetable in the formation of a representative government

December 20: UN Security Council passes Resolution 1386, establishing the International Security Assistance Force (ISAF)

December 22: Karzai government installed in Afghanistan

2002 January 29: President Bush delivers Sate of the Union and identifies "axis of evil," consisting of Iraq, Iran, and North Korea

February 26: President Bush signs top secret intelligence order authorizing disruption activities in Iraq

March: Operation Anaconda is launched in the Sha-i-kot Valley in Afghanistan

April 17: President Bush calls for a "Marshall Plan" for Afghanistan

June 1: President Bush's West Point address emphasizing "pre-emption"

June: Hamad Karzai is selected as head of the Afghan transitional government

July 23: "Downing Street Memo": "facts were being fixed around the policy."

August 26: VP Cheney delivers speech to the Veterans for Foreign Wars (VFW), stating, "[T]here is no doubt that Saddam Hussein now has weapons of mass destruction."

September: National Security Strategy paper released

October: National Intelligence Estimate (NIE) states, "Iraq is reconstituting its nuclear program"

October 7: President Bush gives speech claiming that Iraq has WMD

October 10–11: U.S. Congress votes in favor of Iraq War authorization resolution; the vote is 296–133 in the House and 77–23 in the Senate

October 12: Bali, Indonesia, bombs; 202 killed, 1,500 wounded

November 8: UN Resolution 1441 passes; stipulates that Iraq is in violation of UN Resolution 687, but provides the opportunity to avoid war by cooperating with UN inspection agency, UNMOVIC

November 25: UN weapons inspectors return to Iraq after four year absence

December 7: Iraq issues response ("full disclosure") to UN Resolution 1441 by giving the IAEA 12,000 pages of documents

2003 January 20: National Security Presidential Directive 24 creating ORHA issued; gives control of postwar Iraq to the Department of Defense

January 27: UN weapons inspector Hans Blix reports that Iraq has not cooperated with UNMOVIC

January 28: In his State of the Union Address, President Bush claims that Iraq has WMD

February 5: Secretary of State Powell presents the case against Iraq to the UN Security Council and claims Iraq has weapons of mass destruction

February 25: General Shinseki testifies before the Senate Armed Services Committee; his comments are quickly criticized by Paul Wolfowitz and Donald Rumsfeld

March 1: Al Qaeda leader Khalid Sheik Muhammad is captured in Pakistan

March 1: Turkish Parliament rejects U.S. request to stage forces in Turkey

March 16: General Jay Garner flies to Kuwait to await the occupation of Iraq

March 17: President Bush issues ultimatum to Iraq giving Saddam and his sons forty-eight hours to leave Iraq

March 19: Operation Iraqi Freedom begins

April 9: Baghdad liberated; Saddam's statue in Firdos Square toppled

April 21: ORHA officials led by General Garner arrive in Baghdad

May: Turkish Parliament refuses to approve the transit of American troops through Turkey into Iraq

May 1: President Bush lands on USS *Abraham Lincoln* and declares an end to major combat operations in Iraq; "Mission Accomplished" banner displayed

May 6: Announcement made that Paul Bremer will replace Jay Garner

May 12: Paul Bremer arrives in Iraq and replaces General Garner

May 16: Bremer announces that the establishment of interim government is postponed

May 16: CPA Directive #1 issued; calls for the "de-Baathification" of Iraqi government

May 22: UN Security Council votes to end sanctions in Iraq

May 23: CPA Directive #2 issued; calls for disbanding of Iraqi security forces

June: Iraq Study Group under Dr. David Kay established

July 13: Bremer appoints twenty-five-member Iraqi Governing Council

July 20: U.S. forces kill Saddam's sons, Uday and Qusay, in Mosul

July 23: General Abizaid acknowledges that U.S. forces face "a classical guerilla campaign"

August 9: NATO takes over International Security Force Afghanistan (ISAF)

August 19: Bombing of UN headquarters in Baghdad; Sergio Vieira de Mello killed

August 29: Bombing of Najak shrine; Ayatollah Muhummad Baqir Hakim killed

September 5: Rep. David Obey (D-WI) is the first member of Congress to call for Donald Rumsfeld's resignation

November 15: CPA introduces plan for transition to sovereignty; Ayad Allawi is chosen as the interim prime minister

December 13: Saddam Hussein is captured in Tikrit

2004 January: Afghan *loya jirga* approves new constitution

January 25: David Kay, the CIA's weapons inspector, resigns and testifies that U.S. assumptions about WMD in Iraq were in error; Charles Duelfer replaces Kay

February 2: Commission on WMD (Silberman-Robb) established by President Bush; the next day the British government establishes a commission chaired by Lord Butler

February 5: CIA Director George Tenet concedes that U.S. may have overestimated Iraq's weapons capabilities

March 4: Transitional Administrative Law (Iraqi interim constitution) completed

March 11: Madrid bombings; 192 killed, 1,600 wounded

March 20: Six U.S. soldiers charged for alleged abuses committed against Iraqi prisoners at Abu Ghraib prison

March 31: Crisis in Fallujah; four U.S. contractors killed

April: Shakai Agreement: Pakistani government concludes agreement with the Taliban and tribal leaders; Pakistan agrees to stay in agreed-upon areas; local leaders agree not to attack Pakistani officials

April 15: U.S. issues arrest warrant issued for Moqtada al-Sadr

April 28: Report on Abu Ghraib issued by CBS News

May 8: Iraqi interim constitution, the Transitional Administrative Law, is ratified

May 14: President Bush signs National Security Presidential Directive 36, giving the State Department responsibility for reconstruction in Iraq

June 2: Iraqi Governing Council dissolves itself

June 28: In the Hamdi case, U.S. Supreme Court rules 8–1 that detainees have a right to a lawyer and to challenge their status before a "neutral decision-maker"

June 28: CPA shut down; Bremer departs Iraq and sovereignty is transferred

July: Ayad Allawi becomes Iraqi permanent prime minister

July 1: General George W. Casey, Jr., replaces General Ricardo Sanchez as top U.S. military commander in Iraq

August: Crisis in Najaf, Iraq

September: Taliban rocket attack against President Karzai

September 7: Death toll for U.S. troops in Iraq reaches 1,000

September 30: Charles Duelfer releases report on Iraqi WMD

October 4: U.S. and Iraqi forces battle three days to retake Samarra from Sunni fighters

October 9: Afghan presidential election; Hamad Karzai elected and inaugurated for a five-year term on December 7

November 7: Second siege of Fallujah

2005 January 30: Transitional National Assembly elections; Iraqi Transitional Government headed by President Jalal Talabani and PM Ibrahim al-Jaafari

March 19: U.S. Major General Paul Eaton publishes op-ed in the *New York Times* critical of Rumsfeld; followed by Lieutenant General Gregory Newbold, Major General John Batiste, and Major General Charles Swannack

April 3: Unsuccessful attempt to arrest Moqtada al-Sadr

May 1: President Bush signs National Security Presidential Directive 36, giving the State Department primary responsibility for the reconstruction of Iraq

Summer: U.S. initiates "Anbar Awakening" program working with Sunni tribes

July 7: London subway bombings; 55 killed, 300 wounded

August 6: Mahmoud Ahmadinejad elected as president of Iran

August 29: Hurricane Katrina hits New Orleans

September 5: Afghans elect new parliament which includes ex-Taliban ministers

October: Condoleezza Rice presents U.S. strategy in Iraq as "clear, hold, and build"

October 8: A magnitude 7.6 earthquake strikes Afghanistan, Pakistan, and India, killing an estimated 75,000 people and leaving 2.5 million homeless

October 15: National Assembly ratifies Iraqi constitution

October 18: Saddam Hussein goes on trial

October 26: Death toll for U.S. troops reaches 2,000

November 5: White House issues its report, "National Strategy for Victory in Iraq"

November 19: Haditha incident; 24 Iraqis, some civilian, killed

December 15: National Assembly elections; Iraqi government headed by President Jalal Talabani and PM Nuri al-Maliki

2006 February 22: Al-Askari ("Golden Dome") Mosque in Samarra bombed; Shia respond by killing Sunnis

March: Public opinion polls indicate that a majority of Americans do not support Iraq War

March: Operation Mountain Lion launched by U.S. and Afghan forces in Kunar Province

March 15: Iraq Study Group formed

April 22: Nuri al-Maliki becomes prime minister and forms unity government with Kurds and Shia

May: Operation Mountain Thrust launched by U.S. and Afghan forces in southern Afghanistan

June 7: U.S. air strike kills al Qaeda leader Abu Musab al-Zarqawi

June 29: In *Hamdan v. Rumsfeld*, U.S. Supreme Court rules that the president does not have the power to order that alleged terrorists be tried in military commissions

August 3: General John Abizaid, commander of U.S. forces in the Middle East, warns of the possibility of civil war in Iraq

September 19: Retired General Jack Keane meets with Rumsfeld to make the case for a counterinsurgency approach

September 27: The "council of colonels" begins meeting

October 9: North Korea detonates a nuclear weapon

November: NATO Summit held in Riga, Latvia; tensions concerning Afghan operations

November 5: Saddam Hussein sentenced to death by Iraqi court

November 7: Democrats win majorities in the U.S. House and Senate

November 8: Secretary of Defense Rumsfeld (who had been Bush's longest serving original cabinet member) steps down and is replaced by Robert Gates

November 15: General Abizaid testifies that he opposes sending more U.S. troops to Iraq

December 6: Iraq Study Group issues its report

December 15: New Army/Marine Corps counterinsurgency manual released

December 18: Robert Gates sworn in as secretary of defense

December 19: President Bush says for the first time: "We're not winning, we're not losing in Iraq."

December 30: Saddam Hussein is executed

2007 January 5: White House announces that General Petraeus will take command in Iraq from General George W. Casey, Jr.

January 10: President Bush announces the surge, a buildup of U.S. forces in Iraq

January 26: General Petraeus nominated to implement the surge

February: U.S. sends additional 28,000 troops to Iraq as part of the surge

February 14: President Bush claims that Iran has supplied Iraqi Shia with roadside bombs

March 7: Ryan Crocker becomes ambassador to Iraq, succeeding Zalmay Khalilzad

June: Secretary of Defense Gates does not reappoint JCS Chairman Peter Pace; succeeded by Admiral Mike Mullen

June 10: U.S. arms Sunni Arab groups ("Sons of Iraq") in Anbar Province as part of the "Sunni Awakening"

June 13: Insurgents blow up the two minarets at the Golden Dome Mosque in Samarra

June 25: Sen. Richard Lugar calls for an end to the surge on the Senate floor

July: National Intelligence Council releases report indicating that al Qaeda is the greatest threat to the U.S. and that it is centered in the Federally Administered Tribal Areas of Pakistan

July: Militants at the "Red Mosque" in Islamabad challenge government authority; siege of mosque by government; many deaths

August 29: Moqtada al-Sadr orders ceasefire for his Shia Mahdi army

September 10–11: General Petraeus and Ambassador Crocker testify to Congress about the surge

September 16: Blackwater employees kill 17 Iraqis outside the Green Zone

November 26: President Bush and Prime Minister Maliki issue "Declaration of Principles of U.S.-Iraqi Relations"

December 3: National Intelligence Council issues a report that Iraq abandoned its efforts in 2003 to develop nuclear weapons

December 17: British forces hand over control of Basra Province to Iraqi forces

December 27: Former Pakistani Prime Minister Benazir Bhutto is assassinated

2008 January 9: World Health Organization estimates the number of Iraqi civilian deaths: 150,000

January 12: Iraq parliament approves the participation of some former Baathists to participate in the government

January: Ambassador Crocker: "There is a chance of this breaking down at a whole range of points."

February 22: Moqtada al-Sadr extends ceasefire for his Mahdi army for six more months

March: Prime Minister Maliki launches offensive against Shia militias

March: Admiral Fallon fired as CENTCOM chief

March: General Musharraf steps down as president of Pakistan

March 23: Death toll for U.S. troops reaches 4,000

April: Petraeus and Crocker testify before Congress; Crocker refers to the possible "Lebanonization" of Iraq

April 27: Assassination attempt on Afghan President Hamad Karzai

June 5: Senate Intelligence Committee releases report critical of Bush administration

June 10: U.S. forces kill ten Pakistani Frontier Corps soldiers who were shooting at U.S. troops along Afghan-Pakistani border

June 21: Petraeus issues guidance on counterinsurgency

July: Indian embassy in Kabul is bombed, killing fifty people

July: President Bush issues order authorizing U.S. Predator strikes into Pakistan without the approval of the Pakistani government

August 18: Pakistani President Pervez Musharraf resigns

August 22: U.S. aircraft accidentally kills civilians in Herat Province; Karzai condemns "the unilateral actions of the Coalition Forces"

September 1: U.S. hands over control of Anbar province to Iraq

September 9: Asif Ali Zadari inaugurated as president of Pakistan

September 16: General David Petraeus hands over command of U.S. forces in Iraq to General Ray Odierno

September 20: Bombing of Marriott Hotel in Islamabad; fifty people including two Americans are killed

October: Iraq government begins paying members of the Sunni Awakening

November 4: Barack Obama elected president

November 26: Terrorists from the group Lash-e-Taiba bomb sites in Mumbai, India

November 27: Security agreement calling for the withdrawal of all U.S. troops from Iraq by the end of 2011 is approved

2009 January 20: Barack Obama inaugurated 44th president of the U.S.

January 31: Election of provincial councils in fourteen of Iraq's eighteen provinces

February 27: President Obama announces a new policy toward Iraq and Afghanistan, calling for an increase of forces in Afghanistan and withdrawal of all U.S. combat troops from Iraq by August 31, 2010

April 7: President Obama visits Turkey and Iraq and declares, "It is time for us to transition to the Iraqis."

May 11: General Stanley McChrystal replaces General David McKiernan in Afghanistan

June: British government established an official inquiry to focus on Iraq

June 30: U.S. troops leave urban areas of Iraq

July 17: Ritz-Carlton and Marriott hotels bombed in Jakarta, Indonesia; 9 killed, 50 wounded

August: U.S. drone kills Baitullah Mehsud, a Pakistani Taliban leader

August 18: Richard Holbrooke, U.S. special envoy for Pakistan and Afghanistan, meets with Liaqat Baloch, leaders of Pakistan's Jemaat-I-Islam Party

August 19: According to a *Washington Post*/ABC poll, a majority of Americans do not think the war in Afghanistan is worth fighting

August 20: Afghan elections; observers charge that there are many abuses

August 30: General Stanley McChrystal submits report to President Obama on Afghanistan

November 1: In Afghanistan Abdullah Badullah withdraws from run-off election; Karzai remains president

November 19: Hamad Karzai inaugurated as president of Pakistan

December: Sunni extremists in Karachi, Pakistan, kill 43 Shia

December 1: At West Point, President Obama outlines his strategy for Afghanistan and announces he will send 30,000 more U.S. military to Afghanistan

December 25: A Nigerian national who claims to be affiliated with al Qaeda attempts to blow up an American airliner

2010 January 4: Jordanian double agent kills seven CIA officers in Khost, Afghanistan

February 13: U.S. forces launch the Marjah offensive

March 7: Iraqi parliamentary elections are conducted but no coalition wins a majority

May 1: Attempt by Faisal Shahzad, a Pakistani immigrant in the U.S., to detonate a car bomb in Times Square in New York fails

June: Free-lance journalist publishes article in *Rolling Stone* quoting General Stanley McChrystal and his staff, who are critical of Obama administration

June 23: General McChrystal offers his resignation to President Obama, who accepts it

June 30: General David Petraeus replaces General McChrystal in Afghanistan, and Marine General James Mattis replaces Petraeus at CENTCOM

July 25: Wiki Leaks releases classified documents concerning 91,000 events in Afghanistan and Iraq

August 19: Combat troops withdrawn from Iraq and the number of U.S. troops in Iraq falls below 50,000

September 1: Operation Iraqi Freedom ends and Operation New Dawn begins

November: Wiki Leaks releases 250,000 diplomatic cables

Appendix C: Bibliography

Terrorism, Counterterrorism, and Counterinsurgency

American Political Science Association. "The New U.S. Army/Marine Corps Field Manual as Political Science and Political Praxis." Stephen Biddle, Stathis N. Kalyvas, Wendy Brown, and Douglas A. Ollivant, contributors. *Perspectives on Politics* 6, no. 2 (June 2008): 347–48.

Andrade, Dale, and Lt. Col. James H. Willbanks, USA. "Counterinsurgency Lessons from Vietnam for the Future." *Military Review* (March–April 2006).

Ashcroft, John. *Never Again: Securing America and Restoring Justice*. Nashville, TN: Center Street, 2006.

Aylwin-Foster, Brigadier Nigel. "Changing the Army for Counterinsurgency Operations." *Military Review* (November–December 2005): 2–15.

Baer, Robert. *See No Evil: The True Story of a Ground Soldier in the CIA's War on Terrorism.* New York: Crown, 2002.

Baltazar, Thomas. "The Role of USAID and Development Assistance in Combating Terrorism." *Military Review*, Special Edition (June 2008): 105–7.

Beckett, Ian F. W. *Modern Insurgencies and Counter-Insurgencies: Guerillas and Their Opponents since 1750.* London: Routledge, 2001.

Benjamin, Daniel, and Steven Simon. "America and the New Terrorism." *Survival* 42, no. 1 (Spring 2000): 59–75.

———. *The Age of Sacred Terror*. New York: Random House, 2002.

———. *The Next Attack: The Failure of the War on Terror and a Strategy for Getting It Right.* New York: Times Books, 2005.

Bergen, Peter. *Holy War Inc.: Inside the Secret World of Osama bin Laden.* New York: Free Press, 2002.

———. *The Osama bin Laden I Know: An Oral History of Al Qaeda's Leader.* New York: Free Press, 2006.

Birtle, Andrew J. *U.S. Army Counterinsurgency and Contingency Operations Doctrine, 1942–1976*. Washington, DC: U.S. Army Center of Military History, 2006.

Bowden, Mark. "How to Break a Terrorist." *Atlantic* (May 2007): 54–68.

Brisard, Jean-Charles, with Damien Martinez. *Zarqawi: The New Face of Al-Qaeda*. New York: Other Press, 2005.

Brown, Michael E., Owen R. Cote, Jr., Sean M. Lynn-Jones, and Steven E. Miller. *Contending with Terrorism: Roots, Strategies, and Responses.* Cambridge, MA: MIT Press, 2010.

Bush, George W. "President Bush Visits National Defense University, Discusses Global War on Terror." October 23, 2007; accessed at www.whitehouse.gov.

Byman, Daniel. *Deadly Connections: States that That Sponsor Terrorism.* New York: Cambridge University Press, 2005.

———. *Understanding Proto-Insurgencies.* Santa Monica, CA: RAND, 2007.

Cable, Larry. "Reinventing the Round Wheel: Insurgency, Counter-Insurgency, and Peacekeeping Post Cold War." *Small Wars and Insurgencies* (Autumn 1993).

Caldwell, Dan, and Robert E. Williams, Jr. *Seeking Security in an Insecure World.* Lanham, MD: Rowman and Littlefield, 2006.

Calvert, John. *Sayyid Qutb and the Origins of Radical Islam.* New York: Columbia University Press, 2010.

Cassidy, Robert M. "Back to the Street without Joy." *Parameters* 34 (Summer 2004): 73–83.

———. "The Long Small War: Indigenous Forces for Counterinsurgency." *Parameters* 36 (Spring 2006): 47–62.

———. *Counterinsurgency and the Global War on Terror: Military Culture and Irregular War.* Stanford, CA: Stanford University Press, 2008.

Clarke, Richard A. *Against All Enemies: Inside America's War on Terror.* New York: Simon and Schuster, 2004.

Cohen, Eliot, Conrad Crane, Jan Horvath, and John Nagl. "Principles, Imperatives, Paradoxes of Counterinsurgency." *Military Review* (March/April 2006).

Coll, Steve. *The Bin Ladens: An Arabian Family in the American Century.* New York: Penguin Books, 2008.

Collins, Joseph J. "Nine Years after 9/11: Assessing the War on Terror." *Small Wars Journal* (September 2010); available at smallwarsjournal.com.

Cronin, Audrey Kurth. "How Al-Qaeda Ends: The Decline and Demise of Terrorist Groups." *International Security* 31, no. 1 (Summer 2006): 7–48.

Cronin, Audrey K., and James M. Ludes, eds. *The Campaign against International Terrorism.* Washington, DC: Georgetown University Press, 2003.

Cullison, Alan. "Inside al-Qa'ida's Hard Drive." *Atlantic Monthly* 294, no. 2 (September 2004).

Danner, Mark. *Torture and Truth: America, Abu Ghraib, and the War on Terror.* New York: New York Review of Books, 2004.

Davis, John C. "The Cost of Expediency in Counterinsurgency Operations." *Small Wars Journal* 5 (July 2006).

De Nevers, Renee. "NATO's Security Role in the Terrorist Era." *International Security* 31, no. 4 (Spring 2007): 34–66.

Dunn, David Hastings. "Bush, 11 September and the Conflicting Strategies of the 'War on Terror.'" *Irish Studies in International Affairs* 16 (2005): 11–33.

Fall, Bernard. "The Theory and Practice of Insurgency and Counterinsurgency." *Naval War College Review* (April 1965).

Fearon, James D., and David D. Laitin. "Ethnicity, Insurgency, and Civil War." *American Political Science Review* 97, no. 1 (February 2003): 75–90.

Galula, David. *Counterinsurgency Warfare: Theory and Practice*. New York: Praeger, 1964.

Gelb, Leslie. "How to Leave Afghanistan." *New York Times*, March 13, 2009, p. A23.

Gerges, Fawaz A. *America and Political Islam: Clash of Cultures or Clash of Interests?* New York: Cambridge University Press, 1999.

———. *The Far Enemy: Why Jihad Went Global*. New York: Cambridge University Press, 2005.

Giraldo, Jeanne K., and Harold A. Trinkunas. *Terrorism Financing and State Responses: A Comparative Perspective*. Stanford: Stanford University Press, 2007.

Giustozzi, Antonio. *Koran, Kalashnikov, and Laptop: The Neo-Taliban Insurgency in Afghanistan*. London: Hurst and Company, 2007.

Goldsmith, Jack. *The Terror Presidency: Law and Judgment inside the Bush Administration*. New York: W. W. Norton, 2007.

Gordon, Michael R. "Military Hones a New Strategy on Insurgency." *New York Times*, October 5, 2006, p. A1.

Green, Dan. "Counterinsurgency Diplomacy: Political Advisors at the Operational and Tactical Levels." *Military Review*, Special Edition (June 2008): 108–14.

Greenberg, Karen J., and Joshua L. Dratel, eds. *The Torture Papers: The Road to Abu Ghraib*. Cambridge, UK: Cambridge University Press, 2005.

Hammes, Thomas X. *The Sling and the Stone: On War in the 21st Century*. Osceola, WI: Zenith Press, 2004.

Hardy, Roger. *The Muslim Revolt: A Journey through Political Islam*. New York: Columbia University Press, 2010.

Hayes, Stephen. *The Connection: How al Qaeda's Collaboration with Saddam Hussein Has Endangered America*. New York: Harper Collins, 2004.

Hersh, Seymour M. "The Other War: Why Bush's Afghanistan Problem Won't Go Away." *New Yorker* (April 12, 2004).

———. "Torture at Abu Ghraib." *New Yorker* (May 10, 2004).

———. *Chain of Command: The Road from 9/11 to Abu Ghraib*. New York: HarperCollins, 2004.

———. "The General's Report: How Antonio Taguba, Who Investigated the Abu Ghraib Scandal, Became One of Its Casualties." *New Yorker* (June 25, 2007).

Hoffman, Bruce. *Inside Terrorism*. New York: Columbia University Press, 1998.

———. "From the War on Terror to Global Counterinsurgency." *Current History* 105, no. 693 (December 2006): 423–29.

Hosmer, Stephen T. *The Army's Role in Counterinsurgency and Insurgency*. R-3947-A. Santa Monica, CA: RAND, 1990.

Huda, Qamar-ul. *Crescent and Dove: Peace and Conflict Resolution in Islam.* Washington, DC: United States Institute of Peace Press, 2010.

Ibrahim, Raymond. *The Al Qaeda Reader*. New York: Broadway Books, 2007.

Jacobson, Michael. *The West at War: US and European Counterterrorism Efforts Post-September 11.* Washington, DC: Washington Institute for Near East Policy, 2006.

Jenkins, Brian Michael. "International Terrorism: A New Mode of Conflict." David Carlton and Carlo Schaerf, eds. *International Terrorism and World Security*. London: Croon Helm, 1975.

———. *Will Terrorists Go Nuclear?* Amherst, NY: Prometheus Books, 2008.

Johnson, Thomas H., and M. Chris Mason. "All Counterinsurgency Is Local." *Atlantic Monthly* (October 2008): 36–38.

Jones, Anthony James. *The History and Politics of Counterinsurgency: Resisting Rebellion.* Lexington: University of Kentucky Press, 2004.

Katzman, Kenneth. "Counterterrorism Policy: American Successes." *Middle East Quarterly* 5, no. 4 (December 1998): 45–52.

Keefer, Phillip, and Norman Loayza, eds. *Terrorism, Economic Development and Political Openness.* New York: Cambridge University Press, 2008.

Kepel, Gilles. *Jihad: The Trail of Political Islam.* Cambridge, MA: Harvard University Press, 2003.

———. *The War for Muslim Minds Islam and the West.* Cambridge, MA: Harvard University Press, 2004.

Kepel, Gilles, and Jean-Pierre Milelli, eds. *Al Qaeda in Its Own Words.* Pascale Ghazaleh, trans. Cambridge, MA: Harvard University Press, 2008.

Kilcullen, David. "Countering Global Insurgency." *Journal of Strategic Studies* 28, no. 4 (August 2003): 597–617.

———. "Twenty-eight Articles: Fundamentals of Company-Level Counterinsurgency." *Military Review* 86, no. 3 (May–June 2006): 103–8.

———. "Counter-insurgency Redux." *Survival* 48, no. 4 (December 2006): 111–30.

———. "Subversion, Counter-subversion, and the Campaign against Terrorism in Europe." *Studies in Conflict and Terrorism* 30, no. 8 (August 2007): 647–66.

———. *The Accidental Guerilla: Fighting Small Wars in the Midst of a Big One.* New York: Oxford University Press, 2009.

———. *Counterinsurgency*. New York: Oxford University Press, 2010.

Kilcullen, David, and Andrew McDonal Exum. "Death From Above, Outrage Down Below." *New York Times*, May 17, 2009, p. 13.

Krueger, Alan B. *What Makes a Terrorist: Economics and the Roots of Terrorism.* Princeton: Princeton University Press, 2007.

Lawrence, Bruce, ed. *Messages to the World: The Statements of Osama Bin Laden.* New York: Verso, 2005.

Lawrence, T. E. *Seven Pillars of Wisdom*. New York: Anchor Books, 1926, 1991.

Lesch, David W. *1979: The Year That Shaped the Modern Middle East.* Boulder, CO: Westview Press, 2001.

Lesser, Ian O., et al. *Countering the New Terrorism*. Santa Monica, CA: RAND Corporation, 1999.

Lewis, Bernard. "The Roots of Muslim Rage." *Atlantic Monthly* (September 1990).

———. "What Went Wrong?" *Atlantic Monthly* (January 2002).

———. *What Went Wrong: Western Impact and Middle Eastern Response*. New York: Oxford University Press, 2002.

———. "Freedom and Justice in the Modern Middle East." *Foreign Affairs* (May–June 2005).

Mansoor, Peter R., and Mark S. Ulrich. "A New COIN Center for Gravity Analysis." *Military Review* (September–October 2007): 45–51.

Marlowe, Ann. "The Picture Awaits: The Birth of Modern Counterinsurgency." *World Affairs* (Summer 2009).

Marston, Daniel, and Carter Malkasian, eds. *Counterinsurgency in Modern Warfare*. Oxford: Osprey, 2008.

Mayer, Jane. *The Dark Side: The Inside Story of How the War on Terror Turned into a War on American Ideals*. New York: Doubleday, 2008.

Metz, Steven. *Rethinking Insurgency*. Carlisle Barracks, PA: U.S. Army War College Strategic Studies Institute, 2007.

Metz, Steven, and Raymond Millen. "Insurgency and Counterinsurgency in the 21st Century: Reconceptualizing Threat and Response." *Special Warfare* (February 2005): 6–21.

Miller, Steven E. "Terrifying Thoughts: Power, Order, and Terror after 9/11." *Global Governance* 11: 247–71.

Mockaitis, Thomas R. *The "New" Terrorism: Myths and Reality*. Stanford, CA: Stanford University Press, 2008.

Murray, Williamson, ed. *Strategic Challenges for Counterinsurgency and the Global War on Terror*. Carlisle, PA: Strategic Studies Institute, U.S. Army War College, 2006.

Musallam, Adnan. *From Secularism to Jihad: Sayyid Qutb and the Foundations of Radical Islamism*. New York: Praeger, 2005.

Mylroie, Laurie. *Bush vs. the Beltway: How the CIA and the State Department Tried to Stop the War on Terror*. Washington, DC: Regan, 2003.

Nagl, John. *Learning to Eat Soup with a Knife: Counterinsurgency Lessons from Malaya and Vietnam*. Chicago: University of Chicago Press, 2002.

Ollivant, Douglas, and Eric Chewning. "Producing Victory: Rethinking Conventional Forces in COIN Operations." *Military Review* (July/August 2006).

Packer, George. "Knowing the Enemy." *New Yorker* (December 18, 2006).

Paret, Peter. *French Revolutionary Warfare from Indochina to Algeria: The Analysis of a Political and Military Doctrine*. London: Pall Mall Press, 1964.

Paust, Jordan J. *Beyond the Law: The Bush Administration's Unlawful Responses in the "War" on Terror*. Cambridge, UK: Cambridge University Press, 2007.

Pillar, Paul R. *Terrorism and U.S. Foreign Policy*. Washington, DC: Brookings Institution, 2001.

Posen, Barry R. "The Struggle against Terrorism: Grand Strategy, Strategy, and Tactics." *International Security* 26 (2001/2): 39–55.

Priest, Dana, and William M. Arkin. *Top Secret America: A Washington Post Investigation;* "A Hidden World Growing beyond Control" (July 19, 2010); "National Security Inc." (July 20, 2010); "The Secrets Next Door" (July 21, 2010), *Washington Post*. Available at: http://projects.washingtonpost.com/top-secret-america/articles/.

RAND Corporation. *The RAND Chronology of International Terrorism.* www.rand.org/ise/projects.terrorismdatabase/.

Randal, Jonathan. *Osama: The Making of a Terrorist.* New York: Alfred A. Knopf, 2004.

Record, Jeffrey. *Beating Goliath: Why Insurgencies Win*. Dulles, VA: Potomac Books, 2009.

Sageman, Marc. *Understanding Terror Networks*. Philadelphia: University of Pennsylvania Press, 2004.

———. *Leaderless Jihad: Terror Networks in the Twenty-First Century*. Philadelphia: University of Pennsylvania Press, 2008.

———. "The Next Generation of Terror." *Foreign Policy* (March/April 2008): 37–42.

Scheuer, Michael (as "Anonymous"). *Through Our Enemies' Eyes: Osama bin Laden, Radical Islam and the Future of America.* Washington, DC: Brasseys, 2002.

Scheuer, Michael. *Imperial Hubris: Why the West Is Losing the War on Terror*. Washington, DC: Potomac Books, 2007.

Schultz, Richard, and Andrea Dew. *Insurgents, Terrorists, and Militias: The Warriors of Contemporary Combat.* New York: Columbia University Press, 2006.

Sepp, Kalev I. "Best Practices in Counterinsurgency." *Military Review* (May–June 2005).

Simon, Jeffrey D. *The Terrorist Trap: America's Experience with Terrorism*, 2nd ed. Bloomington: Indiana University Press, 2001.

Smelser, Neil J. *The Faces of Terrorism: Social and Psychological Dimensions*. Princeton: Princeton University Press, 2007.

Stern, Jessica. *The Ultimate Terrorists.* Cambridge, MA: Harvard University Press, 2001.

———. "The Protean Enemy." *Foreign Affairs* 82, no. 4 (July/August 2003): 27–40.

———. *Terror in the Name of God: Why Religious Militants Kill.* New York: HarperPerrenial, 2004.

Talmadge, Caitlin. "Deterring a Nuclear 9/11." *Washington Quarterly* 30, no. 2 (Spring 2007): 21–34.

Thompson, Robert. *Defeating Communist Insurgency: Experiences from Malaya and Vietnam.* London: Chatto and Windus, 1966.

Ucko, David H. *The New Counterinsurgency Era: Transforming the U.S. Military for Modern Wars*. Washington, DC: Georgetown University Press, 2009.

U.S. Army. *Counterinsurgency*. United States Army Field Manual 3–24/United States Marine Corps Warfighting Publication 3–33–5. Washington, DC: Department of the Army, 2006; also published as *The U.S. Army-Marines Corps Counterinsurgency Field Manual.* Chicago: University of Chicago Press, 2007.

U.S. Army Training and Doctrine Command. *A Military Guide to Terrorism in the Twenty-First Century*. TRADOC DSINT Handbook Version 3.0. Ft. Leavenworth, KS: U.S. Army Training and Doctrine Command, 2005.

U.S. Congress. Senate. Committee on Foreign Relations. *Tora Bora Revisited: How We Failed to Get Bin Laden and Why It Matters Today*. Report, 111th Cong., 1st sess., November 30, 2009.

U.S. Congress. Senate. Select Committee on Intelligence and House Permanent Select Committee on Intelligence. *Joint Inquiry into Intelligence Activities before and after the Terrorist Attacks of September 11, 2001*. Senate Report no. 107–351. House Report no. 107–792, December 2002.

U.S. National Commission on Terrorist Attacks on the United States. *The 9/11 Commission Report*. New York: W. W. Norton, 2004.

Walker, David M. *Global War on Terrorism: Observations on Funding, Costs, and Future Commitments*. Washington, DC: Government Accountability Office, 2006.

Wright, Lawrence. *The Looming Tower: Al Qaeda and the Road to 9/11*. New York: Knopf, 2006.

Yoo, John C. *The Powers of War and Peace*. Chicago: University of Chicago Press, 2005.

———. "War and the Constitutional Test." *University of Chicago Law Review* 69 (2005): 1–41.

———. *War by Other Means: An Insider's Account of the War on Terror*. New York: Atlantic Monthly Press, 2006.

Zagorcheva, Dessislave P. "Deterring Terrorism: It Can Be Done." *International Security* 30, no. 3 (Winter 2005–6): 87–123.

Zawahiri, Ayman al. *Knights under the Prophet's Banner*. Laura Mansfield, trans. Old Tappan, NJ: TLG Publications, 2002.

Afghanistan and Pakistan

For a more comprehensive bibliography, see Christian Bleuer, *Afghanistan Analyst Bibliography 2010* (5th edition); available at http://afghanistan-analyst.org/default.aspx.

Abbas, Hassan. *Pakistan's Drift into Extremism: Allah, the Army, and America's War on Terror*. New York: M. E. Sharpe, 2004.

Afghanistan, Islamic Republic of. *Afghanistan National Development Strategy 1387–1391 (2008–2013)*. Kabul: Islamic Republic of Afghanistan, 2008.

Anderson, Jon Lee. *The Lion's Gate: Dispatches from Afghanistan*. New York: Grove Press, 2002.

———. "American Viceroy: Zalmay Khalilzad's Mission." *New Yorker* (December 19, 2006).

———. "Letter from Afghanistan: The Taliban's Opium War." *New Yorker* (July 9, 2007).

Armitage, Richard L., and Samuel R. Berger, Chairs. *U.S. Strategy for Pakistan and Afghanistan*. Independent Task Force Report No. 65. New York: Council on Foreign Relations, 2010.

Asia Foundation. *Afghanistan in 2007: A Survey of the Afghan People*. Kabul: Asia Foundation, 2007.

Aziz, Mazhar. *Military Control in Pakistan: The Parallel State*. London: Routledge, 2009.

Barfield, Thomas. "The Roots of Failure in Afghanistan." *Current History* 107, no. 713 (December 2008): 410–17.

———. *Afghanistan: A Cultural and Political History*. Princeton: Princeton University Press, 2010.

Barno, David. "Fighting 'The Other War': Counterinsurgency Strategy in Afghanistan, 2003–2005." *Military Review* (September–October 2007): 32–44.

Bearden, Milton. "Afghanistan, Graveyard of Empires." *Foreign Affairs* 80, no. 6 (November/December 2001): 17–30.

Belasco, Amy. *The Cost of Afghanistan and Other Global War on Terror Operations since 9/11*. Washington, DC: Congressional Research Service, July 16, 2007.

Berntsen, Gary, and Ralph Pezzullo. *Jawbreaker: The Attack on Bin Laden and Al-Qaeda: A Personal Account by the CIA's Key Field Commander*. New York: Three Rivers Press, 2005.

Biddle, Stephen. *Afghanistan and the Future of Warfare: Implications for Army and Defense Policy*. Carlisle Barracks, PA: U.S. Army War College Strategic Studies Institute, 2002.

———. "Afghanistan and the Future of Warfare." *Foreign Affairs* (March–April 2003).

———. "Is It Worth It? The Difficult Case for War in Afghanistan." *American Interest* (July/August 2009).

Borders, Robert. "Provincial Reconstruction Teams in Afghanistan: A Model for Post-Conflict Reconstruction and Development." *Journal of Development and Social Transformation* 1 (November 2004): 5–12.

Boroumand, Ladan, and Roya Boroumand. "Terror, Islam, and Democracy." *Journal of Democracy* (April 2002).

Bowden, Mark. "The Kabul-Ki Dance." *Atlantic Monthly* (November 2002): 66–87.

Braithwaite, Rodric. "Afghan Diary." *Survival* 51, no. 1 (February–March 2009): 99–118.

Briscoe, Charles H., Richard L. Kiper, James A. Schroder, and Kalev I. Sepp. *Weapons of Choice: U.S. Army Special Operations Forces in Afghanistan*. Fort Leavenworth, KS: Combat Studies Institute, 2002.

Brookings Institution. *Afghanistan Index*. Compiled by Ian S. Livingston, Heather L. Messera, and Michael O'Hanlon. www.brookings.edu/afghanistanindex/.

Campbell, Jason, Michael O'Hanlon, and Jeremy Shapiro. "How to Measure the War." *Policy Review* (October–November 2009): 15–30.

Chayes, Sarah. *The Punishment of Virtue: Inside Afghanistan after the Taliban*. New York: Penguin Books, 2006.

Chin, Warren. "British Counter-Insurgency in Afghanistan." *Defense & Security Analysis* 32, no. 2 (June 2007): 201–25.

Christia, Fotini, and Michael Semple. "Flipping the Taliban: How to Win in Afghanistan." *Foreign Affairs* 88, no. 4 (July/August 2009): 34–45.

Cogan, Charles. "Partners in Time: The CIA and Afghanistan since 1979." *World Policy Journal*, 10, no. 2 (Summer 1993): 73–82.

———. "Afghanistan: Partners in Time." *World Policy Journal* (Fall 2008): 155–56.

Cohen, Craig. *A Perilous Course: U.S. Strategy and Assistance to Pakistan*. Washington, DC: Center for Strategic and International Studies, August 2007.

Cohen, Stephen Philip. "The Nation and the State in Pakistan." *Washington Quarterly* 25, no. 3 (Summer 2002): 109–22.

———. *The Idea of Pakistan*. Washington, DC: Brookings Institution, 2004.

Coll, Steve. *Ghost Wars: The Secret History of the CIA, Afghanistan, and Bin Laden, from the Soviet Invasion to September 10, 2001*. New York: Penguin Press, 2004.

———. "War by Other Means: Is It Possible to Negotiate with the Taliban?" *New Yorker* (May 24, 2010): 42–53.

Collins, Joseph J. *The Soviet Invasion of Afghanistan: A Study in the Use of Force in Soviet Foreign Policy*. Lexington, MA: Lexington Books, 1986.

———. "To Further Afghan Reconciliation: Fight Harder." *Small Wars Journal* (October 2008); available at http://smallwarsjournal.com/blog/2008/10/to-further-afghan-reconciliati/.

———. "Afghanistan: The Path to Victory." *Joint Forces Quarterly* 54 (Third Quarter 2009): 58–61.

Colucci, Craig C. "Committing to Afghanistan: The Case for Increasing U.S. Reconstruction and Stabilization Aid." *Military Review*, Special Edition (June 2008): 90–97.

Cordesman, Anthony H. *The Lessons of Afghanistan: War Fighting, Intelligence, and Force Transformation*. Washington, DC: Center for Strategic and International Studies, 2002.

Cordovez, Diego, and Selig S. Harrison. *Out of Afghanistan: The Inside Story of the Soviet Withdrawal*. New York: Oxford University Press, 1995.

Corera, Gordon. *Shopping for Bombs: Nuclear Proliferation, Global Insecurity, and the Rise and Fall of the A. Q. Khan Network*. New York: Oxford University Press, 2006.

Crews, Robert D., and Amin Tarzi, eds. *The Taliban and the Crisis of Afghanistan*. Cambridge, MA: Harvard University Press, 2008.

Crile, George. *Charlie Wilson's War: The Extraordinary Story of the Largest Covert Operation in History*. New York: Atlantic Monthly Press, 2003.

Crumpton, Henry A. "Intelligence and War: Afghanistan 2001–2." In Jennifer E. Sims and Burton Gelber, eds. *Transforming U.S. Intelligence*. Washington, DC: Georgetown University Press, 2005, pp. 162–79.

Davis, Anthony. "Afghan Security Deteriorates as Taliban Regroup." *Jane's Intelligence Review* 15, no. 5 (May 2003): 10–15.

Dobbins, James F. *After the Taliban: Nation-Building in Afghanistan*. Washington, DC: Potomac Books, 2008.

Donahue, Patrick. "Combating Modern Insurgency: Combined Task Force Devil in Afghanistan." *Military Review*, Special Edition (June 2008): 74–89.

Dupree, Louis. *Afghanistan*. New York: Oxford University Press, 1997.

Edwards, David B. *Heroes of the Age: Moral Fault Lines on the Afghan Frontier*. Berkeley: University of California Press, 1996.

———. *Before the Taliban: Genealogies of the Afghan Jihad*. Berkeley: University of California Press, 2002.

Einfeld, Jann, ed. *Afghanistan*. Detroit: Thomson Gale, 2005.

Enterline, Andrew J., and J. Michael Grieg. "Against All Odds? The History of Imposed Democracy and the Future of Iraq and Afghanistan." *Foreign Policy Analysis* 4: 321–47.

Etzioni, Amatai. "Bottom up Nation Building." *Policy Review*, no. 158 (December 2009 and January 2010): 51–62.

Fair, C. Christine, and Peter Chalk. *Fortifying Pakistan: The Role of U.S. Internal Security Assistance*. Washington, DC: United States Institute of Peace Press, 2006.

Feickert, Andrew. *U.S. and Coalition Military Operations in Afghanistan: Issues for Congress*. Washington, DC: Congressional Research Service, June 6, 2006.

Flynn, Michael T. *Fixing Intel: A Blueprint for Making Intelligence Relevant in Afghanistan*. Working Paper. Washington, DC: Center for New American Security, January 4, 2010.

Friedman, Norman. *Terrorism, Afghanistan, and America's New Way of War*. Annapolis, MD: Naval Institute Press, 2003.

Fukuyama, Francis, ed. *Beyond Afghanistan and Iraq*. Baltimore, MD: Johns Hopkins University Press, 2006.

Gallis, Paul, and Vincent Morelli. *NATO in Afghanistan: A Test of the Atlantic Alliance*. Washington, DC: Congressional Research Service, July 2008.

Ganguly, Sumit. *The Crisis in Kashmir: Portraits of War, Hopes for Peace*. Cambridge: Cambridge University Press, 1997.

———. *Conflict Unending: India-Pakistan Tensions since 1947*. New York: Columbia University Press, 2002.

Ganguly, Sumit, and S. Paul Kapur. *Nuclear Proliferation in South Asia: Crisis Behavior and the Bomb*. New York: Routledge, 2009.

Gannon, Kathy. "Afghanistan Unbound." *Foreign Affairs* 83, no. 3 (2004): 35–46.

Giffin, Michael. *Reaping the Whirlwind: The Taliban Movement in Afghanistan*. London: Pluto Press, 2001.

Giustozzi, Antonio. *Empires of Mud*. New York: Columbia University Press, 2010.

Giustozzi, Antonio, ed. *Decoding the Taliban: Insights from the Afghan Field*. New York: Columbia University Press, 2009.

Goodson, Larry P. *Afghanistan's Endless War: State Failure, Regional Politics, and the Rise of the Taliban*. Seattle: University of Washington Press, 2001.

Grare, Frederic. *Rethinking Western Strategies toward Pakistan: An Action Agenda for the United States and Europe*. Washington, DC: Carnegie Endowment for International Peace, 2005.

Grau, Lester, ed. *The Bear Went over the Mountain: Soviet Combat Tactics in Afghanistan.* Washington, DC: National Defense University Press, 1996.

Gregory, Shaun. "The ISI and the War on Terrorism." *Studies in Conflict and Terrorism* 30, no. 12 (2007): 1013–31.

Griffin, Michael. *Reaping the Whirlwind: The Taliban Movement in Afghanistan.* London: Pluto Press, 2001.

Gutman, Roy. *How We Missed the Story: Osama bin Laden, the Taliban, and the Hijacking of Afghanistan.* Washington, DC: United States Institute of Peace, 2008.

Hammer, Joshua. "After Musharraf." *Atlantic Monthly* (October 2007): 100–14.

Haqqani, Husain. *Pakistan: Between Mosque and Military.* Washington, DC: Carnegie Endowment for International Peace, 2005.

Hastert, Paul L. "Operation Anaconda: Perception Meets Reality in the Hills of Afghanistan." *Studies in Conflict and Terrorism* 28: 11–20.

Hastings, Michael. "The Runaway General." *Rolling Stone* 1108/1109 (July 18–22, 2010).

Human Rights Watch. *"Troops in Contact": Airstrikes and Civilian Deaths in Afghanistan.* New York: Human Rights Watch, September 2008.

Hussain, Rizwan. *Pakistan and the Emergence of Islamic Militancy in Afghanistan.* Aldershot, UK: Ashgate, 2005.

Hussain, Zahid. *Frontline Pakistan: The Struggle with Militant Islam.* New York: Columbia University Press, 2007.

International Crisis Group. *Afghanistan's New Legislature: Making Democracy Work.* Asia Report, no. 116. Brussels: International Crisis Group, May 15, 2006; available at www.cririsgroup.org.

———. *Reforming Afghanistan's Police.* Asia Report, no. 138. Brussels: International Crisis Group, August 30, 2007.

———. *Taliban Propaganda: Winning the War on Words?* Brussels: International Crisis Group, July 24, 2008.

Jalal, Ayesha. *The Sole Spokesman: Jinnah, the Muslim League, and the Demand for Pakistan.* Cambridge: Cambridge University Press, 1985.

Jalali, Ali. "Afghanistan: The Anatomy of an Ongoing Conflict." *Parameters* 31, no. 1 (Spring 2001): 85–98.

———. "The Future of Afghanistan." *Parameters* 36, no. 1 (Spring 2006).

Johnson, Thomas H. "Afghanistan's Post-Taliban Transition: The State of State-Building after War." *Central Asian Survey* 25, nos. 1–2 (March–June 2006): 1–26.

Johnson, Thomas H., and M. Chris Mason. "Understanding the Taliban and Insurgency in Afghanistan." *Orbis* 51, no. 1 (Winter 2007).

———. "No Sign until the Burst of Fire: Understanding the Pakistan-Afghanistan Frontier." *International Security* 32, no. 4 (Spring 2008): 67–68.

Jones, James L., and Thomas R. Pickering, Co-Chairs. *Afghanistan Study Group Report: Revitalizing Our Efforts, Rethinking Our Strategies.* Washington, DC: Center for the Study of the Presidency, January 2008.

Jones, Owen Bennett. *Pakistan: Eye of the Storm*. New Haven: Yale University Press, 2002.

Jones, Seth G. "Averting Failure in Afghanistan." *Survival* 48, no. 1 (Spring 2006): 111–28.

———. "Pakistan's Dangerous Game." *Survival* 49, no. 1 (2007): 15–32.

———. *Counterinsurgency in Afghanistan*. Santa Monica, CA: RAND National Defense Research Institute, 2008.

———. *In the Graveyard of Empires: America's War in Afghanistan*. New York: W. W. Norton, 2009.

———. "It Takes the Villages: Bringing Change from Below in Afghanistan." *Foreign Affairs* 89, no. 3 (May/June 2010): 120–27.

Judah, Tim. "The Taliban Papers." *Survival* 44, no. 1 (Spring 2002): 69–80.

Kagan, Robert, and William Kristol. "A Winning Strategy: How the Bush Administration Changed Course and Won the War in Afghanistan." *Weekly Standard* (November 26, 2001).

Kaplan, Robert. *Soldiers of God: With Islamic Warriors in Afghanistan and Pakistan*. New York: Vintage Books, 2001.

Kapur, S. Paul. "India and Pakistan's Unstable Peace: Why Nuclear South Asia Is Not Like Cold War Europe." *International Security* 30, no. 2 (Fall 2005).

———. "Ten Years of Instability in a Nuclear South Asia." *International Security* 33, no. 2 (Fall 2008).

Khalilzad, Zalmay. "Anarchy in Afghanistan." *Journal of International Affairs* 51, no. 1 (Summer 1997): 37–56.

Khalilzad, Zalmay, and Daniel Byman. "Afghanistan: The Consolidation of a Rogue State." *Washington Quarterly* 23, no. 1 (Winter 2000): 65–78.

Khan, Yasmin. *The Great Partition: The Making of India and Pakistan*. New Haven: Yale University Press, 2008.

Kux, Dennis. *The United States and Pakistan, 1947–2000: Disenchanted Allies*. Washington, DC: Woodrow Wilson Center Press, 2001.

Levy, Adrian, and Catherine Scott-Clark. *Deception: Pakistan, the United States, and the Global Nuclear Weapons Conspiracy*. London: Atlantic Books, 2007.

Lodhi, Maleeha. "The Future of Pakistan-U.S. Relations: Opportunities and Challenges." *INSS Special Report*. Washington, DC: Institute for National Strategic Studies, National Defense University, April 2009.

Loyn, David. *Butcher and Bolt: Two Hundred Years of Foreign Engagement in Afghanistan*. London: Hutchinson, 2009.

Maley, William, ed. *Fundamentalism Reborn? Afghanistan and the Taliban*. London: Hurst and Company, 1988.

———. *Fundamentalism Reborn? Afghanistan and the Taliban*. New York: New York University Press, 1998.

———. *The Afghanistan Wars*. New York: Palgrave, 2002.

———. *Rescuing Afghanistan*. London: Hurst and Company, 2006.

———. *Stabilizing Afghanistan: Threats and Challenges.* Policy Brief no. 68. Washington, DC: Carnegie Endowment for International Peace, 2008.

Maloney, Sean. "Afghanistan: From Here to Eternity?" *Parameters* (Spring 2004).

Manuel, Anja, and P. W. Singer. "A New Model Afghan Army." *Foreign Affairs* 81, no. 4 (July/August 2002): 44–59.

Markey, Daniel. "A False Choice in Pakistan." *Foreign Affairs* 86, no. 4 (July/August 2007): 85–102.

———. *Securing Pakistan's Tribal Belt.* Council Special Report No. 36. New York: Council on Foreign Relations, August 2008.

McChrystal, Stanley A. "Commander's Initial Assessment." Memorandum to Secretary of Defense Robert M. Gates, August 30, 2009; available at www.nytimes.com.

McMaster, H. R. "This Familiar Battleground." *Hoover Digest*, no. 4 (Fall 2009): 92–107.

McNerney, Michael J. "Stabilization and Reconstruction in Afghanistan: Are PRT's a Model or a Muddle?" *Parameters* 35, no. 4 (Winter 2005/2006): 32–46.

Minear, Larry. *Through Veterans' Eyes: The Iraq and Afghanistan Experience.* Dulles, VA: Potomac Books, 2009.

Mullaney, Craig M. *The Unforgiving Minute: A Soldier's Education*. New York: Penguin Press, 2009.

Musharraf, Pervez. *In the Line of Fire: A Memoir*. New York: Simon and Schuster, 2006.

Nagl, John, and Nathaniel Fick. "Counterinsurgency Field Manual: Afghanistan Edition." *Foreign Policy* (January–February 2009).

Nawaz, Shuja. *Crossed Swords: Pakistan, Its Army, and the Wars Within.* London: Oxford University Press, 2008.

Naylor, Sean. *Not a Good Day to Die: The Untold Story of Operation Anaconda.* New York: Berkley Books, 2005.

Neumannn, Ronald E. *The Other War: Winning and Losing in Afghanistan*. Dulles, VA: Potomac Books, 2009.

O'Hanlon, Michael. "Staying Power: The U.S. Mission in Afghanistan beyond 2011." *Foreign Affairs* 89, no. 5 (September/October 2010): 63–79.

O'Hanlon, Michael E., and Hassina Sherjan. *Toughing It Out in Afghanistan*. Washington, DC: Brookings Institution Press, 2010.

Packer, George, "The Last Mission." (Profile of Richard Holbrooke). *New Yorker* (September 28, 2009): 40–56.

Paul, T. V. *The India-Pakistan Conflict: An Enduring Rivalry*. Cambridge, UK: Cambridge University Press, 2005.

Perito, Robert M. *The U.S. Experience with Provincial Reconstruction Teams in Afghanistan: Lessons Identified.* Special Report no. 152. Washington, DC: United States Institute of Peace, October 2005; at http://www.usip.org/files/resources/sr152.pdf/.

Peters, Ralph. "Trapping Ourselves in Afghanistan and Losing Focus on the Essential Mission." *Joint Forces Quarterly* 54 (Third Quarter 2009): 63–67.

Petraeus, David H. "The General's Next War: The FP Interview with Gen. David H. Petraeus." *Foreign Policy* (January/February 2009): 48–50.

Rasanayagan, Angelo. *Afghanistan: A Modern History*. New York: I. B. Taurus, 2005.

Rashid, Ahmed. "The Taliban: Exporting Extremism." *Foreign Affairs* 78, no. 6 (1999): 22–35.

———. *Taliban: Militant Islam, Oil and Fundamentalism in Central Asia*. New Haven: Yale University Press, 2000.

———. "The Mess in Afghanistan." *New York Review of Books*, February 12, 2004.

———. "Afghanistan: Progress since the Taliban." *Asian Affairs* 37, no. 1 (March 2006).

———. *Descent into Chaos: The United States and the Disaster in Pakistan, Afghanistan and Central Asia*. New York: Penguin, 2009.

———. "The Anarchic Republic of Pakistan." *National Interest*, August 24, 2010.

Roberts, Adam. "Doctrine and Reality in Afghanistan." *Survival* 51, no. 1 (February–March 2009): 29–60.

Roe, Andrew M. "To Create a Stable Afghanistan." *Military Review* (November–December 2005).

Rothstein, Hy S. *Afghanistan and the Troubled Future of Unconventional Warfare*. Annapolis, MD: Naval Institute Press, 2006.

Roy, Olivier. *Islam and Resistance in Afghanistan*. Cambridge, UK: Cambridge University Press, 1986.

———. *Afghanistan: From Holy War to Civil War*. Princeton, NJ: Darwin Press, 1995.

Rubin, Barnett R. *The Search for Peace in Afghanistan: From Buffer State to Failed State*. New Haven: Yale University Press, 1995.

———. *The Fragmentation of Afghanistan: State Formation and Collapse in the International System*, 2nd ed. New Haven: Yale University Press, 2002.

———. "Crafting a Constitution for Afghanistan." *Journal of Democracy* (July 2004).

———. *Afghanistan and the International Community: Implementing the Afghanistan Compact*. New York: Council on Foreign Relations, 2006.

———. "Saving Afghanistan." *Foreign Affairs* 86, no. 1 (2007): 57–78.

Rubin, Barnett R., and Andrea Armstrong. "Regional Issues in the Reconstruction of Afghanistan." *World Policy Journal* 20, no. 1 (2003): 31–40.

Rubin, Barnett R., and Ahmed Rashid. "From Great Game to Grand Bargain." *Foreign Affairs* 87, no. 6 (November–December 2008): 30–44.

Sagan, Scott D., ed. *Inside Nuclear South Asia*. Stanford, CA: Stanford University Press, 2009.

Satter, Abdul. *Pakistan's Foreign Policy, 1947–2005: A Concise History*. New York: Oxford University Press, 2007.

Schaffer, Howard B. *The Limits of Influence: America's Role in Kashmir*. Washington, DC: Brookings Institution Press, 2009.

Schofield, Victoria. *Kashmir in Conflict: India, Pakistan, and the Unending War*. New York: I. B. Tauris, 2003.

Schroen, Gary C. *First In: An Insider's Account of How the CIA Spearheaded the War on Terror in Afghanistan*. New York: Presidio Press/Random House, 2005.

Scott, Trent, and John Agoglia. "Getting the Basics Right: A Discussion on Tactical Actions for Strategic Impact in Afghanistan." *Small Wars Journal* (November 2008).

Semple, Michael. *Reconciliation in Afghanistan*. Washington, DC: United States Institute of Peace Press, 2009.

Siddiqa, Ayesha. *Military Inc.: Inside Pakistan's Military Economy*. London: Oxford University Press, 2007.

Simon, Steven. "Can the Right War Be Won? Defining American Interests in Afghanistan." *Foreign Affairs* 88, no. 4 (July/August 2009): 130–37.

Singh, Anita. "Pakistan's Stability/Instability Complex: The Politics and Reverberations of the 2007 November Emergency." *Strategic Studies Quarterly* (Winter 2009): 22–48.

Sinno, Abdulkader H. *Organizations at War in Afghanistan and Beyond*. Ithaca, NY: Cornell University Press, 2007.

Sokolski, Henry D., ed. *Pakistan's Nuclear Future: Worries beyond War*. Carlisle, PA: Strategic Studies Institute, U.S. Army War College, January 2008.

Stanton, Doug. *Horse Soldiers: The Extraordinary Story of a Band of U.S. Soldiers Who Rode to Victory in Afghanistan*. New York: Scribner, 2009.

Synnott, Hilary. "What Is Happening in Pakistan?" *Survival* 51, no. 1 (February–March 2009): 61–80.

Talbot, Ian. *Pakistan: A Modern History*. New York: Palgrave Macmillan, 2005.

Tanner, Stephen. *Afghanistan: A Military History from Alexander the Great to the Fall of the Taliban*. New York: Da Capo Press, 2002.

Tellis, Ashley J. "U.S. Strategy: Assisting Pakistan's Transformation." *Washington Quarterly* 28, no. 1 (Winter 2004–5): 97–116.

———. "The Merits of Dehyphenation: Explaining U.S. Success in Engaging India and Pakistan." *Washington Quarterly* 31, no. 4 (Autumn 2008): 21–42.

———. *Pakistan and the War on Terror: Conflicted Goals, Compromised Performance*. Washington, DC: Carnegie Endowment for International Peace, 2008.

Thier, J. Alexander, ed. *The Future of Afghanistan*. Washington, DC: United States Institute of Peace, 2009.

Thier, J. Alexander, and Azita Ranjbar. *Killing Friends, Making Enemies: The Impact and Avoidance of Civilian Casualties in Afghanistan*. Washington, DC: United States Institute of Peace, July 2008.

Tripathi, Deepak. *Overcoming the Bush Legacy in Iraq and Afghanistan*. Dulles, VA: Potomac Books, 2009.

———. *Breeding Ground: Afghanistan and the Origins of Islamist Terrorism*. Dulles, VA: Potomac Books, 2010.

United Nations. "Letter Dated 5 December 2001 from the Secretary-General Addressed to the President of the Security Council." (Bonn Agreement). UN Security Council Document S/2001/1154, December 5, 2001.

———. *Report of the Secretary General on the Situation in Afghanistan and Its Implications for International Peace and Security*. UN doc A/56/875-S/2002/278.

———. *National Human Development Report for Afghanistan: Security with a Human Face, Challenges and Responsibilities.* Islamabad: United National Development Programme, 2004.

U.S. Congress. Senate. Committee on Foreign Relations. *Afghanistan Stabilization and Reconstruction: A Status Report.* Hearing, January 27, 2004.

U.S. Department of State. *Afghanistan, Autumn 2006: A Campaign at a Crossroads.* Washington, DC: Office of the Coordinator for Counterterrorism, 2006.

U.S. General Accounting Office. *Combating Terrorism: The United States Lacks Comprehensive Plan to Destroy the Terrorist Threat and Close the Safe Haven in Pakistan's Federally Administered Tribal Areas.* Washington, DC: General Accounting Office, April 2008.

———. *Afghanistan Security.* GAO-08–661. Washington, DC: General Accounting Office, June 2008.

———. *Provincial Reconstruction Teams in Afghanistan and Iraq.* GAO-08–905RSU. Washington, DC: General Accounting Office, September 26, 2008.

———. *Provincial Reconstruction Teams in Afghanistan and Iraq.* GAO-09–86R Washington, DC: General Accounting Office, October 1, 2008.

U.S. White House. *White Paper of the Interagency Policy Group's Report on U.S. Policy toward Afghanistan and Pakistan*, March 27, 2009; available at:http://www.whitehouse.gov/assets/documents/Afghanistan-Pakistan_White_Paper.pdf.

Weaver, Mary Anne. *Pakistan: In the Shadow of Jihad and Afghanistan.* New York: Farrar, Straus and Giroux, 2002.

Weinbaum, Marvin G., and Jonathan B. Harder. "Pakistan's Afghan Policies and Their Consequences." *Contemporary South Asia* 16, no. 1 (2008): 25–38.

Weiner, Myron, and Ali Bannazizi. *The Politics of Social Transformation in Afghanistan, Iran, and Pakistan.* Syracuse, NY: Syracuse University Press, 1994.

Wikileaks. "Afghan War Diary, 2004–2010." (Formerly classified documents concerning 91,000 events in the Afghan war); available at: http://wikileaks.org/wiki/Afghan_War_Diary,_2004–2010.

Wirsing, Robert. *Kashmir in the Shadow of War: Regional Rivalries in the Nuclear Age.* New York: M. E. Sharpe, 2003.

Witchell, Sean P. "Pakistan's ISI: The Invisible Government." *International Journal of Intelligence and Counter-Intelligence* 16, no. 1 (Spring 2003): 374–88.

Woodward, Bob. *Obama's Wars.* New York: Simon and Schuster, 2010.

Yousaf, Mohammed, and Mark Adkin. *The Bear Trap: Afghanistan's Untold Story.* Cooper, 1992.

Zaeef, Abdul Salam. *My Life with the Taliban.* New York: Columbia University Press, 2010.

Zahab, Mariam Abou, and Olivier Roy. *Islamist Networks: The Afghan-Pakistan Connection.* John King, trans. New York: Columbia University Press, 2004.

Zulfacar, Maliha. "The Pendulum of Gender Politics in Afghanistan." *Central Asian Survey* 25, nos. 1 and 2 (2006): 27–59.

The Iraq War

Adelman, Ken. "Cakewalk in Iraq." *Washington Post*, February 13, 2002, p. A27.

———. "'Cakewalk' Revisited." *Washington Post*, April 10, 2003.

Ajami, Fouad. "Iraq and the Arabs' Future." *Foreign Affairs* 82, no. 1 (January/February 2003): 2–18.

———. "Blind Liberation." *New Republic* (April 23, 2007): 42–49.

———. "A Measure of Pride: Five Years into the Iraq War, a Better Country Is Emerging." *Wall Street Journal*, March 19, 2008.

Alfonsi, Christian. *Circle in the Sand: Why We Went Back to Iraq*. New York: Doubleday, 2006.

Al-Jabouri, Najim Abed. "Iraqi Security Forces after U.S. Troop Withdrawal: An Iraqi Perspective." *Strategic Forum*, no. 245. Washington, DC: Institute for National Strategic Studies, National Defense University, August 2009.

Allawi, Ali A. *The Occupation of Iraq: Winning the War, Losing the Peace*. New Haven: Yale University Press, 2007.

Ali, Tariq. *Bush in Babylon: The Recolonisation of Iraq*. New York: W. W. Norton, 2003.

Amos, Deborah. *Eclipse of the Sunnis: Power, Exile, and Upheaval in the Middle East*. New York: PublicAffairs, 2010.

Anderson, Jon Lee. *The Fall of Baghdad*. New York: Penguin, 2004.

———. "American Viceroy: Zalmay Khalizad's Mission." *New Yorker* (December 19, 2005).

Anderson, Liam, and Gareth Stansfield. *The Future of Iraq: Dictatorship, Democracy or Division?* London: Palgrave, 2004.

Andres, Richard. "The Afghan Model in Northern Iraq." *Journal of Strategic Studies* 29, no. 3 (June 2006): 395–422.

Arnove, Anthony. *Iraq: The Logic of Withdrawal*. New York: Metropolitan Books, 2007.

Atkinson, Rick. *In the Company of Soldiers: A Chronicle of Combat*. New York: Henry Holt, 2004.

Australia, Government of. *The Report of the Inquiry into Australian Agencies* (Flood Report). Canberra, July 2004.

Bacevich, Andrew J. "The Petraeus Doctrine." *Atlantic Monthly* (October 2008).

Baker, James A., and Lee H. Hamilton, Co-Chairs. *Iraq Study Group Report: The Way Forward—A New Approach*. New York: Vintage Books, 2006.

Baltrusaitis, Daniel. *Coalition Politics and the Iraq War: Determinants of Choice*. Boulder, CO: Lynne Rienner, 2009.

Bamford, James. *A Pretext for War: 9/11, Iraq, and the Abuse of America's Intelligence Agencies*. New York: Doubleday, 2004.

Barnett, Thomas P. M. "The Man between War and Peace." (Profile of Admiral Fallon). *Esquire*, March 2008.

Beckett, Ian F. W. *Insurgency in Iraq: An Historical Perspective*. Strategic Studies Monograph. Carlisle Barracks, PA: U.S. Army War College, January 2005.

Bellavia, David. *House to House*. New York: Free Press, 2007.

Benomar, Jamal. "Constitution-Making after Conflict: Lessons from Iraq." *Journal of Democracy* 15 (April 2004): 81–95.

Bensahel, Nora. "Mission Not Accomplished: What Went Wrong with Iraqi Reconstruction." *Journal of Strategic Studies* 29, no. 3 (June 2006): 453–73.

Bensahel, Nora, et al. *After Saddam: Prewar Planning and the Occupation of Iraq*. Santa Monica, CA: RAND, 2008.

Berger, Samuel R., Brent Scowcroft, William Nash, et al. *In the Wake of War: Improving U.S. Post-Conflict Capabilities*. New York: Council on Foreign Relations, 2005.

Best, Richard A. *U.S. Intelligence and Policymaking: The Iraq Experience*. Report RS21696. Washington, DC: Congressional Research Service, December 2, 2005.

Biddle, Stephen. "Iraq and the Future of Warfare: Implications for Army and Defense Policy." Carlisle, PA: Strategic Studies Institute, U.S. Army War College, August 2003: available at: http://www.globalsecurity.org/military/library/congress/2003_hr/03–10–21warcollege.pdf.

———. *Military Power: Explaining Victory and Defeat in Modern Battle*. Princeton: Princeton University Press, 2004.

———. "Seeing Baghdad, Thinking Saigon." *Foreign Affairs* 85, no. 2 (March/April 2006): 2–14.

———. "Speed Kills? Reassessing the Role of Speed, Precision, and Situation Awareness in the Fall of Saddam." *Journal of Strategic Studies* (February 2007): 3–46.

Biddle, Stephen, et al. *Toppling Saddam: Iraq and Military Transformation*. Carlisle, PA: Strategic Studies Institute, U.S. Army War College, April 2004.

Biddle, Stephen, Michael E. O'Hanlon, and Kenneth M. Pollack. "How to Leave a Stable Iraq." *Foreign Affairs* 87, no. 5 (September/October 2008): 40–58.

Biden, Joseph R., Jr., and Leslie H. Gelb. "Unity through Autonomy." *New York Times*, May 1, 2006, p. A25.

Bilmes, Linda, and Joseph E. Stiglitz. "Encore." *Milken Institute Review* (Fourth Quarter 2006): 76–83.

Blix, Hans. *Disarming Iraq: The Search for Weapons of Mass Destruction*. New York: Pantheon Books, 2004.

Blumenthal, Sidney. *How Bush Rules: Chronicles of a Radical Regime*. Princeton: Princeton University Press, 2006.

Bolton, John. *Surrender Is Not an Option: Defending America at the United Nations and Abroad*. New York: Threshold Editions, 2007.

Boot, Max. "The New American Way of War." *Foreign Affairs* 82, no. 4 (July/August 2003): 41–59.

———. "The Bush Doctrine Lives." *Weekly Standard* (February 16, 2004).

Bouillon, Markus E., David M. Malone, and Ben Roswell, eds. *Iraq: Preventing a New Generation of Conflict*. Boulder, CO: Lynne Rienner, 2007.

Bowden, Mark. "Wolfowitz: The Exit Interviews." *Atlantic Monthly* 296 (July/August 2005).

———. "The Ploy." *Atlantic Monthly* (May 2007): 54–68.

Boyle, Michael. "Utopianism and the Bush Foreign Policy." *Cambridge Review of International Affairs* 17, no. 1 (2004): 81–103.

Bremer, L. Paul, III, "In Iraq, Wrongs Make a Right." *New York Times*, January 13, 2006, p. A23.

———. "What We Got Right in Iraq." *Washington Post*, May 13, 2007, p. B1.

———. "How I Didn't Dismantle Iraq's Army." *New York Times*, September 6, 2007, p. A25.

Bremer, L. Paul, III, with Malcolm McConnell. *My Year in Iraq*. New York: Simon and Schuster, 2006.

Brigham, Robert K. *Is Iraq Another Vietnam?* New York: PublicAffairs, 2006.

———. *Iraq, Vietnam, and the Limits of American Power*. New York: PublicAffairs, 2008.

Brinkley, Paul "A Cause for Hope: Economic Revitalization in Iraq." *Military Review*, Special Edition (June 2008): 64–73.

Briscoe, Charles H., Kenneth Finlayson, et al. *All Roads Lead to Baghdad: Army Special Operations Forces in Iraq.* Fort Bragg, NC: U.S. Army Special Operations Command History Office, 2006.

Brookings Institution. *Iraq Index: Tracking Variables of Reconstruction and Security in Post-Saddam Iraq.* Compiled by Michael O'Hanlon and Ian S. Livingston. http://www.brookings.edu/saban/iraq-index.aspx.

Brown, Todd S. *Battleground Iraq: Journal of a Company Commander*. Washington, DC: U.S. Army Center of Military History, 2007.

Brownstein, Catherine A., and John S. Brownstein. "Estimating Excess Mortality in Post-Invasion Iraq." *New England Journal of Medicine* 358, no. 5 (January 31, 2008): 445–47.

Bumiller, Elisabeth. *Condoleezza Rice: An American Life: A Biography*. New York: Random House, 2007.

Bunker, Robert, and John Sullivan. "Suicide Bombings in Operation Iraqi Freedom." *Military Review* (January–February 2005).

Burgos, Russell. "An N of 1: A Political Scientist in Operation Iraqi Freedom." *Perspectives on Politics* 2, no. 3 (September 2004): 551–56.

———. "Teaching the Iraq War." *PS: Political Science and Politics* (January 2008).

———. "Origins of Regime Change: 'Ideapolitik' on the Long Road to Baghdad, 1993–2000." *Security Studies* 17, no. 2 (April 2008): 221–56.

Burroughs, Bryan, Evgenia Peretz, David Rose, and David Wise. "The Path to War." *Vanity Fair* (May 2004).

Bush, George W. "Remarks by the President at the 2002 Graduation Exercises of the United States Military Academy." West Point, New York, June 1, 2002; available at http://www.whitehouse.gov/news/releases/2002/06/print/20020601–3.html.

———. "Bush's Words to Britons: 'Both Our Nations Serve the Cause of Freedom.'" *New York Times*, November 20, 2003, p. A12.

———. "President's State of the Union Message to Congress and the Nation." *New York Times*, January 29, 2003, p. A12.

———. "President Bush's Address to the Nation on the War on Terror." *New York Times*, September 8, 2003.

———. "President's State of the Union Message to Congress and the Nation." *New York Times*, January 21, 2004, p. A14.

———. "The Inaugural Address: 'The Best Hope for Peace in Our World Is the Expansion of Freedom in All the World.'" *New York Times*, January 21, 2005, pp. A16–17.

———. *Decision Points*. New York: Crown Publishers, 2010.

Butler, Richard. *Saddam Defiant: The Threat of Mass Destruction and the Crisis of Global Security*. London: Weidenfeld and Nicholson, 2000.

Buzzell, Colby. *My War: Killing Time in Iraq*. New York: G. P. Putnam's Sons, 2005.

Byman, Daniel. "Proceed with Caution: U.S. Support for the Iraqi Opposition." *Washington Quarterly* (Summer 1999).

Byman, Daniel, Kenneth Pollack, and Gideon Rose. "Can Saddam Be Toppled?" *Foreign Affairs* (January–February 1999).

Byman, Daniel, Kenneth Pollack, and Matthew Waxman. "Coercing Saddam Hussein: Lessons from the Past." *Survival* (Autumn 1998).

Caldwell, Dan. "Iraq: 'The Wrong War, at the Wrong Time with the Wrong Strategy.'" Columbia International Affairs Online (CIAO), August 2007; available at www.ciao.net.

Campbell, Kenneth J. *A Tale of Two Quagmires: Iraq, Vietnam, and the Hard Lessons of War*. Boulder: Paradigm Publishers, 2007.

Caraley, Demetrios, ed. *American Hegemony: Preventive War, Iraq and Imposing Democracy*. New York: Academy of Political Science, 2004.

Cassidy, John. "Beneath the Sand: Can a Shattered Country Be Rebuilt with Oil?" *New Yorker* (July 14/21, 2003).

Chalabi, Ahmad. "A Democratic Future for Iraq." *Wall Street Journal*, February 27, 1991.

———. "We Can Topple Saddam." *Wall Street Journal*, May 21, 2001.

———. "Iraqis Must Rule Iraq." *Wall Street Journal*, February 19, 2003.

———. "The Future Iraq Deserves." *Wall Street Journal*, December 22, 2004.

Chandrasekaran, Rajiv. *Imperial Life in the Emerald City: Inside Iraq's Green Zone*. New York: Alfred A. Knopf, 2006.

Chehab, Zaki. *Inside the Resistance*. New York: Nation Books, 2005.

Chiarelli, Peter W. "Learning from Our Modern Wars: The Imperatives of Preparing for a Dangerous Future." *Military Review* (September/October 2007): 2–15.

Chiarelli, Peter W., and Patrick Michaelis. "Winning the Peace: The Requirements for Full-Spectrum Operations." *Military Review* (July–August 2005): 4–17.

Chairelli, Peter W., with Stephen M. Smith. "Learning from Our Modern Wars: The Imperatives of Preparing for a Dangerous Future." *Military Review*, Special Edition (June 2008): 36–49.

Cirincione, Joseph, and Jessica R. Mathews. *Iraq: A New Approach.* Washington, DC: Carnegie Endowment for International Peace, August 2002.

Cirincione, Joseph, Jessica R. Mathews, and George Perkovich, with Alexis Orton. *WMD in Iraq: Evidence and Implications.* Washington, DC: Carnegie Endowment for International Peace, January 2004.

Clancy, Tom, with Anthony C. Zinni and Tony Koltz. *Battle Ready.* New York: G. P. Putnam's Sons, 2004.

Clark, Wesley K. *Winning Modern Wars: Iraq, Terrorism, and the American Empire.* New York: PublicAffairs, 2003.

Cloud, David, and Greg Jaffe. *The Fourth Star: Four Generals and the Epic Struggle for the Future of the United States Army.* New York: Crown Publishers, 2009.

Cockburn, Andrew. *Rumsfeld: His Rise, Fall, and Catastrophic Legacy.* New York: Scribner, 2007.

Cockburn, Patrick. *The Occupation: War and Resistance in Iraq.* New York: Verso, 2006.

Cohen, Eliot, and Michael Eisenstadt. *Airpower against Iraq: An Assessment.* Washington, DC: Washington Institute for Near East Policy, 1998.

Cole, Juan. "The United States and Shi'ite Religious Factions in Post-War Iraq." *Middle East Journal* 57, no. 4 (Autumn 2003).

———. "A Shiite Crescent? The Regional Impact of the Iraq War." *Current History* 105 (January 2006): 20–26.

Coll, Steve. "The General's Dilemma: David Petraeus, the Pressures of Politics, and the Road out of Iraq." *New Yorker* (September 8, 2008): 34–47.

Collin, Richard Oliver. "Words of War: The Iraqi Tower of Babel." *International Studies Perspectives* 10 (2009): 245–64.

Collins, Joseph J. "An Open Letter to President Bush." *Armed Forces Journal* (January 2006).

———. "Planning Lessons from Afghanistan and Iraq." *Joint Forces Quarterly*, Issue 42 (2nd quarter, 2006): 10–14.

———. "Beyond the Surge." *Armed Forces Journal* (April 2007): 13.

———. *Choosing War: The Decision to Invade Iraq and Its Aftermath.* Institute for National Strategic Studies Occasional Paper 5. Washington, DC: National Defense University Press, April 2008.

Conway, James. "'Farther and Faster' in Iraq." *U.S. Naval Institute Proceedings* 131, no. 1 (January 2005): 25–30.

Cordesman, Anthony H. *The Iraq War: Strategy, Tactics and Military Lessons.* Westport, CT: Praeger Publishers, 2003.

———. "Iraq's Sunni Insurgents: Looking beyond Al Qa'ida." Washington, DC: Center for Strategic and International and Studies, 2007.

Cornish, Paul, ed. *The Conflict in Iraq, 2003.* London: Palgrave/Macmillan, 2004.

Crahan, Margaret, John Goering, and Thomas G. Weiss, eds. *Wars on Terrorism and Iraq: The US and the World.* London: Routledge, 2004.

Crane, Conrad C., and W. Andrew Terrill. *Reconstructing Iraq: Insights, Challenges, and Missions for Military Forces in a Post-Conflict Scenario*. Carlisle Barracks, PA: Strategic Studies Institute, U.S. Army War College, February 2003.

Crawford, John. *The Last True Story I'll Ever Tell*. New York: Riverhead Books, 2005.

Crocker, Ryan C. "Report to Congress on the Situation in Iraq." Joint Hearing of the Committee on Foreign Affairs and the Committee on Armed Services, September 10, 2007; available at http://www.state.gov/p/nearls/rm/2007/91941.htm.

———. "A Future to Write in Iraq." *Washington Post*, August 31, 2010, p. A17.

Cushman, Thomas, ed. *A Matter of Principle: Humanitarian Arguments for War in Iraq*. Berkeley: University of California Press, 2005.

Daalder, Ivo H., and James M. Lindsay. *America Unbound: The Bush Revolution in Foreign Policy*. Washington, DC: Brookings Institution, 2003.

Danchev, Alex. "The Reckoning: Official Inquiries and the Iraq War." *Intelligence and National Security* 19 (Autumn 2004): 436–66.

Danner, Mark. "Taking Stock of the Forever War." *New York Times Magazine* (September 11, 2003).

———. *The Secret Way to War: The Downing Street Memo and the Iraq War's Buried History*. New York: New York Review of Books, 2006.

———. "Iraq: The War on the Imagination." *New York Review of Books*, December 12, 2006.

Davies, Philip. "Intelligence Culture and Intelligence Failure in Britain and the United States." *Cambridge Review of International Affairs* 17 (October 2004): 495–520.

———. "A Critical Look at Britain's Spy Machinery." *Studies in Intelligence* 49, no. 4 (2005): 41–54.

Davis, Eric. *Memories of State: Politics, History, and Collective Identity in Modern Iraq*. Berkeley: University of California Press, 2005.

Davis, Jack. "The Challenge of Managing Uncertainty: Paul Wolfowitz on Intelligence Policy Relations." *Studies in Intelligence* 39, no. 5 (1996).

———. "Intelligence Analysts and Policymakers: Benefits and Dangers of Tensions in the Relationship." *Intelligence and National Security* 21 (December 2006).

Davis, John W., ed. *Presidential Politics and the Road to the Second Iraq War: From Forty-One to Forty-Three*. New York: Ashgate, 2006.

Dawisha, Adeed. "The Prospects for Democracy in Iraq: Challenges and Opportunities." *Third World Quarterly* 26, nos. 4–5 (2005): 723–37.

Dawisha, Adeed, and Larry Diamond. "Iraq's Year of Voting Dangerously." *Journal of Democracy* 17, no. 2 (April 2006): 89–103.

DeFronzo, James. *The Iraq War: Origins and Consequences*. Boulder, CO: Westview Press, 2009.

Degen, E. J., and Gregory Fremont. *On Point: The United States Army in Operation Iraqi Freedom*. Fort Leavenworth, KS: Combat Studies Institute Press, 2004.

DeLong, Michael, with Noah Lukeman. *Inside CENTCOM: The Unvarnished Truth about the Wars in Afghanistan and Iraq*. New York: Regnery, 2004; Expanded paperback version published as *A General Speaks Out: The Truth about the Wars in Afghanistan and Iraq*. St. Paul, MN: Zenith Press, 2007.

Desch, Michael. "Bush and the Generals." *Foreign Affairs* 86, no. 3 (May/June 2007).

DeYoung, Karen. *Soldier: The Life of Colin Powell*. New York: Vintage, 2006.

Diamond, John. *The CIA and the Culture of Failure: U.S. Intelligence from the End of the Cold War to the Invasion of Iraq*. Stanford: Stanford University Press, 2008.

Diamond, Larry. "Why the United States Should Not Go It Alone." *Hoover Digest* 1 (2003): 82–85.

———. "What Went Wrong in Iraq." *Foreign Affairs* 83, no. 5 (September/October 2004): 34–56.

———. *Squandered Victory: The American Occupation and the Bungled Effort to Bring Democracy to Iraq*. New York: Henry Holt, 2005.

———. "Time for a 'Diplomatic Surge.'" *Hoover Digest*, no. 3 (2008): 15–22.

Diamond, Larry, James Dobbins, Chaim Kaufman, Leslie H. Gelb, and Stephen Biddle. "What to Do in Iraq: A Roundtable." *Foreign Affairs* 85, no. 4 (July/August 2006): 150–69.

Diebel, Terry L. *Foreign Affairs Strategy: Logic for American Statecraft*. New York: Cambridge University Press, 2007.

Djerejian, Edward P., and Frank G. Wisner, Co-Chairs. *Guiding Principles for U.S. Post-Conflict Policy in Iraq*. Working Group Report. New York: Council on Foreign Relations, 2003.

Dobbins, James. "Who Lost Iraq?" *Foreign Affairs* 86, no. 5 (September/October 2007): 61–74.

Dobbins, James, and David Gompert. "Early Days in Iraq: Decisions of the CPA." *Survival* 50, no. 4 (2008): 21–56.

Dobbins, James, Seth G. Jones, Keith Crane, Andrew Rathmell, Brett Steele, Richard Teltschik, and Anga Timilsina. *America's Role in Nation-Building: From Germany to Iraq*. Santa Monica, CA: RAND, 2003.

Dodge, Toby. *Iraq's Future: The Aftermath of Regime Change*. Adelphi Paper 372. London: Routledge for the International Institute for Strategic Studies, 2005.

———. *Inventing Iraq: The Failure of Nation-Building and a History Denied*. New York: Columbia University Press, 2005.

———. "Iraqi Transitions: From Regime Change to State Collapse." *Third World Quarterly* 26, nos. 4–5 (2005): 705–21.

———. "How Iraq Was Lost." *Survival* (Winter 2006–7).

———. "The Causes of U.S. Failure in Iraq." *Survival* (Spring 2007).

Dodge, Toby, and Steven Simon. *Iraq at the Crossroads: State and Society in the Shadow of Regime Change*. Adelphi Paper 354. Oxford: Oxford University Press for the International Institute for Strategic Studies, January 2003.

Donnelly, Thomas. *Operation Iraqi Freedom: A Strategic Assessment*. Washington, DC: AEI Press, 2004.

Dorrien, Gary J. *Imperial Designs: Neoconservatism and the New Pax Americana*. New York: Routledge, 2004.

Draper, Robert. *Dead Certain: The Presidency of George W. Bush*. New York: Free Press, 2007.

Dreasen, Yochi J. "How a 24-Year-Old Got a Job Rebuilding Iraq's Stock Market." *Wall Street Journal*, January 28, 2004.

Drogin, Bob, and John Goetz. "How the U.S. Fell under the Spell of 'Curveball.'" *Los Angeles Times*, November 20, 2005.

Drogin, Bob, and Greg Miller. "Curveball and the Source of Fresh CIA Rancor." *Los Angeles Times*, April 2, 2005.

Drogin, Robert. *Curveball: Spies, Lies, and the Con Man Who Caused a War*. New York: Random House, 2007.

Drumheller, Tyler. *On the Brink: An Insider's Account of How the White House Compromised American Intelligence*. New York: Carroll and Graf, 2006.

Duelfer, Charles. *Hide and Seek: The Search for Truth in Iraq*. New York: PublicAffairs, 2009.

Duffield, John S. W., and Peter J. Dombrowski. *Balance Sheet: The Iraq War and U.S. National Security*. Stanford: Stanford University Press, 2009.

Eaton, Paul D. "A Top-Down Review of the Pentagon." *New York Times*, March 19, 2006.

Edelstein, David M. *Occupation Hazard: Success and Failure in Military Occupation*. Ithaca, NY: Cornell University Press, 2010.

Ekeus, Rolf. "Reassessment: The IISS Strategic Dossier on Iraq's Weapons of Mass Destruction." *Survival* 46, no. 2 (Summer 2004): 73–88.

Eisenstadt, Michael, and Eric Mathewson, eds. *U.S. Policy in Post-Saddam Iraq: Lessons from the British Experience*. Washington, DC: Washington Institute for Near East Policy, 2003.

Ender, Morten G. *American Soldiers in Iraq: McSoldiers or Innovative Professionals?* London: Routledge, 2009.

Enders, David. *Baghdad Bulletin: Dispatches on the American Occupation*. Ann Arbor: University of Michigan Press, 2005.

Ehrenberg, John, J. Patrice McSherry, Jose Ramon Sanchez, and Caroleen Marji Sayej. *The Iraq Papers*. New York: Oxford University Press, 2009.

Etherington, Mark. *Revolt on the Tigris: The al-Sadr Uprising and the Governing of Iraq*. London: Hurst, 2005.

Fallon, William J. "Surge Protector." *New York Times*, July 20, 2008, p. 13.

Fallows, James. "The Fifty-First State?" *Atlantic Monthly* (November 2002): 53–64.

———. "Bush's Lost Year: How the War on Iraq Undermined the War on Terror." *Atlantic Monthly* (October 2004): 68--84.

———. "Why Iraq Has No Army." *Atlantic Monthly* (December 2005).

———. *Blind into Baghdad: America's War in Iraq*. New York: Vintage Books, 2006.

Fassihi, Farnaz. *Waiting for an Ordinary Day: The Unraveling of Life in Iraq*. New York: PublicAffairs, 2009.

Fawn, Rick, and Raymond Hinnebusch, eds. *The Iraq War: Causes and Consequences.* Boulder: Lynn Rienner Publishers, 2006.

Fearon, James. "Iraq's Civil War." *Foreign Affairs* 86, no. 2 (March/April 2007): 2–16.

Feaver, Peter. "Anatomy of the Surge." *Commentary*, April 2008.

Feith, Douglas J. *War and Decision: Inside the Pentagon at the Dawn of the War on Terrorism.* New York: HarperCollins, 2008.

Feldman, Noah. *What We Owe Iraq: War and Ethics of Nation Building.* Princeton: Princeton University Press, 2004.

———. "The Democratic Fatwa: Islam and Democracy in the Realm of Constitutional Politics." *Oklahoma Law Review* 58, no. 1 (Spring 2005).

Ferguson, Charles H. *No End in Sight: Iraq's Descent into Chaos.* New York: PublicAffairs, 2008.

Fick, Nathaniel. *One Bullet Away*. New York: Houghton Mifflin, 2005.

Filkins, Dexter. *The Forever War*. New York: Alfred A. Knopf, 2008.

Finkel, David. *The Good Soldiers*. New York: Farrar, Straus and Giroux, 2009.

Fisher, Louis. "Deciding on War against Iraq: Institutional Failures." *Political Science Quarterly* 118, no. 3 (Fall 2003).

Fleischer, Ari. *Taking Heat: The President, the Press, and My Years in the White House*. New York: William Morris, 2005.

Flippert, Andrew. "The Road to Baghdad: Ideas and Intellectuals in Explanations of the Iraq War." *Security Studies* 15, no. 2 (April–June 2006): 310–52.

Franks, Tommy, with Malcolm McConnell. *American Soldier*. New York: Regan Books, 2004.

Freedman, Lawrence. "War in Iraq: Selling the Threat." *Survival* 46, no. 2 (Summer 2004): 7–49.

———. "Writing of Wrongs." *Foreign Affairs* 5, no. 1 (January–February 2006): 129–34.

———. *A Choice of Enemies: America Confronts the Middle East.* New York: PublicAffairs, 2008.

Freedman, Lawrence, and Efraim Karsh. *The Gulf Conflict, 1990–1991: Diplomacy and War in the New World Order.* Princeton: Princeton University Press, 1993.

French, Peter S., and Jason A. Short, eds. *War and Border Crossings: Ethics when Cultures Clash*. Lanham, MD: Rowman and Littlefield, 2005.

Frum, David. *The Right Man: An Inside Account of the Surprise Presidency of George W. Bush*. London: Random House, 2003.

Fukuyama, Francis. "Nation-Building 101." *Atlantic Monthly* (January–February 2006); available at http://www.theatlantic.com/doc/200401/fukuyama.

———. *America at the Crossroads: Democracy, Power and the Neoconservative Legacy*. New Haven: Yale University Press, 2006.

Gaddis, John Lewis. *Surprise, Security, and the American Experience*. Cambridge, MA: Harvard University Press, 2004.

———. "Grand Strategy in the Second Term." *Foreign Affairs* 84, no. 2 (March–April 2005): 2–15.

Galbraith, Peter W. "How to Get Out of Iraq." *New York Review of Books* 51, no. 8 (May 13, 2004).

———. *The End of Iraq: How American Incompetence Created a War without End*. New York: Simon and Schuster, 2006.

———. "After Iraq: Picking up the Pieces." *Current History* 106 (December 2007): 403–8.

———. *Unintended Consequences: How War in Iraq Strengthened America's Enemies*. New York: Simon and Schuster, 2008.

Gallagher, Matt. *Kaboom: Embracing the Suck in a Savage Little War*. Cambridge, MA: Da Capo, 2010.

Galvin, John Rogers, and David Petraeus. "Uncomfortable Wars: Toward a New Paradigm." *Parameters* 16 (Winter 1986): 2–8.

Gates, Robert M. *From the Shadows: The Ultimate Insider's Story of Five Presidents and How They Won the Cold War*. New York: Simon and Schuster, 1996.

Gavrilis, Major James A. "The Mayor of Ar Rutbah: A Special Forces Account of Post-Conflict Iraq." *Foreign Policy* (November–December 2005).

Gentile, Gian P. "A (Slightly) Better War: A Narrative and Its Defects." *World Affairs* (Summer 2008).

Gellman, Barton. *Angler: The Cheney Vice Presidency*. New York: Penguin Press, 2008.

Gelpi, Christopher, Peter D. Feaver, and Jason Reifler. "Success Matters: Casualty Sensitivity and the War in Iraq." *International Security* (Winter 2005–6).

Gerecht, Reuel Marc. "Liberate Iraq: Is the Bush Administration Serious about Toppling Saddam Hussein?" *Weekly Standard*, May 14, 2001.

Ghareeb, Edmund, and Beth Dougherty. *The Historical Dictionary of Iraq*. Lanham, MD: Scarecrow Press, 2004.

Glees, Anthony, and Philip H. J. Davies. "Intelligence, Iraq and the Limits of Legislative Accountability during Political Crisis." *Intelligence and National Security* 21 (October 2006).

Goetz, John, and Bob Drogin. "'Curveball' Speaks, and a Reputation as a Disinformation Agent Remains Intact." *Los Angeles Times*, June 18, 2008.

Goldberg, Jeffrey. "A Little Learning: What Douglas Feith Knew, and When He Knew It." *New Yorker* (May 9, 2005).

———. "Breaking Ranks: What Brent Scowcroft Tried to Tell Bush." *New Yorker* (October 31, 2005): 54–65.

———. "After Iraq." *Atlantic Monthly* (January/February 2008): 68–79.

Goldfarb, Michael. *Ahmad's War, Ahmad's Peace: Surviving under Saddam, Dying in the New Iraq*. New York: Carroll and Graf, 2005.

Gordon, Michael R., and Bernard E. Trainor. *The Generals' War: The Inside Story of the Conflict in the Gulf*. Boston: Little, Brown, 1995.

———. *Cobra II: The Inside Story of the Invasion and Occupation of Iraq*. New York: Pantheon, 2006.

———. "The Former Insurgent Counterinsurgency." *New York Times Magazine* (September 6, 2007): 35–41.

———. "The Last Battle: The Fight among Iraq's Shiites." *New York Times Magazine* (August 3, 2008): 34–43, 53–55.

Gordon, Philip H., and Michael O'Hanlon. "Should the War on Terrorism Target Iraq?" Policy Brief, no. 53. Washington, DC: Brookings Institution, January 2002.

Gordon, Philip H., and Jeremy Shapiro. *Allies at War: America, Europe and the Crisis over Iraq*. New York: McGraw-Hill, 2004.

———. "The End of the Bush Revolution." *Foreign Affairs* 85, no. 4 (July–August 2006): 75–86.

———. *Winning the Right War: The Path to Security for America and the World*. New York: Times Books, 2007.

Gourevitch, Philip, and Errol Morris. *Standard Operating Procedure*. New York: Penguin Books, 2008; subsequently republished as *The Ballad of Abu Ghraib*. New York: Penguin Books, 2009.

Graham, Bradley. *By His Own Rules: The Ambitions, Successes, and Ultimate Failures of Donald Rumsfeld*. New York: PublicAffairs, 2009.

Graubard, Stephen. *Mr. Bush's War: Adventures in the Politics of Illusion*. New York: Hill and Wang, 1991.

Graveline, Christopher, and Michael Clemens. *The Secrets of Abu Ghraib Revealed*. Dulles, VA: Potomac Books, 2009.

Greenberg, Karen J., and Joshua L. Dratel, eds. *The Torture Papers: The Road to Abu Ghraib*. New York: Cambridge University Press, 2005.

Greenstein, Fred. "The Changing Leadership of George W. Bush: A Pre- and Post-9/11 Comparison." *Presidential Studies Quarterly* 32, no. 2 (June 2002): 387–96.

Gregg, Heather S., Hy S. Rothstein, and John Arquilla. *The Three Circles of War: Understanding the Dynamics of Conflict in Iraq*. Dulles, VA: Potomac Books, 2009.

Guertner, Gary L. "European Views of Preemption in US National Security Policy." *Parameters* 37, no. 2 (Summer 2007): 31–44.

Gurtov, Mel. *Superpower on Crusade: The Bush Doctrine in US Foreign Policy*. Boulder, CO: Lynn Rienner Publishers, 2006.

Gurtov, Mel, and Peter Van Ness, eds. *Confronting the Bush Doctrine: Critical Views from the Asia-Pacific*. London: Routledge, 2005.

Haass. Richard. *The Opportunity: America's Moment to Alter History*. New York: PublicAffairs, 2005.

———. "The New Middle East." *Foreign Affairs* 85, no. 6 (November/December 2006): 2–12.

———. *War of Necessity, War of Choice: A Memoir of Two Iraq Wars*. New York: Simon and Schuster, 2009.

Haley, P. Edward. *Strategies of Dominance: The Misdirection of US Foreign Policy*. Baltimore, MD: Woodrow Wilson Center Press/Johns Hopkins University Press, 2006.

Halper, Stefan, and Jonathan Clarke. *America Alone: The Neo-Conservatives and the Global Order*. Cambridge, UK: Cambridge University Press, 2004.

Hamre, John, et al. *Iraq's Post-Conflict Reconstruction: A Field Review and Recommendations*. Washington, DC: Center for International and Strategic Studies, July 17, 2003.

Hannay, David. "Three Iraqi Intelligence Failures Reconsidered." *Survival* 51, no. 6 (December 2009–January 2010): 13–20.

Hanson, Victor Davis. *Between War and Peace: Lessons from Afghanistan and Iraq*. New York: Random House, 2004.

Hashim, Ahmed. "Insurgency in Iraq." *Small Wars and Insurgencies* 14, no. 3 (2003): 1–22.

———. "Military Power and State Formation in Modern Iraq." *Middle East Policy* 10, no. 4 (2004): 29–47.

———. "Iraq: From Insurgency to Civil War?" *Current History* (January 2005).

———. *Insurgency and Counterinsurgency in Iraq*. Ithaca, NY: Cornell University Press, 2006.

———. "Iraq's Civil War." *Current History* 106 (January 2007): 3–10.

Hayes, Stephen F. "Saddam's al Qaeda Connection." *Weekly Standard* 8, no. 48 (September 1, 2003).

———. "Case Closed: The U.S. Government's Secret Memo Detailing Cooperation between Saddam Hussein and Osama bin Laden." *Weekly Standard* 9, no. 11 (November 24, 2003).

———. *The Connection: How al Qaeda's Collaboration with Saddam Hussein Has Endangered America*. New York: HarperCollins, 2004.

———. *Cheney: The Untold Story of America's Most Powerful and Controversial Vice President*. New York: HarperCollins, 2007.

Hedges, Chris, and Laila Al-Arian. *Collateral Damage: America's War against Iraqi Civilians*. New York: Nation Books, 2008.

Hendrickson, David, and Robert Tucker. "Revisions in Need of Revising: What Went Wrong in the Iraq War?" *Survival* 47, no. 2 (2005): 7–32.

Herman, Arthur. "How to Win in Iraq—and How to Lose." *Commentary* 123, no. 4 (2007): 23–29.

Herring, Eric, and Glen Rangwala. *Iraq in Fragments: The Occupation and Its Legacy*. Ithaca, NY: Cornell University Press, 2007.

Hersh, Seymour M. "Offense and Defense: The Battle between Donald Rumsfeld and the Pentagon." *New Yorker* (April 7, 2003).

———. "Selective Intelligence." *New Yorker* (May 12, 2003).

———. "The War Plans." *New Yorker* (April 17, 2006): 30–37.

Herspring, Dale. *Rumsfeld's Wars: The Arrogance of Power*. Lawrence: University Press of Kansas, 2008.

Hoffman, Bruce. *Insurgency and Counterinsurgency in Iraq*. Occasional Paper OP-127-IPC/CMEPP. Santa Monica, CA: RAND Corporation, 2004.

Hoffman, Frank. "The Marines in Review." *U.S. Naval Institute Proceedings* (May 2005).

Hooker, Gregory. *Shaping the Plan for Operation Iraqi Freedom*. Washington, DC: Washington Institute for Near East Policy, 2005.

Human Rights Watch. *The Graves of al-Mahawill*, May 2003; available at http://hrw.org/reports/2003/iraq0503/.

———. "Violent Response: The US Army in al-Faqllujah." *Middle East Report* 15, no. 7 (June 2003); available at www.hrw.org.

———. "'No Blood, No Foul': Soldiers' Accounts of Detainee Abuse in Iraq." *Human Rights Reports* 28, no. 3 (July 2006); available at www.hw.org/reports/2006/us0706/.

Hybel, Alex Roberto, and Justin Matthew Kaufman. *The Bush Administrations and Saddam Hussein: Deciding on Conflict*. New York: Palgrave Macmillan, 2006.

Ignatieff, Michael. "Why Are We in Iraq? And Liberia? And Afghanistan?" *New York Times Magazine* (September 7, 2003): 38–43.

Ikenberry, John G. "America's Imperial Ambitions." *Foreign Affairs* 77 (September/October 2002).

———. "The End of the Neo-Conservative Moment." *Survival* 46, no. 1 (Spring 2004): 7–22.

International Crisis Group. "Baghdad: A Race against the Clock." *Middle East Briefing* 6 (June 11, 2003); available at wwwlicrc.org.

———. "Governing Iraq." *Middle East Report*, no. 17 (August 25, 2003).

———. "In Their Own Words: Reading the Iraqi Insurgency." *Middle East Report*, no. 50 (February 15, 2006).

———. "The Next Iraq War? Sectarianism and Civil Conflict." *Middle East Report*, no. 52 (February 27, 2006).

———. "Iraq and the Kurds: The Brewing Battle over Kirkuk." *Middle East Report*, no. 58 (July 18, 2006).

———. "Where Is Iraq Heading? Lessons from Basra." *Middle East Report*, no. 67 (June 25, 2007).

International Institute for Strategic Studies. *Iraq's Weapons of Mass Destruction: A Net Assessment*. IISS Strategic Dossier. London: IISS, September 9, 2002.

Isikoff, Michael, and David Corn. *Hubris: The Inside Story of Spin, Scandal, and the Selling of the Iraq War*. New York: Crown Publishing, 2006.

Jabar, Faleh A. "Postconflict Iraq: A Race for Stability, Reconstruction, and Legitimacy." Special Report, no. 120. Washington, DC: U.S. Institute of Peace, May 2004.

Jackson, Mike. *Soldier: The Autobiography*. London: Bantam Press, 2007.

Jamail, Dahr. *The Will to Resist: Soldiers Who Refuse to Fight in Iraq and Afghanistan*. Chicago: Haymarket Books, 2009.

Jehl, Douglas, and David Sanger. "Powell's Case a Year Later: Gaps in Picture of Iraq Arms." *New York Times*, February 1, 2004, p. A10.

Jennings, Ray Salvatore. "The Road Ahead: Lessons in Nation-Building from Japan, Germany, and Afghanistan for Postwar Iraq." *Peaceworks* 49. Washington, DC: U.S. Institute of Peace, 2003.

Jentleson, Bruce W. *With Friends Like These: Reagan, Bush, and Saddam, 1982–1990*. New York: W. W. Norton, 1994.

———. "America's Global Role after Bush." *Survival* 49, no. 3 (Autumn 2007): 179–200.

Jervis, Robert. "Understanding the Bush Doctrine." *Political Science Quarterly* 118, no. 3 (Fall 2003): 365–88.

———. "Why the Bush Doctrine Cannot Be Sustained." *Political Science Quarterly* 120 (Fall 2005).

———. *American Foreign Policy in a New Era*. New York: Routledge, 2005.

———. "Reports, Politics, and Intelligence Failures: The Case of Iraq." *Journal of Strategic Studies* 29 (February 2006): 3–52.

———. "The Remaking of a Unipolar World." *Washington Quarterly* 29, no. 3 (2006–7): 7–19.

———. "War, Intelligence, and Honesty: A Review Essay." *Political Science Quarterly* 123, no. 4 (Winter 2008–9): 645–75.

———. *Why Intelligence Fails: Lessons from the Iranian Revolution and the Iraq War*. Ithaca, NY: Cornell University Press, 2009.

Johnson, David. "Saddam Hussein Sowed Confusion about Iraq's Arsenal as a Tactic of War." *New York Times*, October 7, 2004, p. A22.

Johnson, James Turner. *The War to Oust Saddam Hussein: Just War and the New Face of Conflict*. Lanham, MD: Rowman and Littlefield, 2005.

Judis, John B., and Spencer Ackerman. "The Selling of the Iraq War: The First Casualty." *New Republic* (June 30, 2003).

Kagan, Frederick W. *Finding the Target: The Transformation of American Military Policy*. New York: Encounter Books, 2006.

———. "Iraq Is Not Vietnam: A Pernicious Equivalence." *Policy Review* (January 2006).

Kagan, Kimberly. *The Surge: A Military History*. New York: Encounter Books, 2009.

Kampfner, John. *Blair's Wars*. London: Free Press, 2003.

Kaplan, Lawrence F., and William Kristol. *The War over Iraq: Saddam Hussein's Tyranny and America's Mission*. San Francisco: Encounter Books, 2003.

Kaplan, Robert D. "A Post-Saddam Scenario." *Atlantic Monthly* (November 2002): 88–90.

———. "Five Days in Fallujah: Going In with the Marines." *Atlantic Monthly* (July–August 2005).

———. "What Rumsfeld Got Right." *Atlantic Monthly* (July–August 2008): 64–74.

Karsh, Efraim, and Inari Rautsi. *Saddam Hussein: A Political Biography*. London: Brassey's, 1991.

Katzman, Kenneth. *Iraq: U.S. Efforts to Change the Regime*. Washington, DC: Congressional Research Service, March 22, 2002.

———. *Iraq: Oil for Food Program, International Sanctions, and Illicit Trade*. Report RL30472. Washington, DC: Congressional Research Service, March 21, 2005.

———. *Iraq: U.S. Regime Change Efforts and Post-Saddam Governance*. Report RL31339. Washington, DC: Congressional Research Service, April 5, 2005.

Kaufman, Chaim. "Threat Inflation and the Failure of the Marketplace of Ideas: The Selling of the Iraq War." *International Security* 29, no. 1 (Summer 2004): 5–48.

Kaufman, Robert. *The Bush Doctrine*. Lexington: University Press of Kentucky, 2007.

Kay, David. "Iraq's Weapons of Mass Destruction." *Miller Center Report* 20 (Spring/Summer 2004): 6–14.

Keegan, John. *Iraq War: The Military Offensive, From Victory in 21 Days to the Insurgent Aftermath*. New York: Vintage Press, 2005.

Kegley, Charles W., Jr., and Gregory A. Raymond. "Preventive War and Permissive Normative Order." *International Studies Perspectives* 4, no. 4 (November 2003): 385–94.

———. *After Iraq: The Imperiled American Imperium*. New York: Oxford University Press, 2007.

Keiler, Jonathan. "Who Won the Battle of Fallujah?" *U.S. Naval Institute Proceedings* (January 2005).

Keller, Bill. "The World According to Powell." *New York Times Magazine* (November 25, 2001).

———. "The Sunshine Warrior." (Profile of Paul Wolfowitz) *New York Times Magazine* (September 22, 2002).

Kelly, Michael J. *Ghosts of Halabja: Saddam Hussein and the Kurdish Genocide*. New York: Praeger, 2008.

Kerr, Richard, Thomas Wolfe, Rebecca Donegan, and Aris Pappas. "Collection and Analysis on Iraq: Issues for the US Intelligence Community." *Studies in Intelligence* 49, no. 3 (2005): 47–54.

Khaddur, Majid, and Edmund Ghareeb. *War in the Gulf 1990–1991: The Iraq-Kuwait Conflict and Its Implications*. New York: Oxford University Press, 2002.

Khalilzad, Zalmay, and Paul Wolfowitz. "We Must Lead the Way in Deposing Saddam." *Washington Post*, November 10, 1997, p. C9.

Kinsella, David. *Regime Change: Origins, Execution, and Aftermath of the Iraq War*, 2nd ed. Belmont, CA: Thomson Wadsworth, 2007.

Kitfield, James. *War and Destiny: How the Bush Revolution in Foreign and Military Affairs Redefined American Power*. Washington, DC: Potomac Books, 2005.

Klein, Naomi. "Baghdad Year Zero." *Harper's* (September 2004).

Knights, Michael, ed. *Operation Iraqi Freedom and the New Iraq*. Washington, DC: Washington Institute for Near East Policy, 2004.

———. *Cradle of Conflict: Iraq and the Birth of the Modern U.S. Military*. Annapolis, MD: Naval Institute Press, 2005.

Kohlhaas, Charles A. "War in Iraq: Not Quite a 'War for Oil.'" *National Interest* (March 5, 2003).

Korb, Lawrence, and Caroline Wadhams. "A Critique of the Bush Administration's National Security Strategy." Policy Analysis Brief. Muscatine, Iowa: Stanley Foundation, June 2006.

Krasno, Jean, and James S. Suttering. *The United Nations and Iraq: Defanging the Viper.* New York: Praeger, 2003.

Krauthammer, Charles. *Democratic Realism: An American Foreign Policy for a Unipolar World.* Washington, DC: AEI Press, 2004.

Krebs, Ronald R., and Jennifer K. Lobasz. "Fixing the Meaning of 9/11: Hegemony, Coercion, and the Road to the War in Iraq." *Security Studies* 16, no. 3 (July–September 2007): 409–51.

Krepinevich, Andrew F., Jr. *The Army and Vietnam.* Baltimore, MD: Johns Hopkins University Press, 1988.

———. "How to Win in Iraq." *Foreign Affairs* 84, no. 5 (September/October 2005): 87–104.

Kull, Steven, Clay Ramsey, and Evan Lewis. "Misperception, the Media, and the Iraq War." *Political Science Quarterly* 118 (Winter 2003–4): 569–98.

Kumins, Lawrence. "Iraq Oil: Reserves, Production and Potential Revenues." Washington, DC: Congressional Research Service, September 29, 2003.

Laird, Melvin. "Iraq: Learning the Lessons of Vietnam." *Foreign Affairs* 84, no. 6 (November/December 2005): 22–43.

Lamanna, Lawrence. "Documenting the Differences between American and British Intelligence Reports." *International Journal of Intelligence and Counterintelligence* 20 (Winter 2007): 602–28.

Lampe, John R. "The Lessons of Bosnia and Kosovo for Iraq." *Current History* 671 (March 2004): 113–18.

Laver, Harry S. "Preemption and the Evolution of America's Strategic Defense." *Parameters* 35, no. 2 (2005): 107–20.

Lebovic, James H. *The Limits of U.S. Military Capability: Lessons from Vietnam and Iraq.* Baltimore, MD: Johns Hopkins University Press, 2010.

Lemann, Nicholas. "The Quiet Man: Dick Cheney's Discreet Rise to Unprecedented Power." *New Yorker* (May 7, 2001).

———. "Without a Doubt." *New Yorker* (October 14 and 21, 2002): 164–79.

———. "After Iraq: The Plan to Remake the Middle East." *New Yorker* (November 2, 2003).

Litaker, Eric. "Efforts to Counter the IED Threat." *Marine Corps Gazette* (January 2005).

Litwak, Robert S. *Regime Change: U.S. Strategy through the Prism of 9/11.* Washington, DC, and Baltimore: Woodrow Wilson Center Press and the Johns Hopkins University Press, 2007.

Luban, David. "Preventive War." *Philosophy and Public Affairs* 32, no. 3 (2004): 207–48.

Lynch, Timothy J., and Robert S. Singh. *After Bush: The Case for Continuity in American Foreign Policy.* New York: Cambridge University Press, 2008.

Maass, Peter. "The Salvadorization of Iraq?" *New York Times Magazine* (May 1, 2005).

Mabry, Marcus. *Twice as Good: Condoleezza Rice and Her Path to Power.* New York: Holtzbrinck, 2007.

Mahnken, Thomas. "Spies and Bureaucrats: Getting Intelligence Right." *Public Interest* 81 (Spring 2005).

Mahnken, Thomas G., and Thomas A. Keaney, eds. *War in Iraq: Planning and Execution.* New York: Routledge, 2007.

Makiya, Kanan (Samir al-Khalil). *Republic of Fear: The Politics of Modern Iraq.* Berkeley: University of California Press, 1989.

Malkasian, Carter. "Signalling Resolve, Democratization, and the First Battle of Fallujah." *Journal of Strategic Studies* (June 2006).

Malone, David M. *The International Struggle over Iraq: Politics in the UN Security Council 1980–2005.* London: Oxford University Press, 2006.

Mann, James. *Rise of the Vulcans: The History of Bush's War Cabinet.* New York: Viking, 2004.

Manning, David. "Prime Minister: Your Trip to the U.S." British Government Memo, March 14, 2002; http://www.downingstreetmemo.com.

Mansoor, Peter R. "Spears and Plowshares: Equipping the Force for Operations in Iraq." *RUSI Defense Systems* (Spring 2005): 64–68.

———. *Baghdad at Sunrise: A Brigade Commander's War in Iraq.* New Haven: Yale University Press, 2008.

Marr, Phoebe. "Looking Forward: Can the Untied States Shape a 'New' Iraq?" *Miller Center Report* 19, no. 3 (Fall/Winter 2003): 6–13.

———. *The Modern History of Iraq.* 2nd ed. Boulder, CO: Westview Press, 2004.

Marshall, Joshua Micah. "The Reluctant Hawk: The Skeptical Case for Regime Change in Iraq." *Washington Monthly* (November 2002).

Mayer, Jane. "The Manipulator." *New Yorker* (June 7, 2004).

Mazarr, Michael J. "The Iraq War and Agenda Setting." *Foreign Policy Analysis* 3, no. 1 (January 2007): 1–23.

Mazzetti, Mark. "Spy Agencies Say Iraq War Worsens Terrorism Threat." *New York Times,* September 24, 2006, p. A1.

Mazzetti, Mark, and David E. Sanger. "Bush Advisers See a Failed Strategy against Al Qaeda." *New York Times,* July 18, 2007, p. A1.

McCaffrey, General Barry R. "Visit Iraq and Kuwait 5–11 December 2007." Memorandum for Colonel Michael Meese, December 18, 2007.

———. "Visit Iraq and Kuwait 31 October–6 November 2008." Memorandum for Colonel Michael Meese. November 14, 2008.

McClellan, Scott. *What Happened: Inside the Bush White House and Washington's Culture of Deceit.* New York: PublicAffairs, 2008.

McDowell, David. *The Modern History of the Kurds.* London: I. B. Taurus, 2000.

McMaster, H. R. *Dereliction of Duty: Lyndon Johnson, Robert McNamara, the Joint Chiefs of Staff, and the Lies That Led to Vietnam.* New York: HarperPerrenial, 1998.

———. "On War: Lessons to Be Learned." *Survival* 50, no. 1 (February–March 2008): 19–30.

Mearsheimer, John J., and Stephen M. Walt. "Iraq: An Unnecessary War." *Foreign Policy* 134 (January/February 2003): 51–59.

———. *The Israel Lobby and U.S. Foreign Policy*. New York: Farrar, Straus and Giroux, 2007.

Metz, Helen Chapin, ed. *Iraq: A Country Study*. Washington, DC: Government Printing Office, 1990.

Metz, Steven. "Insurgency and Counterinsurgency in Iraq." *Washington Quarterly* 27, no. 1 (2003–4).

———. *Iraq and the Evolution of American Strategy*. Washington, DC: Potomac Books, 2008.

Michaels, Jim. *A Chance in Hell*. New York: St. Martin's, 2010.

Milbank, Dana. "Colonel Finally Sees the Whites of Their Eyes." *Washington Post*, October 20, 2005.

Miller, James N., and Shawn W. Brimley. *Phased Transition: A Responsible Way Forward and Out of Iraq*. Washington, DC: Center for a New American Security, June 2007.

Miller, T. Christian. "Contractors Outnumber Troops in Iraq." *Los Angeles Times*, July 4, 2007, p. A1.

Military Review. Special Edition—Interagency Reader. Fort Leavenworth, KS: Combined Arms Center, June 2008.

Mitchell, David, and Tansa George Massoud. "Anatomy of Failure: Bush's Decision-Making Process and the Iraq War." *Foreign Policy Analysis* 5, no. 3 (July 2009): 265–86.

Monten, Jonathan. "The Roots of the Bush Doctrine." *International Security* 29 (Spring 2005): 140–53.

Mueller, John. "The Iraq Syndrome." *Foreign Affairs* 84, no. 6 (November/December 2005): 44–54.

Muravchik, Joshua. "The Bush Manifesto." *Commentary* (December 1, 2002).

Murphy, Richard W., Chair. *Winning the Peace: Managing a Successful Transition in Iraq*. Policy Paper. Washington, DC: American University and the Atlantic Council of the United States, January 2003.

Murray, Williamson, and Robert H. Scales, Jr. *The Iraq War: A Military History*. Cambridge, MA: Harvard University Press, 2003.

Myers, Richard B., with Malcolm McConnell. *Eyes on the Horizon: Serving the Front Lines of National Security*. New York: Threshold Editions, 2009.

Myers, Richard, and Richard H. Kohn. "Salute and Disobey: The Military's Place." *Foreign Affairs* (September/October 2007).

Mylroie, Laurie. *The War against America: Saddam Hussein and the World Trade Center Attacks: A Study of Revenge*. New York: HarperCollins, 2001.

Nakash, Yitzhak. *The Shi'is of Iraq*, rev. ed. Princeton: Princeton University Press, 2003.

———. "The Shi'ites and the Future of Iraq." *Foreign Affairs* 82, no. 4 (July–August 2003): 17–26.

Newbold, Lieutenant General Greg. "Why Iraq Was a Mistake." *Time* (April 17, 2006).

Newhouse, John. *Imperial America: The Bush Assault on the World.* New York: Alfred A. Knopf, 2003.

Newnham, Randall. "'Coalition of the Bribed and Bullied?' U.S. Economic Linkage and the Iraq War Coalition." *International Studies Perspectives* 9 (2008): 183–200.

O'Hanlon, Michael E. "Iraq without a Plan." *Policy Review* 128 (December 2004–January 2005): 33–45.

O'Hanlon, Michael E., and Kenneth Pollack. "A War We Just Might Win." *New York Times*, July 30, 2007.

Ollivant, Douglas A., and Eric D. Chewning. "Producing Victory: Rethinking Conventional Forces in COIN Operations." *Military Review* (July/August 2006): 50–59.

Orr, Robert C., ed. *Winning the Peace.* Washington, DC: Center for Strategic and International Studies Press, 2004.

O'Sullivan, Christopher D. *Colin Powell: American Power and Intervention from Vietnam to Iraq*. Lanham, MD: Rowman and Littlefield, 2009.

O'Sullivan, Meghan. *Iraq: Time for a Modified Approach*. Washington, DC: Brookings Institution, 2001.

Packer, George. *The Assassins' Gate: America in Iraq*. New York: Farrar, Straus and Giroux, 2005.

———. "Letter from Iraq: The Lesson of Tal Afar." *New Yorker* (March 10, 2006).

———. "Knowing the Enemy." *New Yorker* (December 18, 2006).

———. "Betrayed: The Iraqis Who Trusted America the Most." *New Yorker* (March 26, 2007).

———. *Interesting Times: Writings from a Turbulent Decade*. New York: Farrar, Straus and Giroux, 2009.

Pearson, Graham S. *The Search for Iraq's Weapons of Mass Destruction: Inspection, Verification, and Non-Proliferation*. New York: Palgrave Macmillan, 2005.

Peleg, Ilan. *The Legacy of George W. Bush's Foreign Policy: Moving beyond Neoconservatism.* Boulder, CO: Westview Press, 2009.

Pemberton, Miriam, and William D. Hartung, eds. *Lessons from Iraq: Avoiding the Next War*. Boulder, CO: Paradigm Publishers, 2008.

Perito, Robert M. *Provincial Reconstruction Teams in Iraq*. Special Report 185. Washington, DC: United States Institute of Peace, March 2007.

Petraeus, David Howell. *The American Military and the Lessons of Vietnam: A Study of Military Influence and the Use of Force in the Post-Vietnam Era*. Doctoral dissertation. Woodrow Wilson School of Public and International Affairs, Princeton University, 1987.

———. "Lessons of History and Lessons of Vietnam." In Lloyd J. Matthews and Dale E. Brown, eds. *Assessing the Vietnam War*. McLean, VA: Pergamon-Brassey's, 1987, pp. 171–88.

———. "Military Influence and the Post-Vietnam Use of Force." *Armed Forces and Society* 15 (Summer 1989): 489–505.

———. "Battling for Iraq." *Washington Post,* September 26, 2004.

———. "Learning Counterinsurgency: Observations from Soldiering in Iraq." *Military Review* (January–February 2006): 2–12.

Pfiffner, James P. "Did President Bush Mislead the Country in His Arguments for War with Iraq?" *Presidential Studies Quarterly* 34, no. 1 (March 2004): 25–46.

Phillips, David L. *Losing Iraq: Inside the Postwar Reconstruction Fiasco.* Boulder, CO: Westview Press, 2005.

Phythian, Mark. "The Perfect Intelligence Failure? U.S. Pre-War Intelligence on Iraqi Weapons of Mass Destruction." *Politics & Polity* 34 (June 2006): 400–424.

Pickering, Thomas R. "Does the UN Have a Role in Iraq?" *Survival* 50, no. 1 (February–March 2008): 133–42.

Pillar, Paul. "Intelligence, Policy, and the War in Iraq." *Foreign Affairs* 85, no. 2 (March–April 2006): 15–28.

Pincus, Walter. "1,000 Iraqis a Day Flee Violence, U.N. Group Finds." *Washington Post,* November 24, 2006.

Podhoretz, Norman. "The War against World War IV." *Commentary* 119, no. 2 (February 2005): 23.

———. "Is the Bush Doctrine Dead?" *Commentary* 122, no. 2 (September 2006): 17–31.

Polk, William R. *Understanding Iraq.* New York: HarperCollins, 2005.

Pollack, Kenneth M. *The Threatening Storm: The Case for Invading Iraq.* New York: Random House, 2002.

———. "Next Stop Baghdad?" *Foreign Affairs* 81 (March/April 2002): 32–47.

———. "Spies, Lies, and Weapons: What Went Wrong." *Atlantic Monthly* (January–February 2004).

Porch, Douglas. "Occupational Hazards: Myths of 1945 & US Iraq Policy." *National Interest* 72 (Summer 2003): 35–47.

Posen, Barry. "Exit Strategy: How to Disengage from Iraq in 18 Months." *Boston Review* (January/February 2006); available at bostonreview.net/BR31.1/posen.html.

Powell, Colin L. "A Strategy of Partnership." *Foreign Affairs* 83, no. 1 (January–February 2004): 22–34.

Powell, Colin L., with Joseph Persico. *My American Journey.* New York: Random House, 1995.

Powers, Thomas. "War and Its Consequences." *New York Review of Books,* March 27, 2003.

Prados, John. *Hoodwinked: The Documents That Reveal How Bush Sold Us a War.* New York: New Press, 2004.

Preble, Chris, ed. *Exiting Iraq: Why the U.S. Must End the Military Occupation and Renew the War against Al Qaeda.* Washington, DC: Cato Institute, 2004.

Prestowitz, Clyde. *Rogue Nation: American Unilaterialism and the Failure of Good Intentions.* New York: Basic Books, 2003.

Prichard, Tim. *Ambush Alley: The Most Extraordinary Battle of the Iraq War.* New York: Random House, 2005.

Priest, Dana. *The Mission*. New York: W. W. Norton, 2003.

Purdum, Todd S. *A Time of Our Choosing: America's War in Iraq*. New York: Times Books, 2004.

Rampton, Sheldon, and John Stauber. *Weapons of Mass Deception: The Uses of Propaganda in Bush's War on Iraq*. New York: Penguin, 2003.

Rathmell, Andrew. "Planning Post-Conflict Reconstruction in Iraq: What Can We Learn?" *International Affairs* 81, no. 5 (2005).

Record, Jeffrey. "The Bush Doctrine and the War with Iraq." *Parameters* 33 (Spring 2003): 4–21.

———. "Bounding the Global War on Terrorism." Carlisle Barracks, PA: Strategic Studies Institute, U.S. Army War College, December 2003.

———. "Threat Confusion and Its Penalties." *Survival* 46, no. 2 (Summer 2004): 51–72.

———. *Dark Victory: America's Second War against Iraq*. Annapolis, MD: Naval Institute Press, 2004.

———. *Wanting War: Why the Bush Administration Invaded Iraq*. Dulles, VA: Potomac Books, 2009.

Record, Jeffrey, and W. Andrew Terrill. *Iraq and Vietnam: Differences, Similarities, and Insights*. Carlisle Barracks, PA: U.S. Army War College, May 2004.

Reese, Colonel Timothy R. "It's Time for the US to Declare Victory and Go Home." Memorandum from the Chief, Baghdad Operations Advisory Team, Baghdad, Iraq, July 31, 2009; www.nytimes.com.

Renshon, Stanley Allen, and Peter Suedfeld. *Understanding the Bush Doctrine: Psychology and Strategy in an Age of Terrorism*. New York: Routledge, 2007.

Reynolds, Nicholas. *Basrah, Baghdad, and Beyond: The U.S. Marine Corps in the Second Iraq War*. Annapolis, MD: U.S. Naval Institute Press, 2005.

Rhodes, Edward. "The Imperial Logic of Bush's Liberal Agenda." *Survival* 45, no. 1 (Spring 2003): 131–53.

Rice, Condoleezza. "Promoting the National Interest." *Foreign Affairs* 79, no. 1 (January–February 2000): 45–62.

———. "Rethinking the National Interest: American Realism for a New World." *Foreign Affairs* 87, no. 4 (July/August 2008): 2–27.

Ricks, Thomas E. *Fiasco: The American Military Adventure in Iraq*. New York: Penguin Press, 2006.

———. *The Gamble: General David Petraeus and the American Military Adventure in Iraq, 2006–2008*. New York: Penguin Press, 2009.

Rieff, David. "Blueprint for a Mess: How the Bush Administration's Prewar Planners Bungled Postwar Iraq." *New York Times Magazine* (November 2, 2003): 28–44.

Riggs, Richard. "Where Are the Weapons of Mass Destruction?" *U.S. Naval Institute Proceedings* (March 2004).

Risen, James. "The Struggle for Iraq: Intelligence Ex-Inspector Says CIA Missed Disarray in Iraqi Arms Program." *New York Times*, January 26, 2004.

———. *State of War: The Secret History of the CIA and the Bush Administration*. New York: Free Press, 2006.

Ritter, Scott. *Endgame: Solving the Iraq Problem Once and for All.* New York: Simon and Schuster, 1999.

———. "The Case for Iraq's Qualitative Disarmament." *Arms Control Today* (June 2000).

Roberts, Adam. "Law and the Use of Force after Iraq." *Survival* 45, no. 2 (Summer 2003): 31–56.

Roberts, Les, Riyadh Lafta, Richard Garfield, Jamal Khudhairi, and Gilbert Burnham. "Mortality after the 2003 Invasion of Iraq: A Cross Sectional Cluster Sample Survey." *Lancet* 368, issue 9545 (October 21, 2006): 1421–28.

Robinson, Linda. *Tell Me How This Ends: General David Petraeus and the Search for a Way Out of Iraq.* New York: PublicAffairs, 2008.

———. "What Petraeus Understands." www.ForeignPolicy.com, September 2008.

Robison, Sam. "George W. Bush and the Vulcans: Leader-Advisor Relations and America's Response to the 9/11 Attacks." In Mark Schafer and Stephen G. Walker, eds. *Beliefs and Leadership in World Politics: Methods and Applications of Operational Code Analysis.* New York: Palgrave/Macmillan, 2006, pp. 101–24.

Rose, David. "Neo Culpa: Now They Tell Us." *Vanity Fair* (November 3, 2006).

Rosen, Gary, ed. *The Right War: The Conservative Debate on Iraq*. New York: Cambridge University Press, 2005.

Rosen, Nir. "The Death of Iraq." *Current History* 106 (December 2007): 409–13.

———. *In the Body of the Green Bird: The Triumph of Martyrs in Iraq.* London: Free Press, 2006; updated version published as *The Triumph of the Martyrs: A Reporter's Journey into Occupied Iraq*. Washington, DC: Potomac Books, 2008.

Ross, Dennis B. *Statecraft: And How to Restore America's Standing in the World*. New York: Farrar, Straus and Giroux, 2007.

Roston, Aram. *The Man Who Pushed America to War: The Extraordinary Life, Adventures, and Obsessions of Ahmad Chalabi*. New York: Nation Books, 2008.

Roth, Ken. *War in Iraq: Not a Humanitarian Intervention*. World Report 2004. New York: Human Rights Watch, 2004; http://hrw.org/wr2k4/3.htm#_Toc58744952.

Rove, Karl. "Bush Was Right When It Mattered Most." *Wall Street Journal*, January 22, 2009, p. A15.

———. *Courage and Consequence: My Life as a Conservative in the Fight.* New York: Threshold Editions, 2010.

Rubin, Trudy. *Willful Blindness: The Bush Administration and Iraq*. Philadelphia: Philadelphia Inquirer, 2004.

Rumsfeld, Donald. "Transforming the Military." *Foreign Affairs* 81, no. 3 (May/June 2002).

———. *Known and Unknown: A Memoir*. New York: Sentinel, 2011.

Ryan, Maria. "Inventing the 'Axis of Evil': The Myth and Reality of US Intelligence and Policy-Making After 9/11." *Intelligence and National Security* 17, no. 4 (Winter 2002).

———. "Filling in the 'Unknowns': Hypothesis-Based Intelligence and the Rumsfeld Commission." *Intelligence and National Security* 21 (April 2006): 286–315.

Rycroft, Matthew. "Memo to David Manning, July 23." Reprinted in *New York Review of Books,* June 9, 2005, p. 71.

Sanchez, Ricardo, and Donald T. Philips. *Wiser in Battle: A Soldier's Story.* New York: Harper, 2008.

Sands, Philippe. *Lawless World: The Whistle-Blowing Account of How Bush and Blair Are Taking the Law into Their Own Hands.* New York: Penguin, 2006.

Scarborough, Rowan. *Rumsfeld's War: The Untold Story of America's Anti-Terrorist Commander.* Washington, DC: Regnery, 2004.

Schlesinger, Arthur, Jr. "Eyeless in Iraq." *New York Review of Books* 50 (October 9, 2003).

Schuman, Howard, and Amy Corning. "Comparing Iraq to Vietnam." *Public Opinion Quarterly* 70, no. 1 (Spring 2006): 78–87.

Schwarzkopf, H. Norman, with Peter Petre. *It Doesn't Take a Hero: The Autobiography.* New York: Bantam Books, 1992.

Scowcroft, Brent. "Don't Attack Saddam." *Wall Street Journal,* August 15, 2002, p. A19.

———. "Getting the Middle East Back on Our Side." *New York Times,* January 4, 2007, p. A23.

Seierstad, Asne. *A Hundred and One Days: A Baghdad Journal.* New York: Basic Books, 2006.

Shadid, Anthony. *Night Draws Near: Iraq's People in the Shadow of America's War.* New York: Henry Holt and Company, 2005.

Shawcross, William. *Allies: The U.S., Britain, Europe and the War in Iraq.* New York: PublicAffairs, 2004.

Shelton, Hugh, with Ronald Levinson and Malcolm McConnell. *Without Hesitation: The Odyssey of an American Warrior.* New York: St. Martin's, 2010.

Shinseki, General Erik K. "End of Tour Memorandum." Memorandum to the Secretary of Defense, June 10, 2003.

Shuster, Richard. "The Iraq Survey Group." *Journal of Strategic Studies* 31 (April 2008): 231–33.

Sifry, Micah L., and Christopher Cerf, eds. *The Iraq War Reader: History, Documents, Opinions.* New York: Touchstone, 2003.

Simon, Steven N. *After the Surge: The Case for U.S. Military Disengagement from Iraq.* Council Special Report, no. 23. New York: Council on Foreign Relations, February 2007.

———. "The Price of the Surge: How the U.S. Is Hastening Iraq's Demise." *Foreign Affairs* 87, no. 3 (May/June 2008): 57–76.

Singer, P. W. "Outsourcing War." *Foreign Affairs* 84, 2 (March/April 2005): 119–33.

Skidmore, David. "Understanding the Unilateralist Turn in US Foreign Policy." *Foreign Policy Analysis* 1, no. 2 (2005): 207–28.

Smidt, Corwin E. "Religion and American Attitudes toward Islam and an Invasion of Iraq." *Sociology of Religion* 66, no. 3 (Fall 2005): 243–62.

Sobel, Richard, Peter Furia, and Bethany Barratt, eds. *Public Opinion and International Intervention: Lessons from the Iraq War.* Dulles, VA: Potomac Books, 2009.

Solomon, Lewis D. *Paul D. Wolfowitz: Visionary Intellectual, Policymaker, and Strategist.* Westport, CT: Praeger, 2007.

Special Inspector General for Iraq Reconstruction. *Hard Lessons: The Iraq Reconstruction Experience.* New York: Bernan, 2009.

Spiegel, Peter. "Investigation Fills in Blanks on How War Groundwork Was Laid." *Los Angeles Times*, April 6, 2007, p. A10.

Stansfield, Gareth R. V. *Iraqi Kurdistan: Political Development and Emergency Democracy.* London: Routledge Curzon, 2003.

———. *Iraq: People, History, Politics.* Cambridge, UK: Polity, 2007.

Stauber, John. *Weapons of Mass Deception: The Uses of Propaganda in Bush's War on Iraq.* New York: Penguin, 2003.

Steele, Jonathan. *Defeat: Why America and Britain Lost Iraq.* Berkeley, CA: Counterpoint, 2008.

Steinberg, James. "The Bush Foreign Policy Revolution." *New Perspectives Quarterly* 20, no. 3 (Summer 2003): 5–14.

Steinbruner, John. "Confusing Ends and Means: The Doctrine of Coercive Pre-emption." *Arms Control Today* (January–February 2003).

Stephenson, James. *Losing the Golden Hour: An Insider's View of Iraq's Reconstruction.* Washington, DC: Potomac Books, 2007.

Stiglitz, Joseph E., and Linda J. Bilmes. *The Three Trillion Dollar War: The True Cost of the Iraq Conflict.* New York: W. W. Norton, 2008.

Strachan, Hew. "Strategy and the Limitation of War." *Survival* 50, no. 1 (February–March 2008): 31–54.

Sultan, Khaled bin. *Desert Warrior: A Personal View of the Gulf War by the Joint Forces Commander.* New York: HarperCollins, 1995.

Suskind, Ron. *The Price of Loyalty: George W. Bush, the White House, and the Education of Paul O'Neill.* New York: Simon and Schuster, 2004.

———. "Faith, Certainty and the Presidency of G. W. Bush." *New York Times Magazine* (October 17, 2004).

———. *The One Percent Doctrine: Deep Inside America's Pursuit of Its Enemy since 9/11.* New York: Simon and Schuster, 2007.

———. *The Way of the World: A Story of Truth and Hope in an Age of Extremism.* New York: HarperCollins, 2008.

Synnott, Hilary. "State-Building in Southern Iraq." *Survival* (Summer 2005).

Tannenhaus, Sam. "Interview with Paul Wolfowitz." *Vanity Fair*, May 9, 2003.

Tenet, George, with Bill Harlow. *At the Center of the Storm: My Years at the CIA.* New York: HarperCollins, 2007.

Tavernise, Sabrina, and Donald G. McNeil, Jr. "Iraqi Dead May Total 600,000, Study Says." *New York Times,* October 11, 2006, p. A16.

Trevan, Tim. *Saddam's Secrets: The Hunt for Iraq's Hidden Weapons.* London: HarperCollins, 1999.

Treverton, Gregory F. "Intelligence: The Achilles Heel of the Bush Doctrine." *Arms Control Today* (July–August 2003).

———. *Intelligence for an Age of Terror.* New York: Cambridge University Press, 2009.

Unger, Craig. *House of Bush, House of Saud: The Secret Relationship between the World's Two Most Powerful Dynasties.* New York: Scribner, 2004.

———. *The Fall of the House of Bush.* New York: Scribner, 2007.

United Kingdom. House of Commons. Defence Committee. *Iraq: An Initial Assessment of Post-Conflict Operations.* Sixth Report of Session 2004–5, vol. 1, March 16, 2005.

United Kingdom. House of Commons. Foreign Affairs Committee. *The Decision to Go to War in Iraq:* Ninth Report of Session 2002–2003, vol. I Report, July 3, 2003.

United Kingdom. House of Commons. Intelligence and Security Committee. *Iraqi Weapons of Mass Destruction—Intelligence and Assessments.* Cmnd [Command] 5972, September 2003.

United Kingdom. House of Commons. *Review of Intelligence on Weapons of Mass Destruction.* Report of a Committee of Privy Councillors (Butler Report), July 14, 2004.

United Kingdom. *The Iraq Inquiry.* Sir John Chilcot, Chairman. Evidence and testimonies available at: http://www.iraqinquiry.org.uk/transcripts.aspx/.

United Kingdom. Parliament. Joint Intelligence Committee. *International Terrorism: War with Iraq,* February 2003.

United Nations. *The Political Transition in Iraq: Report of the Fact-Finding Mission.* New York: United Nations, February 23, 2004.

U.S. Agency for International Development. *Iraq's Legacy of Terror: Mass Graves,* January 2004; available at www.usaid.gov/iraq/pdf/iraq_mass_graves.pdf.

U.S. Army. *On Point: The United States Army in Operation Iraqi Freedom.* Fort Leavenworth, KS: Combined Arms Center, Center for Lessons Learned, August 2004.

———. *On Point II: Transition to the New Campaign.* Fort Leavenworth, KS: Combined Arms Center, Center for Lessons Learned, June 2008.

———. *A Different Kind of War.* Fort Leavenworth, KS: Combat Studies Institute, 2009.

U.S. Central Intelligence Agency. "National Intelligence Estimate: Prospects for Iraq, Saddam and Beyond." National Intelligence Estimate (NIE) 93–42. December 1993.

———. "National Intelligence Estimate: Iraq's Continuing Programs for Weapons of Mass Destruction." October 2002.

———. "Principal Challenges in Post-Saddam Iraq." National Intelligence Council Report, January 2003.

———. Directorate of Intelligence. "Continuous Learning in the DI: May 2004 Review of Analytic Tradecraft Fundamentals." Sherman Kent School. *Tradecraft Review* 1 (August 2004).

———. *Comprehensive Report of the Special Adviser to the DCI on Iraq's WMD* (Duelfer Report), September 30, 2004; available at www.cia.gov/cia/reports/iraq_wmd_2004/index.html.

U.S. Commission on the Intelligence Capabilities of the United States Regarding Weapons of Mass Destruction. *Report to the President*, Laurence H. Silberman and Charles S. Robb, Co-Chairs. March 31, 2005; www.wmd.gov/report.

U.S. Congress. Congressional Research Service. *Iraq: Weapons Threat, Compliance, Sanctions, and U.S. Policy*, updated December 10, 2002.

———. Elaine Halchin. *The Coalition Provisional Authority (CPA): Origin, Characteristics and Institutional Authorities*, 2005.

———. *The Cost of Iraq, Afghanistan, and Other Global War on Terror Operations since 9/11.* Report to Congress no. RI 33110, updated June 23, 2008.

U.S. Congress. House of Representatives. *The Iraq Liberation Act.* 105th Cong., 2nd sess., H.R. 4655.

U.S. Congress. Joint Economic Committee. *War at Any Price? The Total Economic Costs of the War beyond the Federal Budget.* 110th Cong., 1st sess. (November 2007).

U.S. Congress. Senate. Armed Services Committee. *Lessons Learned during Operations in Afghanistan and Iraq.* Hearings, 108th Cong., 1st sess. (July 9, 2003).

———. *Operational Lessons Learned from Operation Iraqi Freedom.* October 2, 2003.

———. *Hearing on the Status of Iraqi Weapons of Mass Destruction and Related Programs.* 108th Cong., 2nd sess., January 28, 2004.

U.S. Congress. Senate. Foreign Relations Committee. *Hearing on Stabilization and Reconstruction Efforts.* 108th Cong., 1st sess., May 22, 2003.

U.S. Congress. Senate. Select Committee on Intelligence. *Report on the U.S. Intelligence Community's Prewar Intelligence Assessment on Iraq.* 108th Cong., 2nd sess., July 7, 2004.

———. *Report of the Select Committee on Intelligence on Postwar Findings about Iraq's WMD Programs and Links to Terrorism and How They Compare with Prewar Assessments,* September 8, 2006.

———. *The Use by the Intelligence Community of Information Provided by the Iraqi National Congress,* September 8, 2006.

———. *Report on Prewar Intelligence Assessments about Postwar Iraq.* 110th Cong., 1st sess. May 31, 2007.

———. *Report on Whether Public Statements Regarding Iraq by U.S. Government Officials Were Substantiated by Intelligence Information,* June 2008.

U.S. Department of Defense. Inspector General. *Review of Pre-Iraqi War Activities of the Office of the Under-Secretary for Policy.* Report No. 07-INTELL-04. Available at http: www.fas.org.irp.agency/dod/ig020907-dec;.pdf.

———. *Measuring Stability and Security in Iraq.* Report to Congress, December 2007.

U.S. Department of State. *Iraq Weekly Status Report.* Available at: http://www.state.gov/p/nea/rls/rpt/iraqstatus/.

———. "New State Department Releases on the 'Future of Iraq' Project." *Electronic Briefing Book*, no. 198. Washington, DC: National Security Archive, September 1, 2006.

U.S. Director of National Intelligence. *National Intelligence Estimate: Prospects for Iraq's Stability: A Challenging Road Ahead*, January 2007; available at www.dni.gov/press_releases/.

U.S. Government Accountability Office. *Rebuilding Iraq: Status of DoD's Reconstruction Programs*, 2006.

———. *Rebuilding Iraq: Governance, Security, Reconstruction, and Financing Challenges.* GAO-06-697T, April 25, 2006.

———. *Securing, Stabilizing, and Rebuilding Iraq: Iraqi Government Has Not Met Most Legislative, Security, and Economic Benchmarks.* Report to Congressional Committees, September 2007.

U.S. Office of the Special Inspector General for Iraq. Stewart W. Bowen, Jr., Chair. *Hard Lessons: The Iraq Reconstruction Experience.* Washington, DC, 2008.

U.S. The White House. *National Security Strategy of the United States*, September 2002; available at www.whitehouse.gov/nsc/nss.html.

———. *National Strategy for Victory in Iraq*, November 30, 2005; www.whitehouse.gov/infocus/iraq/iraq_national_strategy_20051130.pdf.

———. *The National Security Strategy of the United States of America.* Washington, DC: The White House, March 16, 2006.

Urquhart, Brian. "Hidden Truths." *New York Review of Books*, March 25, 2004.

Veritas: Journal of Army Special Forces History. Issue on Special Forces operations in the Iraq War, Winter 2005.

Wallsten, Scott, and Katrina Kosec. "The Iraq War: The Economic Costs." *Milken Institute Review* (Third Quarter, 2006): 16–23.

Walzer, Michael, and Nicolaus Mills, eds. *Getting Out: Historical Perspectives on Leaving Iraq*. Philadelphia: University of Pennsylvania Press, 2009.

Weisberg, Jacob. *The Bush Tragedy*. New York: Random House, 2008.

West, Bing. *The March Up: Taking Baghdad with the United States Marines*. New York: Bantam, 2004.

———. *No True Glory: A Frontline Account of the Battle for Fallujah*. New York: Bantam, 2005.

———. *The Strongest Tribe: War, Politics, and the Endgame in Iraq*. New York: Random House, 2008.

West, Nigel. "The UK's Not Quite So Secret Services." *International Journal of Intelligence and Counter Intelligence* 18 (Spring 2005): 23–30.

Western, Jon. "The War over Iraq: Selling the War to the American Public." *Security Studies* 14, no. 1 (January–February 2005): 106–39.

White, Jeffrey. *Iraq Fights Its War 'Outside-In.'*" Washington, DC: Washington Institute for Near East Policy, 2003.

———. *War in Iraq: A Preliminary Assessment.* Washington, DC: Washington Institute for Near East Policy, 2003.

———. *Faces of Battle: The Insurgents at Fallujah*. Washington, DC: Washington Institute for Near East Policy, 2004.

Wikileaks. *The Iraq War Logs*. www.wikileaks.org.

Wilkerson, Lawrence B. "The White House Cabal." *Los Angeles Times,* October 25, 2005, p. B 11.

Wilkie, Andrew. *Axis of Deceit: The Story of the Intelligence Officer Who Risked All to Tell the Truth about WMD and Iraq.* Melbourne, Australia: Black Inc. Agenda, 2004.

Williams, Kayla. *Love My Rifle More Than You.* New York: W. W. Norton, 2005.

Wilson, Joseph. "What I Didn't Find in Africa." *New York Times,* July 6, 2003, p. 9.

———. *The Politics of Truth: Inside the Lies that Led to War and Betrayed My Wife's CIA Identity*. New York: Carroll and Graf, 2004.

Wolfowitz, Paul, and Zalmay Khalilzad. "Overthrow Him." *Weekly Standard*, December 1, 1997, p. 14.

Wood, Trish, ed. *What Was Asked of Us: An Oral History of the Iraq War by the Soldiers Who Fought.* Boston: Little Brown, 2007.

Woods, Kevin, with Michael R. Pease, Mark E. Stout, Williamson Murray, and James G. Lacy. *Iraq: Perspectives Project: A View of Operation Iraqi Freedom from Saddam's Senior Leadership.* Joint Center for Operational Analysis, U.S. Joint Forces Command, March 2006.

Woods, Kevin, James Lacey, and Williamson Murray. "Saddam's Delusions: The View from the Inside." *Foreign Affairs* 85, no. 3 (May–June 2006): 2–27.

Woodward, Bob. *Bush at War*. New York: Simon and Schuster, 2002.

———. *Plan of Attack*. New York: Simon and Schuster, 2004.

———. *State of Denial: Bush at War, Part III*. New York: Simon and Schuster, 2006.

———. *The War Within: A Secret White House History, 2006–2008*. New York: Simon and Schuster, 2008.

Wright, Donald P., and Timothy R. Reese, *On Point II: Transition to the New Campaign: The United States Army in Operation Iraqi Freedom, May 2003–January 2005*. Fort Leavenworth, KS: U.S. Army Combined Arms Center, 2008.

Wright, Evan. *Generation Kill*. New York: Putnam, 2004.

Yaphe, Judith S. "War and Occupation in Iraq: What Went Right? What Could Go Wrong?" *Middle East Journal* 57 (Summer 2003).

———. "After the Surge: Next Steps in Iraq?" *Strategic Forum*, no. 230. Washington, DC: Institute for National Strategic Studies, National Defense University, February 2008.

———. "Iraq: Are We There Yet?" *Current History* 107, no. 713 (December 2008): 403–9.

Yingling, Paul. "A Failure in Generalship." *Armed Forces Journal* (May 2007).

Zimmerman, David. *The Sandbox*. New York: Soho, 2010.

Zinni, Tony, and Tony Koltz. *The Battle for Peace*. New York: Palgrave, 2006.

Zucchino, David. *Thunder Run: The Armored Strike to Capture Baghdad*. New York: Atlantic Monthly Press, 2004.

Notes and Index

Notes

Preface and Acknowledgments

1. Dan Caldwell, "The Wrong War at the Wrong Time with the Wrong Strategy," Columbia International Affairs Online, August 2007; available at www.ciaonet.org.

2. Joseph J. Collins, *Choosing War: The Decision to Invade Iraq and Its Aftermath,"* Occasional Paper 5 (Washington, DC: National Defense University Press, April 2008).

3. President Obama quoted by Jeff Zeleny, "The Medal of Honor Is Given to Hero of Afghan Battle," *New York Times,* September 18, 2009, p. A17.

Chapter 1

1. David Howell Petraeus, *The American Military and the Lessons of Vietnam: A Study of Military Influence and the Use of Force in the Post-Vietnam Era,* doctoral dissertation, Princeton University, 1987, p. 104.

Chapter 2

1. Joel S. Fetzer and J. Christopher Soper, *Muslims and the State in Britain, France, and Germany* (New York: Cambridge University Press, 2005).

2. Osama bin Laden, "Declaration of Jihad against the Americans Occupying the Land of the Two Holy Sanctuaries," in Gilles Kepel and Jean-Pierre Milelli, eds., *Al Qaeda in Its Own Words* (Cambridge, MA: Harvard University Press, 2008), pp. 47–48.

3. Fawaz A. Gerges, *The Far Enemy: Why Jihad Went Global* (New York: Cambridge University Press, 2005), p. 257.

4. Vali Nasr, *The Shia Revival: How Conflicts within Islam Will Shape the Future* (New York: W. W. Norton, 2006).

5. Thomas Friedman, *From Beirut to Jerusalem* (New York: Farrar, Straus and Giroux, 1989).

6. Osama bin Laden quoted by Christopher M. Blanchard, "Al Qaeda: Statements and Evolving Ideology," *CRS Report for Congress,* June 20, 2005 (Washington, DC: Congressional Research Service, 2005), p. 7.

7. Daniel Benjamin and Steven Simon, *The Age of Sacred Terror* (New York: Random House, 2002), p. 47.

8. Michael Walzer, *The Revolution of the Saints: A Study in the Origins of Radical Politics* (Cambridge, MA: Harvard University Press, 1982).

9. Osama bin Laden, "The Betrayal of Palestine," in Bruce Lawrence, ed., *Messages to the World: The Statements of Osama bin Laden* (New York: Verso, 2005), p. 11.

10. Taqi al-Din ibn Taymiyya quoted by Osama bin Laden, "The World Islamic Front," February 23, 1998, in Lawrence, *Messages to the World*, pp. 60–61.

11. Lawrence Wright, *The Looming Tower: Al-Qaeda and the Road to 9/11* (New York: Vintage, 2006), pp. 72–73.

12. Benjamin and Simon, *The Age of Sacred Terror*, p. 53.

13. Wright, *The Looming Tower*, p. 170.

14. John Calvert, *Sayyid Qutb and the Origins of Radical Islamism* (New York: Columbia University Press, 2010), p. 1; see also Adnan Musallam, *From Secularism to Jihad: Sayyid Qutb and the Foundations of Radical Islamism* (New York: Praeger, 2005).

15. Sayyid Qutb quoted by Wright, *The Looming Tower*, p. 27.

16. Muslim Brotherhood credo quoted by Benjamin and Simon, *The Age of Sacred Terror*, p. 57.

17. Lawrence, *Messages to the World*, note 3, p. 16.

18. Benjamin and Simon, *The Age of Sacred Terror*, p. 448.

19. Ibid., p. 62; Calvert, *Sayyid Qutb*, p. 278.

20. Sabrina Tavernise, "Mystical Form of Islam Suits Sufis in Pakistan," *New York Times*, February 26, 2010, p. A4.

21. David Fromkin, *A Peace to End All Peace: The Fall of the Ottoman Empire and the Creation of the Modern Middle East* (New York: Henry Holt, 1989).

22. T. E. Lawrence, *Seven Pillars of Wisdom* (New York: Anchor Books, 1991).

23. T. E. Lawrence, "27 Articles," quoted by Thomas E. Ricks, *Fiasco: The American Military Adventure in Iraq* (New York: Penguin Press, 2006), p. 318.

24. Raul Hilberg, *The Destruction of the European Jews*, 3rd ed. (New Haven: Yale University Press, 2003).

25. Lawrence Freedman, *A Choice of Enemies: America Confronts the Middle East* (New York: PublicAffairs, 2008), p. 18.

26. Ibid., p. 23.

27. Ibid., pp. 23–24.

28. Ahmed Rashid, *Taliban: Militant Islam, Oil and Fundamentalism in Central Asia* (New Haven: Yale University Press, 2001), p. 96.

29. David W. Lesch, *1979: The Year That Shaped the Modern Middle East* (Boulder, CO: Westview Press, 2001).

30. Toast by President Carter at a state dinner, Tehran, December 31, 1977.

31. Gary Sick, *All Fall Down: America's Tragic Encounter with Iran* (New York: Random House, 1986).

32. Yaroslav Trofimov, *The Siege of Mecca: The 1979 Uprising at Islam's Holiest Shrine* (New York: Anchor Books, 2007).

33. Wright, *Looming Tower*, p. 108.

34. Benjamin and Simon, *The Age of Sacred Terror*, p. 90.

35. Tamim Al-Barghoti, *The Umma and the Dawla: The Nation State and the Arab Middle East* (London: Pluto Press, 2008).

36. Seth P. Tillman, *The United States in the Middle East: Interests and Obstacles* (Bloomington: Indiana University Press, 1982).

37. Donald M. Goldstein and Katherine V. Dillon, eds., *The Pearl Harbor Papers: Inside the Japanese Plans* (Dulles, VA: Brassey's, 2000).

38. Daniel Yergin, *The Prize: The Epic Quest for Oil, Money, and Power* (New York: Free Press, 1993).

Chapter 3

1. Stephen P. Cohen, *The Idea of Pakistan* (Washington, DC: Brookings, 2004).

2. "The General's Next War," interview with General David H. Petraeus, *Foreign Policy* (January–February 2009): p. 48.

3. Adam Roberts, "Doctrine and Reality in Afghanistan," *Survival* 51, no. 1 (February–March 2009): p. 52.

4. David Kilcullen, *The Accidental Guerilla: Fighting Small Wars in the Midst of a Big One* (Ithaca, NY: Oxford University Press, 2009), p. 41.

5. Barack Obama quoted by Bob Woodward, *Obama's Wars* (New York: Simon and Schuster, 2010).

6. George Tenet with Bill Harlow, *At the Center of the Storm: My Years at the CIA* (New York: HarperCollins, 2007).

7. U.S. National Commission on Terrorist Attacks upon the United States, *9/11 Commission Final Report* (New York: W. W. Norton, 2004), p. 369.

8. George W. Bush, "State of the Union Address," *New York Times*, January 21, 2004.

9. Steve Coll, *Ghost Wars: The Secret History of the CIA, Afghanistan, and bin Laden, from the Soviet Invasion to September 10, 2001* (New York: Penguin Press, 2004), p. 305.

10. General Anthony Zinni, testimony to the Senate Armed Services Committee, February 29, 2000, quoted by Coll, ibid., p. 508.

11. Comments by the Honorable Anne Patterson, U.S. ambassador to Pakistan, Pacific Council on International Policy, Los Angeles, March 5, 2010.

12. Owen Bennett Jones, *Pakistan: Eye of the Storm* (New Haven: Yale University Press, 2002), p. 137.

13. Cohen, *The Idea of Pakistan*, p. 52.

14. Mohammad Ayub Khan, *Diaries of Field Marshal Mohammad Ayub Khan*, edited and annotated by Craig Baxter (New York: Oxford University Press, 2007), p. 506.

15. Henry D. Sokolski, ed., *Pakistan's Nuclear Future: Worries beyond War* (Carlisle, PA: Strategic Studies Institute, U.S. Army War College, 2008).

16. Ahmed Rashid, *Descent into Chaos: The U.S. and the Disaster in Pakistan, Afghanistan, and Central Asia* (New York: Penguin Books, 2004), p. 219.

17. Comments by the Honorable Anne Patterson, U.S. Ambassador to Pakistan, Pacific Council on International Policy, Los Angeles, March 5, 2010.

18. Arnold J. Toynbee, *Between Oxus and Jumna* (Oxford: Oxford University Press, 1961), p. 131.

19. Ahmed Rashid, *Taliban: Militant Islam, Oil and Fundamentalism in Central Asia* (New Haven: Yale University Press, 2001), p. 7.

20. Kilcullen, *The Accidental Guerilla*, p. 44.

21. Rashid, *Taliban*, p. 37.

22. Quoted in Seth G. Jones, *In the Graveyard of Empires: America's War in Afghanistan* (New York: W. W. Norton, 2009), p. 7.

23. Quoted in Henrik Bering, "Fighting Clever," *Policy Review* (June and July 2009): p. 96.

24. Quoted ibid., p. 97.

25. Rashid, *Taliban*, p. 11.

26. Central Intelligence Agency, *World Factbook*; available at www.cia.gov/library/pulications/the-world-factbook/index.html.

27. Louis Dupree, *Afghanistan* (New York: Oxford University Press, 1997), p. 452.

28. Quoted ibid._

29. Ibid., p. 477.

30. Richard F. Nyrop and Donald M. Seekins, eds., *Afghanistan: A Country Study* (Washington, DC: U.S. Government Printing Office, 1986), p. 63.

31. Personal communication from Joseph J. Collins to the author, March 28, 2010.

32. Nyrop and Seekins, *Afghanistan*, p. 66.

33. Alvin Z. Rubinstein, *Soviet Policy toward Turkey, Iran, and Afghanistan: The Dynamics of Influence* (New York: Praeger, 1982), p. 104.

34. Top secret memo "Regarding Events in Afghanistan during 27–28 December 1979," from Y. Andropov, A. Gromyko, D. Ustinov, and V. Ponomarev to the Central Committee of the Communist Party of the Soviet Union, in *The Intervention in Afghanistan and the Fall of Détente*, 1995 Nobel Symposium, Oslo, Norway, September 17–20, 1995, tab 6.

35. Secret memorandum from Zbigniew Brzezinski to President Carter, December 26, 1979, p. 1, in *The Intervention in Afghanistan and the Fall of Détente*, tab 9.

36. Jimmy Carter, *Keeping Faith: Memoirs of a President* (New York: Bantam Books, 1982), p. 472.

37. Milt Bearden and James Risen, *The Main Enemy: The Inside Story of the CIA's Final Showdown with the KGB* (New York: Random House, 2003), p. 234.

38. Coll, *Ghost Wars*, p. 59.

39. Rashid, *Taliban*, p. 38.

40. Joe Lokey, "Global Focus on Landmines in Afghanistan," http://maic.jmu.edu/JOURNAL/5.3/features/joe_lokey/joe_lokey.htm.

41. Angela Rasanayagam, *Afghanistan: A Modern History* (New York: I. B. Taurus, 2005), p. 115.

42. Mao Zedong, *On Guerilla Warfare* (Urbana: University of Illinois Press, 2000).

43. Bearden and Risen, *The Main Enemy*, p. 341.

44. Rashid, *Taliban*, p. 85.

45. Bearden and Risen, *The Main Enemy*, p. 154.

46. Robert Gates, *From the Shadows: The Ultimate Insider's Story of Five Presidents and How They Won the Cold War* (New York: Simon and Schuster, 1996), p. 199.

47. See ibid.; Coll, *Ghost Wars*, pp. 104–5.

48. Coll, *Ghost Wars*, p. 93.

49. Jones, *In the Graveyard of Empires*, p. 37.

50. Rashid, *Taliban*, p. 130.

51. Ibid., p. 129.

52. George Crile, *Charlie Wilson's War: The Extraordinary Story of the Largest Covert Operation in History* (New York: Atlantic Monthly Press, 2003).

53. Quoted in Bearden and Risen, *The Main Enemy*, p. 249.

54. Coll, *Ghost Wars*, p. 11.

55. Richard A. Clarke, "*Against All Enemies: Inside America's War on Terror* (New York: Free Press, 2004), p. 50.

56. Mikhail Gorbachev, *Memoirs* (New York: Doubleday, 1995), p. 138.

57. "Gorbachev on 1989," interview by Katrina Vanden Heuvel and Stephen F. Cohen, *The Nation*, October 28, 2009; available at www.thenation.com/doc/20091116/kvh_cohen.

58. Gorbachev, *Memoirs*, p. 249.

59. Barnett R. Rubin, *The Search for Peace in Afghanistan: From Buffer State to Failed State* (New Haven: Yale University Press, 1995), p. 7.

60. Raymond L. Garthoff, *Détente and Confrontation: American-Soviet Relations from Nixon to Reagan* (Washington, DC: Brookings Institution Press, 1994), p. 1022.

61. Charles G. Cogan, "Partners in Time: The CIA and Afghanistan since 1979," *World Policy Journal* 10, no. 2 (1993): p. 81.

62. Rubin, *The Search for Peace in Afghanistan*, p. 7.

63. Henry S. Bradsher, *Afghanistan and the Soviet Union* (Durham, NC: Duke University Press, 1985), pp. 24–25; Rashid, *Taliban*, p. 18.

64. Lawrence Freedman, *A Choice of Enemies: America Confronts the Middle East* (New York: PublicAffairs, 2008), p. 88.

65. Clarke, *Against All Enemies*, p. 50.

66. George P. Shultz, *Turmoil and Triumph: My Years as Secretary of State* (New York: Charles Scribner's Sons, 1993), p. 987.

67. Rashid, *Taliban*, p. 89.

68. Ibid., pp. 17–18.

69. Ibid., p. 33.

70. Ibid., pp. 120–21.

71. Ibid., p. 122.

72. Rashid, *Descent into Chaos*, p. 319.

73. Speech by Prime Minister Tony Blair to the Labour Party Conference, Brighton, October 2, 2001.

74. Jason Campbell, Michael O'Hanlon, and Jeremy Shapiro, "How to Measure the War," *Policy Review* (October and November, 2009): p. 27.

75. Rashid, *Descent into Chaos*, p. 317.

76. Thomas H. Johnson, "Financing Afghan Terrorism: Thugs, Drugs, and Creative Movement of Money," in Jeanne K. Giraldo and Harold A. Trinkunas, eds., *Terrorism Financing and State Responses: A Comparative Perspective* (Stanford: Stanford University Press, 2007), p. 98.

77. Jones, *In the Graveyard of Empires*, p. 195.

78. The Soviet government tried and convicted Powers of espionage, and the U.S. government gained his release by trading him for several Soviet spies. After he was released, Powers became a helicopter pilot for a Los Angeles radio station reporting on traffic conditions. While doing this, he crashed into power lines and was killed.

79. Coll, *Ghost Wars*, p. 221.

80. Bearden and Risen, *The Main Enemy*, p. 236.

81. Coll, *Ghost Wars*, p. 283.

82. Ibid., p. 287.

83. *Washington Post*, October 7, 1996.

84. Gary C. Schroen, *First In: An Insider's Account of How the CIA Spearheaded the War on Terror in Afghanistan* (New York: Ballantine Books, 2005), pp. 48, 65.

85. Gary Berntsen and Ralph Pezzulo, *Jawbreaker: The Attack on Bin Laden and Al-Qaeda: A Personal Account by the CIA's Field Commander* (New York: Three Rivers Press, 2005), p. 63.

86. Ibid., p. 49.

87. Coll, *Ghost Wars*, p. 228.

88. Schroen, *First In*, p. 56.

89. Coll, *Ghost Wars*, p. 201.

90. Daniel Benjamin and Steven Simon, *The Age of Sacred Terror* (New York: Random House, 2002), p. 242.

91. John Prados, *Safe for Democracy: The Secret Wars of the CIA* (Chicago: Ivan R. Dee, 2006), p. 491; Coll, *Ghost Wars*, p. 337.

92. Paul Richter, "Troops Could Face Missiles U.S. Sent Afghanistan in '80s," *Los Angeles Times*, October 6, 2001, p. A12.

93. Clarke, *Against All Enemies*, p. 52.

94. Coll, *Ghost Wars*, 337.

95. Schroen, *First In*, p. 67.

Chapter 4

1. T. E. Lawrence, "The Changing East," originally published in *The Round Table* (September 1920); reprinted in Malcolm Brown, ed., *T. E. Lawrence in War and Peace:*

An Anthology of the Military Writings of Lawrence of Arabia (London: Greenhill Books, 2005), p. 255.

2. Charles Tripp, *A History of Iraq*, 3rd ed. (New York: Cambridge University Press, 2007), p. 8.

3. Ibid., p. 40.

4. William R. Polk, *Understanding Iraq* (New York: HarperCollins, 2005), p. 99.

5. Kenneth M. Pollack, *The Threatening Storm: The Case for Invading Iraq* (New York: Random House, 2002), p. 12.

6. Lord Curzon quoted by Polk, *Understanding Iraq*, p. 64.

7. Tripp, *A History of Iraq*, p. 191.

8. Polk, *Understanding Iraq*, p. 159.

9. Jerrold M. Post, "Saddam Hussein of Iraq: A Political Psychology Profile," in Jerrold Post, ed., *The Psychological Assessment of Political Leaders* (Ann Arbor: University of Michigan Press, 2003), p. 344.

10. Tripp, *A History of Iraq*, p. 217.

11. Pheobe Marr, *The Modern History of Iraq* (Boulder, CO: Westview Press), p. 245.

12. Kanan Makiya, *Republic of Fear* (Berkeley: University of California Press, 1998), p. 72.

13. Pollack, *The Threatening Storm*, p. 20.

14. Michael J. Kelly, *Ghosts of Halabja: Saddam Hussein and the Kurdish Genocide* (New York: Praeger, 2008).

15. Patrick Tyler, "Poison Gas Kills Hundreds," *Washington Post*, March 21, 1988, pp. A1, A36.

16. Polk, *Understanding Iraq*, pp. 134–35.

17. Judith Miller and Laurie Mylroie, *Saddam Hussein and the Crisis in the Gulf* (New York: Times Books, 1990), p. 124.

18. Pollack, *The Threatening Storm*, p. 24.

19. See Energy Information Administration, Department of Energy, Table 5.4: Petroleum Imports by Country of Origin, 1960–2008, http://www.eia.doe.gov/emeu/aer/txt/ptb0504.html.

20. Colin Powell with Joseph E. Persico, *My American Journey* (New York: Random House, 1995), p. 459.

21. "The Gulf War," *Frontline*, Public Broadcasting System; http://www.pbs.org/wgbh/pages/frontline/gulf/

22. Tripp, *A History of Iraq*, p. 242.

23. Sarah Graham-Brown, *Sanctioning Saddam: The Politics of Intervention in Iraq* (London: I. B. Taurus, 1999).

24. Bruce Jentleson, *With Friends Like These: Reagan, Bush, and Saddam, 1982–1990* (New York: W. W. Norton, 1994), p. 45.

25. Saddam Hussein quoted in the *Observer*, October 21, 1990; cited by Lawrence Freedman and Efraim Karsh, *The Gulf Conflict, 1990–1991: Diplomacy and War in the New World Order* (Princeton: Princeton University Press, 1993), p. 45.

26. Bob Woodward, *The Commanders* (New York: Simon and Schuster, 2003), pp. 206–7.

27. The Iraqi transcript of the meeting between Saddam and Ambassador Glaspie was published in the *International Herald Tribune*, September 17, 1990.

28. Ambassador Glaspie's interpretation of her meeting with Saddam is presented in her testimony in U.S. Congress, Senate, Foreign Relations Committee, *Hearings*, March 20, 1991.

29. Quoted in Powell with Persico, *My American Journey*, p. 466.

30. Margaret Thatcher quoted in *The Gulf War*, Frontline.

31. Quoted by Freedman and Karsh, *The Gulf Conflict*.

32. Mohamed Heikal, *Illusions of Triumph: An Arab View of the Gulf War* (New York: HarperCollins, 1992), p. 16.

33. "Oral History: General Charles Horner," *The Gulf War*, Frontline, PBS; available at http://www.pbs.org/wgbh/pages/frontline/gulf/oral/horner/1.html.

34. James A. Baker III with Thomas M. DeFrank, *The Politics of Diplomacy: Revolution, War and Peace, 1989–1992* (New York: Putnam, 1995).

35. Powell with Persico, *My American Journey*, p. 486.

36. Polk, *Understanding Iraq*, p. 152.

37. James Baker quoted in Michael R. Gordon and Bernard Trainor, *The Generals' War: The Inside Story of the Conflict in the Gulf* (Boston: Little, Brown, 1995), p. 416.

38. *The Gulf War*, Frontline, PBS.

39. George H. W. Bush quoted in Gordon and Trainor, *The Generals' War*, p. 416.

40. Graham-Brown, *Sanctioning Saddam*. p. 23.

41. Author's interview with a U.S. member of UNSCOM inspection team.

42. Charles Duelfer, *Hide and Seek: The Search for Truth in Iraq* (New York: PublicAffairs, 2009),p. 97.

43. Comment by Paul Wolfowitz, "Deepening Crisis," *The News Hour*, November 11, 1998; available at http://www.pbs.org/newshour/bb/middle_east/July–dec98/iraq_11-11.html/.

44. Letter from Project for the New American Century to President William Jefferson Clinton, January 26, 1998, quoted by Douglas J. Feith, *War and Decision: Inside the Pentagon at the Dawn of the War on Terrorism* (New York: HarperCollins, 2008), p. 195.

45. "How the Accord Will Work: Special Group Is Set Up," *New York Times*, February 24, 1998, p. A8.

46. Barton Gellman, "Why Now? U.S. Says Iraq Determined Timing," *Washington Post*, December 17, 1998, p. A1.

47. Senator Trent Lott quoted in the *Los Angeles Times*, December 17, 1998, p. A46.

48. Lawrence, "The Changing East," p. 265

Chapter 5

1. Walter Laqueur, *The Age of Terrorism* (Boston: Little Brown, 1987), p. 72.

2. Brian Jenkins quoted by Jonathan R. White, *Terrorism: An Introduction* (Pacific Grove, CA: Brooks/Cole, 1991), p. 5.

3. United States Code, Title 22, Section 2656f(d).

4. Numbers 31:17–18; see also Deuteronomy 7:1–2 and 20:10–17.

5. Ward Thomas, "Norms and Security: The Case of International Assassination," *International Security* 25, no. 1 (Summer 2000): pp. 105–33.

6. See the State Department site at www.state.gov/s/ct/c14151.htm/.

7. From unpublished FBI data cited by Paul Pillar, *Terrorism and U.S. Foreign Policy* (Washington, DC: Brookings Institution Press, 2001), pp. 18–19.

8. Ibid., p. 5; Steve Coll, *Ghost Wars: The Secret History of the CIA, Afghanistan, and Bin Laden, from the Soviet Invasion to September 10, 2001* (New York: Penguin Press, 2004), p. 254.

9. Bruce Hoffman, "Terrorism Trends and Prospects," in Ian Lesser et al., eds., *Countering the New Terrorism* (Santa Monica, CA: RAND Corporation, 1999), p. 11.

10. Pillar, *Terrorism and U.S. Foreign Policy*, p. 31.

11. U.S. Department of State, *Patterns of Global Terrorism 1999* (Washington, DC: Government Printing Office, 2000), p. 2.

12. Omar Saghi, "Osama Bin Laden, the Iconic Orator," in Gilles Kepel and Jean-Pierre Milelli, eds., *Al Qaeda in Its Own Words* (Cambridge, MA: Harvard University Press, 2008), p. 20.

13. Osama bin Laden quoted by Richard Bulliet and Fawaz A. Gerges, eds., "A Recruiting Tape of Osama bin Laden: Excerpts and Analyses," Columbia International Affairs Online at www.ciaonet.org.

14. John Calvert, *Sayyid Qutb and the Origins of Radical Islamism* (New York: Columbia University Press, 2010), p. 290.

15. Steven Coll, *The Bin Ladens: An Arabian Family in the American Century* (New York: Penguin Books, 2009).

16. Nasir Al-Bahri quoted ibid., p. 253.

17. Fawaz A. Gerges, *The Far Enemy: Why Jihad Went Global* (New York: Cambridge University Press, 2005), p. 18.

18. Bruce Lawrence, ed., *Messages to the World: The Statements of Osama bin Laden* (New York: Verso, 2005), p. 76.

19. For a sampling of Azzam's writings, see "Part II: Abdullah Azzam," in Kepel and Milelli, *Al Qaeda in Its Own Words*, pp. 81–146.

20. Daniel Benjamin and Steven Simon, *The Age of Sacred Terror* (New York: Random House, 2002), p. 99.

21. Lawrence Wright, *The Looming Tower: Al-Qaeda and the Road to 9/11* (New York: Vintage, 2006), p. 204.

22. Coll, *The Bin Ladens,* p. 340; Lawrence Freedman, *A Choice of Enemies: America Confronts the Middle East* (New York: PublicAffairs, 2008), p. 347; Gerges, *The Far Enemy*, p. 137; Lawrence, *Messages to the World*, p. 76.

23. Osama bin Laden, "Declaration of Jihad," August 23, 1996, in Lawrence, *Messages to the World*, p. 26.

24. Gerges, *The Far Enemy*, pp. 13, 183.

25. Ibid., p. 139.

26. Osama bin Laden quoted by Wright, *The Looming Tower,* p. 179.

27. Osama bin Laden, "The Betrayal of Palestine," December 29, 1994, in Lawrence, *Messages to the World*, p. 7.

28. Lawrence, "Introduction," *Messages to the World*, p. xiii.

29. Coll, *The Bin Ladens,* p. 409.

30. Mark Bowden did not mention this in his book and later movie, *Black Hawk Down: A Story of Modern War* (New York: Penguin Books, 2000), but later accounts note that al Qaeda members advised Mohammed Aidid's soldiers; U.S. National Commission on Terrorist Attacks upon the United States, *Final Report*, hereafter cited as *9/11 Commission Final Report* (New York: W. W. Norton, 2004), pp. 59–60; and Benjamin and Simon, *Age of Sacred Terror*, p. 132.

31. Richard A. Clarke, *Against All Enemies: Inside America's War on Terror* (New York: Free Press, 2004), p. 79.

32. Journalist Steve Coll (*The Bin Ladens*, p. 403) concludes, "Osama Bin Laden was not identified as Yousef's direct patron, then or later," and Lawrence Wright (*The Looming Tower*, p. 279) claims, "[B]in Laden was not connected" to the bombing.

33. *9/11 Commission Final Report,* p. 73.

34. Ibid., p. 171.

35. Undated NSC memo cited ibid., p. 183.

36. Coll, *The Bin Ladens,* p. 411.

37. *9/11 Commission Final Report*, p. 88.

38. "The World Islamic Front," February 23, 1998, in Lawrence, *Messages to the World*, pp. 60–61.

39. Bin Laden, "Declaration of Jihad," August 23, 1996, quoted in Lawrence, *The Looming Tower,* p. 23. The full statement can also be found in the *Washington Post* at www.washingtonpost.com.ac2/wp-dyn/A4342–2110Sep21/.

40. Osama bin Laden, "World Islamic Front Statement Urging Jihad against Jews and Crusaders," in Kepel and Milelli, *Al Qaeda in Its Own Words,* p. 55; also in Lawrence, *Messages to the World*, p. 61.

41. John Kelsay, *Arguing the Just War in Islam* (Cambridge, MA: Harvard University Press, 2008); Michael Walzer, *Just and Unjust Wars: A Philosophical Argument with Historical Illustrations* (New York: Basic Books, 1977).

42. Bin Laden, "Declaration of Jihad," in Lawrence, *Messages to the World,* p. 30.

43. Gerges, *The Far Enemy*, p. 188.

44. Gary Berntsen and Ralph Pezzullo, *Jawbreaker: The Attack on bin Laden and Al-Qaeda: A Personal Account by the CIA's Key Field Commander* (New York: Three Rivers Press, 2005), p. 48.

45. Brian Jenkins, "International Terrorism: A New Mode of Conflict," in David Carlton and Carlo Schaerf, eds., *International Terrorism and World Security* (London: Croon Helm, 1975).

46. Steven Simon and Daniel Benjamin, "America and the New Terrorism," *Survival* 42, no. 1 (Spring 2000), p. 71 (emphasis in the original).

47. Ian O. Lesser, "Countering the New Terrorism: Implications for Strategy," in Lesser, *Countering the New Terrorism,* p. 87; see also ch. 2, "The Foundations of the New Terrorism," in *9/11 Commission Final Report*, pp. 47–70.

48. David Kilcullen, *The Accidental Guerilla: Fighting Small Wars in the Midst of a Big One* (New York: Oxford University Press, 2009).

49. Samuel R. Berger quoted in U.S. Congress, Senate Select Committee on Intelligence and House Permanent Select Committee on Intelligence, *Joint Inquiry into Intelligence Activities before and after the Terrorist Attacks of September 11, 2001,* Senate Report no. 107–351. House Report no. 107–792, December 2002, p. 305; hereafter cited as *Joint Inquiry into Intelligence Activities.*

50. Ibid., pp. 305–6; *9/11 Commission Final Report,* pp. 194, 351; Hugh Shelton with Ronald Levinson and Malcolm McConnell, *Without Hesitation: The Odyssey of an American Warrior* (New York: St. Martin's, 2010).

51. Richard C. Clarke quoted in *Joint Inquiry into Intelligence Activities*, p. 305.

52. Gary C. Schroen, *First In: An Insider's Account of How the CIA Spearheaded the War on Terror in Afghanistan* (New York: Ballantine Books, 2007), p. 12.

53. Clarke, *Against All Enemies*, p. 209.

54. Coll, *Ghost Wars*, pp. 109–10.

55. Ibid., p. 114.

56. "Dossiers of Rebel Field Commanders," January 1, 2001, Cold War International History Project, Woodrow Wilson International Center for Scholars, Washington, DC.

57. Ahmed Rashid, *Taliban: Militant Islam, Oil and Fundamentalism in Central Asia* (New Haven: Yale University Press, 2000), p. 82.

58. "Dossiers of Rebel Field Commanders"; Coll, *Ghost Wars*, p. 114.

59. "Dossiers of Rebel Field Commanders."

60. Robert M. Gates, *From the Shadows: The Ultimate Insider's Story of Five Presidents and How They Won the Cold War* (New York: Simon and Schuster, 1996), p. 429.

61. Benjamin and Simon, *The Age of Sacred Terror*, pp. 138, 338.

62. Tim Weiner, *Legacy of Ashes: The History of the CIA* (New York: Anchor Books, 2007), p. 548.

63. Wright, *The Looming Tower*, p. 163.

64. Abdullah Azzam, "Join the Caravan," in Kepel and Milelli, *Al Qaeda in Its Own Words*, p. 113.

65. Freedman, *A Choice of Enemies*, p. 347.

66. Clarke, *Against All Enemies*, p. 210.

67. Berntsen and Pezzullo, *Jawbreaker*, p. 623; Ahmed Rashid, *Descent into Chaos: The U.S. and the Disaster in Pakistan, Afghanistan, and Central Asia* (New York: Penguin Books, 2009), p. 20.

68. Seth G. Jones, *In the Graveyard of Empires: America's War in Afghanistan* (New York: W. W. Norton, 2009), p. 46; Berntsen and Pezzullo, *Jawbreaker*, p. 49.

69. Ahmad Shah Masud, "A Message to the People of the United States of America," U.S. Congress, Senate, Committee on Foreign Relations, Committee Hearing, October 8, 1998.

70. Rashid, *Descent into Chaos*, p. 21.

71. *9/11 Commission Final Report*, p. 187.

72. The accounts in this paragraph are from the author's notes taken at the Annual Conference of the International Institute of Strategic Studies, Geneva, Switzerland, September 13–14, 2001.

73. Daniel Benjamin and Steven Simon, "At War with a Wraith," *Washington Post*, September 14, 2001, p. A37.

74. This account of the events of September 11 is based on the *9/11 Commission Final Report*, pp. 1–46.

75. Ibid., p. 45.

76. Bob Woodward, *Plan of Attack* (New York: Simon and Schuster, 2004), p. 45.

77. Ibid., p. 24.

78. John Ashcroft, *Never Again: Securing America and Restoring Justice* (Nashville, TN: Center Street, 2006).

79. George W. Bush quoted by James Harding, "Conflicting Views from Two Bush Camps," *Financial Times*, March 20, 2003.

80. Robert Jervis, "Understanding the Bush Doctrine," in Demetrios Caraley, ed., *American Hegemony: Preventive War, Iraq and Imposing Democracy* (New York: Academy of Political Science, 2004), p. 17.

81. George W. Bush, "President's State of the Union Message to Congress and the Nation," *New York Times*, January 21, 2004, p. A15.

82. "President Bush's Address on Terrorism before a Joint Meeting of Congress," *New York Times*, September 21, 2001, p. B4.

83. Jacob Weisberg, *The Bush Tragedy* (New York: Random House, 2008), p. 103.

84. Ibid.

85. George W. Bush quoted by Ron Suskind, "Faith, Certainty and the Presidency of George W. Bush," *New York Times Magazine*, October 17, 2004, p. 50.

86. George Tenet with Bill Harlow, *At the Center of the Storm: My Years at the CIA* (New York: HarperCollins, 2007), p. 129.

87. Mullah Omar quoted in Gerges, *The Far Enemy*, p. 196.

88. Bill Clinton quoted in Coll, *Ghost Wars*, p. 537.

Chapter 6

1. Alexander L. George, "Domestic Constraints and Regime Change in U.S. Foreign Policy: The Need for Policy Legitimacy," in Ole R. Holsti, Randolph Siverson, and Alexander L. George, eds., *Change in the International System* (Boulder, CO: Westview Press, 1980).

2. Dan Caldwell, ed., *Henry Kissinger: His Personality and Policies* (Durham, NC: Duke University Press, 1983).

3. Jacob Weisberg, *The Bush Tragedy* (New York: Random House, 2008), p. xxiii.

4. Author's interviews with several prep school and college classmates of George W. Bush; Nicholas D. Kristof, "Ally of an Older Generation amid the Tumult of the 60's," *New York Times*, June 19, 2000, p. A1.

5. Weisberg, *The Bush Tragedy*, p. xvi.

6. "Bush Fell Short on Duty at Guard: Records Show Pledges Unmet," *Boston Globe*, September 8, 2004.

7. George W. Bush, "Chapter 1: Quitting," *Decision Points* (New York: Crown Books, 2010), pp. 1–34; the quotation is from p. 33.

8. Weisberg, *The Bush Tragedy*, p. 60.

9. Alan Cooperman, "Openly Religious, to a Point," *Washington Post*, September 9, 2004, p. A1.

10. George W. Bush quoted by Bob Woodward, *Plan of Attack* (New York: Simon and Schuster, 2004), p. 91.

11. George W. Bush quoted by Bob Woodward, *State of Denial: Bush at War, Part III* (New York: Simon and Schuster, 2006), p. 334.

12. George W. Bush quoted by Ron Suskind, "Faith, Certainty and the Presidency of George W. Bush," *New York Times Magazine*, October 17, 2004, p. 51.

13. George W. Bush quoted by David Brooks, "Heroes and History," *New York Times*, July 17, 2007, p. A21.

14. Jim Wallis quoted by Suskind, "Faith, Certainty and the Presidency of George W. Bush," p. 50.

15. "Excerpts from Platform Approved by Republican National Convention," *New York Times*, August 1, 2000, p. A16.

16. "Excerpts from Bush's Remarks on National Security and Arms Control," *New York Times*, May 24, 2000, p. A19.

17. "No Honeymoon Likely for New President's Foreign Policy Team," *New York Times*, January 20, 2002, p. A13.

18. Brent Scowcroft quoted by Nicholas Lemann, "Without a Doubt," *New Yorker*, October 14, 21, 2002, p. 164.

19. Condoleezza Rice, "Promoting the National Interest," *Foreign Affairs* 79, no. 1 (January–February 2000): pp. 45–62.

20. George W. Bush quoted by Karen DeYoung, *Soldier: The Life of Colin Powell* (New York: Alfred A. Knopf, 2006), p. 295.

21. Keith A. Hansen, *The Comprehensive Test Ban Treaty: An Insider's Perspective* (Stanford: Stanford University Press, 2006).

22. Lawrence Freedman, *A Choice of Enemies: America Confronts the Middle East* (New York: PublicAffairs, 2008).

23. Ivo H. Daalder and James M. Lindsay, *America Unbound: The Bush Revolution in Foreign Policy* (Washington, DC: Brookings, 2003).

24. Ibid., p. 15.

25. Jame Mann, *Rise of the Vulcans: The History of Bush's War Cabinet* (New York: Viking, 2004), pp. 209–15.

26. Michael Gordon and Bernard Trainor, *Cobra II: The Inside Story of the Invasion and Occupation of Iraq* (New York: Pantheon, 2006), p. 63.

27 Paul Wolfowitz quoted in Thomas Ricks, *Fiasco: The American Military Adventure in Iraq* (New York: Penguin Press, 2006), p. 7.

28. Wolfowitz quoted ibid.

29 Mann. *Rise of the Vulcans.*

30. Ibid., pp. xvxvi.

31. George W. Bush, "State of the Union Address," January 2002.

32. Dick Cheney, speech to the Council on Foreign Relations, Washington, DC, January 29, 2002.

33. Ted Sorensen, *Counselor: A Life at the Edge of History* (New York: HarperCollins, 2008), pp. 325–27.

34. Edward Rhodes, "The Imperial Logic of Bush's Liberal Agenda," *Survival* 45, no. 1 (Spring 2003): p. 134.

35. Weisberg, *The Bush Tragedy*, p. 198.

36. George W. Bush, "President Delivers Graduation Speech at West Point," June 1, 2002; available at http://www.whitehouse.gove/news/releases/2002/06/print/20020601–3.html/.

37. Dennis B. Ross, *Statecraft and How to Restore America's Standing in the World* (New York: Farrar, Straus and Giroux, 2007).

38. The White House, *A National Security Strategy for a New Century*, published in October 1998, December 1999, and December 2000.

39. The White House, *National Security Strategy of the United States*, September 2002; available at www.whitehouse.gov/nsc/nss.html.

40. John Lewis Gaddis, *Surprise, Security, and the American Experience* (Cambridge, MA: Harvard University Press, 2004).

41. Robert G. Kaufman, *In Defense of the Bush Doctrine* (Lexington: University Press of Kentucky, 2007), pp. 157–84.

42. Rhodes, "The Imperial Logic of Bush's Liberal Agenda," p. 140.

43. John G. Ikenberry, "America's Imperial Ambitions," *Foreign Affairs* 77 (September/October 2002).

44. Joseph S. Nye, Jr., *Soft Power: The Means to Success in World Politics* (New York: PublicAffairs, 2004).

45. Gaddis, *Surprise, Security, and the American Experience*; Kaufman, *In Defense of the Bush Doctrine.*

46. Rhodes, "The Imperial Logic of Bush's Liberal Agenda"; Mel Gurtov, *Superpower on Crusade: The Bush Doctrine in US Foreign Policy* (Boulder, CO: Lynne Rienner, 2006).

47. "Excerpts: Charlie Gibson Interviews Sarah Palin," http://abcnews.go.com/Politics/Vote2008/story?id=5782924&page=4.

48. Weisberg, *The Bush Tragedy*.

49. Robert Dallek and Robert Jervis, "Preventive Attacks Fail Test of History," *Los Angeles Times*, October 20, 2002, p. M2.

50. Kaufman, *In Defense of the Bush Doctrine*, p. 92.

51. Robert S. Litwak, *Regime Change: U.S. Strategy through the Prism of 9/11* (Washington and Baltimore: Woodrow Wilson Center Press and Johns Hopkins University Press, 2007), p. 67.

52. Quoted by Dallek and Jervis, "Preventive Attacks Fail Test of History," p. M2.

53. President Eisenhower quoted by John F. Stacks, *Scotty: James B. Reston and the Rise and Fall of American Journalism* (Boston: Little Brown, 2003), p. 133.

54. Jervis quoted in Caraley, *American Hegemony*, p. 11.

55. Ken Adelman quoted in "Six Degrees of Preemption," *Washington Post*, September 29, 2002, p. B2.

56. George W. Bush, "President's State of the Union Message to Congress and the Nation," *New York Times*, January 21, 2004, p. A14.

57. Ricks, *Fiasco*, p. 348.

58. Dick Cheney quoted by Daalder and Lindsay, *America Unbound*, p. 119.

59. Bush, "President's State of the Union Message," 2004, p. A14.

60. Quoted in Timothy Garton Ash, *New York Times*, September 22, 2002, p. A4.

61 Ross, *Statecraft*, p. 5.

62. Bush, second "State of the Union Address," quoted by Weisberg, *The Bush Tragedy*, p. 215.

63. Bush, "State of the Union Address," 2004, p. A14.

64. Douglas J. Feith, *War and Decision: Inside the Pentagon at the Dawn of the War on Terrorism* (New York: HarperCollins, 2008), p. 234 (emphasis in the original).

65. Jane Mayer, *The Dark Side: The Inside Story of How the War on Terror Turned into a War on American Ideals* (New York: Doubleday, 2008), p. 50.

66. Dana Milbank, "In Cheney's Shadow, Counsel Pushes the Conservative Cause," *Washington Post*, October 11, 2004, p. A21.

67. Memorandum from John Yoo, Deputy Assistant Attorney General, Office of Legal Counsel, to Timothy Flanigan, Deputy Counsel to the President, "The President's Constitutional Authority to Conduct Military Operations against Terrorists and Nations Supporting Them," September 25, 2001, reprinted in Karen J. Greenberg and Joshua L. Dratel, eds., *The Torture Papers: The Road to Abu Ghraib* (New York: Cambridge University Press, 2005), pp. 3–24.

68. Jack Goldsmith, *The Terror Presidency: Law and Judgment inside the Bush Administration* (New York: W. W. Norton, 2007), p. 102.

69. Colin Powell quoted by Mayer, *The Dark Side*, p. 87.

70. "Interview with Lewis 'Scooter' Libby," *Larry King Weekend*, CNN, February 16, 2002, quoted by Barton Gellman, *Angler: The Cheney Vice Presidency* (New York: Penguin Press, 2008), p. 96.

71. Gellman, *Angler*, p. 313.

Chapter 7

1. Ron Suskind, "Faith, Certainty and the Presidency of George W. Bush," *New York Times Magazine*, October 17, 2004, p. 51.

2. Thomas Ricks, *Fiasco: The American Military Adventure in Iraq* (New York: Penguin Press, 2006), p. 111.

3. Dennis Ross, *Statecraft and How to Restore America's Standing in the World* (Farrar, Straus and Giroux, 2007), p. 125 (emphasis in the original).

4. Seth G. Jones, *In the Graveyard of Empires: America's War in Afghanistan* (New York: W. W. Norton, 2009), p. 131.

5. Hamid Karzai led the anti-Pashtuns fighting the Taliban in the south and was almost killed in a friendly fire incident. Author's interviews.

6. Richard Clarke, *Against All Enemies: Inside America's War on Terror* (New York: Free Press, 2004), p. 32.

7. George Tenet with Bill Harlow, *At the Center of the Storm: My Years at the CIA* (New York: HarperCollins, 2007), p. 306.

8. Michael DeLong with Noah Lukeman, *Inside CENTCOM: The Unvarnished Truth about the Wars in Afghanistan and Iraq* (New York: Regnery, 2004), p. 19.

9. Ibid., p. 20.

10. George W. Bush quoted by Bob Woodward, *Bush at War* (New York: Simon and Schuster, 2002), p. 99.

11. Bob Woodward, *Plan of Attack* (New York: Simon and Schuster, 2004), p. 2; see also Tommy Franks with Malcolm McConnell, *American Soldier* (New York: Regan Books, 2004), p. 315.

12. Quoted in George Packer, *The Assassins' Gate: America in Iraq* (New York: Farrar, Straus and Giroux, 2005), p. 45.

13. George W. Bush quoted by Walter Pincus and Dana Milbank, "Bush Reasserts Hussein-Al Qaeda Link," *Washington Post*, June 17, 2004; available at http://www.washingtonpost.com/wp-dyn/articles/A48970-2004Jun17.html/.

14. Tenet with Harlow, *At the Center of the Storm*, p. 341.

15. Ibid., p. 310.

16. George W. Bush quoted by Jonathan S. Landay, Warren P. Strobel, and John Walcott, "Doubts Cast on Efforts to Link Saddam and Al-Qaeda," Knight Ridder/Tribune News Service, March 3, 2004.

17. David L. Phillips, *Losing Iraq: Inside the Postwar Reconstruction Fiasco* (Boulder, CO: Westview Press, 2005), p. 159.

18. Douglas J. Feith, *War and Decision: Inside the Pentagon at the Dawn of the War on Terrorism* (New York: Harper, 2008), p. 215.

19. Paul Pillar quoted by Michael R. Gordon and Bernard E. Trainor, *Cobra II: The Inside Story of the Invasion and Occupation of Iraq* (New York: Pantheon, 2006), p. 127.

20. Thomas E. Ricks and Walter Pincus, "Pentagon Plans Major Changes in U.S. Strategy," *Washington Post*, May 7, 2001, p. A1.

21. Gordon and Trainor, *Cobra II*, p. 46.

22. Dale R. Herspring, *Rumsfeld's Wars: The Arrogance of Power* (Lawrence: University Press of Kansas, 2008), p. 13.

23. Gordon and Trainor, *Cobra II*, p. 4; DeLong with Lukeman, *Inside CENTCOM*, p. 70.

24. Gordon and Trainor, *Cobra II*, p. 28; Charles H. Ferguson, *No End in Sight: Iraq's Descent into Chaos* (New York: PublicAffairs, 2008), p. 25; Herspring, *Rumsfeld's Wars*, p. 124.

25. Franks with McConnell, *American Soldier*, pp. 331, 348.

26. DeLong with Lukeman, *Inside CENTCOM*, p. 66.

27. Franks with McConnell, *American Soldier*, p. 329.

28. Ibid., pp. 165, 400.

29. Author's confidential interview with a CIA official.

30. Herspring, *Rumsfeld's Wars*, p. 87.

31. Ricks, *Fiasco*, p. 75.

32. Franks with McConnell, *American Soldier*, p. 167–68.

33. Ken Adelman, "Cakewalk in Iraq," *Washington Post*, Feburary 13, 2002, p. A27.

34. Gordon and Trainor, *Cobra II*, pp. 101–2.

35. The Levin-Shinseki exchange is reprinted in Ricks, *Fiasco*, p. 97.

36. Author's interviews with generals who led previous occupations in Bosnia and Kosovo.

37. Rowan Scarborough, "Wolfowitz Criticizes 'Suspect' Estimate of Occupation Force," *Washington Times*, February 28, 2003, p. A1.

38. Donald Rumsfeld, Press Conference, February 27, 2003, quoted by Ferguson, *No End in Sight*, p. 32.

39. "End of Tour Memorandum" from General Erik Shinseki to Secretary of Defense Donald Rumsfeld, June 10, 2003.

40. Ricardo Sanchez and Donald T. Phillips, *Wiser in Battle: A Soldier's Story* (New York: Harper, 2008), p. 157.

41. Herspring, *Rumsfeld's Wars*, p. 125.

42. Gordon and Trainor, *Cobra II*, p. 116.

43. David Rieff, "Blueprint for a Mess: How the Bush Administration's Prewar Planners Bungled Postwar Iraq," *New York Times Magazine*, November 2, 2003, p. 58.

44. Franks with McConnell, *American Soldier*, p. xiii.

45. Paul Wolfowitz quoted by Karen DeYoung, *Soldier: The Life of Colin Powell* (New York: Alfred A. Knopf, 2006), pp. 460–61.

46. Dick Cheney on *Meet the Press*, March 16, 2003.

47. Woodward, *Plan of Attack*, pp. 22, 259; see also Michael R. Gordon, "Faulty Intelligence Misled Troops at War's Start," *New York Times*, October 20, 2004, p. A1.

48. Kanan Makiya quoted in Ari Fleischer, *Taking Heat: The President, the Press, and My Years in the White House* (New York: HarperCollins, 2005), p. 298.

49. "Post-War Planning Non-Existent," Knight-Ridder, October 17, 2003, quoted in Herspring, *Rumsfeld's Wars*, p. 127.

50. Marc Garlasco quoted in Ferguson, *No End in Sight*, p. 37.

51. Quoted in L. Paul Bremer with Malcolm McConnell, *My Year in Iraq: The Struggle to Build a Future of Hope* (New York: Simon and Schuster, 2006), p. 36.

52. Ruth Benedict, *The Chrysanthemum and the Sword: Patterns of Japanese Culture* (New York: Houghton Mifflin, 1946). I am indebted to Frank Hawke for pointing this out to me.

53. Powell quoted in Woodward, *Plan of Attack*, p. 22.

54. Feith, *War and Decision*, pp. 239–41.

55. Aram Roston, *The Man Who Pushed America to War: The Extraordinary Life, Adventures, and Obsessions of Ahmad Chalabi* (New York: Nation Books, 2008), p. 33.

56. Ricks, *Fiasco*, p. 57.

57. DeLong with Lukeman, *Inside CENTCOM*, p. 80.

58. Franks with McConnell, *American Soldier*, p. 421.

59. DeLong with Lukeman, *Inside CENTCOM*, p. 80.

60. Marc Garlasco quoted by Ferguson, *No End in Sight*, p. 43.

61. Ahmad Chalabi quoted by David Sanger, "A Seat of Honor Lost to Open Political Warfare," *New York Times*, May 21, 2004, p. A1.

62. Ferguson, *No End in Sight*, p. 41.

63. Roston, *The Man Who Pushed America to War*, p. 340.

64. Peter Galbraith, *The Fall of Iraq: How American Incompetence Created a War without End* (New York: Simon and Schuster, 2006), pp. 86–87.

65. Dean Acheson, *Present at the Creation: My Years in the State Department* (New York: W. W. Norton, 1969), p. 293.

66. Dick Cheney quoted in *Time*, October 14, 2002, p. 34.

67. National Intelligence Council, "Can Iraq Ever Become a Democracy?" January 2003; cited by Tenet with Harlow, *At the Center of the Storm*, p. 425.

68. George W. Bush quoted by Woodward, *Plan of Attack*, p. 405.

69. Ricks, *Fiasco*, p. 15.

70. "Bush Economic Aide Says Cost of Iraq War May Top $100 Billion," *Wall Street Journal*, September 16, 2002.

71. Scott McClellan, *What Happened: Inside the Bush White House and Washington's Culture of Deception* (New York: PublicAffairs, 2008), p. 123.

72. Joseph E. Stiglitz and Linda J. Bilmes, *The Three Trillion Dollar War: The True Cost of the Iraq Conflict* (New York: W. W. Norton, 2008).

73. Colonel John Agoglia quoted by Ferguson, *No End in Sight*, p. 41.

74. Wolfowitz quoted in Bob Herbert, "George Bush's Trillion Dollar War," *New York Times*, March 23, 2006, p. A27.

75. Bremer with McConnell, *My Year in Iraq*, p. 112.

76. Ricks, *Fiasco*, p. 85.

77. Quoted in Herspring, *Rumsfeld's Wars*, p. 163.

78. *Comprehensive Report of the Special Adviser to the DCI on Iraq's WMD* (Duelfer Report), September 30, 2004.

79. Robert Jervis, "Understanding the Bush Doctrine," *Political Science Quarterly* 118, no. 3 (Fall 2003); Ross, *Statecraft*, p. 125.

80. Tenet with Harlow, *At the Center of the Storm*, p. 493.

Chapter 8

1. Frederick the Great, *Instruction to His Generals*, iv, 1747 quoted in Robert Debs Heinl, Jr., ed., *Dictionary of Military and Naval Quotations* (Annapolis, MD: U.S. Naval Institute, 1966), p. 160.

2. Dana Priest and William M. Arkin, "Top Secret America: A Hidden World, Growing beyond Control," *Washington Post*, July 19, 2010; available at http://projects.washingtonpost.com/top-secret-america/articles/.

3. David Kahn, *The Codebreakers: The Comprehensive History of Secret Communication from Ancient Times to the Internet* (New York: Scribner, 1996).

4. Charles Duelfer, *Hide and Seek: The Search for Truth in Iraq* (New York: PublicAffairs, 2009), p. 470.

5. "In Cheney's Words: The Administration Case for Removing Saddam Hussein," *New York Times*, August 27, 2002.

6. Dino A. Brugioni, *Eyeball to Eyeball: The Inside Story of the Cuban Missile Crisis* (New York: Random House, 1993).

7. Gregory F. Treverton, *Intelligence for an Age of Terror* (New York: Cambridge University Press, 2009), p. 7.

8. Ibid., p. 54.

9. F. W. Winterbotham, *The Ultra Secret* (New York: Dell, 1994); Ronald W. Clark, *The Man Who Broke Purple* (London: Weidenfeld and Nicholson, 1977).

10. Nathan Aseng, *Navajo Code Talkers: America's Secret Weapon in World War II* (New York: Walker and Company, 1992); William C. Meadows, *The Comanche Code Talkers of World War II* (Austin: University of Texas Press, 2002). I am indebted to Frank Hawke for pointing this out to me.

11. U.S. Commission on the Terrorist Attacks upon the United States, *9/11 Commission Final Report* (New York: W. W. Norton, 2004), p. 86.

12. See, for example, Milt Bearden and James Risen, *The Main Enemy: The Inside Story of the CIA's Final Showdown with the KGB* (New York: Random House, 2003).

13. Numbers 13.

14. Oleg Vladimirovich Penkovskii, *The Penkovskii Papers* (New York: Collins, 1965); U.S. Central Intelligence Agency, *Preparing for Martial Law: Through the Eyes of Col. Ryszard Kuklinski*, booklet and CD-ROM (Washington, DC: Central Intelligence Agency, n.d.).

15. Ronald Radosh, *The Rosenberg File*, 2nd ed. (New Haven: Yale University Press, 1997).

16. Steve Coll, *Ghost Wars: The Secret History of the CIA, Afghanistan, and bin Laden, from the Soviet Invasion to September 10, 2001* (New York: Penguin Press, 2004), p. 278.

17. Stephen Philip Cohen, *The Idea of Pakistan* (Washington, DC: Brookings Institution, 2004), p. 100.

18. Coll, *Ghost Wars*, p. 492.

19. Lawrence Wright, *The Looming Tower: Al-Qaeda and the Road to 9/11* (New York: Vintage Books, 2006), p. 301.

20. Richard N. Haass, *War of Necessity, War of Choice: A Memoir of Two Iraq Wars* (New York: Simon and Schuster, 2009), p. 189.

21. James Bamford, *The Puzzle Palace: Inside the National Security Agency, America's Most Secret Intelligence* Organization (New York: Penguin, 1983); James Bamford, *Body of Secrets: Anatomy of the Ultra-Secret National Security Agency* (New York: Doubleday, 2001).

22. James Risen, *State of War: The Secret History of the CIA and the Bush Administration* (New York: Free Press, 2006), p. 48.

23. George Cahlink, "National Security: Breaking the Code," *Government Executive* (September 1, 2001), http://www.govexec.com/features/0901/0901s6.htm, quoted by Treverton, *Intelligence for an Age of Terror*, p. 106.

24. Priest and Arkin, "Top Secret America."

25. Gina Kolata, "Veiled Messages of Terrorists May Lurk in Cyberspace," *New York Times*, October 30, 2001.

26. Mark M. Lowenthal, *Intelligence: From Secrets to Policy*, 4th ed. (Washington, DC: CQ Press, 2009), p. 96; Jeffrey T. Richelson, *The US Intelligence Community*, 5th ed. (Boulder, CO: Westview Press, 2008), pp. 245–72.

27. U.S. Commission on the Intelligence Capabilities of the United States Regarding Weapons of Mass Destruction, *Report to the President*, Laurence H. Silberman and Charles S. Robb, Co-Chairs, March 31, 2005, p. 16.

28. Admiral Sergei Gorshkov, *The Seapower of the State*, 2nd ed. (Annapolis, MD: Naval Institute Press, 1979).

29. Barton Whaley, *Operation BARBAROSSA* (Cambridge, MA: MIT Press, 1974); David Stahel, *Operation Barbarossa and Germany's Defeat in the East* (New York: Cambridge University Press, 2009).

30. Roberta Wohlstetter, *Pearl Harbor: Warning and Decision* (Stanford: Stanford University Press, 1962).

31. For an example of the U.S. government's concern with the problem of surprise attack, see the declassified study directed by J. R. Killian and completed in 1955 entitled *Meeting the Threat of Surprise Attack*; reprinted in Declassified Documents Reference System, *Retrospective Collection* (Arlington, VA: Carollton Press, 1977); see also James R. Killian, Jr., *Sputnik, Scientist, and Eisenhower* (Cambridge, MA: MIT Press, 1977), pp. 67–93.

32. Agranat Commission Report, http://www.knesset.gov.il/lexicon/eng/agranat_eng.htm/.

33. Richard Betts, "Analysis, War and Decision: Why Intelligence Failures Are Inevitable," *World Politics* 31, no. 1 (October 1978).

34. Ronald Kessler, *The CIA at War: Inside the Secret Campaign against Terror* (New York: St. Martin's Griffin, 2003), p. 89.

35. Coll, *Ghost Wars*, p. 316.

36. Ibid., p. 572.

37. Charles G. Cogan, "Partners in Time: The CIA and Afghanistan since 1979," *World Policy Journal* 10, no. 2 (1993): p. 74.

38. Gary C. Schroen, *First In: An Insider's Account of How the CIA Spearheaded the War on Terror in Afghanistan* (New York: Ballantine Books, 2005), p. 56. For the account of Schroen's successor, see Gary Berntsen and Ralph Pezzulo, *Jawbreaker: The Attack on Bin Laden and Al-Qaeda: A Personal Account by the CIA's Field Commander* (New York: Three Rivers Press, 2005).

39. Henry A. Crumpton, "Intelligence and War: Afghanistan, 2001–2002," in Jennifer E. Sims and Burton Gerber, eds., *Transforming U.S. Intelligence* (Washington, DC: Georgetown University Press, 2005), p. 163.

40. These statistics are from ibid., p. 162.

41. "Cell Phone Tracking Helped Find al-Zaqawi," CNN, June 10, 2006; http://www.cnn.com/2006/WORLD/meast/06/09/iraq.al.zarqawi/.

42. Coll, *Ghost Wars*, p. 521.

43. Julian E. Barnes, "Military Refines a 'Constant Stare against Our Enemy,'" *Los Angeles Times*, November 2, 2009, p. A14.

44. Ibid., p. A1.

45. "The Year of the Drone," New America Foundation, http://counterterrorism.newamerica.net/drones.

46. Elisabeth Bumiller, "U.S. to Provide Spy Drones to Pakistan," *New York Times*, February 22, 2010, p. A8.

47. Michah Zenko, *Between Threats and War: U.S. Discrete Military Operations in the Post-Cold War World* (Stanford: Stanford University Press, 2010).

48. Risen, *State of War*, pp. 89, 143.

49. L. Paul Bremer with Malcolm McConnell, *My Year in Iraq: The Struggle to Build a Future of Hope* (New York: Simon and Schuster, 2006), p. 107.

50. Richard Haass, *The Opportunity: America's Moment to Alter History's Course* (New York: PublicAffairs, 2005), p. 187.

51. Comments by General Wesley Clark, "Six Degrees of Preemption," www.washingtonpost.com, posted September 29, 2002, p. B2.

52. David Kay quoted by Max Boot, "The Bush Doctrine Lives," *Weekly Standard*, February 16, 2004.

53. Robert Jervis, *Why Intelligence Fails: Lessons from the Iranian Revolution and the Iraq War* (Ithaca, NY: Cornell University Press, 2010, p. 134 (emphasis in the original).

54. David Johnston, "Saddam Hussein Sowed Confusion about Iraq's Arsenal as a Tactic of War," *New York Times*, October 7, 2004, p. A22.

55. Jervis, *Why Intelligence Fails*, p. 134.

56. Risen, *State of War*, p. 112.

57. Quoted by Elisabeth Bumiller and James Dao, "Cheney Says Peril of a Nuclear Iraq Justifies Attack," *New York Times*, August 27, 2002, p. A8. In his memoirs, George Tenet (p. 315) noted: "The [Cheney] speech went well beyond what our analysis could support."

58. National Intelligence Estimate, *Iraq's Continuing Programs for Weapons of Mass Destruction*, NIE 2002–16HC, October 2002; available at http://www.gwu.edu/~nsarchiv/NSAEBB/NSAEBB129/index.htm.

59. Michael DeLong with Noah Lukeman, *A General Speaks Out: The Truth about the Wars in Afghanistan and Iraq* (St. Paul, MN: Zenith Press, 2007), p. 68.

60. *The Independent*, January 30, 2003, quoted by Mark Bowden, "Wolfowitz: The Exit Interviews," *Atlantic Monthly* (July/August 2005): p. 114.

61. King Abdullah and Hosni Mubarak quoted by Tommy Franks with Malcolm McConnell, *American Soldier* (New York: Regan Books, 2004), pp. 418–19.

62. Robert Drogin, *Curveball: Spies, Lies, and the Con Man Who Caused a War* (New York: Random House, 2007); see also George Tenet with Bill Harlow, *At the Center of the Storm: My Years at the CIA* (New York: HarperCollins, 2007), pp. 375–83; and Risen, *State of War*, pp. 115–19.

63. Quoted in Risen, *State of War*, p. 116.

64. John Goetz and Bob Drogin, "Curveball Lies Low and Denies It All," *Los Angeles Times*, June 18, 2008, p. A1.

65. Tenet with Harlow, *At the Center of the Storm*, pp. 397–98.

66. Richard Perle quoted in Thomas Ricks, *Fiasco: The American Military Adventure in Iraq* (New York: Penguin Press, 2006), p. 54.

67. Peter Spiegel, "Investigation Fills in Blanks on How War Groundwork Was Laid," *Los Angeles Times*, April 6, 2007, p. A10. The inspector general of the Department of Defense investigated the operations of Feith's Office of Special Plans and released a report critical of it in April 2007. Feith responds to this report in his memoirs and on a website, www.dougfeith.com.

68. Seymour Hersh, "Selective Intelligence," *New Yorker*, May 12, 2003.

69. Tenet with Harlow, *At the Center of the Storm*, p. 321.

70. Treverton, *Intelligence for an Age of Terror*, p. 176.

71. For the text of the DOD Inspector General's report, see www.levin.senate.gov.

72. Jean Krasno and James S. Sutterin, *The United Nations and Iraq: Defanging the Viper* (New York: Praeger, 2003).

73. Author's interviews with UN weapons inspectors.

74. Duelfer, *Hide and Seek*, p. 217.

75. Franks with McConnell, *American Soldier*, pp. xiv–xv.

76. Judith Miller and Michael R. Gordon, "U.S. Says Hussein Intensifies Quest for A-Bomb Parts," *New York Times*, September 8, 2002, p. A1.

77. Condoleezza Rice quoted by Ricks, *Fiasco*, p. 58.

78. "Secretary Rumsfeld's Interview on Face the Nation," September 8, 2002, transcript, p. 1.

79. U.S. Commission on the Intelligence Capabilities of the United States Regarding Weapons of Mass Destruction, *Report to the President*, Laurence H. Silberman and Charles S. Robb, Co-Chairs, March 31, 2005.

80. Joseph Wilson, *The Politics of Truth: A Diplomat's Memoir: Inside the Lies That Led to War and Betrayed My Wife's CIA Identity* (New York: Carroll and Graf, 2004).

81. James Risen, "C.I.A. Aides Feel Pressure in Preparing Iraqi Reports," *New York Times*, March 23, 2003, p. B10.

82. Joseph Wilson, "What I Didn't Find in Africa," *New York Times*, July 6, 2003.

83. Douglas Jehl and David E. Sanger, "Powell's Case, a Year Later: Gaps in Picture of Iraq Arms," *New York Times*, February 1, 2004, p. A10.

84. Sam Tannenhaus, "Interview with Paul Wolfowitz," *Vanity Fair*, June 2003.

85. Haass, *War of Necessity, War of Choice*, p. 231.

86. *The 9/11 Commission Final Report*, p. 229.

87. *New York Times*, February 2002; cited by John B. Judis and Spencer Ackerman, "The Selling of the Iraq War," *New Republic Online*, June 30, 2003, p. 3.

88. President George W. Bush quoted by David L. Phillips, *Losing Iraq: Inside the Postwar Reconstruction Fiasco* (Boulder, CO: Westview Press, 2005), p. 65.

89. Paul Pillar quoted by Scott Shane, "Ex-CIA Official Says Iraq Data Was Distorted," *New York Times*, February 11, 2006, p. A6; see also Paul Pillar, "Intelligence, Policy, and the War in Iraq," *Foreign Affairs* 85, no. 2 (March–April 2006), pp. 15–28.

90. Phillips, *Losing Iraq*, p. 159.

91. Tenet with Harlow, *At the Center of the Storm*, p. 310.

92. Ibid., pp. 317, 348.

93. Robert Jervis, "War, Intelligence, and Honesty: A Review Essay," *Political Science Quarterly* 123 (Winter 2008).

94. Public Law 107–306, November 27, 2002.

95. *The 9/11 Commission Final Report.*

96. Michael Krepon, *Better Safe Than Sorry: The Ironies of Living with the Bomb* (Stanford: Stanford University Press, 2009). p. 94.

97. Richard Butler, *Saddam Defiant: The Threat of Mass Destruction and the Crisis of Global Security* (London: Weidenfeld and Nicholson, 2000).

98. Tim Weiner, *Legacy of Ashes: The History of the CIA* (New York: Anchor Books, 2007), p. 565.

99. Hans Blix, *Disarming Iraq: The Search for Weapons of Mass Destruction* (New York: Pantheon Books, 2004).

100. Walter Pincus and Dana Milbank, "Arms Hunt in Iraq to Get New Focus; Next Chief Named for Effort," *Washington Post*, January 24, 2004, p. A1.

101. U.S. Commission on the Intelligence Capabilities of the United States Regarding Weapons of Mass Destruction, *Report to the President.*

102. Quoted in Weiner, *Legacy of Ashes*, p. 572; see also Richard Kerr, Thomas Wolfe, Rebecca Donegan, and Aris Pappas, "Collection and Analysis on Iraq: Issues for the US Intelligence Community," *Studies in Intelligence* 49, no. 3 (2005): pp. 47–54.

103. U.S. Congress, Senate, Select Committee on Intelligence, *Report on the U.S. Intelligence Community's Prewar Intelligence Assessment on Iraq*, 108th Cong., 2nd sess., July 7, 2004.

104. U.K., House of Commons, Committee of Privy Counselors, *Review of Intelligence on Weapons of Mass Destruction* (The Butler Report), July 14, 2004; available at http://www.butlerreview.org.uk/index.

105. Philip Davies, "Intelligence Culture and Intelligence Failure in Britain and the United States," *Cambridge Review of International Affairs* 17 (October 2004): pp. 495–520.

106. Government of Australia, *The Report of the Inquiry into Australian Agencies* (The Flood Report), July 2004.

107. "Report Answers Questions on Iraq," and "Dutch War Inquiry Colours UK Investigation," Radio Netherlands Worldwide (RNW), January 14, 2010; available at http://www.rnw.nl/english/article/report-answers-questions-iraq/.

108. "About the Inquiry," *The Iraq Inquiry;* available at http://www.iraqinquiry.org.uk/about.aspx.

109. Ricks, *Fiasco*, p. 53.

110. Tenet with Harlow, *At the Center of the Storm*, pp. 236–37.

111. For Duelfer's personal account of the Iraq Survey group, see Duelfer, *Hide and Seek.*

112. George W. Bush quoted by Mike Allen and Dana Priest, "Report Discounts Iraqi Arms Threat," *Washington Post* (October 6, 2004), p. A1.

113. Duelfer, *Hide and Seek.*

114. Unnamed senator quoted ibid., p. 454.

115. Ahmed S. Hashim, *Insurgency and Counterinsurgency in Iraq* (Ithaca, NY: Cornell University Press, 2006), p. 320.

116. Duelfer, *Hide and Seek*, p. 246.

117. Ibid., p. 248.

118. Jervis, *Why Intelligence Fails;* Richard Betts, *Enemies of Intelligence: Knowledge and Power in American National Security* (New York: Columbia University Press, 2007).

Chapter 9

1. George Tenet with Bill Harlow, *At the Center of the Storm: My Years at the CIA* (New York: HarperCollins, 2007), p. 309.

2. Mark Danner, *The Secret Way to War: The Downing Street Memo and the Iraq War's Buried History* (New York: New York Review of Books, 2006); see also Don Van Atta, Jr., "Bush Was Set on Path to War, Memo by British Adviser Says," *New York Times*, March 27, 2006, p. A1.

3. There are several histories of the military aspects of early war planning and the invasion, including Michael R. Gordon and Bernard E. Trainor, *Cobra II: The Inside Story of the Invasion and Occupation of Iraq* (New York: Pantheon, 2006); Thomas E. Ricks, *Fiasco: The American Military Adventure in Iraq* (New York: Penguin Press, 2006); John Keegan, *The Iraq War* (New York: Alfred A. Knopf, 2004); and Williamson Murray and Robert H. Scales, Jr., *The Iraq War: A Military History* (Cambridge, MA: Harvard University Press, 2003).

4. George H. W. Bush and Brent Scowcroft, *A World Transformed* (New York: Knopf, 1998), p. 489.

5. General H. Norman Schwarzkopf with Peter Petre, *The Autobiography: It Doesn't Take a Hero* (New York: Bantam, 1992), p. 498.

6. Richard N. Haass, *War of Necessity, War of Choice: A Memoir of Two Iraq Wars* (New York: Simon and Schuster, 2009), p. 131.

7. For a description of this policy, see the article by Clinton's assistant for national security affairs, Anthony Lake, "Confronting Backlash States," *Foreign Affairs* (March/April 1994).

8. National Commission on Terrorist Attacks on the United States, *9/11 Commission Final Report* (New York: W. W. Norton, 2004), pp. 116–17, 131–33.

9. Bill Clinton, *My Life* (New York: Knopf, 2004), p. 799.

10. Madeleine Albright with Bill Woodward, *Madame Secretary* (New York: Miramax Books, 2003), p. 374.

11. Mark Mazzetti, "Outsiders Hired as C.I.A. Planned to Kill Jihadists," *New York Times*, August 20, 2009, p. A1.

12. "How Far Americans Would Go to Fight Terror," *Christian Science Monitor*, November 14, 2001.

13. Remarks of John Major in *Official Record* (House of Commons), January 15, 22, 1991, quoted by Lawrence Freedman and Efraim Karsh, *The Gulf Conflict, 1990–1991: Diplomacy and War in the New World Order* (Princeton: Princeton University Press, 1993), p. 411.

14. ABC Television, *The Guardian*, February 26, 1991, quoted by Freedman and Karsh, *The Gulf Conflict*, p. 412.

15. Judith Miller and Laurie Mylroie, *Saddam and the Crisis in the Gulf* (New York: Times Books, 1990), p. 117.

16. These are described by Robert Baer, *See No Evil: The True Story of a Ground Soldier in the CIA's War on Terrorism* (New York: Three Rivers Press, 2002).

17. Ibid., pp. 198–99; Ronald Kessler, *The CIA at War: Inside the Secret Campaign against Terror* (New York: St. Martin's Griffin, 2003).

18. Talabani quoted in Kessler, *The CIA at War*, p. 197.

19. Aram Roston, *The Man Who Pushed America to War: The Extraordinary Life, Adventures, and Obsessions of Ahmad Chalabi* (New York: Nation Books, 2008), p. 106.

20. Ibid., p. 118.

21. *New Republic*, December 7, 1998.

22. Daniel Byman, Kenneth Pollack, and Gideon Rose, "The Rollback Fantasy," *Foreign Affairs* (January/February 1999).

23. Bradley Graham, *By His Own Rules: The Ambitions, Successes, and Ultimate Failures of Donald Rumsfeld* (New York: PublicAffairs, 2009), p. 307.

24. Richard Andres, "The Afghan Model in Northern Iraq," *Journal of Strategic Studies* 29, no. 3 (June 2006): pp. 395–422.

25. U.S. Army and U.S. Marine Corps, *Counterinsurgency Field Manual* (Chicago: University of Chicago Press, 2007), p. 2.

26. David Kilcullen, *The Accidental Guerilla: Fighting Small Wars in the Midst of a Big One* (New York: Oxford University Press, 2009), p. 73.

27. Gordon and Trainor, *Cobra II*, p. 4.

28. Tommy Franks with Malcolm McConnell, *American Soldier* (New York: Regan Books, 2004), p. 394.

29. George W. Bush, speech at the Citadel, South Carolina, September 23, 1999.

30. Quoted by Graham, *By His Own Rules*, p. 208.

31. Quoted ibid., p. 277.

32. Donald Rumsfeld, *Annual Report to the President and the Congress*, 2002, quoted ibid., p. 326.

33. Donald Rumsfeld, "Transforming the Military," *Foreign Affairs* 81, no. 3 (May/June 2002).

34. Quoted in Graham, *By His Own Rules*, p. 325.

35. Doug Stanton, *Horse Soldiers: The Extraordinary Story of a Band of U.S. Soldiers Who Rode to Victory in Afghanistan* (New York: Simon and Schuster, 2009).

36. For an excellent analysis, see Joseph J. Collins, *Choosing War: The Decision to Invade Iraq and Its Aftermath*, Institute for National Strategic Studies Occasional Paper 5 (Washington, DC: National Defense University Press, April 2008).

37. Bob Woodward, *Plan of Attack* (New York: Simon and Schuster, 2004), p. 437.

38. Tenet with Harlow, *At the Center of the Storm*, p. 308.

39. Haass, *War of Necessity, War of Choice*, p. 6.

40. U.S. Joint Chiefs of Staff, *Joint Operations*, Joint Publication 3-0 (Washington, DC: U.S. Joint Chiefs of Staff, September 17, 2006), p. xxi.

41. Dick Cheney quoted by Dale R. Herspring, *Rumsfeld's Wars: The Arrogance of Power* (Lawrence: University Press of Kansas, 2008), p. 58.

42. Steven Cambone quoted in Frederick Kagan, *Finding the Target: The Transformation of American Military Policy* (New York: Encounter Books, 2006), p. 346.

43. John M. Broder, "Filling Gaps in Iraq, Then Finding a Void at Home," *New York Times*, July 17, 2007, p. A1.

44. James Glanz, "Contractors Outnumber U.S. Troops in Afghanistan." *New York Times*, September 2, 2009, p. A8.

45. Tenet with Harlow, *At the Center of the Storm*, p. 399.

46. Ahmed S. Hashim, *Insurgency and Counter-Insurgency in Iraq* (Ithaca, NY: Cornell University Press, 2006), p. 292.

47. Nir Rosen quoted by Charles H. Ferguson, *No End in Sight: Iraq's Descent into Chaos* (New York: PublicAffairs, 2008), p. 136.

48. Franks with McConnell, *American Soldier*, p. 442.

49. Quoted by Michael Isikoff and David Corn, *Hubris: The Inside Story of Spin, Scandal, and the Selling of the Iraq War* (New York: Crown, 2006), pp. 196–97.

50. See, for example, L. Paul Bremer III with Malcolm McConnell, *My Year in Iraq* (New York: Simon and Schuster, 2006); Rajiv Chandrasekaran, *Imperial Life in the Emerald City: Inside Iraq's Green Zone* (New York: Alfred A. Knopf, 2006); Larry Diamond, *Squandered Victory: The American Occupation and the Bungled Effort to Bring Democracy to Iraq* (New York: Henry Holt, 2005); George Packer, *The Assassins' Gate: America in Iraq* (New York: Farrar, Straus and Giroux, 2005); David L. Phillips, *Losing Iraq: Inside the Postwar Reconstruction Fiasco* (Boulder, CO: Westview, 2005); and Ricardo Sanchez and Donald T. Phillips, *Wiser in Battle: A Soldier's Story* (New York: Harper, 2008).

51. Ryan Crocker quoted by Thomas E. Ricks, *The Gamble: General David Petraeus and the American Military Adventure in Iraq, 2006–2008* (New York: Penguin Press, 2009), p. 32.

52. Max Boot, *The Savage Wars of Peace: Small Wars and the Rise of American Power* (New York: Basic Books, 2003).

53. Maxwell Taylor, *The Uncertain Trumpet* (New York: Harper Brothers, 1960); Henry A. Kissinger, *Nuclear Weapons and Foreign Policy* (New York: Harper and Row, 1957).

54. Roger Hilsman, *To Move a Nation: The Politics of Foreign Policy in the Administration of John F. Kennedy* (New York: Doubleday, 1967), p. 413.

55. William C. Westmoreland, *A Soldier Reports* (New York: Doubleday, 1976), p. 38.

56. David H. Hackworth and Julie Sherman, *About Face: The Odyssey of an American Warrior* (New York: Simon and Schuster, 1989), p. 431 (emphasis in the original).

57. General Harold K. Johnson, U.S. Army Military History Institute Senior Officer Oral History Project, vol. III, section XII (April 23, 1973), pp. 8–9, quoted by John A. Nagl, *Learning to Eat Soup with a Knife: Counterinsurgency Lessons from Malaya and Vietnam* (Chicago: University of Chicago Press, 2002), p. 128.

58. Hackworth, *About Face*, p. 431.

59. Personal communication to the author.

60. Robert S. Thompson, *No Exit from Vietnam* (London: Chatto and Sindus, 1969), p. 136, quoted by Nagl, *Learning to Eat Soup with a Knife*, p. 209.

61. H. R. McMaster, *Dereliction of Duty: Lyndon Johnson, Robert McNamara, the Joint Chiefs of Staff, and the Lies That Led to Vietnam* (New York: HarperPerrenial, 1997), p. 146.

62. Nagl, *Learning to Eat Soup with a Knife*, pp. 175, 208.

63. David Howell Petraeus, *The American Military and the Lessons of Vietnam: A Study of Military Influence and the Use of Force in the Post-Vietnam Era*, doctoral dissertation, Princeton University, 1987; available from University Microfilms, Ann Arbor, MI.

64. Ibid., p. 308; see also p. 108.

65. CNN, U.S., "Iraq Insurgency in Its 'Last Throes,' Cheney Says," June 20, 2005; at http://articles.cnn.com/2005–05–30/us/cheney.iraq_1_weapons-inspectors-al-zarqawi-iraq-insurgency?_s=PM:US.

66. President Bush quoted by Ricks, *The Gamble*, p. 14.

67. U.S., White House, *National Strategy for Victory in Iraq* (Washington, DC: White House, November 5, 2005).

68. Peter Feaver, "Anatomy of the Surge," *Commentary*, April 2008.

69. Ibid.

70. Ricks, *The Gamble*.

71. Linda Robinson, *Tell Me How This Ends: General David Petraeus and the Search for a Way Out of War* (New York: PublicAffairs, 2008).

72. David Petraeus and James Amos with a foreword by John Nagl, *The US Army, Marine Corps, Counterinsurgency Field Manual* (Chicago: University of Chicago Press, 2007).

73. Kilcullen quoted by Ricks, *The Gamble*, p. 163.

74. Petraeus, *The American Military and the Lessons of Vietnam*, p. 239.

75. Andrew Card quoted by Graham, *By His Own Rules*, pp. 671–72.

76. B. H. Liddell Hart, *Strategy*, 2nd ed. (New York: Frederick A. Praeger, 1967), p. 335.

77. Hedley Bull, "Strategic Studies and Its Critics," *World Politics*, 20, no. 4 (July 1968): p. 593.

78. T. E. Lawrence quoted by Ricks, *Fiasco*, p. 253.

79. Franks with McConnell, *American Soldier*, p. 239. This is a paraphrase of the German General von Moltke the elder's observation: "No plan of operations extends with certainty beyond the first encounter with the enemy's main strength."

Chapter 10

1. Richard N. Haass, *The Opportunity: America's Moment to Alter History's Course* (New York: PublicAffairs, 2005), p. 193.

2. Ahmed S. Hashim, *Insurgency and Counter-Insurgency in Iraq* (Ithaca, NY: Cornell University Press, 2006), p. 264.

3. James Dobbins et al., *America's Role in Nation-Building: From Germany to Iraq* (Santa Monica, CA: RAND Corporation, 2003).

4. Ibid., p. 154.

5. Paul Wolfowitz on "Face the Nation," CBS, November 18, 2001; available at http://www.defenselink.mil/transcript.aspx?transcriptid=2442/.

6. Adam Roberts, "Doctrine and Reality in Afghanistan," *Survival* 51, no. 1 (February–March 2009), p. 40.

7. Seth G. Jones, *In the Graveyard of Empires: America's War in Afghanistan* (New York: W. W. Norton, 2009), p. 118.

8. Eric Schmitt, "In Afghanistan: What's Past and What's Still to Come," *New York Times*, October 13, 2002, section 4, p. 5.

9. Gary C. Schroen, *First In: An Insider's Account of How the CIA Spearheaded the War on Terror in Afghanistan* (New York: Presidio Press/Random House, 2005), pp. 380–81.

10. Ibid., p. 381.

11. Richard Armitage quoted by Jones, *In the Graveyard of Empires*, p. 127.

12. Among the best accounts of postwar reconstruction in Iraq are Ali A. Allawi, *The Occupation of Iraq: Winning the War, Losing the Peace* (New Haven: Yale University Press, 2007); Nora Bensahel, "Mission Not Accomplished: What Went Wrong with Iraqi Reconstruction," *Journal of Strategic Studies* 29, no. 3 (June 2006): pp. 453–73; L. Paul Bremer, III, with Malcolm McConnell, *My Year in Iraq* (New York: Simon and Schuster, 2006); Larry Diamond, *Squandered Victory: The American Occupation and the Bungled Effort to Bring Democracy to Iraq* (New York: Henry Holt, 2005); George Packer, *The Assassins' Gate: America in Iraq* (New York: Farrar, Straus and Giroux, 2005); David L. Phillips, *Losing Iraq: Inside the Postwar Reconstruction Fiasco* (Boulder, CO: Westview Press, 2005); and Rajiv Chandrasekaran, *Imperial Life in the Emerald City: Inside Iraq's Green Zone* (New York: Alfred A. Knopf, 2006).

13. Two of the best accounts of the early military aspects of the Iraq War are Michael R. Gordon and Bernard E. Trainor, *Cobra II: The Inside Story of the Invasion and Occupation of Iraq* (New York: Pantheon, 2006), p. 464; and Thomas E. Ricks, *Fiasco: The American Military Adventure in Iraq* (New York: Penguin Press, 2006), p. 221.

14. Ricks, *Fiasco*, p. 115.

15. These quotations are from the hearing of the Senate Foreign Relations Committee, February 11, 2003, quoted by Phillips, *Losing Iraq*, p. 122.

16. Dobbins et al., *America's Role in Nation-Building*; Edward P. Djerejian and Frank G. Wisner, Co-Chairs, *Guiding Principles for U.S. Post-Conflict Policy in Iraq* (New York: Council on Foreign Relations, February 2003); John Hamre et al., *Iraq's Post-Conflict Reconstruction: A Field Review and Recommendations* (Washington, DC: Center for International and Strategic Studies, July 17, 2003); Richard W. Murphy, Chair, *Winning the Peace: Managing a Successful Transition in Iraq* (Washington, DC: American University and the Atlantic Council of the United States, January 2003); Conrad C. Crane and W. Andrew Terrill, *Reconstructing Iraq: Insights, Challenges, and Missions for Military*

Forces in a Post-Conflict Scenario (Carlisle, PA: Strategic Studies Institute, U.S. Army War College, February 2003); Michael Eisenstadt and Eric Mathewson, eds., *U.S. Policy in Post-Saddam Iraq: Lessons from the British Experience* (Washington, DC: Washington Institute on Near East Policy, 2003).

17. "New State Department Releases on the 'Future of Iraq' Project," *Electronic Briefing Book No. 198* (Washington, DC: National Security Archive, September 2006); available at http://www.gwu.edu/~nsarchiv/NSAEBB/NSAEBB198/index.htm. For comments on the project, see Gordon and Trainor, *Cobra II*, p. 159; Ricks, *Fiasco*, p. 102; Phillips, *Losing Iraq*, p. 5.

18. George Tenet with Bill Harlow. *At the Center of the Storm: My Years at the CIA* (New York: HarperCollins, 2007), p. 419; Ricardo S. Sanchez with Donald T. Phillips, *Wiser in Battle: A Soldier's Story* (New York: HarperCollins, 2008), p. 171.

19. Michael Gordon, "The Strategy to Secure Iraq Did Not Foresee a 2nd War," *New York Times*, October 19, 2004.

20. Ambassador James Dobbins quoted by Robin Wright, "Series of US Fumbles Blamed for Turmoil in Postwar Iraq," *Washington Post*, April 11, 2004, p. 15.

21. Steven S. Simon, *After the Surge: The Case for U.S. Military Disengagement from Iraq*, CSR Report no. 23 (New York: Council on Foreign Relations, 2007), p. 4.

22. Ibid.

23. Garner quoted in Ricks, *Fiasco*, p. 102.

24. Gordon and Trainor, *Cobra II*, p. 159; Ricks, *Fiasco*, p. 102; Chandrasekaran, *Imperial Life in the Emerald City*, p. 37.

25. Roger Cohen, "The MacAuthur Lunch," *Washington Post*, August 27, 2007, p. 17, quoted by Joseph J. Collins, *Choosing War: The Decision to Invade Iraq and Its Aftermath*, Institute for National Strategic Studies, Occasional Paper 5 (Washington, DC: National Defense University Press, April 2008), pp. 18–19.

26. Charles Ferguson, *No End in Sight: Iraq's Descent into Chaos* (New York: PublicAffairs, 2008), p. 293.

27. Bremer with McConnell, *My Year in Iraq*, p. 10.

28. Phillips, *Losing Iraq*, p. 134.

29. Patrick Tyler, "New Policy in Iraq to Authorize G.I.s to Shoot Looters," *New York Times*, May 14, 2003, p. A1.

30. Rumsfeld quoted by Ferguson, *No End in Sight*, p. 135.

31. Packer, *The Assassins' Gate*, p. 139.

32. Quoted in Diamond, *Squandered Victory*, p. 288.

33. Major General Paul Eaton quoted in Ferguson, *No End in Sight*, p. 114.

34. Richard Armitage quoted ibid., p. 127.

35. Lieutenant General Jay Garner quoted by Michael R. Gordon, "The Strategy to Security Iraq Did Not Foresee a 2nd War," *New York Times*, October 19, 2004.

36. Bremer with McConnell, *My Year in Iraq*, p. 106 (emphasis in the original).

37. Gordon and Trainor, *Cobra II*, p. 497.

38. "Coalition Provisional Authority Order Number 1: De-Ba'athification of Iraqi Society," May 16, 2003; text reprinted in Ferguson, *No End in Sight*, pp. 150–51.

39. Chandrasekaran, *Imperial Life in the Emerald City*, p. 69; Packer, *The Assassins' Gate*, p. 195; Tenet with Harlow, *At the Center of the Storm*, p. 426; Bremer with McConnell, *My Year in Iraq*, pp. 45, 57.

40. Bremer with McConnell, *My Year in Iraq*, p. 297.

41. Recommendation 27 in James A. Baker and Lee H. Hamilton, Co-Chairs, *Iraq Study Group Report: The Way Forward—A New Approach* (New York: Vintage Books, 2006), p. 65.

42. Sanchez with Phillips, *Wiser in Battle*, p. 185.

43. Dale R. Herspring, *Rumsfeld's Wars: The Arrogance of Power* (Lawrence: University Press of Kansas, 2008), p. 146.

44. The text of CPA Order Number 2 is included as an appendix in Gordon and Trainor, *Cobra II*, pp. 586–90; and in Ferguson, *No End in Sight*, pp. 164–67.

45. Bremer with McConnell, *My Year in Iraq*, p. 27.

46. Ricks, *Fiasco*, p. 161.

47. Gordon and Trainor, *Cobra II*, p. 483; Ferguson, *No End in Sight*, p. 199; Herspring, *Rumsfeld's Wars*, p. 147.

48. Ricks, *Fiasco*, p. 161.

49. John Hamre, Chairman, *Iraq's Post-Conflict Reconstruction: A Field Review and Recommendations*, July 17, 2003, quoted by Bremer with McConnell, *My Year in Iraq*, p. 114.

50. General Jay Garner quoted by Ferguson, *No End in Sight*, p. 199.

51. Tenet with Harlow, *At the Center of the Storm*, p. 429.

52. Tommy Franks with Malcolm McConnell, *American Soldier* (New York: Regan Books, 2004), p. 441; Bremer with McConnell, *My Year in Iraq*, p. 223; Ferguson, *No End in Sight*, p. 192.

53. Peter R. Mansoor, *Baghdad at Sunrise: A Brigade Commander's War in Iraq* (New Haven: Yale University Press, 2008), p. 106.

54. Tenet with Harlow, *At the Center of the Storm*, p. 428; James Risen, *State of War: The Secret History of the CIA and the Bush Administration* (New York: Free Press, 2006), p. 3.

55. Robert Draper, *Dead Certain: The Presidency of George W. Bush* (New York: Free Press, 2007), p. 211; on this point, see also Risen, *State of War*, p. 3.

56. "Letter from L. Paul Bremer to George W. Bush," May 22, 2003; http://www.nytimes.com/ref/washington/04bremer-text1.html?ref=washington.

57. Edmund L. Andrews, "Envoy's Letters Counter Bush on Dismantling of Iraq Army," *New York Times*, September 4, 2007, p. A1.

58. Gordon and Trainor, *Cobra II*, p. 485.

59. General Jay Garner quoted in Ferguson, *No End in Sight*, p. 94.

60. Charles Duelfer, *Hide and Seek: The Search for Truth in Iraq* (New York: PublicAffairs, 2009), p. 311.

61. Diamond, *Squandered Victory,* p. 91.

62. Franks with McConnell, *American Soldier,* p. 421.

63. Noah Feldman quoted by Packer, *The Assassins' Gate,* p. 77.

64. Yochi J. Dreazen, "How a 24-Year-Old Got a Job Rebuilding Iraq's Stock Market," *Wall Street Journal*, January 28, 2004, p. A1; Chandrasekaran, *Imperial Life in the Emerald City,* pp. 95–99.

65. Packer, *The Assassins' Gate,* p. 184.

66. Tenet with Harlow, *At the Center of the Storm,* p. 423.

67. Heather Coyne quoted by Ferguson, *No End in Sight*, p. 305.

68. Colonel Paul Hughes quoted by Ferguson ibid., p. 284.

69. Jacob Weisberg, *The Bush Tragedy* (New York: Random House, 2008), p. 101.

70. Baker and Hamilton, *Iraq Study Group Report,* p. 92.

71. Major General Paul Eaton quoted by Ferguson, *No End in Sight*, p. 279.

72. Paul Pillar quoted ibid., p. 297.

73. Gerald Burke quoted ibid., p. 246.

74. Michael Moss quoted ibid., p. 247.

75. Colonel T. X. Hammes, USMC, quoted by Packer, *The Assassins' Gate,* p. 307.

76. Ferguson, *No End in Sight*, p. 345.

77. Bremer with McConnell, *My Year in Iraq,* p. 397.

78. Diamond, *Squandered Victory,* p. 226.

79. Douglas J. Feith, *War and Decision: Inside the Pentagon at the Dawn of the War on Terrorism* (New York: Harper, 2008), p. 497.

80. Joseph R. Biden, Jr., and Leslie Gelb, "Unity through Autonomy in Iraq," *New York Times*, May 1, 2006, p. A25.

81. Robert M. Perito, *The U.S. Experience with Provincial Reconstruction Teams in Afghanistan,* Special Report 152 (Washington, DC: United States Institute of Peace, October 2005), p. 2.

82. Timothy K. Deady, "Lessons from a Successful Counterinsurgency: The Philippines, 1899–1902," *Parameters* 35 (Spring 2005): p. 57.

83. Michael J. McNerney, "Stabilization and Reconstruction in Afghanistan: Are PRTs a Model or a Muddle?" *Parameters* (Winter 2005–6): p. 37.

84. U.S. Government Accountability Office, "Provincial Reconstruction Teams in Afghanistan and Iraq," October 1, 2008, p. 2.

85. McNerney, "Stabilization and Reconstruction in Afghanistan," p. 37.

86. Ibid., p. 40.

87. Robert M. Perito, *Provincial Reconstruction Teams in Iraq,* Special Report 185 (Washington, DC: United States Institute of Peace, March 2007), p. 7.

88. Mansoor, *Baghdad at Sunrise*, p. 54.

89. Thomas E. Ricks, *The Gamble: General David Petraeus and the American Military Adventure in Iraq, 2006–2008* (New York: Penguin Press, 2009), p. 38.

90. Bradley Graham, *By His Own Rules: The Ambitions, Successes, and Ultimate Failures of Donald Rumsfeld* (New York: PublicAffairs, 2009), pp. 609–11.

91. For a useful source, see U.S. Army, *PRT Playbook: Tactics, Techniques, and Procedures* (Fort Leavenworth, KS: Center for Army Lessons Learned, September 2007).

92. Commander Larry Legere quoted by Jones, *Graveyard of Empires*, p. 296.

93. Ahmed Rashid, *Descent into Chaos: The U.S. and the Disaster in Pakistan, Afghanistan, and Central Asia* (New York: Penguin Books, 2009), p. 195.

Chapter 11

1. Lawrence Freedman, "War in Iraq: Selling the Threat," *Survival* 46, no. 2 (Summer 2004): p. 9.

2. For a history of the NSC, see David Rothkopf, *Running the World: The Inside Story of the National Security Council and the Architects of American Power* (New York: PublicAffairs, 2005).

3. Michael R. Gordon and Bernard E. Trainor, *Cobra II: The Inside Story of the Invasion and Occupation of Iraq* (New York: Pantheon Books, 2006), p. 38. This view is echoed by a number of others including Bob Woodward, *State of Denial: Bush at War, Part III* (New York: Simon and Schuster, 2006), p. 391; Jane Mayer, *The Dark Side: The Inside Story of How the War on Terror Turned into a War on American Ideals* (New York: Doubleday, 2008), pp. 53, 62.

4. Stephen F. Hayes, *Cheney: The Untold Story of America's Most Powerful and Controversial Vice President* (New York: HarperCollins, 2007), p. 305.

5. Quoted by Mayer, *The Dark Side*, p. 60; see also Jack Goldsmith, *The Terror Presidency: Law and Judgment Inside the Bush Administration* (New York: W. W. Norton, 2007), pp. 86–88.

6. Samuel Alito quoted by Jess Bravin, "Rule of Law, Judge Alito's View of the Presidency: Expansive Powers," *Wall Street Journal*, January 5, 2006.

7. John C. Yoo, *The Powers of War and Peace* (Chicago: University of Chicago Press, 2005).

8. Barton Gellman, *Angler: The Cheney Vice Presidency* (New York: Penguin Press, 2008), p. 137.

9. President George W. Bush quoted ibid., p. 318.

10. Mayer, *The Dark Side*, p. 152.

11. Bradley Graham, *By His Own Rules: The Ambitions, Successes, and Ultimate Failures of Donald Rumsfeld* (New York: PublicAffairs, 2009), p. 316.

12. Woodward, *State of Denial*, p. 127; see also Charles H. Ferguson, *No End in Sight: Iraq's Descent into Chaos* (New York: PublicAffairs, 2008), p. 82; George Packer, *The Assassins' Gate: America in Iraq* (New York: Farrar, Straus and Giroux, 2005), p. 124.

13. Richard B. Myers with Malcolm McConnell, *Eyes on the Horizon: Serving on the Front Lines of National Security* (New York: Threshold Books, 2009).

14. Graham, *By His Own Rules*, p. 274.

15. Ibid., pp. 275, 320; Thomas E. Ricks, *Fiasco: The American Military Adventure in Iraq* (New York: Penguin Press, 2006), p. 89.

16. See, for example, Major General Paul Eaton, "A Top-Down Review of the Pentagon," *New York Times*, March 16, 2006; Lieutenant General Greg Newbold, "Why Iraq Was a Mistake," *Time*, April 17, 2006; Major General John Batiste, "A Case for Accountability," *Washington Post*, April 19, 2006.

17. Memorandum from General Barry R. McCaffrey to Colonel Michael Meese, "After Action Report," December 18, 2007, p. 10.

18. James Fallows, "Blind into Baghdad," *Atlantic Monthly* 293, no. 1 (January–February 2004): p. 65.

19. Graham, *By His Own Rules*, p. 345.

20. Ibid.

21. Woodward, *State of Denial*, pp. 316–17.

22. Rumsfeld quoted in Graham, *By His Own Rules*, p. 521.

23. Transcript, Press Conference at the Department of Defense, April 14, 2004; http://transcripts.cnn.com/TRANSCRIPTS/0404/15/lol.04.html.

24. Peter R. Mansoor, *Baghdad at Sunrise: A Brigade Commander's War in Iraq* (New Haven: Yale University Press, 2008), p. 288 (emphasis in the original).

25. Quoted in Karen DeYoung, *Soldier: The Life of Colin Powell* (New York: Alfred A. Knopf, 2006), p. 520.

26. Lawrence B. Wilkerson, "The White House Cabal," *Los Angeles Times*, October 25, 2005, p. B11; see also Dana Milbank, "Colonel Finally Sees the Whites of Their Eyes," *Washington Post*, October 20, 2005.

27. Ferguson, *No End in Sight*, p. 71.

28. Quoted in Ricks, *Fiasco*, pp. 102–3.

29. DeYoung, *Soldier*, p. 332.

30. Charles Duelfer, *Hide and Seek: The Search for Truth in Iraq* (New York: PublicAffairs, 2009), p. 197.

31. Tommy Franks with Malcolm McConnell, *American Soldier* (New York: Regan Books, 2004), p. 376.

32. Dennis B. Ross, *Statecraft and How to Restore America's Standing in the World* (New York: Farrar, Straus and Giroux, 2007).

33. George Tenet with Bill Harlow, *At the Center of the Storm: My Years at the CIA* (New York: HarperCollins, 2007), p. 350.

34. George W. Bush quoted ibid.

35. James Risen, *State of War: The Secret History of the CIA and the Bush Administration* (New York: Free Press, 2006), p. 111.

36. Franks with McConnell, *American Soldier*, p. 281; General Franks expresses his negative opinion of Feith in similar terms on page 362.

37. Woodward, *State of Denial*, p. 265.

38. Packer, *The Assassins' Gate*, p. 325; see also Ferguson, *No End in Sight*, p. 295.

39. Ricardo Sanchez and Donald T. Phillips, *Wiser in Battle: A Soldier's Story* (New York: Harper, 2008), p. 314.

40. Dale R. Herspring, *Rumsfeld's Wars: The Arrogance of Power* (Lawrence: University Press of Kansas, 2008), p. 147; Feith noted: "I thought the CPA's dissolution of the Iraqi army was a sound decision under the circumstances, properly reasoned through by Bremer and Slocombe. I still do. But the decision became associated with a number of unnecessary problems, including the apparent lack of interagency review." Douglas J. Feith, *War and Decision: Inside the Pentagon at the Dawn of the War on Terrorism* (New York: HarperCollins, 2008), p. 433.

41. Larry Diamond, *Squandered Victory: The American Occupation and the Bungled Effort to Bring Democracy to Iraq* (New York: Henry Holt, 2005), p. 29.

42. DeYoung, *Soldier*, p. 10; see also Packer, *The Assassins' Gate*, pp. 444–45.

43. Ross, *Statecraft*, pp. 121, 139.

44. Woodward, *State of Denial*, p. 379.

45. Franks with McConnell, *American Soldier*, p. 544.

46. Tenet with Harlow, *At the Center of the Storm*, p. 308.

47. Bob Woodward, *Plan of Attack* (New York: Simon and Schuster, 2004), p. 437.

48. Gregory F. Treverton, *Intelligence for an Age of Terror* (New York: Cambridge University Press, 2009), p. 91.

49. Woodward, *State of Denial*, p. 312.

50. Quoted in DeYoung, *Soldier*, p. 477.

51. Woodward, *State of Denial*, p. 330.

52. Quoted in Risen, *State of War*, p. 64.

53. Tenet with Harlow, *At the Center of the Storm*, p. 447.

54. Risen, *State of War*, p. 64.

55. Ross, *Statecraft*, p. 139.

56. Richard N. Haass, *War of Necessity, War of Choice: A Memoir of Two Iraq Wars* (New York: Simon and Schuster, 2009), p. 185.

57. Jacob Weisberg, *The Bush Tragedy* (New York: Random House, 2008), p. 206; see also Graham, *By His Own Rules*, p. 345.

58. Gellman, *Angler*, p. 189.

59. Woodward, *State of Denial*, p. 87.

60. "President's State of the Union Message to Congress and the Nation," *New York Times*, January 29, 2003, p. A12.

61. Tenet with Harlow, *At the Center of the Storm*, pp. 449–78.

62. Stephen J. Hadley quoted in Scott McClellan, *What Happened: Inside the Bush White House and Washington's Culture of Deception* (New York: PublicAffairs, 2008), p. 177.

63. Richard A. Clarke, *Against All Enemies: Inside America's War on Terror* (New York: Free Press, 2004), p. 234.

64. Stephen J. Hadley quoted by Bob Woodward, "Secret Reports Countered Bush Optimism," *Washington Post*, October 1, 2006, p. A1.

65. Bob Woodward, *The War Within: A Secret White House History, 2006–2008* (New

York: Simon and Schuster, 2008), p. 279; Thomas E. Ricks, *The Gamble: General David Petraeus and the American Military Adventure in Iraq, 2006–2008* (New York: Penguin Press, 2009), pp. 98–101.

66. Linda Robinson, *Tell Me How This Ends: General David Petraeus and the Search for a Way Out of Iraq* (New York: PublicAffairs, 2008), p. 21.

67. Senate Joint Resolution 23, "Authorization for Use of Military Forces," September 14, 2001.

68. Karlyn Brown, "America and the War on Terror," (Washington, DC: American Enterprise Institute, July 24, 2008).

69. Myers with McConnell, *Eyes on the Horizon*, p. 167.

70. Chuck Hagel with Peter Kaminsky, *America: Our Next Chapter: Tough Questions, Straight Answers* (New York: HarperCollins, 2008), p. 53.

71. Ricks, *Fiasco*, p. 85.

72. Senator Hillary Rodham Clinton quoted by Ricks, *Fiasco*, p. 385.

73. Representative Ike Skelton ibid., p. 386.

74. Ibid., p. 387.

75. General Zinni quoted in Tom Clancy with Anthony Zinni and Tony Koltz, *Battle Ready* (New York: G. P. Putnam's Sons, 2004), p. 426.

76. McClellan, *What Happened*, p. 210.

Chapter 12

1. For example, see Joshua 9, verses 6 and 15: "And they went to Joshua in the camp at Gilgal, and said to him, and to the men of Israel, 'We have come from a far country; so now make a covenant with us.'…And Joshua made peace with them, and made a covenant with them, to let them live."

2. Michael Howard, "Strategy of the Grand Alliance, 1941–1945," lecture at Stanford University, May 22, 1967.

3. For an excellent history of this event, see Mary Elise Sarotte, *1989: The Struggle to Create Post-Cold War Europe* (Princeton: Princeton University Press, 2009).

4. Vladimir Putin quoted in Bob Woodward, *Plan of Attack* (New York: Simon and Schuster, 2004), p. 118.

5. Douglas J. Feith, *War and Decision: Inside the Pentagon at the Dawn of the War on Terrorism* (New York: Harper, 2008), p. 126.

6. National Commission on Terrorist Attacks upon the United States, *9/11 Commission Final Report* (New York: W. W. Norton, 2003), p. 29.

7. Sheikh Saleh bin Luheidan quoted in "Supreme Judicial Council Comments on Terrorism," *Saudi Arabia* 18, no. 10 (Washington, DC: Royal Embassy of Saudi Arabia, October 2001), p. 2.

8. "Testimony of Binyamin Netanyahu," U.S. House of Representatives, Government Reform Committee, September 24, 2001.

9. George W. Bush, "Address on Terrorism," *New York Times*, September 21, 2001, p. B4.

10. Speech by Tony Blair, Labour Party Conference, Brighton, UK, October 2, 2001.

11. George W. Bush, "Bush's Words to Britons: 'Both Our Nations Serve the Cause of Freedom,'" *New York Times*, November 20, 2003, p. A12.

12. Bush, "Address on Terrorism."

13. Linda D. Kozaryn, "Rumsfeld Thanks NATO as AWACS Planes Head Home," http://www.defense.gov/news/newsarticle.aspx?id=44105.

14. James Risen, *State of War: The Secret History of the CIA and the Bush Administration* (New York: Free Press, 2006), p. 34; Jane Mayer, *The Dark Side: The Inside Story of How the War on Terror Turned into a War on American Ideals* (New York: Doubleday, 2008), pp. 130–31.

15. Richard A. Oppel, Jr., Mark Mazzetti, and Souad Midhennet, "Suicide Bomber in Afghanistan a Double Agent," *New York Times*, January 5, 2010, p. A1.

16. George Tenet with Bill Harlow, *At the Center of the Storm: My Years at the CIA* (New York: HarperCollins, 2007), p. 129.

17. Wesley Clark, remarks at UCLA, January 22, 2007.

18. Donald H. Rumsfeld, "A New Kind of War," *New York Times*, September 27, 2001, p. A25.

19. Dick Cheney, *Meet the Press*, March 16, 2003, quoted by Ivo H. Daalder and James M. Lindsay, *America Unbound: The Bush Revolution in Foreign Policy* (Washington, DC: Brookings Institution, 2003), p. 136.

20. Dick Cheney, *Face the Nation*, March 16, 2003, quoted in Daalder and Lindsay, *America Unbound*, p. 136.

21. Bradley Graham, *By His Own Rules: The Ambitions, Successes, and Ultimate Failures of Donald Rumsfeld* (New York: PublicAffairs, 2009), p. 386.

22. Thomas E. Ricks, *Fiasco: The American Military Adventure in Iraq* (New York: Penguin Press, 2006), p. 346.

23. Personal communication to the author.

24. U.S. Department of State, *Country Reports on Human Rights Practices*. Hearings before the House Subcommittee on International Operations and Human Rights, Committee on International Relations, February 25, 2000, 196th Cong., 2nd sess. (Washington, DC: Government Printing Office, 2000).

25. Ali A. Allawi, *The Occupation of Iraq: Winning the War, Losing the Peace* (New Haven: Yale University Press, 2007), p. 214.

26. Steven Coll, *Ghost Wars: The Secret History of the CIA, Afghanistan, and Bin Laden, from the Soviet Invasion to September 10, 2001* (New York: Penguin Press, 2004), p. 420.

27. Memorandum from George Tenet to President George W. Bush, December 18, 2000, quoted in Tenet with Harlow, *At the Center of the Storm*, p. 129.

28. Seth G. Jones, *In the Graveyard of Empires: America's War in Afghanistan* (New York: W. W. Norton, 2009), p. 250.

29. Donald Rumsfeld quoted ibid., p. 250.

30. Polls cited by David L. Phillips, *Losing Iraq: Inside the Postwar Reconstruction Fiasco* (Boulder, CO: Westview Press, 2005), p. 118.

31. Quoted ibid., p. 120.

32. Ricardo Sanchez and Donald T. Phillips, *Wiser in Battle: A Soldier's Story* (New York: Harper, 2008), p. 240.

33. Bill Clinton, *My Life* (New York: Alfred A. Knopf, 2004), p. 799.

34. Secret cable from the Secretary of State to American Embassy in Islamabad, Pakistan, "Deputy Secretary Armitage's Meeting with General Mahmud," September 13, 2001; declassified as a result of Freedom of Information request by the National Security Archive; available at http://www.gwu.edu/~nsarchiv/NSAEBB/NSAEBB325/doc05.pdf/.

35. Transcript of Martin Smith interview with Richard Armitage, July 20, 2006, quoted by Jones, *In the Graveyard of Empires*, p. 88.

36. Secret cable from Ambassador Wendy Chamberlain to Secretary of State Powell, "Musharraf," September 13, 2001; declassified as a result of Freedom of Information request by the National Security Archive; available at http://www.gwu.edu/~nsarchiv/NSAEBB/NSAEBB325/doc06.pdf.

37. Seth G. Jones interview with Ambassador Wendy Chamberlain quoted in Jones, *Graveyard of Empires*, p. 88.

38. Lord Curzon quoted by Scott Atran, "To Best Al Qaeda, Look to the East," *New York Times*, December 13, 2009, p. A11.

39. Author's interviews with U.S. military personnel stationed on the Afghan-Pakistani border.

40. Craig M. Mullaney, *The Unforgiving Minute: A Soldier's Education* (New York: Penguin Press, 2009), p. 288.

41. Nicholas Kulish, "Dutch Government Collapses over Its Stance on Troops for Afghanistan," *New York Times*, February 21, 2010, p. 12.

Chapter 13

1. "Cheney Roars Back: The Nightline Interview during His Trip to Iraq," ABC News, December 18, 2005; http://abcnews.go.com/Nightline/IraqCoverage/story?id=1419206.

2. Thomas E. Ricks, *The Gamble: General David Petraeus and the American Military Adventure in Iraq, 2006–2008* (New York: Penguin Press, 2009), p. 8.

3. "Testimony of Ambassador Ryan Crocker," Joint Hearing, September 10, 2007.

4. Interview with the author.

5. Linda Robinson, *Tell Me How This Ends: General David Petraeus and the Search for a Way Out of War* (New York: PublicAffairs, 2008), 14.

6. James A. Baker III and Lee H. Hamilton, Co-Chairs, *The Iraq Study Group Report* (New York: Vintage Books, 2006), p. xiii.

7. Ibid., p. ix.

8. Ibid., p. 65.

9. Ibid., p. 73.

10. Peter Feaver, "Anatomy of the Surge," *Commentary*, April 2008.

11. Robinson, *Tell Me How This Ends*, p. 34.

12. David Petraeus and James Amos with a foreword by John Nagl, *The US Army, Marine Corps, Counterinsurgency Field Manual* (Chicago: University of Chicago Press, 2007); also published as U.S. Army, *Counterinsurgency*, United States Army Field Manual 3–24/United States Marine Corps Warfighting Publication 3–33–5 (Washington, DC: Department of the Army, 2006).

13. John Nagl, *Learning to Eat Soup with a Knife: Counterinsurgency Lessons from Malaya and Vietnam* (Chicago: University of Chicago Press, 2002).

14. Conrad Crane and W. Andrew Terrill, *Reconstructing Iraq: Insights, Challenges, and Missions for Military Forces in a Post-Conflict Scenario* (Carlisle Barracks, PA: Strategic Studies Institute, U.S. Army War College, February 2003).

15. John A. Nagl, "Foreword to the University of Chicago Press Edition," *The U.S. Army-Marines Corps Counterinsurgency Field Manual*, p. xiii.

16. Ibid., paragraphs I–148 through I–157, pp. 48–50.

17. H. R. McMaster, *Dereliction of Duty: Lyndon Johnson, Robert McNamara, the Joint Chiefs of Staff, and the Lies That Led to Vietnam* (New York: HarperPerrenial, 1998).

18. Harry G. Summers, *On Strategy: A Critical Analysis of the Vietnam War* (San Francisco: Presidio Press, 1995).

19. George Packer, "Letter from Iraq: The Lesson of Tal Afar," *New Yorker*, March 10, 2006.

20. Peter R. Mansoor, *Baghdad at Sunrise: A Brigade Commander's War in Iraq* (New Haven: Yale University Press, 2008).

21. Robinson, *Tell Me How This Ends*, p. 27.

22. Stephen Biddle, *Military Power: Explaining Victory and Defeat in Modern Battle* (Princeton: Princeton University Press, 2006).

23. Andrew F. Krepinevich, Jr., *The Army and Vietnam* (Baltimore: Johns Hopkins University Press, 1988).

24. Andrew F. Krepinevich, Jr., "How to Win in Iraq," *Foreign Affairs* 84, no. 5 (September/October 2005): pp. 87–104.

25. In their book *Four Generals and the Epic Struggle for the Future of the United States Army* (New York: Crown Publishers, 2009), David Cloud and Greg Jaffe note that George W. Casey, Jr., and John Abizaid favored a traditional military strategy in Iraq while David Petraeus and Peter Chiarelli favored a counterinsurgency strategy.

26. Major General Peter W. Chiarelli and Major Patrick R. Michaelis, "Winning the Peace: The Requirement for Full-Spectrum Operations," *Military Review* (July–August 2005): pp. 4–17.

27. Ricks, *The Gamble*, p. 104; Robinson, *Tell Me How This Ends*, p. 27.

28. Colonel Bob Killebrew quoted in Ricks, *The Gamble*, p. 104.

29. Lieutenant Colonel Paul Yingling, "A Failure of Generalship," *Armed Forces Journal*, May 2007.

30. Colonel J. B. Burton, "The Officer Critical Skills Retention Bonus"; available at http://smallwarsjournal.com/blog/2007/07/the-officer-critical-skills-re-1/.

31. Author's interview with an Army officer who worked closely with the 4th Infantry Division during his deployment to Iraq in 2004–5.

32. Ricks, *The Gamble*, p. 131.

33. Thomas X. Hammes, *The Sling and the Stone: On War in the 21st Century* (Osceola, WI: Zenith Press, 2004).

34. Colonel T. X. Hammes quoted by Packer, "Letter from Iraq."

35. Robinson, *Tell Me How This Ends*, p. 69.

36. Robert Thompson, *Defeating Communist Insurgency: Experiences from Malaya and Vietnam* (London: Chatto and Windus, 1966).

37. Colonel H. R. McMaster quoted by Packer, "Letter from Iraq" (emphasis in the original).

38. Ricks, *The Gamble*, p. 60.

39. George W. Bush quoted in "More to Iraq Story than Violence," CNN, March 20, 2006; http://www.cnn.com/2006/POLITICS/03/20/bush.iraq/index.html.

40. Ricks, *The Gamble*, p. 160.

41. "Statement of Ambassador Ryan C. Crocker, U.S. Congress, Joint Hearing of the Committee on Foreign Affairs and the Committee on Armed Services," September 10, 2007, transcript.

42. For a good description of Sittar Abu Risha's role in the Anbar Awakening, see Jim Michaels, *A Chance in Hell* (New York: St. Martin's, 2010). Sittar was killed in a roadside bomb attack in 2007.

43. David Kilcullen quoted in Ricks, *The Gamble*, p. 71.

44. Ibid., p. 72.

45. General David Petraeus quotation, ibid.

46. Ibid., p. 123.

47. Letter from General David Petraeus to Members of Multi-National Force Iraq, March 15, 2007, p. 1.

48. Karen DeYoung, *Soldier: The Life of Colin Powell* (New York: Alfred A. Knopf, 2006), p. 459.

49. David Ignatius, "A Farewell Warning on Iraq," *Washington Post*, January 18, 2008, p. B7.

50. General Petraeus and Ambassador Crocker quoted by Robinson, *Tell Me How This Ends*, p. 149.

51. "Testimony of General David Petraeus," U.S. Congress, House of Representatives, Committee on Foreign Affairs, April 2008.

52. Ricks, *The Gamble*, p. 271.

53. William J. Fallon, "Surge Protector," *New York Times*, July 20, 2008, p. 13.

54. Memorandum from General Barry R. McCaffrey to Colonel Michael Meese, "Visit to Iraq and Kuwait, 31 October–6 November 2008," p. 5.

55. Kilcullen quoted by Ricks, *The Gamble*, p. 163.

56. Thomas Ricks, "Understanding the Surge in Iraq and What's Ahead," Foreign Policy Research Institute, Philadelphia, May 29, 2009.

57. Vali Nasr quoted by Michael R. Gordon, *New York Times*, August 3, 2008, p. 55.

58. Bob Woodward, *Obama's Wars* (New York: Simon and Schuster, 2010).

59. Memorandum from General Stanley A. McChrystal to Secretary of Defense Robert Gates, "COMISAF's Initial Assessment," August 30, 2006; available at www.nyt.com/, p. 2–12.

60. Memorandum from General Stanley A. McChrystal to Secretary of Defense Robert Gates, p. 1–1.

61. Michael Hastings, "The Runaway General," *Rolling Stone*, June 22, 2010.

62. Carl von Clausewitz, *On War*, Book I, Chapter VII, Michael Howard and Peter Paret, translators (Princeton: Princeton University Press, 1989).

63. Dexter Filkins, "Afghans Offer Jobs to Taliban if They Defect," *New York Times*, November 11, 2009, p. A1.

64. Steve Coll, "War by Other Means: Is It Possible to Negotiate with the Taliban?" *New Yorker*, May 24, 2010.

65. David Howell Petraeus, *The American Military and the Lessons of Vietnam: A Study of Military Influence and the Use of Force in the Post-Vietnam Era*, doctoral dissertation, Princeton University, 1987, p. 239.

66. T. Christian Miller, "Contractors Outnumber Troops in Iraq," *Los Angeles Times*, July 4, 2007, p. A1.

67. John M. Broder, "Filling Gaps in Iraq, Then Finding a Void at Home," *New York Times*, July 17, 2007, p. A1.

68. Dana Priest and William M. Arkin, "National Security Inc.," *Washington Post*, July 20, 2010.

Chapter 14

1. David Howell Petraeus, *The American Military and the Lessons of Vietnam: A Study of Military Influence and the Use of Force in the Post-Vietnam Era*, doctoral dissertation Princeton, University, 1987, p. 10.

2. Quoted by H. R. McMaster, "This Familiar Battleground," *Hoover Digest*, no. 4 (Fall 2009), 100.

3. John Keegan quoted in the *Los Angeles Times*, October 14, 2001, p. M6.

4. T. E. Lawrence, "Twenty-seven Articles," *The Arab Bulletin*, August 20, 1917; available at http://wwi.lib.byu.edu/index.php/The_27_Articles_of_T.E._Lawrence/.

5. David Kilcullen, "Twenty-eight Articles: Fundamentals of Company-level Counterinsurgency," in *Counterinsurgency* (New York: Oxford University Press, 2010), pp. 29–50.

6. This was the conclusion of a National Intelligence Estimate; see Mark Mazzetti, "Spy Agencies Say Iraq War Worsens Terror Threat," *New York Times*, September 24, 2006, p. A1.

7. Rajiv Chandrasekaran, *Imperial Life in the Emerald City: Inside Iraq's Green Zone* (New York: Alfred A. Knopf, 2006), p. 246.

8. Brookings Institution, "Arab Public Opinion Polls," released annually, conducted by Shibley Telhami and Zogby International; available at http://www.brookings.edu/reports/2010/0805_arab_opinion_poll_telhami.aspx.

9. Leslie Gelb with Richard Betts, *The Irony of Vietnam: The System Worked* (Washington, DC: Brookings, 1979).

10. Dana Priest and William Arkin, "Top Secret America," *Washington Post*, July 20, 2010.

11. Mike McConnell quoted by Bob Woodward, *Obama's Wars* (New York: Simon and Schuster, 2010).

12. Robert S. Norris and Hans M. Kristensen, "Global Nuclear Stockpiles, 1945–2006," *Bulletin of the Atomic Scientists* 62, no. 4 (July–August 2006), pp. 64–66.

13. Dan Caldwell and Robert E. Williams, Jr., *Seeking Security in an Insecure World*, 2nd ed. (Lanham, MD: Rowman and Littlefield, 2011).

14. The classic consideration of levels of analysis in international relations is Kenneth Waltz, *Man, the State, and War* (New York: Columbia University Press, 1959).

15. Kenneth Waltz, *Theory of International Politics* (New York: McGraw Hill, 1979), p. 112.

16. Russell Weigley, *The American Way of War: A History of United States Military Strategy and Policy* (New York: Macmillan, 1974).

17. "New State Department Releases on the 'Future of Iraq' Project," National Security Archive, September 1, 2006; available at http://www.gwu.edu/~nsarchiv/NSAEBB/NSAEBB198/index.htm.

18. Carl von Clausewitz quoted by Thomas Ricks, *Fiasco: The American Military Adventure in Iraq* (New York: Penguin Press, 2006), p. 59.

19. Memorandum from General Stanley A. McChrystal to Secretary of Defense Robert Gates, "COMISAF's Initial Assessment," August 30, 2006; available at www.nyt.com/, p. D-1.

20. William D. Baker and John R. Oneal, "Patriotism or Opinion Leadership: The Nature and Origin of the 'Rally Round the Flag' Effect," *Journal of Conflict Resolution* 45 (2001).

21. Ricks, *Fiasco*, p. 85.

22. Clinton Rossiter, *The American Presidency* (New York: Harcourt Brace, 1956).

23. Alexander L. George and William E. Simons, eds., *The Limits of Coercive Diplomacy*, 2nd ed. (Boulder, CO: Westview Press, 1994).

24. "Testimony of General George Casey," U.S. Senate, Armed Services Committee, September 29, 2005.

25. Seth G. Jones, *In the Graveyard of Empires: America's War in Afghanistan* (New York: W. W. Norton, 2009), p. 153.

26. George W. Bush, *Decision Points* (New York: Crown, 2010), pp. 170–71.

27. David Fromkin, "The Strategy of Terrorism," *Foreign Affairs* (July 1975): p. 697.

28. Stephen Flynn, *The Edge of Disaster: Rebuilding a Resilient Nation* (New York: Random House, 2007).

29. Douglas J. Feith, *War and Decision: Inside the Pentagon at the Dawn of the War on Terrorism* (New York: Harper, 2008), p. 127.

30. Ahmed Rashid, *Descent into Chaos: The U.S. and the Disaster in Pakistan, Afghanistan, and Central Asia* (New York: Penguin, 2008), p. 383.

31. Memorandum from General Stanley A. McChrystal to Secretary of Defense Robert Gates, p. 2–10.

Index

Abbisid Caliphate, 54, 59
Abdullah, King (of Jordan), 141
Abdullah bin Abdul Azziz, King (of Saudi Arabia), 13, 66
Abizaid, John, 168, 180, 193, 225, 231, 234
Abraham Lincoln, USS, 162
Abrams, Creighton, 167
Abrams, Elliott, 96
Abu Ghraib, 204–5, 256, 263
Acheson, Dean, 91, 123, 165
Adams, John Quincy, 92
Addington, David, 107–8, 191
Adelman, Kenneth, 105, 117, 163
Afghanistan, 89, 172, 254; Afghan-Soviet War, 74, 83; bin Laden's move to, 77; intelligence concerning, 136–39; relationship to Pakistan, 30–31; state sponsor of terrorism, 72; Sufism, 18; U.S. attack, 6
Agoglia, Paul, 124
Agranat Commission (Israel), 135
Ahmed, Mahmoud, 219
Airborne Warning and Control System (AWACS), 88, 212
Ajami, Fouad, 121
Al-Aqsa Mosque, 78
Albright, Madeleine, 94, 155–56
Alexander the Great, 31, 35
Ali, Rashid, 55
Al Kifah Center (Brooklyn), 76
Allawi, Ali, 181, 217, 252
Allawi, Ayad, 13, 121, 157, 181, 198
Al Qaeda, 44, 89, 178, 187, 222; and Afghanistan, 30; assassination of Massoud, 85, 112; attacks on U.S. naval ships, 80–81; founding, 75; linked to Iraq, 146
Aluminum tubes, 144
Alwan, Rafid Ahmed. *See* "Curveball"
Amin, Hafizullah, 37–38
Anbar Province, 235
Anglo-Afghan wars, 31, 35
Ani, Ahmad Khalil Ibrahim Samir al-, 146
Annan, Kofi, 69
Ansar al-Islam, 114
Arab-Israeli conflict, 10, 20–23
Arkin, William, 132
Armitage, Richard, 68, 96, 99, 173, 177, 195, 200, 201, 219
Asad, Hafez al-, 56
Ashcroft, John, 87
Assassination, 71, 155–58
Atef, Mohammed, 137
Atta, Mohammed, 146
Australia, 105, 150, 216
"axis of evil," 99–100
AWACS. *See* Airborne Warning and Control System
Awakening Council, 235
Aziz, Tariq, 63–65
Azzam, Abdullah, 74–76, 84
Azziz bin Baz, Sheik Abd al-, 76

Baath Party: in Iraq, 58, 66, 178; in Syria, 56
Baer, Robert, 156

Baghdad Pact. *See* Central Treaty Organization
Baker, James, III, 63–66, 226
Bakr, Abu, 18
Bakr, Hasan al-, 58
Balawi, Humam Khalil Abu-Mulal al-, 213
Barno, David, 186
Barzani, Massoud, 121, 157
Bearden, Milt, 39–40, 49
Begin, Menachem, 24
Benedict, Ruth, 119–20
Benjamin, Daniel, 14–17, 79, 83, 86
Berger, Samuel, 81
Berntsen, Gary, 50
Betts, Richard, 135, 152
Bhutto, Benazir, 40, 219, 239
Bhutto, Zulfiqar Ali, 48
Biddle, Stephen, 201, 231
Biden, Joseph, 174, 184, 204, 242
Bin Laden Brothers for Contracting and Industry, 25, 77
Bin Laden, Muhammad bin Awad, 74
Bin Laden, Osama, 11, 13, 44, 73, 112, 158, 251; in Afghanistan, 51; attempts to assassinate, 155–58; desecration of Saudi Arabia by infidels, 11, 78; education, 74; influence of Taqi al-Din ibn Taymiyya, 14–15; "Jewish-Crusader" alliance, 75–76; use of religion, 26; views on *jihad*, 13
Blackwater (contractors), 156
Blair, Tony, 47, 114, 154, 211–12
Blix, Hans, 149
Bolton, John, 68, 192, 195
Boot, Max, 96
Bosnia, 76, 172, 209, 261
Bremer, L. Paul, III, 124, 139, 176–83, 198, 233, 238, 260
Brzezinski, Zbigniew, 38, 91, 258
Burke, Gerald, 183
Burton, J. B., 232
Bush, George Herbert Walker, 48, 51–52, 61–63, 66, 92–93, 156, 203, 253, 265; plot to assassinate, 68, 81, 98; policy toward Saddam, 5, 154–55, 248
Bush, George W., 94, 124, 237, 248, 261; background, 92–95; 9/11 and Iraq, 113, 146; optimistic assumptions, 125; religious views, 87–88, 93; response to 9/11, 87–88; responsibility of, 170; unilateralism, 95
Bush, Laura, 92–93
Bush Doctrine, 103–8
Butler, Frederick Edward Robin (Lord Butler of Brockwell), 150
Butler, Richard, 69
Byrd, Robert, 257

Calvert, John, 16–17, 74
Cambone, Steven, 163
Canada, 210, 212, 214, 217, 222
Card, Andrew, 87, 170, 194
Carter, Jimmy, 24, 28, 38, 93, 258
Casey, George, 231, 260
Casey, William, 40–41, 129, 136
Central Intelligence Agency (CIA), 38, 41, 51, 62, 69, 129, 135, 150, 157, 196, 198; assassination plots, 156–58; establishment of, 130; Forward Operating Base Chapman, 213; 9/11 and Iraq, 114; operations in Afghanistan, 82, 89, 112, 116, 136–39; overthrow of Mossadegh, 23; paramilitary forces, 112, 116; relations with FBI, 143; rendition, 212
Central Treaty Organization (CENTO), 55, 203
Chalabi, Ahmed, 121–22, 142–43, 146, 157, 181, 198, 252; in charge of "de-Baathification," 178–79
Chamberlain, Wendy, 219–20
Cheney, Richard, 65–66, 99–100, 105, 123, 163, 175, 190, 194–97, 213, 237, 258; as "assertive nationalist," 96; belief in secrecy, 107; on intelligence, 128; Iraqi reception of U.S. troops, 119; "last throes" of insurgency, 168, 225; policy on detainees and torture, 170; as secretary of defense, 75–76, 97; weapons of mass destruction, 140

Chiarelli, Peter, 231, 236
Chicago, University of, 97, 142
Chilcot, John, 150
China, People's Republic of, 9, 33, 61, 93, 103, 108, 128, 133, 203
China, Republic of (Taiwan), 93, 103
Christopher, Warren, 91
CIA. *See* Central Intelligence Agency
Civil Operations and Rural Development Support (CORDS), 185
Clark, Wesley, 118, 140, 170, 213
Clarke, Richard, 44, 52, 76–77, 82, 84, 113, 201
Clarridge, Duane R. ("Dewey"), 138
Clash of civilizations, 78, 86
Clausewitz, Carl von, 242, 247, 256
Clinton, Hillary, 91, 204–5
Clinton, William Jefferson, 66, 68–70, 76, 81, 93, 95, 98, 217, 219; policy toward al Qaeda, 90, 155
Coalition Provisional Authority (CPA), 119, 164, 181–83, 197; CPA Order Number 1, 178, 181–83, 226, 254; CPA Order Number 2, 179–80, 254
Cogan, Charles, 136
Cohen, Eliot, 201, 231
Cohen, Stephen Philip, 30, 32
Cold war, 39, 47, 49, 93, 122–23, 131
Cole, USS, 81
Coll, Steve, 39, 50, 131, 136
Collins, Joseph J., xii, 36–37, 118
Commander's Emergency Response Program (CERP), 233
Condor Project, 67
Congress, 69, 202–6; Goldwater-Nichols legislation, 101; Petraeus and Crocker testimony, 239
Containment, strategy of, 101, 154–55
Contractors, 156, 243
"Council of colonels," 227–31
Counterinsurgency, 158–59, 228–43; *U.S. Army and Marine Corps Field Manual*, 158, 169, 229–30
Counterterrorism, 173
Coyne, Heather, 182
Crane, Conrad, 169, 229
Crocker, Ryan, xii, 164, 225, 238–39
Crumpton, Henry, 137
Cuba, 72; Bay of Pigs, 104, 157; Cuban missile crisis, 100, 104, 129, 132–33
"Curveball" (Codename for Rafid Ahmed Alwan), 141, 146
Curzon, George Nathaniel (Lord Curzon), 33, 55, 220
Czech Republic, 105, 209; Mohammad Atta in Prague, 146

Daalder, Ivo, 96, 195
Dallek, Robert, 104
Daoud Khan, Mohammad, 36
Davids, Willibrord, 150
Dearlove, Richard, 114, 147, 154
"De-Baathification," 178–79, 226
Debray, Regis, 83
Defense Policy Guidance (1992), 97
DeLong, Michael, 115–16, 122, 140
Democracy promotion, 29, 106, 123, 239, 253
Deterrence, 101, 154–55
Deutsch, John, 136
DeYoung, Karen, 196, 198
Diamond, Larry, 184
Dobbins, James, 175–76
Dobriansky, Paula, 99
Donovan, William, 129
Dostum, Aburrashid, 44, 82, 84
Downing, Wayne, 194
Drone unmanned aerial vehicle (UAV), 138–39, 251
Dubs, Adolph, 24
Duelfer, Charles, 125, 128, 151–52, 196
Dulles, John Foster, 91
Dupree, Louis, 36–37
Durand Line, 31

Eagleberger, Lawrence, 91
Eaton, Paul, 177, 182
Edwards, John, 204
Egypt, 16, 57, 67, 76–77, 83, 135, 208, 212
Eikenberry, Karl, 265

Eisenhower, Dwight David, 104, 153, 165
Ekeus, Rolf, 148–49
ElBaradei, Mohammed, 144

Fahd, King (of Saudi Arabia), 66, 76
Faisal, King (of Iraq), 55
Faisal, Turki al-, 31
Fallon, William J., 240
FBI, 129–30; and the CIA, 143, 148
Feaver, Peter, 168, 227
Federally Administered Tribal Areas (FATA), 239
Feith, Douglas J., 99, 106, 174, 180, 198, 201, 210, 264; neoconservative, 96; 9/11 and Iraq, 114, 142
Feldman, Noah, 181
Ferguson, Charles, 122, 176
Filkins, Dexter, 242
Flanigan, Timothy, 107
Flood, Philip, 150
Foreign Affairs, 94, 157, 161, 231
France, 20, 63, 214, 217, 221; arms deals with Iraq, 61
Franks, Tommy, 113–14, 122, 162, 170, 198; "catastrophic success," 164; "cats in a sack," 196; opposed to disbanding Iraqi army, 180; on the Powell Doctrine, 160; weapons of mass destruction, 143
Frederick the Great, 127
Freedman, Lawrence, 21, 44, 86, 150, 189
Friedman, Thomas, 13
Frist, Bill, 228–29
Fromkin, David, 264
Fulbright, William J., 204, 257
Future of Iraq Project, 120, 174–76, 256

Gaddis, John Lewis, 102
Galbraith, Peter, 122, 125, 184
Galula, David, 169, 229
Garlasco, Mark, 119, 122
Garner, Jay, 175–79, 192–93
Gates, Robert, 41, 83, 139, 241
Gelb, Leslie, 184
Gellman, Barton, 108, 191
Gerges, Fawaz, 74–75, 79
Germany, 63, 119–20, 172, 208, 214, 217, 221; Zimmermann Telegram, 127–28
Ghazi, King (of Iraq), 55
Glaspie, April, 62, 342nn27, 28
Goldsmith, Jack, 107
Gorbachev, Mikhail, 42, 63–64, 251
Gordon, Michael, 144, 178, 180, 190
Gore, Albert, 93
Gromov, Boris, 42, 44
Grossman, Marc, 174
Guevara, Ernesto ("Che"), 83
Gulf War (1990–91), 51, 159, 253, 255; cost of, 65, 123–24; ultimatum to Iraq, 65

Haass, Richard N., 96, 132, 140, 145, 155, 171; decision to go to war with Iraq, 154, 162; on NSC, 200
Habash, George, 22, 72
Hackworth, David, 166
Hadith (sayings or deeds of Muhammad), 15
Hadley, Stephen, 99, 179, 196, 200–202
Hagel, Chuck, 204
Haig, Alexander, 91
Hajj (pilgrimage), 10
Halabja, 60, 67
Hallen, Jay, 181
Hamilton, Lee, 147, 226
Hammes, T. X., 183, 233
Hamre, John, 180
Haq, Abdul, 44
Haqqani, Jalaluddin, 44
Haram al-Sharif (Temple Mount), 18
Hart, Basil Liddell, 170
Hashim, Ahmed, 151, 163
Hastings, Michael, 375n61
Hawkins, Steve, 117
Hazaras, 44, 82
Heisbourg, Francois, 86
Hekmatyar, Gulbuddin, 44, 49–50, 84
Herbits, Steve, 194
Hersh, Seymour, 142–43
Herspring, Dale, 118, 179
Hilsman, Roger, 165

"Hind" (codename for Soviet MI-24D helicopter gunship), 39
Hitler, Adolf, 59, 63, 105
Homeland Security, Department of, 147–48
Horan, Hume, 119
Horner, Charles, 64
Howard, Michael, 208
Hughes, Paul, 182
Human rights, 27–29, 216, 263
Huntington, Samuel, 5, 74
Hussein, King (of Jordan), 22, 212–13
Hussein, Saddam, 18, 23, 25, 70; biography, 57–61; capture of, 115; intelligence about, 132; "malignant narcissism," 59; nationalization of Iraq Petroleum Company, 56; Tikrit, 13, 58; use of religion by, 26, 59

Ignatius, David, 238
INC. *See* Iraq National Congress
India, 31–33, 49, 84, 103; 1965 war with Pakistan, 32, 47–48; 1974 detonation of nuclear device, 48
Insurgency: definition, 158
Intelligence: cost of, 127; human (HUMINT), 131–32, 136; image (IMINT), 132–33, 138; measurement and signature (MASINT), 133–34; open source (OSINT), 133; problem of "stove-piping," 143; signals (SIGINT), 132, 136–38; technical (TECHINT), 133
International Atomic Energy Agency (IAEA), 148
International Security Force Afghanistan (ISAF), 214, 256, 264–65
Inter-Services Intelligence (ISI) directorate, 40–41, 49, 51, 131, 136, 219
Iqbal, Muhammad, 33
Iran, 27, 44, 55, 60, 77, 84, 96, 99, 212, 249; hostage crisis, 24, 66; state sponsor of terrorism, 72
Iran-Contra scandal, 191, 200
Iran-Iraq War, 58, 60–62, 73
Iraq, 72, 96, 99, 254; cost of war, 124
Iraq National Congress (INC), 121–22, 142–43, 157
Iraq Petroleum Company, 56
Iraq Study Group, 179, 182, 226–27, 237
Iraqi National Accord, 121
ISAF. *See* International Security Force Afghanistan
ISI. *See* Inter-Services Intelligence directorate
Islamic Jihad, 99
Islamism, 9–10, 13, 19, 25–26, 74; use of technology, 77
Israel, 28, 212; Arab-Israeli conflict, 10; attack on Osirak reactor, 104; founding of, 20
Italy, 216–17, 225

Jahiliyya (paganism), 17
Jamaat-e-Islami, 25, 40
James, Kay Coles, 182
Japan, 119–20, 172, 208, 253
Jefferson, Thomas, 92, 207
Jenkins, Brian, 71, 79
Jerusalem, 18–19
Jervis, Robert, 87, 104–5, 140, 147
Jihad, 13, 14, 39, 41, 74, 77–78, 178, 210–11
Johnson, Harold K., 166
Johnson, Lyndon, 251
Jones, Owen Bennett, 31
Jones, Seth, 173, 260
Jordan, 55–56, 142, 212–13

Kagan, Robert, 96, 231
Kahn, David, 128
Karmal, Babrak, 38
Karzai, Hamid, 121, 137; donation to the Taliban, 50; November 2009 election, 241
Kashmir, 32, 44, 136
Kaufman, Robert, 102, 104
Kay, David, 140, 149, 151, 200
KDP. *See* Kurdish Democratic Party
Kean, Thomas, 147
Keane, Jack, 168, 201, 227–31
Keegan, John, 247

Kennedy, John F., 165–66
Kennedy, Paul, 153
Kenya, 76, 79, 81, 155
Kerr, Richard, 150
Kerry, John, 204
Khalilzad, Zalmay, 50, 97, 176, 238
Khalis, Yunis, 44
Khan, Amanullah, 36
Khan, Genghis, 35
Khan, Mohammad Ayub, 32
Khan, Yahya, 48
Khomeini, Ayatollah Ruhollah, 37, 77
Kilcullen, David, 30, 79–80, 158–59, 235; "accidental guerillas," 79–80; "counterrevolution in military affairs," 169, 240; "Twenty-eight Articles," 247
Killebrew, Bob, 231
Kissinger, Henry A., 22, 48, 91, 96, 165, 190
Korbel, Josef, 94
Korean War, 4, 165, 254
Kosovo, 94, 118, 172, 209, 214, 261
Krauthammer, Charles, 96
Krepinevich, Andrew, 115, 231–32, 234
Kristol, William, 96
Kuklinski, Ryszard, 131
Kurdish Democratic Party (KDP), 121, 157–58
Kurds, 56, 59–60, 66–68, 156, 184, 216
Kuwait, 26, 55–56, 61–65, 68, 70, 73–74, 194

Lake, Anthony, 156
Laqueur, Walter, 71
Lasswell, Harold, 184
Lawrence, T. E., 19–20, 53, 70, 169, 229; definition of tactics, 170; "Twenty-seven Articles," 19–20, 247
League of Arab States, 22–23
League of Nations, 91
Lebanon, 20, 23, 83
Legere, Larry, 187
Le Monde, 86, 222
Levin, Carl, 117
Lewinsky, Monica, 69–70
Lewis, Bernard, 74
Libby, Lewis ("Scooter"), 97, 99, 195–96, 201; convicted of lying to the FBI, 145; link between 9/11 and Iraq, 114, 147; neoconservative, 96
Lindsay, James M., 96, 195
Lindsay, Lawrence, 124
Litwak, Robert, 104
Libya, 72, 76
Looting of Baghdad, 176–77
Los Angeles International Airport millennium bombing plot, 79, 81
Lott, Trent, 70
Loya Jirga, 36
Luheidan, Saleh bin, 211
Lute, Douglas, 231

MacArthur, Douglas, 118, 120
MacFarland, Sean, 234–37
MacKinder, Halford, 30
Madison, James, 92
Madrassa, 45
Majlis (conclave), 18
Major, John, 156
Makiya, Kanan, 59, 119
Maktab al-Khadamat (Services Office), 75–76
Malik, Pahlawan, 44
Maliki, Nuri al-, 181, 236, 239
Mansoor, Peter, xii, 180, 186–87, 194, 230
Mao Zedong, 39, 83
Marshall, George C., 100, 207; Marshall Plan, 3, 171, 255
Massoud, Ahmed, 49–52, 82–85; assassination of, 85, 112, 137
Mattis, James, 169, 229, 242
Mayer, Jane, 190
McCaffrey, Barry, 117–19, 168, 193, 229, 240
McCain, John, 240
McChrystal, Stanley, 113, 241–42, 256, 265
McClellan, Scott, 124, 205
McConnell, Michael, 250
McKiernan, David, 180
McLaughlin, John, 201
McMaster, H. R., 167, 230, 232, 234
Mecca, 11, 19, 23, 25, 37, 48
Miller, Judith, 60, 144

Military commissions, 192
Ministry of Intelligence and Security (MOIS), 50, 84
Miscik, Jami, 196–97
Monroe, James, 92
Morocco: first country to recognize the U.S., 9
Mossadegh, Muhammed, 23
Mubarak, Hosni, 62, 77, 141
Muhammad, 10, 18–19, 59
Mujahideen, 39, 41–43, 49–51, 73–4, 77–79, 83, 136, 203, 219, 259
Mullaney, Craig, 220
Mullen, Mike, 239
Muravchik, Joshua, 96
Musharraf, Pervez, 219–20, 239
Muslim Brotherhood, 17, 24–25, 51, 74, 83, 212
Muslim Youth Organization, 83
Mutawain (religious police), 16
Myers, Richard B., 159, 192–93, 203
Mylroie, Laurie, 60

Nadir Shah, Mohammed (King of Afghanistan), 36
Nagl, John, 167, 169, 229, 232, 235
Nash, William, 117–18
Nasr, Vali, 12
Nasser, Gamal Abdel, 21, 59
"Nation-building," 94, 172, 261
National Intelligence Council (NIC), 123, 248
National Intelligence Estimate (NIE), 140
National missile defense, 96
National Security Act (1947), 130, 190, 199
National Security Agency (NSA), 132, 250
National Security Council (NSC), 190, 197–99, 227
National Security Strategy (2002), 101–3, 153–54
National Strategy for Victory in Iraq, 168, 227
NATO (North Atlantic Treaty Organization), 4, 55, 86, 88, 102, 171, 208–9, 214, 222–24, 265
Neoconservatives ("neocons"), 68–69, 96, 106, 123
Netanyahu, Binyamin, 211
Netherlands, 216–17, 222, 225
Newbold, Greg, 159
Niger, 144, 197, 201
9/11 attacks on U.S., 85–88; link to Iraq, 113–14
9/11 Commission, 30, 77–78, 86, 146–48
Nixon, Richard M., 48, 96
"No fly zone" (in Iraq), 66–67
North Korea, 72, 96, 100, 249
Northern Alliance, 50–51, 82, 89, 112, 116, 137, 210, 255
NSC. *See* National Security Council
Nye, Joseph, 5, 103

Obama, Barack, 30, 240–43, 249
Odierno, Ray, 232–33, 237
Office of Legal Counsel (OLC), 191–92
Office for Reconstruction and Humanitarian Assistance (ORHA), 175–77
Office of Special Plans (U.S. Department of Defense), 142–43
Office of Strategic Services (OSS), 40, 129–30
Oil: discovery in Kirkuk (1927), 54; discovery in Saudi Arabia (1938), 56; to pay for Iraqi reconstruction, 124; U.S. as exporter and importer, 26–27
Omar, Mullah Muhammad, 18, 45, 89, 112, 158, 251
Operation Desert Fox, 69, 98
Operation Desert Storm, 115–16. *See also* Gulf War (1990–91)
OPLAN (Operational Plan) 1003-98, 115–16, 159, 163
Organization of Petroleum Exporting Countries (OPEC), 29, 57, 62
ORHA. *See* Office for Reconstruction and Humanitarian Assistance
Osirak (Iraqi nuclear reactor), 61, 104
O'Sullivan, Meghan, 193
Ottoman Empire, 19, 54, 56, 247

Pace, Peter, 179, 192–93, 227, 230, 239
Pachachi, Adnan, 198
Pahlavi, Mohammad Reza Shah, 23–24, 28
Pakistan, 30–32, 55, 83, 221, 264–65; and drones, 138–39; mutual defense agreement with U.S., 47; 1965 war with India, 47–48; opium production, 46–47; reluctant U.S. ally, 219–20; support for *mujahideen*, 44
Palestine, 10, 18, 20
Palestinian Liberation Organization (PLO), 23
Palin, Sarah, 103
Panjshir Valley, 51–52, 82–83, 137
Pashtuns, 36, 45, 82
Patriotic Union of Kurdistan (PUK), 121, 157–58, 216
Patterson, Anne, 31
Pearl Harbor, 26, 85, 87
Penkovskii, Oleg, 131
Perle, Richard, 69, 97, 195; criticism of CIA, 142; defense of Ahmed Chalabi, 121; neoconservative, 96
Petraeus, David Howell, 4, 30, 167–69, 228–40, 242, 247
Pew Global Attitudes Project, 220–21
Pillar, Paul, 72, 114, 146
Plame, Valerie, 144
Plato, 60, 61
Poland, 131, 209, 214
Polk, George, 58, 60
Popular Front for the Liberation of Palestine (PFLP), 22, 72
Post, Jerrold, 58–59
Powell, Colin, 64–65, 91, 97–99, 107, 179, 192, 198–99, 232; criticism of Paul Wolfowitz, 120; opinion of Richard Cheney, 195; Powell Doctrine, 5, 64, 160, 167; as pragmatic internationalist, 96; presentation to the UN on weapons of mass destruction, 141, 144–45; and Turkey, 218–19
Powers, Gary, 47, 340n78
Predator. *See* Drone unmanned aerial vehicle
Preemption, 101
Pressler Amendment, 48, 203
Preventive war, 101, 103–4, 140
Priest, Dana, 132
Project for a New American Century, 68–69, 98
Provincial Reconstruction Team (PRT), 185–88, 261
PUK. *See* Patriotic Union of Kurdistan
Putin, Vladimir, 88, 210

Quaid-I-Azam University, 25
Quran, 10, 14–16
Qutb, Sayyid, 16–19, 74, 83

Rabbani, Burhanuddin, 44, 49, 51, 83
Rabin, Yitzhak, 24
RAND Corporation, 172–74, 176, 178
Rashid, Ahmed, 35, 40, 46, 83–84, 187–88
Rawalpindi, Treaty of, 35
Reagan, Ronald, 24, 40, 48, 62, 92, 191
Reaper (MQ-9). *See* Drone unmanned aerial vehicle
Ressam, Ahmed ("millennium bomber"), 79
"Revolution in military affairs" (RMA), 89, 96, 114–19, 159–62, 169–70, 242
Rhodes, Edward, 100
Rice, Condoleezza, 93–94, 113, 179, 199, 258; "clear, hold, and build" strategy, 234; decision to go to war against Iraq, 154; as NSC adviser, 199–200; Provincial Reconstruction Teams (PRT), 186–87; "smoking gun, mushroom cloud" warning, 144; Vulcans, 98–99
Ricks, Thomas, 111, 116, 125, 150, 204–5, 216, 225, 237, 240, 257; Iraq war plan, 173–74
Risha, Sittar Abu, 235, 374n42
RMA. *See* "Revolution in military affairs"
Roberts, Adam, 30
Robinson, Linda, 225
Rolling Stone, 241–42, 256

Roosevelt, Franklin Delano, 87, 91, 129, 240, 249
Rosen, Nir, 163
Ross, Dennis, 105–6, 111, 200
Rossiter, Clinton, 258
Roston, Aram, 121–22, 157
Rubin, James, 86
Rumsfeld, Donald, 68, 89, 97, 99, 144, 158–60, 170, 175, 180, 193, 198, 213, 227, 258; as "assertive nationalist," 96; "catastrophic success," 164; comparison to Robert McNamara, 192; "dead enders," 168; distrust of CIA, 142; favored "de-Baathification," 178; "freedom's untidy," 177; "hillbilly armor," 194; 9/11 and Iraq, 113; "old" and "new" Europe, 105; resignation, 169, 237; Rumsfeld Commission, 142; transformation, 169–70
Russia, 20, 73, 88, 210, 221
Russo-Japanese War, 134

Sabah, al- (ruling family of Kuwait), 13, 63
Sadat, Anwar, 22–24
Sadr, Moqtada al-, 239
Saghi, Omar, 73
Salafis, 14, 16, 18, 44, 77, 211
Samarra, 56, 225
Sanchez, Ricardo, 118, 179, 238
Saud, King Abdul Azziz al- (founder and first king of Saudi Arabia), 13, 74
Saudi Arabia, 11, 13, 16, 27, 55–56, 64, 73, 77–78, 136, 253; and Saddam Hussein, 61; discovery of oil, 16, 74
Sayyaf, Abdurrab Rasul, 83
Schoomaker, Peter, 231
Schroen, Gary, 50–52, 136–37, 173
Schwarzkopf, Norman, 98, 155
Scowcroft, Brent, 94, 154–55, 190, 201–2
SCUD missiles, 67
Separation of church and state, 10–11, 26
Shah of Iran. *See* Pahlavi, Mohammad Reza Shah
Sharia (Islamic law), 10–11, 18–19, 45–46, 211
Shelton, Henry, 81–82, 113, 115, 167
Shevardnadze, Eduard, 42, 44, 63
Shia Islam, 25, 156; in the Ottoman Empire, 54–56; tensions with Sunnis, 11–12, 23, 59; repression by Saddam Hussein, 67
Shinseki, Eric, 117–19, 160, 163, 167, 178, 193
Shutz, George, 198, 258
Silberman-Robb Commission. *See* Weapons of Mass Destruction Commission
Simon, Steven, 14–17, 79, 83, 86
Sistani, Grand Ayatollah Ali al-, 179
Six Day War (June 1967), 21–22
Skelton, Ike, 205
Slocombe, Walter, 180, 198
Solarz, Stephen, 69
Somalia, 76, 94, 172, 261
"Sons of Iraq," 36, 235–36
South Korea, 95, 216
Soviet Union, 37–42, 55, 73, 83, 128, 132, 208; relations with Iraq, 61
Spain, 216–17, 220, 225
Special Forces, 89, 112, 116, 137, 158, 161, 166, 187, 258
Stalin, Josef, 26, 59
Stanford University, 94
State, Department of, 121, 175, 178, 185–87, 189, 192, 197–98
Steganography, 133
Stiglitz, Joseph, 248
Stinger surface-to-air missile, 41, 52, 139
Sudan, 72, 76, 78, 81; U.S. attack on pharmaceutical plant, 79
Suez Canal, 21–22, 208
Sufi Islam, 18
The Sullivans, USS, 80–81
Sultan, Prince (of Saudi Arabia), 75
Summers, Harry, 230, 232
"Sunni Awakening," 235–36
Sunnis, 11–12, 59
"Surge": in Afghanistan, 240–43; civilian, 261; in Iraq, 237–40
Surprise attack, 134–35, 355n31
Suskind, Ron, 111

Swannack, Charles, 232–33
Sykes-Picot Agreement, 54
Symington Amendment, 48
Syria, 20, 55–56, 57, 72, 89, 135, 212, 226, 233

Taiwan. *See* China, Republic of
Tajikistan, 76
Talabani, Jalal, 121, 157
Tal Afar, 234–35
Taliban, 45–46, 49–50, 77, 82, 84, 89, 187, 222, 241, 255
Tanzania, 79, 81, 155
Taraki, Nur Mohammed, 37
Taymiyya, Taqi al-Din al-, 13–15, 17, 25, 74
Tenet, George, 88, 113, 120, 150–51, 180, 196, 200, 213; decision to go to war in Iraq, 162, 199; "Feith-based" analysis, 143; no linkage between 9/11 and Iraq, 114; policy built on hope, 126; postwar planning for Iraq, 163; warning of al Qaeda threat, 217
Terrorism: definitions, 71; law enforcement approach to dealing with, 73, 77; the "new terrorism," 79; state sponsors of, 72
Thatcher, Margaret, 63, 66
Thompson, Robert, 166–67, 169, 229
Tora Bora, 77, 89, 112, 264
Toynbee, Arnold, 33
Trainor, Bernard, 178, 180, 190
Transformation of defense. *See* "Revolution in military affairs"
Treverton, Gregory, 129, 143, 199
Tripp, Charles, 54, 59
Truman, Harry S., 20, 87, 118, 262
Turabi, Hassan al-, 76–77
Turkey, 19, 55, 216–18, 221
Turner, Stansfield, 136
Tyler, Patrick, 60

U-2 aircraft, 47, 132, 138, 203
UAV. *See* Drone unmanned aerial vehicle
Ukraine, 216
"Unitary executive" (theory of presidential power), 107, 262
United Arab Emirates (UAE), 62
United Kingdom, 20, 55, 68, 105, 208, 211–12, 214–15, 217, 222
United Nations (UN), 20, 22, 32, 69, 91; UN Security Council Resolution 687, 64, 67
UN Monitoring, Verification, and Inspection Commission (UNMOVIC), 149
UN Special Commission on Iraq (UNSCOM), 67–69, 143, 148–49
U.S. Agency for International Development (USAID), 175, 185, 187, 261
U.S. Army and Marine Corps Counter-insurgency Field Manual, 169, 229–30; definition of insurgency, 158
U.S. Army War College, 164, 174
U.S. Military Academy (West Point), 100, 153, 165, 228, 230
Uzbekistan, 138, 210

Van Buren, Martin, 92
Vance, Cyrus, 91, 258
Versailles: conference, 54; Treaty, 95
Vessey, John, 169
Vietnam War, 4, 39, 64, 86, 92, 159–, 166–67, 175, 185, 195, 228–32, 234, 247, 249, 254, 257, 265; casualties, 64–65; Gulf of Tonkin Resolution, 204; "Vietnam syndrome," 41
Vulcans (foreign policy advisory group), 98–99, 196, 200

Wag the Dog (movie), 70
Wahhab, Muhammed ibn Abd al-, 13, 15–17, 25, 74
Wahhabis, 16, 45, 210–11
Wallis, Jim, 93
Waltz, Kenneth, 5, 255
Warrantless wiretapping, 107–8, 263
Warrick, Tom, 174–76, 192–93
Washington, George, 207
"Weapons of mass destruction" (WMD), 100, 140–47, 250–51

Weapons of Mass Destruction Commission (Silberman-Robb Commission), 134, 140, 149–50
Weigley, Russell, 255
Weinberger, Caspar, 5, 198, 258
Weisberg, Jacob, 92, 100, 103, 182, 200
Westmoreland, William, 167
Wilkerson, Larry, 195
Wilson, Charlie, 41
Wilson, Joseph, 144
Wilson, Woodrow, 3, 27, 54, 91, 106, 127–28, 259
WMD. *See* "Weapons of mass destruction"
Wohlstetter, Albert, 97
Wohlstetter, Roberta, 134
Wolfowitz, Paul, 68, 99, 113, 119, 142, 155, 157, 180, 193, 196, 198, 201, 205; and Afghanistan, 172; cost of Iraqi reconstruction, 124; criticism of General Shinseki, 117–18; invasion plan for Iraq, 115–19; professional background, 97–98; weapons of mass destruction, 140, 145
Woodward, Bob, 93, 106, 162, 190, 199, 241, 250
World Trade Center: 1993 attack, 76–77, 344n32; 2001 attack, 85–87
World War I, 3, 19, 54–55, 60, 127–28, 165, 208, 259–60
World War II, 20, 55, 60, 63, 119–20, 129–30, 165, 208, 254–55, 259
Wright, Lawrence, 15, 83–84, 131–32

Yakis, Yasar, 218
Yale University, 92, 97, 200
"Yellow cake" (uranium oxide), 144, 197, 201
Yemen, 76, 80–81
Yingling, Paul, 232
Yom Kippur War (October 1973), 22, 28–29, 135
Yoo, John, 107, 191–92
Yousef, Ramzi, 76–77

Zahir, Shah Mohammed (King of Afghanistan), 36, 82
Zakheim, Dov, 196
Zapatero, Jose Luis Rodriquez, 220
Zarqawi, Abu Musab al-, 137–38, 241
Zawahiri, Ayman al-, 13, 75–76, 213
Zia ul-Haq, Muhammad, 22, 48
Zimmermann Telegram, 127–28
Zinni, Anthony, xi, 31, 115, 122, 157, 159, 162–63, 167, 205